On Literary Intention

On Literary Intention

CRITICAL ESSAYS SELECTED
AND INTRODUCED BY
DAVID NEWTON-DE MOLINA

But this is enough to direct those who may
have overlooked the author's intention.

SWIFT *A Tale of a Tub*
'An Apology for the Author'

o

EDINBURGH
AT THE UNIVERSITY PRESS
1976

© 1976
Edinburgh University Press

ISBN 0 85224 275 1

Printed in Great Britain by
W & J Mackay Limited, Chatham

Publisher's Note
Apart from the correction of obvious printer's errors
(and in one case extensive revision by the author)
the texts of these essays have been reprinted from
previous editions, not necessarily the first
editions cited in the Acknowledgements.
This accounts for certain discrepancies
in the wording of quotations.

o

Contents

Contents

vi

Introduction

These essays illustrate the relevance and irrelevance of questions about authorial *intention* in literary criticism. The debate by literary theorists on 'intention' increases our comprehension of relationships among several kinds of recurrent questions that literary critics ask of literary works in countless specific instances of their applied criticism. Something of the *dialectic* of critical activity seems to have been illuminatingly caught, unlike those theoretical debates which become, if not utterly arid, so profitless that we return to them less and less. The questions reflected at different theoretical levels are amongst those that arise, repeatedly and irresistibly, at crucial moments of much practical critical activity: stubbornly and spontaneously recurrent precisely because they *are* (within their due limits) criticism. Such vitality belongs only to the finest and most fortunate examples of theoretical criticism, to which we return, whatever their limitations, thankful for their usefulness—the best fate any theorizing about literature can hope for.

A central focus is on a recent critical term of terms: *meaning*. The meaning of literary 'meaning', as of a word like 'understanding' or 'intention' itself, is pursued by questions that address the familiar triangle of (i) author, (ii) work, and (iii) reader. Redpath writes that 'it seems that a poem may mean something different from what the poet intended it to mean, may mean less than the poet intended it to mean, may mean more than he intended it to mean; may perhaps sometimes mean substantially what he intended'. By varying this, we might say that a literary work may mean something different from what a *reader* understands it to mean, may mean less than a reader understands it to mean . . . and so on. And if we want to see how such alternatives might or might not interrelate in particular cases, then the kinds of theoretical discussion we shall most need must include the best in the debate about authorial intention: lucid explorations of the dialectic of difference, difference-

and-identity, and identity of meanings for authors', works' and readers' meanings.

The debate has often started by trying to come to terms with proclaimed differences between author ('the author's meaning') and work ('the work's meaning'), or between author and reader ('the reader's meaning'): hence between reader and work. But difference and sameness are inseparable dialectical twins: they will always coexist in any particular critical synthesis. So if it is said that an initial stimulus to debate has come from explicating implications of difference rather than of identity, we really mean differences that (at first) seem *total* or *radical*.

Historically, the need to reply to Wimsatt and Beardsley's classic essay 'The Intentional Fallacy' has been the catalytic stimulus: dissentient critics have repeatedly re-opened the debate by confronting its ambiguously *negative* pronouncement. The essay became one of the 'three negatives' in Wimsatt's *Verbal Icon*:[1] three negations—innovative oppositions of critical idiom, strategic New Critical promulgations—placed as timely antitheses to various inherited theses. The roots reached back, through the rich deposits of the immediately preceding generation of critics, to the ferment of modernism. In 'The Intentional Fallacy', a handbreadth beneath the surface, we readily sense the accumulated debts to the revolutionary writings of the post-Romantic poet-critics and the critical renaissance they provoked; but this indebtedness had undergone a sea-change. Any historically derived critical principles had been shaped into a statement that sounded deceptively like a logically derived set of alternatives: 'We argued that the design or intention of the author is neither available nor desirable as a standard for judging the success of a work of literary art, and it seems to us that this is a principle which goes deep into some differences in the history of critical attitudes.' How deep? Which differences? Which attitudes? Barrett's paraphrase is that 'these authors maintain that the artist's intentions are not relevant. If he has failed to realize his intentions, then the internal evidence of the work will not reveal what they were; and, even if external evidence is available, this does not tell us anything about the meaning of the work but only what the artist meant it to mean. If, on the other hand, he succeeds in his intentions, then the intended meaning and the meaning of the work as it stands coincide: it means what it is intended to mean.'[2] But if logical aplomb may have contributed to the success of Wimsatt and Beardsley's formulation, its welcome precision ought not to cause us to lose sight of the fact that the arguments suscitated by the 'fallacy' are not always wholly like logical arguments in some important senses of the word 'logical'. Yet it would appear to be generally true of literary critical arguments that they *cannot* be predominantly like logical arguments in some senses of 'logical': they are both like and unlike some kinds of logical argument, just as they are like and unlike some kinds of philosophical argument. William Righter, who speaks of literary criticism's mélange of 'logic and illogic',[3] has brilliantly reminded us that this is, indeed, the necessary and perfectly proper state of affairs. Literary criticism has 'its own realm of discourse' where any 'rigid use of logical models'[4] is scarcely paramount. There is much to be found in the arguments surrounding 'The Intentional Fallacy' that is logical: but the logic is very often the logic peculiar to literary criticism. In other words, we once more enter 'a region', as Abrams says of criticism generally, 'where the rules are uncodified and elusive', but which at its most interesting 'possesses just the kind of rationality it needs to achieve its own purposes'.[5] In short: like all good literary critical arguments the best arguments here often display their own kind of logic.

Hough remarks that the 'modern discussion of intention in a literary context begins with Wimsatt and Beardsley's article': 'This critical monument has by now disintegrated, as a result of its own internal contradictions, of direct assaults upon it, and of more philosophical consideration of meaning and intention in a non-literary context. But the ruined site remains, haunted by the memory of an ill-defined New Critical doctrine that the intention of the author (which sometimes means his biography, sometimes his plan of work) is irrelevant (or unavailable, or both) to the interpretation (or evaluation) of a work of literature. This blunderbuss utterance could be, indeed has been, analysed into a variety of propositions, some plainly untrue, some true but on the verge of being truisms, and some doubtful. A typical literary-critical doctrine, in fact. In spite of contradictions and inconsistencies its operational purport is, however, tolerably clear—we are not to ask questions about what the author intended, but only questions about what the words mean.' Discussion has taken the form of attempts at rejecting *tamen usque recurret* 'The Intentional Fallacy'. Critics have severally reconfronted its tonic, outlandish negative injunction. They have agreed and dis-agreed about the sorts of questions and answers that criticism—Wimsatt and Beardsley seem to suggest—either cannot or ought not to include at different levels and in different moments. As a result, critical energies were fruitfully channelled into a much more ex-tensive exploration of the whole disturbingly equivocal matter of the relevance and irrelevance of 'intention' than would otherwise have been the case.

Critics have asked: What if questions and answers about intention *are* entertained in ways that 'The Intentional Fallacy' is interpreted as declaring they should not be? But their antithetical impulse has not unmasked Wimsatt and Beardsley's essay as simply another ill-conceived and transient slogan—one of the major abandoned Latinisms of a critical sect (comparison with the fate of 'the affective fallacy' underlines this). And any polemical tints have gradually paled into insignificance: 'The Intentional Fallacy' can now be regarded as fortunately initiating what turns out to have been—like so many fertile critical ideas in their historical evolution—an unplanned but ultimately co-operative endeavour. Thanks to Wimsatt and Beardsley's seminal ukase a fresh speculative instrument, the focal concept 'intention', has been adapted and refined for critical uses. Because of it, we are better able to express discriminations of 'intentionalism' and 'anti-intentionalism' (and there must be both) in our own analyses and syntheses. Without it, we would still have more or less dumbly experienced the consequences of 'intention', but would not have inherited an array of valuable argument and counter-argument—the nexus of problems and puzzles embodied in these essays' highly specific idioms and tones that *are* our critical instrument. Without the competing explicators of 'the intentional fallacy' and their competing explications, implications would have stayed implicit. The nature of literary intention would have been what it always was; but when would we have so fully known and been able to contemplate it in all the length and breadth of its critical unity? The words of Merleau-Ponty in another context seem apt: 'Comment tracer une limite entre ce qu'il a pensé et ce qu'on a pensé à partir de lui,—entre ce que nous lui devons et ce que nos interprétations lui prêtent? Ses successeurs, il est vrai, appuient là où il passait vivement, laissent dépérir ce qu'il expliquait soigneuse-ment . . . mais enfin c'est encore lui qui les éveille à leurs pensées les plus propres, qui les anime dans leur agression contre lui . . . .'[6]

We are aware of the theoretical vigour (and theoretical dangers) latent in a distinction between 'internal' and 'external' evidence as a general critical metaphor for the zigzag education of taste. We may ask: What is 'inside' and what is 'outside' a literary work? What is 'inside' and 'outside' all literary works (literature)? What is 'inside' and 'outside' literary criticism? But we also know, from the nature of the case, that any compact summary will gravely mislead if it even suggests that critics can move triumphantly or in idyllic unison from one answer to the next; that they can literally decide what is inside and outside a literary work, or literature, or criticism. A general metaphor about *intrinsic* and *extrinsic* criticism has been deployed at different times by different critics in attempts at expressing what criticism is: what ought or ought not to belong to different aspects and different kinds of their own or others' critical activity. For literary critics, discussion of intention, too, may easily radiate back into different visions of the *raison d'être* of criticism itself: into criticism of criticism. And such metacriticism will analytically survey general notions and particular instances of what a literary work or even literature is: that is, what 'literary work' or 'literature' may mean, and what they ought to mean.

What matters is the relevance and irrelevance of questions and answers about intention—relevance and irrelevance to what? Obviously, to interpretation; but also to the transcending distinction between (i) interpretation and (ii) evaluation. The arguments have their vivid interest because they lend a characteristic salience to two critical moments intertwined in the perennial difficulties of determining (a) *what* we judge (interpretation of meaning) and (b) what we *judge* (evaluation of meaning).

And we may detect *en filigrane* in this debate (as in others) aspects of a double insight. Interpretation ought always to be (as it were) logically prior to evaluation—albeit evaluation ultimately transcends the putative neutrality of interpretation *qua* construed meaning; but the significant fact remains that in particular interpretations of literary works, as in interpretations of other works of art or other kinds of interpretation, this logical condition of priority may tend to elide the full human importance of an awkward truth: that the relevant information upon which we base particular interpretations is not always prior *in time* to particular evaluations. For how and when do we decide what is and what is not 'relevant'? So, in extremely various ways, interpretation does not always seem to be psychologically prior to evaluation. All the evidence never can be shown to have been made available. Time has no stop. Some evidence may simply never be available: it may not exist. And it is this kind of uncertainty that makes us speak of the gathering of evidence in the first place, and makes us say, afflicted by aporia mild or chronic, that unless evaluations are to be eternally postponed they must always be accepted, in some senses, as generically provisional.

Hirsch, for example, has the following sentence in 'Objective Interpretation': 'Understanding (and therefore interpretation, in the strict sense of the word) is both logically and psychologically prior to what is generally called criticism.' But other critics might wish to put this differently, should there seem to be other things to say about our experience of psychological priorities—something equally necessary that we want to add about *a priori* judgments and *a posteriori* revisions, which is not mere theoretical confusion. The following memorable passage throws light on this:

I will not expatiate here on the relation between understanding and valuing, in reference to literary criticism, for I do not wish to incur . . . [the] . . . charge of elaborating a 'dialectic' for its own sake. And anyway I find the whole subject very puzzling —as who does not, who is interested in the definition of criticism? On the one hand, valuing in the sense which matters to the literary critic, is not simply like awarding a certificate, or afixing a price-tag; it seems to refer to something which controls from the start the whole process of critical reading; on the other hand, I cannot believe that one recognizes the value of a work by a pre-reflective intuition: the very word 'judgement' that we tend to use ('value-judgement') carries the suggestion of a reflective act, a decision. (And we might say that a valuation based on a misunderstanding of a poem is not, in an important sense, a valuation of *that* poem.) It seems, then, that understanding is, at least conceptually, distinct from valuing; that it is a prior requisite. But it does not follow from this (so to speak) logical priority, that as a temporal, psychological process 'understanding' precedes 'valuing'; and indeed I think few would accept that account, who recollect what the actual reading of a great poem is like: how it grows in the mind as the mind grows in comprehension of it, how it comes to be possessed by its reader and in turn possesses him. And so I have to grant that the distinction between understanding and valuing, as commonly stated or implied, strikes no real root in the experience of any lover of literature. There can be no doubt that Mr Eliot, and Coleridge before him, speak for many when they declare that it is possible to admire and enjoy and be moved by poetry which in a strict sense one doesn't, and may not even want to, 'understand'. And in the same anti-academic spirit we may retort to our self-appointed enlighteners that many of the poems they affect to explicate or surround with 'facts about' them, we *already* understand, and that any 'help' they may offer will make no difference, since we will not *let* it make any. And I can sympathize all too easily with the mood in which one answers the question: 'What is the correct text of that poem? Which is the correct interpretation?' by saying, 'That which is most beautiful; that which gives me most pleasure.' But I also have my share of that impulse which I will not dignify by calling it anything other than *curiosity*, to find out what the poet actually wrote, and what he probably meant it to mean—if I may perpetrate this 'intentionalism' without qualification or discussion. And I can only say that I think the teaching at the University should minister at one time or another to both kinds of reader; or rather, to the same reader according to his different states of mind, and his different purposes. And the ideal historian of literature would be that reader *in excelsis*. He would be a critic; reading his authors, he would know what the actual historian may not know: how to tell the quick from the dead. But the poet, and the critic, must have wherewithal to discriminate. And they may want other information too; wisdom is a higher and better thing than information, but it is not the same thing; and the wise man may show his wisdom in consenting to inform himself.[7]

Meanwhile, above all in the language of criticism, we ought to insert that 'meaning' (like 'understanding') is a word that, in different contexts and with different nuances, torques and intonations, shades little by little from something nearly equivalent to neutrally construed meaning into something much nearer to, or identical with, valued meaning. To understand a meaning that a critic values is not the same thing as to understand a meaning he does not value (or is indifferent to), although it is still a kind of understanding, still a kind of meaning.

Without overstepping the bounds of an introduction, let it be said that 'understanding', in the heart of a critic's experience or writings, may be an abstraction stretched to cover something we might ultimately (or initially) want to call pleasure or appreciation. Or better still: ecstasy, wonder, love. And this comes *before* all else. 'What more felicitie can fall to creature,/Than to enioy delight with libertie . . .?' We are never unaware of the principle of stylistic decorum that tells us we will need other registers of expression for this, when the metalanguage of the debate about intention reaches its inevitable limits, although we know that it is only by having such limits imposed that the debate is able to focus beneficially on its specific somethings rather than uselessly on everything and nothing. 'No theory', as Abrams reminds us, 'is adequate to tell the whole story, for each one has limits correlative with its powers. As a speculative instrument, it has its particular angle and focus of vision, and what for one speculative instrument is an indistinct or blank area requires an alternative speculative instrument if it is to be brought into sharp focus for inspection.'[8]

I think that some of the later aphorisms of T. S. Eliot genially compress part of what is implied by the 'peculiar mystery of the marriage between thought and feeling that is consummated [in literary art]', to borrow a phrase from Ronald Peacock.[9] 'To understand a poem', Eliot wrote, 'comes to the same thing as to enjoy it for the right reasons. One might say that it means getting from the poem such enjoyment as it is capable of giving: to enjoy a poem under a misunderstanding as to what it is, is to enjoy what is merely a projection of our own mind. So difficult a tool to handle is language, that "to enjoy" and "to get enjoyment from" do not seem to mean quite the same thing: that to say that one "gets enjoyment from" poetry does not sound quite the same as to say that one "enjoys poetry". And indeed, the very meaning of "joy" varies with the object inspiring joy; different poems, even, yield different satisfactions. It is certain that we do not fully enjoy a poem unless we understand it; and on the other hand, it is equally true that we do not fully understand a poem unless we enjoy it.'[10] Only a shallow reading will take at its face value Eliot's characteristic comment about language being a difficult tool. What *is* difficult, on the other hand, inheres in the sublime achievements of art itself: where success is a waking pleasure in illusion, and illusion a magical harmony of intellect and feeling.

But if we remark a kind of stylistic stretching of 'understanding', we may also see something like it *mutatis mutandis* in uses of 'misunderstanding': our 'mistakes' and 'errors'. Literally speaking, understanding and misunderstanding, like interpretation and misinterpretation, are no more obscurely related than any pair of antonyms: getting something wrong is merely the logical obverse of getting it right. To recognize that we have misunderstood a meaning or meanings which we previously supposed we had understood is an ineluctable way of noticing the *process* of understanding: one name for the negative moments which (we hope) antithetically define the positive moments of augmented understanding. *Recto* and *verso*. To have to alter our earlier evaluations also, in the light of subsequently revealed 'misunderstandings', is merely a way of voicing the process of evaluation, of saying that it consists partly in revaluations and devaluations of past evaluations.

Psychologically, however, we know the inner cost of our revisions and mutations: the difficulty of recognizing some of our 'mistakes' and 'errors'—perhaps even our resistance to doing so. And so we might want other registers of expression to say so. The vulnerability of all our judgments, the nature and depth of our critical responsibilities, emerge poignantly and unavoidably. At times, evidence or lack of evidence, premise or lack of premise, about an author or his intentions, do not, if true, permit us in all conscience to continue valuing a work in the same ways—ways that might in the past have gone deep into our critical allegiances, themselves earned at considerable cost against earlier setbacks and lesser 'misunderstandings'. More mundanely, our vanity will be injured if our previous constatations of response are impugned. There is our wretched misery, at all events, whose obsessive adhesiveness we shall scarcely underestimate. Walter Jackson Bate, for instance, has a hard sentence about prejudice: 'to pursue it with a shrewd and honest imagination would involve a more drastic questioning of ourselves—of our stock responses, of our confidence in our ability to respond immediately, without the help and security of a given context, to what we all say we most deeply value—than most of us care to indulge.'[11] At all events, in these and many other ways, although we realize that, logically, evaluations must change in major or minor ways when facts or premises structuring facts change, psychologically we also realize that it may be against our wishes and our earlier 'understanding' (pleasure, appreciation, ecstasy, wonder, love) that change *must* come.

How might we best express the sense of loss of experience *not* validated? At times a sense of *disappointment* seems adequate. And, once alive to the matter, we will as readily remark the absence of expressions of disappointment (or how fleeting they can be!) as their presence, if only because full confessions of failures to validate evaluations are less common than apparent success stories. At other times, correspondingly difficult to acknowledge either to ourselves or to others, are experiences or anticipations of disappointments so intense or major that *chagrin* or *mortification* might better express the extent of the disillusionment we, as critics, risk when the vanity of our previous 'understanding' is revealed, or seems threatened with revelation as 'misunderstanding'. As I have said, it is often just as much the motivated *absence* of adequate expression of such reversals that prompts us to puzzle over the writings of particular critics. We may witness the sheer resourcefulness of rationalization and its legerdemain. For here is a source of the shame or guilt we can all suffer, confronted with the inadequacies of our own publications: public imperfections harder to evade than the fugitive and, we hope, venial self-deceptions that accompany our unrecorded *obiter dicta*.

As a coda there is even that facet of critical responsibility Hirsch's most recent paper puts generally as an imperative for critics: we can find moral analogues for the sense of *duty* we have in knowing that we ought to respect and have regard for authorial meaning—especially if the meanings are not the meanings we think we needed or thought we would prefer. If they are the author's meanings, per-

perhaps some ethical constraint impels us to do them justice. This is part of critics' recognitions and failures to recognize *whose* meanings they mean; and part of what we all mean when we speak of liberty and license in interpretation.

Doubtless, criticism offers numberless examples of the synthesis Hough describes: 'Neither "the words on the page" nor "the intentions of the author" can alone reveal the significance of a work of literature, and no adequate interpretation of a poem has ever been made by the exclusive pursuit of either of these phantoms.' Sometimes we have certainly 'been presented with false alternatives—to explore the complexities of the inspectable text without extraneous aid, or to recover the uninspectable intentions of the author. Each method has claimed to be sufficient and to exclude the other [whereas] neither the presented surface of the text nor the inferred intention of the author is a sufficient basis for interpretation, and that so far from being mutually exclusive they are complementary.' One way of looking at the debate about authorial intention, compatible with the realities of critical synthesis, is to say that it captures something of the double light, the chequered shade, which, in the temporal systole and diastole of 'internal' and 'external' evidence, and in the setting and the changing of perspectives, *is* the ambivalent interplay of impulses we simplify and call our sense of duty to fact and our sense of transcending value.

One word for the way in which information and evaluation must complement each other and yet must, in specific cases, overrule or undermine each other (remember the scrutiny of 'expression' and the idiom of 'sincerity' and 'authenticity' in 'The Intentional Fallacy') is *irony*. Two halves of a double antithesis strive against each other. In 'Genesis' Wimsatt thinks that 'the statement in our essay of 1946 should certainly have read: "The design or intention of the author is neither available nor desirable as a standard for judging either the meaning or the value of a work of literary art".' Against this ironizing negative there flows an equally protean positive: the design or intention of the author *is* available *and* desirable. What emerges from their mutual conflict contributes to the definition of criticism: What is 'available' or not? What is 'desirable' or not? And what do we know or not know, what do we need or not need, affirming and denying general theses and particular truths about 'design', 'intention', 'author', 'standard', 'judging', 'meaning', 'value' and 'work of literary art'?

It is an editor's duty to avoid too much unnecessary commentary. Assured of the co-operation and goodwill of all concerned it would

be invidious to say more and to presume to speak at length on behalf
of authors who have been invited, and have so kindly consented, to
speak for themselves. The reader can be relied upon to confirm his
own suspicion that, especially in some cases, arguments ought to be
considered in the necessary contexts of wider critical oeuvres.

It is a pleasure, not a duty, to express my gratitude to each one of
the contributors for their generosity in granting permission to reproduce their work in this format, and for encouragement and
advice without which this volume would not have been possible.

I would like to express heartfelt thanks to Wallace Robson. I am
also most grateful to Alastair Fowler for invaluable comments on the
nascent anthology and for his generosity in contributing the essay
published here for the first time.

And lastly express what cannot be expressed. My debt to my wife
Marie-José:

> *Toy qui a veu l'excellence de celle*
> *Qui rend le ciel sur l'Escosse envieux,*
> *Dy hardiment, contentez vous mes yeux,*
> *Vous ne verrez jamais chose plus belle.*

DAVID NEWTON-DE MOLINA
UNIVERSITY OF
EDINBURGH
MAY 1974

o

1. W. K. Wimsatt (with M. C. Beardsley) *The Verbal Icon: Studies in the Meaning of Poetry* (Lexington 1954) p. xi.
2. C. Barrett, ed. *Collected Papers on Aesthetics* (Oxford 1965) p. xiii.
3. W. Righter *Logic and Criticism* (London 1963) p. 3.
4. M. H. Abrams 'What's the Use of Theorizing about the Arts?' in M. W. Bloomfield, ed. *In Search of Literary Theory* (Ithaca and London 1972) pp. 53 and 33.
5. Abrams, p. 53.
6. M. Merleau-Ponty *La Prose du monde*, ed. C. Lefort (Paris 1969) p. 130.
7. W. W. Robson *Critical Essays* (London 1966) pp. 18–19.
8. Abrams, p. 25.
9. R. Peacock *Criticism and Personal Taste* (Oxford 1972) p. 100.
10. T. S. Eliot 'The Frontiers of Criticism' (1956) in *On Poetry and Poets* (London 1957) p. 115.
11. W. Jackson Bate *The Burden of the Past and the English Poet* (London 1971) p. 74. Occasionally, the spectre of the principle of least effort assumes its most cynical aspect. We then remember one of Avenarius' sentences: 'Noch deutlicher fast als im theoretischen Denken zeigt sich in der Kunst die Bestimmung des Verhältnisses der Mittel zu der Leistung durch das Prinzip des kleinsten Kraftmasses' (R. Avenarius *Philosophie als Denken der Welt gemäss dem Prinzip des kleinsten Kraftmasses*, third edition, Berlin 1917, p. 75, note 14).

W. K. WIMSATT and M. C. BEARDSLEY

The Intentional Fallacy

> He owns with toil he wrote the following scenes;
> But, if they're naught, ne'er spare him for his pains:
> Damn him the more; have no commiseration
> For dullness on mature deliberation.
>
> WILLIAM CONGREVE Prologue to *The Way of the World*

The claim of the author's 'intention' upon the critic's judgment has been challenged in a number of recent discussions, notably in the debate entitled *The Personal Heresy*, between Professors Lewis and Tillyard. But it seems doubtful if this claim and most of its romantic corollaries are as yet subject to any widespread questioning. The present writers, in a short article entitled 'Intention' for a *Dictionary*[1] of literary criticism, raised the issue but were unable to pursue its implications at any length. We argued that the design or intention of the author is neither available nor desirable as a standard for judging the success of a work of literary art, and it seems to us that this is a principle which goes deep into some differences in the history of critical attitudes. It is a principle which accepted or rejected points to the polar opposites of classical 'imitation' and romantic expression. It entails many specific truths about inspiration, authenticity, biography, literary history and scholarship, and about some trends of contemporary poetry, especially its allusiveness. There is hardly a problem of literary criticism in which the critic's approach will not be qualified by his view of 'intention.'

'Intention,' as we shall use the term, corresponds to *what he intended* in a formula which more or less explicitly has had wide acceptance. 'In order to judge the poet's performance, we must know *what he intended.*' Intention is design or plan in the author's mind. Intention has obvious affinities for the author's attitude toward his work, the way he felt, what made him write.

We begin our discussion with a series of propositions summarized and abstracted to a degree where they seem to us axiomatic.

1. A poem does not come into existence by accident. The words of a poem, as Professor Stoll has remarked, come out of a head, not out of a hat. Yet to insist on the designing intellect as a *cause* of a poem is not to grant the design or intention as a *standard* by which the critic is to judge the worth of the poet's performance.

2. One must ask how a critic expects to get an answer to the question about intention. How is he to find out what the poet tried to do? If the poet succeeded in doing it, then the poem itself shows what he was trying to do. And if the poet did not succeed, then the poem is not adequate evidence, and the critic must go outside the poem—for evidence of an intention that did not become effective in the poem. 'Only one *caveat* must be borne in mind,' says an eminent intentionalist[2] in a moment when his theory repudiates itself; 'the poet's aim must be judged at the moment of the creative act, that is to say, by the art of the poem itself.'

3. Judging a poem is like judging a pudding or a machine. One demands that it work. It is only because an artifact works that we infer the intention of an artificer. 'A poem should not mean but be.' A poem can *be* only through its *meaning*—since its medium is words—yet it *is*, simply *is*, in the sense that we have no excuse for inquiring what part is intended or meant. Poetry is a feat of style by which a complex of meaning is handled all at once. Poetry succeeds because all or most of what is said or implied is relevant; what is irrelevant has been excluded, like lumps from pudding and 'bugs' from machinery. In this respect poetry differs from practical messages, which are successful if and only if we correctly infer the intention. They are more abstract than poetry.

4. The meaning of a poem may certainly be a personal one, in the sense that a poem expresses a personality or state of soul rather than a physical object like an apple. But even a short lyric poem is dramatic, the response of a speaker (no matter how abstractly conceived) to a situation (no matter how universalized). We ought to impute the thoughts and attitudes of the poem immediately to the dramatic *speaker*, and if to the author at all, only by an act of biographical inference.

5. There is a sense in which an author, by revision, may better achieve his original intention. But it is a very abstract sense. He intended to write a better work, or a better work of a certain kind, and now has done it. But it follows that his former concrete intention was not his intention. 'He's the man we were in search of, that's true,' says Hardy's rustic constable, 'and yet he's not the man we were in search of. For the man we were in search of was not the man we wanted.'

'Is not a critic,' asks Professor Stoll, 'a judge, who does not explore his own consciousness, but determines the author's meaning or intention, as if the poem were a will, a contract, or the constitution? The poem is not the critic's own.' He has accurately diagnosed two forms of irresponsibility, one of which he prefers. Our view is yet different. The poem is not the critic's own and not the author's (it is detached from the author at birth and goes about the world beyond his power to intend about it or control it). The poem belongs to the public. It is embodied in language, the peculiar possession of the public, and it is about the human being, an object of public knowledge. What is said about the poem is subject to the same scrutiny as any statement in linguistics or in the general science of psychology.

A critic of our *Dictionary* article, Ananda K. Coomaraswamy, has argued[3] that there are two kinds of inquiry about a work of art: (i) whether the artist achieved his intentions; (ii) whether the work of art 'ought ever to have been undertaken at all' and so 'whether it is worth preserving.' Number (ii), Coomaraswamy maintains, is not 'criticism of any work of art *qua* work of art,' but is rather moral criticism; number (i) is artistic criticism. But we maintain that (ii) need not be moral criticism: that there is another way of deciding whether works of art are worth preserving and whether, in a sense, they 'ought' to have been undertaken, and this is the way of objective criticism of works of art as such, the way which enables us to distinguish between a skillful murder and a skillful poem. A skillful murder is an example which Coomaraswamy uses, and in his system, the difference between the murder and the poem is simply a 'moral' one, not an 'artistic' one, since each if carried out according to plan is 'artistically' successful. We maintain that (ii) is an inquiry of more worth than (i), and since (ii) and not (i) is capable of distinguishing poetry from murder, the name 'artistic criticism' is properly given to (ii).

o   o   o

It is not so much a historical statement as a definition to say that the intentional fallacy is a romantic one. When a rhetorician of the first century A D writes: 'Sublimity is the echo of a great soul,' or when he tells us that 'Homer enters into the sublime actions of his heroes' and 'shares the full inspiration of the combat,' we shall not be surprised to find this rhetorician considered as a distant harbinger of romanticism and greeted in the warmest terms by Saintsbury. One may wish to argue whether Longinus should be called romantic, but there can hardly be a doubt that in one important way he is.

Goethe's three questions for 'constructive criticism' are 'What did the author set out to do? Was his plan reasonable and sensible, and how far did he succeed in carrying it out?' If one leaves out the middle question, one has in effect the system of Croce—the culmination and crowning philosophic expression of romanticism. The beautiful is the successful intuition-expression, and the ugly is the unsuccessful; the intuition or private part of art is *the* aesthetic fact, and the medium or public part is not the subject of aesthetic at all.

> The Madonna of Cimabue is still in the Church of Santa Maria Novella; but does she speak to the visitor of to-day as to the Florentines of the thirteenth century?
>
> *Historical interpretation* labours . . . to reintegrate in us the psychological conditions which have changed in the course of history. It . . . enables us to see a work of art (a physical object) as its *author saw it* in the moment of production.[4]

The first italics are Croce's, the second ours. The upshot of Croce's system is an ambiguous emphasis on history. With such passages as a point of departure a critic may write a nice analysis of the meaning or 'spirit' of a play by Shakespeare or Corneille—a process that involves close historical study but remains aesthetic criticism—or he may, with equal plausibility, produce an essay in sociology, biography, or other kinds of non-aesthetic history.

o o o

> I went to the poets; tragic, dithyrambic, and all sorts. . . . I took them some of the most elaborate passages in their own writings, and asked what was the meaning of them. . . . Will you believe me? . . . there is hardly a person present who would not have talked better about their poetry than they did themselves. Then I knew that not by wisdom do poets write poetry, but by a sort of genius and inspiration.

That reiterated mistrust of the poets which we hear from Socrates may have been part of a rigorously ascetic view in which we hardly wish to participate, yet Plato's Socrates saw a truth about the poetic mind which the world no longer commonly sees—so much criticism, and that the most inspirational and most affectionately remembered, has proceeded from the poets themselves.

Certainly the poets have had something to say that the critic and professor could not say; their message has been more exciting: that poetry should come as naturally as leaves to a tree, that poetry is the lava of the imagination, or that it is emotion recollected in tranquillity. But it is necessary that we realize the character and authority of such testimony. There is only a fine shade of difference between such expressions and a kind of earnest advice that authors often give. Thus Edward Young, Carlyle, Walter Pater:

> I know two golden rules from *ethics*, which are no less golden in *Composition*, than in life. 1. *Know thyself*; 2dly, *Reverence thyself*.

> This is the grand secret for finding readers and retaining them: let him who would move and convince others, be first moved and convinced himself. Horace's rule, *Si vis me flere*, is applicable

4

in a wider sense than the literal one. To every poet, to every writer, we might say: Be true, if you would be believed.

Truth! there can be no merit, no craft at all, without that. And further, all beauty is in the long run only *fineness* of truth, or what we call expression, the finer accommodation of speech to that vision within.

And Housman's little handbook to the poetic mind yields this illustration:

Having drunk a pint of beer at luncheon—beer is a sedative to the brain, and my afternoons are the least intellectual portion of my life—I would go out for a walk of two or three hours. As I went along, thinking of nothing in particular, only looking at things around me and following the progress of the seasons, there would flow into my mind, with sudden and unaccountable emotion, sometimes a line or two of verse, sometimes a whole stanza at once.

This is the logical terminus of the series already quoted. Here is a confession of how poems were written which would do as a definition of poetry just as well as 'emotion recollected in tranquillity'—and which the young poet might equally well take to heart as a practical rule. Drink a pint of beer, relax, go walking, think on nothing in particular, look at things, surrender yourself to yourself, search for the truth in your own soul, listen to the sound of your own inside voice, discover and express the *vraie vérité*.

It is probably true that all this is excellent advice for poets. The young imagination fired by Wordsworth and Carlyle is probably closer to the verge of producing a poem than the mind of the student who has been sobered by Aristotle or Richards. The art of inspiring poets, or at least of inciting something like poetry in young persons, has probably gone further in our day than ever before. Books of creative writing such as those issued from the Lincoln School are interesting evidence of what a child can do.[5] All this, however, would appear to belong to an art separate from criticism—to a psychological discipline, a system of self-development, a yoga, which the young poet perhaps does well to notice, but which is something different from the public art of evaluating poems.

Coleridge and Arnold were better critics than most poets have been, and if the critical tendency dried up the poetry in Arnold and perhaps in Coleridge, it is not inconsistent with our argument, which is that judgment of poems is different from the art of producing them. Coleridge has given us the classic 'anodyne' story, and tells what he can about the genesis of a poem which he calls a 'psychological curiosity,' but his definitions of poetry and of the poetic quality 'imagination' are to be found elsewhere and in quite other terms.

It would be convenient if the passwords of the intentional school, 'sincerity,' 'fidelity,' 'spontaneity,' 'authenticity,' 'genuineness,' 'originality,' could be equated with terms such as 'integrity,' 'relevance,' 'unity,' 'function,' 'maturity,' 'subtlety,' 'adequacy,' and other more precise terms of evaluation—in short, if 'expression' always meant aesthetic achievement. But this is not so.

'Aesthetic' art, says Professor Curt Ducasse, an ingenious theorist of expression, is the conscious objectification of feelings, in which an intrinsic part is the critical moment. The artist corrects the objectification when it is not adequate. But this may mean that the earlier attempt was not successful in objectifying the self, or 'it may also mean that it was a successful objectification of a self which, when it confronted us clearly, we disowned and repudiated in favor of another.'[6] What is the standard by which we disown or accept the self? Professor Ducasse does not say. Whatever it may be, however, this standard is an element in the definition of art which will not reduce to terms of objectification. The evaluation of the work of art remains public; the work is measured against something outside the author.

o   o   o

There is criticism of poetry and there is author psychology, which when applied to the present or future takes the form of inspirational promotion; but author psychology can be historical too, and then we have literary biography, a legitimate and attractive study in itself, one approach, as Professor Tillyard would argue, to personality, the poem being only a parallel approach. Certainly it need not be with a derogatory purpose that one points out personal studies, as distinct from poetic studies, in the realm of literary scholarship. Yet there is danger of confusing personal and poetic studies; and there is the fault of writing the personal as if it were poetic.

There is a difference between internal and external evidence for the meaning of a poem. And the paradox is only verbal and superficial that what is (1) internal is also public: it is discovered through the semantics and syntax of a poem, through our habitual knowledge of the language, through grammars, dictionaries, and all the literature which is the source of dictionaries, in general through all that makes a language and culture; while what is (2) external is private or idiosyncratic; not a part of the work as a linguistic fact: it consists of revelations (in journals, for example, or letters or reported conversations) about how or why the poet wrote the poem—to what lady, while sitting on what lawn, or at the death of what friend or brother.

6

There is (3) an intermediate kind of evidence about the character of the author or about private or semiprivate meanings attached to words or topics by an author or by a coterie of which he is a member. The meaning of words is the history of words, and the biography of an author, his use of a word, and the associations which the word had for *him*, are part of the word's history and meaning.[7] But the three types of evidence, especially (2) and (3), shade into one another so subtly that it is not always easy to draw a line between examples, and hence arises the difficulty for criticism. The use of biographical evidence need not involve intentionalism, because while it may be evidence of what the author intended, it may also be evidence of the meaning of his words and the dramatic character of his utterance. On the other hand, it may not be all this. And a critic who is concerned with evidence of type (1) and moderately with that of type (3) will in the long run produce a different sort of comment from that of the critic who is concerned with (2) and with (3) where it shades into (2).

The whole glittering parade of Professor Lowes' *Road to Xanadu*, for instance, runs along the border between types (2) and (3) or boldly traverses the romantic region of (2). '*Kubla Khan*,' says Professor Lowes, 'is the fabric of a vision, but every image that rose up in its weaving had passed that way before. And it would seem that there is nothing haphazard or fortuitous in their return.' This is not quite clear—not even when Professor Lowes explains that there were clusters of associations, like hooked atoms, which were drawn into complex relation with other clusters in the deep well of Coleridge's memory, and which then coalesced and issued forth as poems. If there was nothing 'haphazard or fortuitous' in the way the images returned to the surface, that may mean (a) that Coleridge could not produce what he did not have, that he was limited in his creation by what he had read or otherwise experienced, or (b) that having received certain clusters of associations, he was bound to return them in just the way he did, and that the value of the poem may be described in terms of the experiences on which he had to draw. The latter pair of propositions (a sort of Hartleyan association-ism which Coleridge himself repudiated in the *Biographia*) may not be assented to. There were certainly other combinations, other poems, worse or better, that might have been written by men who had read Bartram and Purchas and Bruce and Milton. And this will be true no matter how many times we are able to add to the brilliant complex of Coleridge's reading. In certain flourishes (such as the sentence we have quoted) and in chapter headings like 'The Shaping Spirit,' 'The Magical Synthesis,' 'Imagination Creatrix,' it may be

7

that Professor Lowes pretends to say more about the actual poems than he does. There is a certain deceptive variation in these fancy chapter titles; one expects to pass on to a new stage in the argument, and one finds—more and more sources, more and more about 'the streamy nature of association.'[8]

'Wohin der Weg?' quotes Professor Lowes for the motto of his book. 'Kein Weg! Ins Unbetretene.' Precisely because the way is *unbetreten*, we should say, it leads away from the poem. Bartram's *Travels* contains a good deal of the history of certain words and of certain romantic Floridian conceptions that appear in *Kubla Khan*. And a good deal of that history has passed and was then passing into the very stuff of our language. Perhaps a person who has read Bartram appreciates the poem more than one who has not. Or, by looking up the vocabulary of *Kubla Khan* in the *Oxford English Dictionary*, or by reading some of the other books there quoted, a person may know the poem better. But it would seem to pertain little to the poem to know that *Coleridge* had read Bartram. There is a gross body of life, of sensory and mental experience, which lies behind and in some sense causes every poem, but can never be and need not be known in the verbal and hence intellectual composition which is the poem. For all the objects of our manifold experience, for every unity, there is an action of the mind which cuts off roots, melts away context—or indeed we should never have objects or ideas or anything to talk about.

It is probable that there is nothing in Professor Lowes' vast book which could detract from anyone's appreciation of either *The Ancient Mariner* or *Kubla Khan*. We next present a case where preoccupation with evidence of type (3) has gone so far as to distort a critic's view of a poem (yet a case not so obvious as those that abound in our critical journals).

In a well known poem by John Donne appears this quatrain:

> Moving of th' earth brings harmes and feares,
>   Men reckon what it did and meant,
> But trepidation of the spheares,
>   Though greater farre, is innocent.

A recent critic in an elaborate treatment of Donne's learning has written of this quatrain as follows:

> He touches the emotional pulse of the situation by a skillful allusion to the new and the old astronomy. . . . Of the new astronomy, the 'moving of the earth' is the most radical principle; of the old, the 'trepidation of the spheres' is the motion of the greatest complexity. . . . The poet must exhort his love to quietness and calm upon his departure; and for this

purpose the figure based upon the latter motion (trepidation), long absorbed into the traditional astronomy, fittingly suggests the tension of the moment without arousing the 'harmes and feares' implicit in the figure of the moving earth.[9]

The argument is plausible and rests on a well-substantiated thesis that Donne was deeply interested in the new astronomy and its repercussions in the theological realm. In various works Donne shows his familiarity with Kepler's *De Stella Nova*, with Galileo's *Siderius Nuncius*, with William Gilbert's *De Magnete*, and with Clavius' commentary on the *De Sphaera* of Sacrobosco. He refers to the new science in his Sermon at Paul's Cross and in a letter to Sir Henry Goodyer. In *The First Anniversary* he says the 'new philosophy calls all in doubt.' In the *Elegy on Prince Henry* he says that the 'least moving of the center' makes 'the world to shake.'

It is difficult to answer argument like this, and impossible to answer it with evidence of like nature. There is no reason why Donne might not have written a stanza in which the two kinds of celestial motion stood for two sorts of emotion at parting. And if we become full of astronomical ideas and see Donne only against the background of the new science, we may believe that he did. But the text itself remains to be dealt with, the analyzable vehicle of a complicated metaphor. And one may observe: (i) that the movement of the earth according to the Copernican theory is a celestial motion, smooth and regular, and while it might cause religious or philosophic fears, it could not be associated with the crudity and earthiness of the kind of commotion which the speaker in the poem wishes to discourage; (ii) that there is another moving of the earth, an earthquake, which has just these qualities and is to be associated with the tear-floods and sigh-tempests of the second stanza of the poem; (iii) that 'trepidation' is an appropriate opposite of earthquake, because each is a shaking or vibratory motion; and 'trepidation of the spheres' is 'greater far' than an earthquake, but not much greater (if two such motions can be compared as to greatness) than the annual motion of the earth; (iv) that reckoning what it 'did and meant' shows that the event has passed, like an earthquake, not like the incessant celestial movement of the earth. Perhaps a knowledge of Donne's interest in the new science may add another shade of meaning, an overtone to the stanza in question, though to say even this runs against the words. To make the geocentric and heliocentric antithesis the core of the metaphor is to disregard the English language, to prefer private evidence to public, external to internal.

o o o

If the distinction between kinds of evidence has implications for the historical critic, it has them no less for the contemporary poet and his critic. Or, since every rule for a poet is but another side of a judgment by a critic, and since the past is the realm of the scholar and critic, and the future and present that of the poet and the critical leaders of taste, we may say that the problems arising in literary scholarship from the intentional fallacy are matched by others which arise in the world of progressive experiment.

The question of 'allusiveness,' for example, as acutely posed by the poetry of Eliot, is certainly one where a false judgment is likely to involve the intentional fallacy. The frequency and depth of literary allusion in the poetry of Eliot and others has driven so many in pursuit of full meanings to the *Golden Bough* and the Elizabethan drama that it has become a kind of commonplace to suppose that we do not know what a poet means unless we have traced him in his reading—a supposition redolent with intentional implications. The stand taken by F. O. Matthiessen is a sound one and partially forestalls the difficulty.

> If one reads these lines with an attentive ear and is sensitive to their sudden shifts in movement, the contrast between the actual Thames and the idealized vision of it during an age before it flowed through a megalopolis is sharply conveyed by that movement itself, whether or not one recognizes the refrain to be from Spenser.

Eliot's allusions work when we know them—and to a great extent even when we do not know them, through their suggestive power.

But sometimes we find allusions supported by notes, and it is a nice question whether the notes function more as guides to send us where we may be educated, or more as indications in themselves about the character of the allusions. 'Nearly everything of importance . . . that is apposite to an appreciation of *The Waste Land*,' writes Matthiessen of Miss Weston's book, 'has been incorporated into the structure of the poem itself, or into Eliot's Notes.' And with such an admission it may begin to appear that it would not much matter if Eliot invented his sources (as Sir Walter Scott invented chapter epigraphs from 'old plays' and 'anonymous' authors, or as Coleridge wrote marginal glosses for *The Ancient Mariner*). Allusions to Dante, Webster, Marvell, or Baudelaire doubtless gain something because these writers existed, but it is doubtful whether the same can be said for an allusion to an obscure Elizabethan:

> The sound of horns and motors, which shall bring
> Sweeney to Mrs. Porter in the spring.

'Cf. Day, *Parliament of Bees*:' says Eliot,

> When of a sudden, listening, you shall hear,

A noise of horns and hunting, which shall bring
Actaeon to Diana in the spring,
Where all shall see her naked skin.

The irony is completed by the quotation itself; had Eliot, as is quite conceivable, composed these lines to furnish his own background, there would be no loss of validity. The conviction may grow as one reads Eliot's next note: 'I do not know the origin of the ballad from which these lines are taken: it was reported to me from Sydney, Australia.' The important word in this note—on Mrs Porter and her daughter who washed their feet in soda water—is 'ballad.' And if one should feel from the lines themselves their 'ballad' quality, there would be little need for the note. Ultimately, the inquiry must focus on the integrity of such notes as parts of the poem, for where they constitute special information about the meaning of phrases in the poem, they ought to be subject to the same scrutiny as any of the other words in which it is written. Matthiessen believes the notes were the price Eliot 'had to pay in order to avoid what he would have considered muffling the energy of his poem by extended connecting links in the text itself.' But it may be questioned whether the notes and the need for them are not equally muffling. F. W. Bateson has plausibly argued that Tennyson's *The Sailor Boy* would be better if half the stanzas were omitted, and the best versions of ballads like *Sir Patrick Spens* owe their power to the very audacity with which the minstrel has taken for granted the story upon which he comments. What then if a poet finds he cannot take so much for granted in a more recondite context and rather than write informatively, supplies notes? It can be said in favor of this plan that at least the notes do not pretend to be dramatic, as they would if written in verse. On the other hand, the notes may look like unassimilated material lying loose beside the poem, necessary for the meaning of the verbal symbol, but not integrated, so that the symbol stands incomplete.

We mean to suggest by the above analysis that whereas notes tend to seem to justify themselves as external indexes to the author's *intention*, yet they ought to be judged like any other parts of a composition (verbal arrangement special to a particular context), and when so judged their reality as parts of the poem, or their imaginative integration with the rest of the poem, may come into question. Matthiessen, for instance, sees that Eliot's titles for poems and his epigraphs are informative apparatus, like the notes. But while he is worried by some of the notes and thinks that Eliot 'appears to be mocking himself for writing the note at the same time that he wants to convey something by it,' Matthiessen believes that the 'device' of epigraphs 'is not at all open to the objection of not being sufficiently structural.' 'The *intention*,' he says, 'is to enable the poet to secure a condensed expression in the poem itself.' 'In each case the epigraph is *designed* to form an integral part of the effect of the poem.' And Eliot himself, in his notes, has justified his poetic practice in terms of intention.

> The Hanged Man, a member of the traditional pack, fits my purpose in two ways: because he is associated in my mind with the Hanged God of Frazer, and because I associate him with the hooded figure in the passage of the disciples to Emmaus in Part V. . . . The man with Three Staves (an authentic member of the Tarot pack) I associate, quite arbitrarily, with the Fisher King himself.

And perhaps he is to be taken more seriously here, when off guard in a note, than when in his Norton Lectures he comments on the difficulty of saying what a poem means and adds playfully that he thinks of prefixing to a second edition of *Ash Wednesday* some lines from *Don Juan*:

> I don't pretend that I quite understand
> My own meaning when I would be *very* fine;
> But the fact is that I have nothing planned
> Unless it were to be a moment merry.

If Eliot and other contemporary poets have any characteristic fault, it may be in *planning* too much.

Allusiveness in poetry is one of several critical issues by which we have illustrated the more abstract issue of intentionalism, but it may be for today the most important illustration. As a poetic practice allusiveness would appear to be in some recent poems an extreme corollary of the romantic intentionalist assumption, and as a critical issue it challenges and brings to light in a special way the basic premise of intentionalism. The following instance from the poetry of Eliot may serve to epitomize the practical implications of what we have been saying. In Eliot's *Love Song of J. Alfred Prufrock*, toward the end, occurs the line: 'I have heard the mermaids singing, each to each,' and this bears a certain resemblance to a line in a Song by John Donne, 'Teach me to heare Mermaides singing,' so that for the reader acquainted to a certain degree with Donne's poetry, the critical question arises: Is Eliot's line an allusion to Donne's? Is Prufrock thinking about Donne? Is Eliot thinking about Donne? We suggest that there are two radically different ways of looking for an answer to this question. There is (i) the way of poetic analysis and exegesis, which inquires whether it makes any sense if Eliot-Prufrock *is* thinking about Donne. In an earlier part of the poem, when Prufrock asks, 'Would it have been worth while, . . . To have squeezed the universe into a ball,' his words take half their sadness and irony from certain energetic and passionate lines of Marvell *To His Coy Mistress*. But the exegetical inquirer may wonder whether mermaids considered as 'strange sights' (to hear them is in Donne's poem analogous to getting with child a mandrake root) have much to do with Prufrock's mermaids, which seem to be symbols of romance and dynamism, and which incidentally have literary authentication, if they need it, in a line of a sonnet by Gérard de Nerval. This method of inquiry may lead to the conclusion that the given resemblance between Eliot and Donne is without significance and is better not thought of, or the method may have the disadvantage of providing no certain conclusion. Nevertheless, we submit that this is the true and objective way of criticism, as contrasted to what the very uncertainty of exegesis might tempt a second kind of critic to undertake: (ii) the way of biographical or genetic inquiry, in which, taking advantage of the fact that Eliot is still alive, and in the spirit of a man who would settle a bet, the critic writes to Eliot and asks what he meant, or if he had Donne in mind. We shall not here weigh the probabilities—whether Eliot would answer that he meant nothing at all, had nothing at all in mind—a sufficiently good answer to such a question—or in an unguarded moment might furnish a clear and, within its limit, irrefutable answer. Our point is that such an answer to such an inquiry would have nothing to do with the poem *Prufrock*; it would not be a critical inquiry. Critical inquiries, unlike bets, are not settled in this way. Critical inquiries are not settled by consulting the oracle.

THEODORE REDPATH

The Meaning of a Poem

Like some of the other lecturers on this course,[1] I intend in my lectures not to render an account of recent British philosophy on my subject, but to try to exemplify a way of thinking characteristic of at least one trend in recent British thought. The way of thinking is one which I believe I have learned by studying philosophy at Cambridge: but I do not wish to attribute either my method or my conclusions to any one of the Cambridge philosophers under whom I have studied, i.e. Moore, Broad, Wittgenstein, Wisdom or Russell. None of these philosophers have, in any case, discussed questions of aesthetics very much: and so even someone trained in philosophy at Cambridge, if he tries to philosophize about problems in aesthetics, is under the disadvantage of moving in a field uncharted by them. The only Cambridge philosophers who have recently discussed aesthetics at all largely are C. K. Ogden and I. A. Richards, and while I have certainly learned much from them, as so many others have, I have neither followed their methods nor come to their conclusions.

The problems I have chosen for discussion are problems that have interested British aestheticians recently, though I would not pretend that this interest in them is peculiar to this country. The problems I shall discuss in this first lecture concern aesthetic interpretation: those I shall discuss in the second lecture concern aesthetic evaluation. That has seemed to me a fair division.

Let me make a start on the first problem, then, which is this: 'Is the meaning of a poem the meaning the poet intended it to have?' Some high modern authorities would certainly reply to this question in the negative. Roger Fry, for instance, speaking of works of art in general, once said: 'I'm certain that the only meanings that are worth anything in a work of art, are those that the artist himself knows nothing about'.[2] Let us look into the question.

It is perhaps first worth asking what evidence there could be as to the meaning that the poet intended his poem to have. Some theorists would maintain that there can be no evidence, external or internal, as to what the poet intended his poem to mean, where that meaning would differ from the meaning of the poem as it stands. The American literary theorists, Professors Monroe C. Beardsley and W. K. Wimsatt, Jr., for instance, who have given this problem careful attention, maintain (1) that 'to pretend that the author's aim can be detected internally in the work even where it is not realized . . . is merely a self-contradictory proposition', and (2) that 'there can be no evidence, internal or external, that the author has conceived something which he did not execute'.

Both these statements seem to me to be false.

I think that it is sometimes possible to detect from inspection of a poem, particularly in the case of an inferior poem, that the poet has not said exactly what he meant to say; that is, that the poem, as it stands, does not mean exactly what the poet intended it to mean. Thus the claim 'that the author's aim can be detected internally in the work even where it is not realized', so far from being self-contradictory, is, in my view, not even false, but, on the contrary, absolutely valid, in some cases.

Again, I believe, contrary to (2), that there can be both internal *and* external evidence 'that the author had conceived something which he did not execute'. I have spoken in the last paragraph of the internal evidence; but there could easily be external evidence as well. We have, for example, a poet's own word about the process of poetic creation. Shelley, in his *Defence of Poetry*, writes in terms of great generality: 'when composition begins, inspiration is already on the decline, and the most glorious poetry that has ever been communicated to the world is probably a feeble shadow of the original conceptions of the poet'. This seems to me itself evidence of great weight. A poet is telling us that the words of poets do not mean what they were intended to mean. He is even taking precisely the opposite view to that of Professors Beardsley and Wimsatt, and telling us that poems *never* mean what they were intended to mean. Perhaps that is forgivable romantic exaggeration, but it might be as well not to feel too sure. In any case we ought, I think, to take it as evidence that *sometimes* poems do not mean what they were intended to mean. Again, when a poet changes expressions in a poem during revision, is that not sometimes[3] because he considers that the words he is rejecting do not express as well as the new words, what he meant? A mere change would not by itself be evidence; but the setting of the words in the poem *might* be the only additional factor requiring consideration, to make it clear that the old words did not express what the poet meant. On the other hand, other evidence *might* be required, and might actually be *forthcoming*, e.g. the poet might himself tell us that the old expressions did not convey what he had meant, and he might even tell us *how* they failed to do so.

Thus both of the assertions of Professors Beardsley and Wimsatt seem to me to be wrong. There could be evidence, both internal and external, as to the meaning that the poet intended a poem to have, even where that meaning would differ from the meaning of the poem as it stands. On the other hand, there seems to be definite point in what they say with regard to internal evidence. If it is clear 'from within the four corners of the poem itself' (to adapt an expression from English legal interpretation to new purposes), that some of the words in the poem do not convey the poet's meaning, then at all events the poem as a whole has at least revealed the poet's meaning. Might there not therefore be colour for saying that the poem as a whole, as it stands, *does* convey the poet's meaning? And would it not be an easy step from that to saying that the poem as a whole has the meaning that the poet intended it to have? There is some plausibility in this. All the same, the last step, at least, would be a dangerous one. And I believe the second step would also be objectionable. The indication as to what the poet really intended the poem to mean might be a mere hint here and there, and in that case it would surely be a mistake to say that the poem *as a whole* conveyed the meaning the poet intended it to convey, when the greater part of it did not?

Let us leave this point now, and go on to another point about the assertions of Professors Beardsley and Wimsatt. There was an important difference between assertions (1) and (2). The first poured ridicule on the claim that the author's aim *can be detected* internally in the work even when it is not realized. The second expressed the larger opinion that there *can be no evidence that* the author had conceived something which he did not execute. Now Shelley's statement seems to me, as I have said, strong evidence in favour of the view that authors have at least sometimes intended their works to mean something different from what they do in fact mean: but it is no evidence that *what* the authors intended their works to mean *can be detected* either by internal or by external evidence. Shelley might well have admitted that 'the original conceptions' of the poet could not be detected by readers of his poem, and might even have agreed that the poet himself could not say in what way the poem as it stands differs from his 'original conception'. Possibly, then, Professors Beardsley and Wimsatt could have enlisted Shelley's support of their first point, even though he was a powerful adversary of their second point. But Shelley's statement as it stands does not give their first point any support either. He says nothing about a poet's subsequent knowledge of his 'original conceptions'. In any case, though, surely a poet might sometimes be able to recapture his 'original conceptions', and to describe them to some extent, even though he had failed to express them in the poem which he actually wrote?

Alternatively, even if a poet could never do *this*, surely, before writing his poem, he might have acquiesced in the reduction of his intentions to something which he could easily *describe*, yet failed to *express* in the poem?

My own view, then, is that there could be both internal and external evidence of the meaning which the poet intended a poem to have, even where that meaning differed from the meaning of the poem as it stands. This is also *part* of an answer to the original question: 'Is the meaning of a poem the meaning the poet intended it to have?' If I am right, we should at least answer to this: 'Not always'.

That by no means exhausts the matter, though. We must go on to ask whether the meaning of a poem is *ever* the meaning the poet intended it to have. T. S. Eliot, in an article in *The Partisan Review* (November–December 1942), writes (on p. 457): 'There may be much more in a poem than the author was aware of'. It is important to notice that Eliot does not say that there *must* be much more in a poem than the author was aware of, or even that there *is always* much more in a poem than the author is aware of, but only that there *may* be much more in a poem than the author is aware of. He leaves open the possibility that in *some* poems there is neither more nor less than the author was aware of. This is perhaps the point at which to say a brief word as to the relation between 'being aware of' a meaning, and 'intending' a meaning. In the most common sense of the terms 'intention' and 'intended', the sense in which it would be reasonable to take the term 'intended' in the question we are considering, a meaning in a poem being written could not be 'intended' without the poet 'being aware of' it. So that when Eliot says that there may be much more in a poem than the author was aware of, we must take it that he is at least saying that there may be much more in a poem than the author intended. That statement we may, I think, accept. It seems very unlikely that in the case of every poem that has ever been written, the poet has always intended everything that the poem means, especially if we take the 'meaning' of the poem in a full sense, such as that described by Professor I. A. Richards in his book *Practical Criticism*, i.e. as including intellectual, emotive, tonal and intentional elements. It seems very unlikely that every poet in writing every poem has been in full conscious control of all these.[4] Even in the case of *good* poems it seems that poets are at least sometimes, as Socrates found them to be, 'like prophets and oracular persons, who say many fine things without knowing what it is that they are saying'. There may be much more in a poem, then, than the author intended.

But *must* there be more in a poem than the author intended? To answer in the affirmative would be to enunciate a necessary proposition, which ought immediately to be suspect. What is there to exclude the *possibility* that, substantially at least, there may be in some poems neither more nor less than the author intended? It is difficult, even in comparatively simple cases, to tell for certain whether this is so: but a probable estimate would seem often possible.

So far then, it seems that a poem may mean something different from what the poet intended it to mean, may mean less than the poet intended it to mean, may mean more than he intended it to mean; may perhaps sometimes mean substantially what he intended.

But if this is so, it would certainly seem that the poet's intention cannot be used as a *universal* criterion of the meaning of a poem, and can hardly even always be used as a *leading* criterion in the search for the meaning even if that intention can easily be discovered, which may often not be the case. On the other hand, the probable intention of the poet does at least sometimes afford a criterion by which to judge whether a certain meaning which is attributed to a poem is probably correct or not. The situation is therefore confusing. Is part of the confusion due to the fact that the use of the term 'intention' or 'intended', in the question under consideration, lets in such awkward cases as those envisaged by Shelley? Very possibly. While admitting, then, that in such cases the meaning of a poem is not the meaning the poet intended it to have, let us try to clear up the rest of the situation by asking a slightly different question, namely: 'Is the meaning of a poem what the poet *meant* by it?' Some people would say: 'Yes, certainly, otherwise it would not be the poet's poem'. Professor G. E. Moore expressed such a view to me about two years ago when I was discussing this very point with him. He said that he did not see how a poem could be called the poem of the poet who wrote it, unless it meant what the poet meant by it. (I should not like to misrepresent that fine philosopher's views about anything, and I cannot help thinking that he must have had *good* poems in mind: for it seems to me that a *bad* poem could only too easily mean something different from what the poet meant by it.) In the opposite camp to that of those who would say that the meaning of a poem *is* what the poet meant by it, we might expect to find those who would say that the meaning of a poem is *never* what the poet meant by it; but I think the population of such a camp would be rather sparse. On the other hand, there would, I believe, be plenty of people who would maintain that, although the meaning of a poem may often be what the poet meant by it, that would he a pure contingency; on the ground that the meaning of the poem itself is neither more nor less than the meaning it has for an intelligent and sensitive reader or for intelligent and sensitive readers, who understand the language in which it is written. In this camp, as can be seen, there would be included both people who consider that a poem has *one* meaning, and people who consider that it has *many* meanings, the meanings, namely, that it would have for all the intelligent and sensitive readers who come to read it. There is, in my opinion, a crippling objection to this view, namely, that even intelligent and sensitive readers are liable to make mistakes. Yet another camp would be represented by the late John Dewey, who, in his book *Art as Experience*, writes as follows: 'It is absurd to ask what an artist "really" meant by his product; he himself would find different meanings in it at different days and hours and in different stages of his own development. If he could articulate, he would say "I meant just *that*, and *that* means whatever you or anyone can honestly, that is in virtue of your own vital experience, get out of it".'[5] This position of Dewey's is a somewhat curious one. Substantially, he seems to be mediating between the two opposing camps by saying that the meanings of the work *are* what the artist meant by it: while, on the other hand, there are many meanings, and what these meanings are is determined by what he calls 'whatever anyone can honestly, that is, in virtue of that person's vital experience, get out of it'. Dewey, it will be noticed, alleges that the artist 'would say' all those things. Now that is an empirical proposition which I, for one, believe to be untrue. Those things are indeed what Dewey would have *liked* the artist to say: but it is more than doubtful whether artists are all and always so liberal. Still, we must not undervalue Dewey's point. Even if artists *would not* always say those things, perhaps those are the things they *ought* to say. Yet, facing this suggestion, we can legitimately ask: 'Why should they? Why *should* a poet say: "I meant by my poem everything anyone can honestly, that is in virtue of that person's vital experience, get out of it"?' At least in one important sense it would seem fantastic to suggest, for instance, that Shakespeare *meant* by his plays just everything which that vital Professor, George Wilson Knight, to take one person only, may 'honestly' get out of them at any time. It might not be wholly unreasonable, though this also would take some swallowing, to say that Shakespeare's *plays* 'meant' all these things; but it appears to me ridiculous to suppose that *Shakespeare himself* 'meant' all these things by them. A better attitude on that point would seem to me to be expressed by Mr Eliot's remarks that there may be much more in a poem than the author was aware of. Even if Shakespeare himself might be forced, were he alive, to confess that he *ought* to have meant all these things by his plays, there seems no good reason why, were he alive, he *ought* to *confess*, that he *did* mean them. Dewey's position, then, seems to me to be untenable, but it is, nevertheless, an instructive one to consider. Dewey is trying to satisfy two apparently conflicting urges which many of us who consider these matters cannot help feeling. We do not want to have to say, when we think of or come across a satisfying interpretation of a good poem, that it does not matter at all whether this is what the poet *meant* by the poem. On the other hand, we do not wish to say that what the poem means to different people, however sensitive and intelligent, is always precisely the same. Dewey tries to satisfy both these urges by saying that the poem means many different things, and that the poet meant by his poem all of them. Now I feel certain that many people, like me, will not be satisfied by his attempt. Many of us do not want to have to say that a poet means utterly disparate, even contrary or contradictory things, by his poem, according as readers, even sensitive and intelligent[6] readers, may interpret his poem in disparate, contrary or even contradictory ways.

We should be willing to admit that a poem may really mean disparate things to different intelligent and sensitive readers: that a poem may sometimes even mean *contrary* or even *contradictory* things to different intelligent and sensitive readers, but it does not follow from such propositions, that the poet *meant* all these disparate, contrary or contradictory things by his poem. The puzzle is, which are we going to call '*the* meaning' of the poem, *in an unqualified way*, what it means to the readers, or what the poet meant by it? The prize term '*the* meaning' seems to float between the two parties, like a balloon floating above two parties of children, each of which wishes to reach and appropriate it. Some people faced withour present puzzle about the meaning of a poem, might feel like applying a needle-point to the balloon, and denying that there is such a thing as '*the* meaning' of a poem at all. Yet this would not be satisfying either, for it would make nonsense of all those occasions on which readers ask each other such questions as: 'What do *you* think this poem means?' or 'What do *you* take the meaning of this poem to be?' and so on. It might be claimed that all such questions are pseudo-questions: but that would take a great deal of showing, and they would in any case be very queer pseudo-questions, for they time and again receive answers which entirely satisfy the questioners. Again, there are other contexts in which we constantly speak of 'the meaning' of a poem. You may remember, for instance, that in the early part of this lecture I frequently spoke of 'the meaning' of a poem, and distinguished it from such things as 'what the poet intended his poem to mean', as if I knew what 'the meaning' of a poem was. To speak of 'the meaning' of a poem, in this unperturbed way, is, I would claim, a legitimate thing for us to do on many occasions. We many of us know what 'the meaning' of a poem is, in the sort of way in which St Augustine said he knew what time was, in the passage in the *Confessions*,[7] often quoted by Wittgenstein in his lectures:[8] 'What is time? If you don't ask me, I know: but if you ask me, I don't know.' We are many of us familiar *enough* with what we could call 'the meaning' of a poem, but it is hard indeed to give an analysis of that concept. Not so hard, however, to see the shortcomings of certain analyses or parts of analyses which may be proposed. For instance, from what we know of 'the meaning' of a poem it seems to me that we could not be satisfied with an analysis so strictly tied to the poet as one which might be suggested by Moore's remark: or with one so freely accommodating to the reactions of readers as the analysis proposed by Dewey. In this respect, at least, the meaning of a *poem* is not unlike the meaning of a *word*. A word uttered by some-one on some occasion may not mean what the speaker meant by it; and it may not mean what it means for many intelligent and sensitive hearers who know the language:[9] though each of these possibilities is perhaps *in general* less likely in the case of a word than in the case of a sentence, and less likely in the case of a sentence than in the case of a poem.

Although there are many further difficulties that could be con-sidered, let me make a rough constructive suggestion, which may help towards a satisfactory analysis: Perhaps the meaning of a poem is a class of similar experiences, one or other of which those words in that order and arranged in that form, *ought* to evoke in a reader familiar with the language (or languages) in which the poem is written.[10]

Some such account would seem to accord with our practice of asking such questions as 'What is the full meaning of this poem?' On this account the question would be tantamount to asking: 'What set of experiences ought the poem to evoke in a reader?' It would also satisfy the desire to restrict that welter of allowable meanings which Dewey would permit. It would further fulfil the wish to distinguish between what the poet intended to mean or actually did mean by his poem, and what his poem in fact means. The account certainly seems to have these advantages: but accounts of this sort are only too liable to be wrong.

Before concluding I wish to do two things: (1) to distinguish this rough suggestion of mine from a suggestion made by Professor I.A.Richards in his epoch-making book *Principles of Literary Criticism*, first published in 1924; (2) to make one or two comments on the form of my suggestion, and, in particular, to consider briefly (very briefly, I fear) what factors would decide what experiences the words of a poem *ought to evoke*.

First, then, as to the distinction between the present suggestion and that of Professor I. A. Richards. In *Principles of Literary Criticism*[11] Richards writes that 'the only workable way of defining a poem' is as 'a class of experiences which do not differ in any character more than a certain amount, varying for each character, from a standard experience', adding that we might take as this standard experience 'the relevant experience of the poet when contemplating the completed composition'. Now the idea of a class of experiences seems to me very important in this connection, and I have gratefully borrowed the idea from Richards, but I cannot agree with the use he has made of it here, and, as I hope will be clear, I have, in my suggestion, made a very different use of it. There is indeed much to be said about Richards's interesting definition, but at present I only want to draw attention to two points on which my suggestion differs from it. First, Richards is offering a suggestion for the definition of *a poem*, not of *the meaning of a poem*. This is not a trivial point. I believe that the Riccardian suggestion leads into difficulties. We want to speak of being able to *read* poems, and *write* poems, and we cannot very well say that we read experiences or even (except in an elliptical way) that we write experiences. When we read a poem we read *words*, and when we write a poem we write *words*. We also want to be able to speak of the words *of* a poem, and we cannot very well speak of the words *of* a class of experiences. And there are other such difficulties. To define a *poem* as a class of experiences is to fail to conform to common usage, and there seems here no sufficient justification for that failure to conform. It would seem better to think of a poem as a set of symbols (generally, and certainly for our purpose, *words*) functioning within a language system. Yet some philosophers and aestheticians certainly seem to feel driven to think of *poems* as *experiences*. This may perhaps be due to some phobia that otherwise they would have to consider them as marks on paper, or mere sounds in the air. John Dewey in *Art as Experience* seems to exhibit this phobia. Another acute writer who seems to have suffered from it was A. C. Bradley. Bradley writes:[21] 'Poetry being poems, we are to think of a poem as it actually exists; and, without aiming here at accuracy, we may say that an actual poem is a succession of experiences—sounds, images, thoughts, emotions—through which we pass when we read as poetically as we can'. What Bradley has done here is simply invent or take over an artificial sense of the word 'poem', to connote a succession of experiences. This must be what he has done, if we are to interpret his remark charitably: since other-wise what he would be saying would be nonsense. This can easily be seen. For I take it that what we read 'as poetically as we can', is a *poem*. And, if so, he would be saying that 'an actual poem is a succession of experiences through which we pass when we read a succession of experiences through which we pass when we read a succession of experiences through which we pass when we read . . .' and so on, *ad infinitum*, which would seem to be absurd. But there is no need to be caught in the dichotomy that a poem is *either* marks on paper (or sounds in the air) *or* experiences. There is a third alterna-tive, namely, that a poem is *words*, symbols, functioning within a language system. The poem can, and does indeed, in my view, con-sist of *words*. The *meaning* of the poem, on the other hand, may well be *experiences*, and, indeed, that is my suggestion.

I now want to pass to my second point of dissent from Richards's suggestion. I cannot agree that the standard experience should be taken to be the relevant experience of the poet when contemplating the completed composition. That cannot be right, I think. The poet may sometimes never contemplate the completed composition: he might even die before he could do so. If the poem were a long one he might never think over the whole thing again. There are many possible forms of this objection. Another objection was seen by Richards himself, who added in a footnote that the poet might be dissatisfied without reason. But there are other difficulties, too. Even the *relevant* experience of the poet when contemplating the com-pleted composition, may fail in adequacy to the full meanings of the words of the poem. The contemplating poet may be no more infallible as a judge of the meaning of his creation than the creating poet was.

This is a convenient point at which to pass to my concluding remarks:

If we take seriously the suggestion I have made that perhaps the meaning of a poem is a class of similar experiences[13] which those words in that order and in that form *ought* to evoke in a reader familiar with the language in which the poem is written, we must obviously consider the question as to what factors would decide what experiences the words of a poem *ought* to evoke. One factor, I suggest, is the meanings of the words in that order in the language system which prevailed *at the time when they were written*. If the words or the order would have been novel at that time, evidence such as other writings of the poet, or even statements of intention, may be relevant: and these may also be relevant in cases of ambiguity. There may be other sorts of evidence relevant in such cases, e.g. known influences, evidence of literary imitation and allusion. Even in these cases of novelty and ambiguity, though, there may be limits to the pains we ought to take to ascertain *what the poet meant* by his poem, as a means of finding out what the poem *means*. Sometimes, where a poet attaches a novel sense to a word, or intends the word to have a special novel effect, this may not come out in the poem as it stands, and we certainly sometimes say that if the poet intended the word to bear that sense or to have that effect, he should have made it clearer, for it does not bear that sense or have that effect in the poem as it stands. The words of the poem do not mean what he meant by them. And it seems to me often legitimate that we should say such things. In such cases the only experiences which the poem ought to evoke in us are not the same as those the poet intended his readers to have. Again, sometimes we say that we are not sure what certain words of a poem mean, that their meaning is obscure, whereas at other times we say quite confidently that the meaning of the words is clear enough, though we are certain that they do not mean what the poet meant by them. In the latter case we definitely think that this is a defect in the poem. In the former case (the case of obscurity) we sometimes regard it as a defect, but not always; and whether we regard it as a defect or not, we sometimes look further, and try to find out what the words *do* mean, and this we may succeed in doing, either by making use of internal evidence or even by making use of external evidence. On the other hand, sometimes we refuse to make use of external evidence: we say that the meaning of a poem cannot be given to it by the external evidence; that that would be *importing* a meaning into the poem which it has not got in its own right. We seem, therefore, in some cases more inclined, and in some cases less inclined, to regard the meaning of a poem as being something other than the meaning which the words would naturally have borne or would naturally bear, in the language system in which the poem was written. We seem in some cases more inclined, and in some cases less inclined, to attach importance in determining what is the meaning of a poem, to what the poet meant by it. I suggest that there is no universal rule that we ought to attach the same importance in all cases to what the poet meant by his poem, in determining the meaning of the poem: but that the degree of importance we should attach to it in any particular case is a matter for *aesthetic decision*. The *meaning* of a poem, then, like its value, is something which we shall only arrive at if we make a right aesthetic decision. The meaning of the poem, moreover, will correspond to that right decision, in making which we have given their due weight (whether by careful consideration or by some more or less automatic process) to the different factors involved, in determining that class of experiences one or other of which the words of the poem, in that order, and in that form, *ought to evoke* in a reader familiar with the language (or languages) in which the poem is written.

E.D.HIRSCH, Jr
Objective Interpretation

The fact that the term 'criticism' has now come to designate all commentary on textual meaning reflects a general acceptance of the doctrine that description and evaluation are inseparable in literary study. In any serious confrontation of literature it would be futile, of course, to attempt a rigorous banishment of all evaluative judgment, but this fact does not give us the license to misunderstand or misinterpret our texts. It does not entitle us to use the text as the basis for an exercise in 'creativity' or to submit as serious textual commentary a disguised argument for a particular ethical, cultural, or aesthetic viewpoint. Nor is criticism's chief concern—the present relevance of a text—a strictly necessary aspect of textual commentary. That same kind of theory which argues the inseparability of description and evaluation also argues that a text's meaning is simply its meaning 'to us, today.' Both kinds of argument support the idea that interpretation is criticism and vice versa. But there is clearly a sense in which we can neither evaluate a text nor determine what is means 'to us, today' until we have correctly apprehended what it means. Understanding (and therefore interpretation, in the strict sense of the word) is both logically and psychologically prior to what is generally called criticism. It is true that this distinction between understanding and evaluation cannot always show itself in the finished work of criticism—nor, perhaps, should it—but a general grasp and acceptance of the distinction might help correct some of the most serious faults of current criticism (its subjectivism and relativism) and might even make it plausible to think of literary study as a corporate enterprise and a progressive discipline.

No one would deny, of course, that the more important issue is not the status of literary study as a discipline but the vitality of literature—especially of older literature—in the world at large. The critic is right to think that the text should speak to us. The point which needs to be grasped clearly by the critic is that a text cannot be made to speak to us until what it says has been understood. This is not an argument in favor of historicism as against criticism—it is simply a brute ontological fact. Textual meaning is not a naked given like a physical object. The text is first of all a conventional representation like a musical score, and what the score represents may be construed correctly or incorrectly. The literary text (in spite of the semimystical claims made for its uniqueness) does not have a special ontological status which somehow absolves the reader from the demands universally imposed by all linguistic texts of every description. Nothing, that is, can give a conventional representation the status of an immediate given. The text of a poem, for example, has to be construed by the critic before it becomes a poem for him. Then it is, no doubt, an artifact with special characteristics. But before the critic construes the poem it is no artifact for him at all, and if he construes it wrongly, he will subsequently be talking about the wrong artifact, not the one represented by the text. If criticism is to be objective in any significant sense, it must be founded on a self-critical construction of textual meaning, which is to say, on objective interpretation.

The distinction I am drawing between interpretation and criticism was one of the central principles in the now vestigial science of hermeneutics. August Boeckh, for example, divided the theoretical part of his *Encyclopädie* into two sections, one devoted to *Interpretation* (*Hermeneutik*) and the other to *Kritik*. Boeckh's discussion of his distinction is illuminating: interpretation is the construction of textual meaning as such; it explicates (*legt aus*) those meanings, and only those meanings, which the text explicitly or implicitly represents. Criticism, on the other hand, builds on the results of interpretation; it confronts textual meaning not as such, but as a component within a larger context. Boeckh defined it as 'that philological function through which a text is understood not simply in its own terms and for its own sake, but in order to establish a relationship with something else, in such a way that the goal is a knowledge of this relationship itself.'[1] Boeckh's definition is useful in emphasizing that interpretation and criticism confront two quite distinct 'objects,' for this is the fundamental distinction between the two activities. The object of interpretation is textual meaning in and for itself and may be called the *meaning* of the text. The object of criticism, on the other hand, is that meaning in its bearing on something else (standards of value, present concerns, etc.), and this object may therefore be called the *significance* of the text.

The distinction between the meaning and the significance of a text was first clearly made by Frege in his article 'Über Sinn und Bedeutung,' where he demonstrated that although the meanings of two texts may be different, their referent or truth-value may be identical.[2] For example, the statement, 'Scott is the author of *Waverley*,' is true and yet the meaning of 'Scott' is different from that of 'the author of *Waverley*.' The *Sinn* of each is different, but the *Bedeutung* (or one aspect of *Bedeutung*—the designatum of 'Scott' and 'author of *Waverley*') is the same. Frege considered only cases where different *Sinne* have an identical *Bedeutung*, but it is also true that the same *Sinn* may, in the course of time, have different *Bedeutungen*. For example, the sentence, 'There is a unicorn in the garden,' is prima facie false. But suppose the statement were made when there *was* a unicorn in the garden (as happened in Thurber's imaginative world); the statement would be true; its relevance would have shifted. But true or false, the meaning of the proposition would remain the same, for unless its *meaning* remained self-identical, we would have nothing to label true or false. Frege's distinction, now widely accepted by logicians, is a special case of Husserl's general distinction between the inner and outer horizons of any meaning. In the next section I shall try to clarify Husserl's concept and to show how it applies to the problems of textual study and especially to the basic assumptions of textual interpretation.

My purpose is primarily constructive rather than polemical. I would not willingly argue that interpretation should be practiced in strict separation from criticism. I shall ignore criticism simply in order to confront the special problems involved in construing the meaning or *Sinn* of a text. For most of my notions I disclaim any originality. My aim is to revive some forgotten insights of literary study and to apply to the theory of interpretation certain other insights from linguistics and philosophy. For although the analytical movement in criticism has permanently advanced the cause of intrinsic literary study, it has not yet paid enough attention to the problem of establishing norms and limits in interpretation. If I display any argumentative intent, it is not, therefore, against the analytical movement, which I approve, but only against certain modern theories which hamper the establishment of normative principles in interpretation and which thereby encourage the subjectivism and individualism which have for many students discredited the analytical movement. By normative principles I mean those notions which concern the nature of a correct interpretation. When the critic clearly conceives what a correct interpretation is in principle, he possesses a guiding idea against which he can measure his construction. Without such a guiding idea, self-critical or objective interpretation is hardly possible. Current theory, however, fails to provide such a principle. The most influential and representative statement of modern theory is *Theory of Literature* by Wellek and Warren, a book to which I owe much. I ungratefully select it (especially Chap. 12) as a target of attack, both because it is so influential and because I need a specific, concrete example of the sort of theory which requires amendment.[3]

The Two Horizons of Textual Meaning

The metaphorical doctrine that a text leads a life of its own is used by modern theorists to express the idea that textual meaning changes in the course of time.[4] This theory of a changing meaning serves to support the fusion of interpretation and criticism and, at the same time, the idea that present relevance forms the basis for textual commentary. But the view should not remain unchallenged, since if it were correct, there could be no objective knowledge about texts. Any statement about textual meaning could be valid only for the moment, and even this temporary validity could not be tested, since there would be no permanent norms on which validating judgments could be based. While the 'life' theory does serve to explain and sanction the fact that different ages tend to interpret texts differently, and while it emphasizes the importance of a text's present relevance, it overlooks the fact that such a view undercuts *all* criticism, even the sort which emphasizes present relevance. If the view were correct, criticism would not only lack permanent validity, but could not even claim current validity by the time it got into print. Both the text's meaning and the tenor of the age would have altered. The 'life' theory really masks the idea that the reader construes his own, new meaning instead of that represented by the text.

The 'life' theory thus implicitly places the principle of change squarely where it belongs, that is, not in textual meaning as such, but in changing generations of readers. According to Wellek, for example, the meaning of the text changes as it passes 'through the minds of its readers, critics, and fellow artists.'[5] Now when even a few of the norms which determine a text's meaning are allotted to readers and made dependent on their attitudes and concerns, it is evident that textual meaning must change. But is it proper to make textual meaning dependent upon the reader's own cultural givens? It may be granted that these givens change in the course of time, but does this imply that textual meaning itself changes? As soon as the reader's outlook is permitted to determine what a text means, we have not simply a changing meaning but quite possibly as many meanings as readers.

Against such a reductio ad absurdum, the proponent of the current theory points out that in a given age many readers will agree in their construction of a text and will unanimously repudiate the accepted interpretation of a former age. For the sake of fair-mindedness, this presumed unanimity may be granted, but must it be explained by arguing that the text's meaning has changed? Recalling Frege's distinction between *Sinn* and *Bedeutung*, the change could be explained by saying that the meaning of the text has remained the same, while the significance of that meaning has shifted.[6] Contemporary readers will frequently share similar cultural givens and will therefore agree about what the text means to them. But might it not be the case that they agree about the text's meaning 'to them' because they have first understood its meaning? If textual meaning itself could change, contemporary readers would lack a basis for agreement or disagreement. No one would bother seriously to discuss such a protean object. The significance of textual meaning has no foundation and no objectivity unless meaning itself is unchanging. To fuse meaning and significance, or interpretation and criticism, by the conception of an autonomous, living, changing meaning does not really free the reader from the shackles of historicism; it simply destroys the basis both for any agreement among readers and for any objective study whatever.

The dilemma created by the fusion of *Sinn* and *Bedeutung* in current theory is exhibited as soon as the theorist attempts to explain how norms can be preserved in textual study. The explanation becomes openly self-contradictory: 'It could be scarcely denied that there is [in textual meaning] a substantial *identity* of "structure" which has remained the *same* throughout the ages. This *structure*, however, is dynamic: it *changes* throughout the process of history while passing through the minds of its readers, critics, and fellow artists.'[7] First the 'structure' is self-identical; then it changes! What is given in one breath is taken away in the next. Although it is a matter of common experience that a text appears different to us than it appeared to a former age, and although we remain deeply convinced that there *are* permanent norms in textual study, we cannot properly explain the facts by equating or fusing what changes with what remains the same. We must distinguish the two and give each its due.

A couplet from Marvell, used by Wellek to suggest how meaning changes, will illustrate my point:[8]

My vegetable love should grow
Vaster than empires and more slow.

Wellek grants that 'vegetable' here probably means more or less what we nowadays express by 'vegetative,' but he goes on to suggest that we cannot avoid associating the modern connotation of 'vegetable' (what it means 'to us'). Furthermore, he suggests that this enrichment of meaning may even be desirable. No doubt, the associated meaning *is* here desirable (since it supports the mood of the poem), but Wellek could not even make his point unless we could distinguish between what 'vegetable' probably means as used in the text and what it commonly means to us. Simply to discuss the issue is to admit that Marvell's poem probably does not imply the modern connotation, for if we could not separate the sense of 'vegetative' from the notion of an 'erotic cabbage,' we could not talk about the difficulty of making the separation. One need not argue that the delight we may take in such new meanings must be ignored. On the contrary, once we have self-critically understood the text, there is little reason to exclude valuable or pleasant associations which enhance its significance. However, it is essential to exclude these associations in the process of interpretation, that is, in the process of understanding what a text means. The way out of the theoretical dilemma is to perceive that the meaning of a text does not change and that the modern, different connotation of a word like 'vegetable' belongs, if it is to be entertained at all, to the constantly changing significance of a text's meaning.

It is in the light of the distinction between meaning and significance that critical theories like T. S. Eliot's need to be viewed.[9] Eliot, like other modern critics, insists that the meaning of a literary work changes in the course of time, but, in contrast to Wellek, instead of locating the principle of change directly in the changing outlooks of readers, Eliot locates it in a changing literary tradition. In his view, the literary tradition is a 'simultaneous' (as opposed to temporal) order of literary texts which is constantly rearranging itself as new literary works appear on the public scene. Whenever a new work appears it causes a rearrangement of the tradition as a whole, and this brings about an alteration in the meaning of each component literary text. For example, when Shakespeare's *Troilus* entered the tradition, it altered not only the meaning of Chaucer's *Troilus*, but also, to some degree, the meaning of every other text in the literary tradition.

If the changes in meaning Eliot speaks of are considered to be changes in significance, then his conception is perfectly sound. And indeed, by definition, Eliot is speaking of significance rather than meaning, since he is considering the work in relation to a larger realm, as a component rather than a world in itself. It goes without saying that the character of a component considered as such changes whenever the larger realm of which it is a part changes. A red object will appear to have different color qualities when viewed against differently colored backgrounds. The same is true of textual meaning. But the meaning of the text (its *Sinn*) does not change any more than the hue and saturation of the red object changes when seen against different backgrounds. Yet the analogy with colored objects is only partial: I can look at a red pencil against a green blotting pad and perceive the pencil's color in that special context without knowing the hue and saturation of either pencil or blotter. But textual meaning is a construction, not a naked given like a red object, and I cannot relate textual meaning to a larger realm until I have construed it. Before I can judge just how the changed tradition has altered the significance of a text, I must understand its meaning or *Sinn*.

This permanent meaning is, and can be, nothing other than the author's meaning. There have been, of course, several other definitions of textual meaning—what the author's contemporaries would ideally have construed, what the ideal present-day reader construes, what the norms of language permit the text to mean, what the best critics conceive to be the best meaning, and so on. In support of these other candidates, various aesthetic and psychological objections have been aimed at the author: first, his meaning, being conditioned by history and culture, is too confined and simple; second, it remains, in any case, inaccessible to us because we live in another age, or because his mental processes are private, or because he himself did not know what he meant. Instead of attempting to meet each of these objections separately, I shall attempt to describe the general principle for answering all of them and, in doing so, to clarify further the distinction between meaning and significance. The aim of my exposition will be to confirm that the author's meaning, as represented by his text, is unchanging and reproducible. My problem will be to show that, although textual meaning is *determined* by the psychic acts of an author and realized by those of a reader, textual meaning itself must not be *identified* with the author's or reader's psychic acts as such. To make this crucial point, I shall find it useful to draw upon Husserl's analysis of verbal meaning.

In his chief work, *Logische Untersuchungen*, Husserl sought, among other things, to avoid an identification of verbal meaning with the psychic acts of speaker or listener, author or reader, but to do this he did not adopt a strict, Platonic idealism by which meanings have an actual existence apart from meaning experiences. Instead, he affirmed the objectivity of meaning by analyzing the observable relationship between it and those very mental processes in which it is actualized, for in meaning experiences themselves, the objectivity and constancy of meaning are confirmed.

Husserl's point may be grasped by an example from visual experience.[10] When I look at a box, then close my eyes, and then reopen them, I can perceive in this second view the identical box I saw before. Yet, although I perceive the same box, the two acts of seeing are distinctly different—in this case, temporally different. The same sort of result is obtained when I alter my acts of seeing spatially. If I go to another side of the room or stand on a chair, what I actually 'see' alters with my change in perspective, and yet I still 'perceive' the identical box; I still understand that the *object* of my seeing is the same. Furthermore, if I leave the room and simply recall the box in memory, I still understand that the *object* I remember is identical with the object I saw. For if I did not understand that, how could I insist that I was remembering? The examples are paradigmatic: All events of consciousness, not simply those involving visual perception and memory, are characterized by the mind's ability to make modally and temporally different *acts* of awareness refer to the same *object* of awareness. An object for the mind remains the same even though what is 'going on in the mind' is not the same. The mind's object therefore may not be equated with psychic processes as such; the mental object is self-identical over against a plurality of mental acts.[11]

The relation between an act of awareness and its object Husserl calls 'intention,' using the term in its traditional philosophical sense, which is much broader than that of 'purpose' and is roughly equivalent to 'awareness.' (When I employ the word subsequently, I shall be using it in Husserl's sense.)[12] This term is useful for distinguishing the components of a meaning experience. For example, when I 'intend' a box, there are at least three distinguishable aspects of that event. First, there is the object as perceived by me; second, there is the act by which I perceive the object; and finally, there is (for physical things) the object which exists independently of my perceptual act. The first two aspects of the event Husserl calls 'intentional object' and 'intentional act' respectively. Husserl's point, then, is that *different* intentional acts (on different occasions) 'intend' an *identical* intentional object.

The general term for all intentional objects is meaning. Verbal meaning is simply a special kind of intentional object, and like any other one, it remains self-identical over against the many different acts which 'intend' it. But the noteworthy feature of verbal meaning is its supra-personal character. It is not an intentional object for simply one person, but for many—potentially for all persons. Verbal meaning is, by definition, *that aspect of a speaker's 'intention' which, under linguistic conventions, may be shared by others.* Anything not sharable in this sense does not belong to the verbal intention or verbal meaning. Thus, when I say, 'The air is crisp,' I may be thinking, among other things, 'I should have eaten less at supper,' and 'Crisp air reminds me of my childhood in Vermont,' and so on. In certain types of utterance such unspoken accompaniments to meaning may be sharable, but in general they are not, and therefore they do not generally belong to verbal meaning. The nonverbal aspects of the speaker's intention Husserl calls 'experience' and the verbal ones 'content.' However, by content he does not mean simply intellectual content, but all those aspects of the intention—cognitive, emotive, phonetic (and in writing, even visual)—which may be conveyed to others by the linguistic means employed.[13]

Husserl's analysis (in my brief exposition) makes the following points then: Verbal meaning, being an intentional object, is unchanging, that is, it may be reproduced by different intentional acts and remains self-identical through all these reproductions. Verbal meaning is the sharable content of the speaker's intentional object. Since this meaning is both unchanging and interpersonal, it may be reproduced by the mental acts of different persons. Husserl's view is thus essentially historical, for even though he insists that verbal meaning is unchanging, he also insists that any particular verbal utterance, written or spoken, is historically determined. That is to say, the meaning is determined once and for all by the character of the speaker's intention.[14]

Husserl's views provide an excellent context for discussing the central problems of interpretation. Once we define verbal meaning as the content of the author's intention (which for brevity's sake I shall call simply the author's 'verbal intention'), the problem for the interpreter is quite clear: he must distinguish those meanings which belong to that verbal intention from those which do not belong. This problem may be rephrased, of course, in a way that nearly everyone will accept: the interpreter has to distinguish what a text implies from what it does not imply; he must give the text its full due, but he must also preserve norms and limits. For hermeneutic theory, the problem is to find a *principle* for judging whether various possible implications should or should not be admitted.

I describe the problem in terms of implication, since, for practical purposes, it lies at the heart of the matter. Generally, the explicit meanings of a text can be construed to the satisfaction of most readers; the problems arise in determining inexplicit or 'unsaid' meanings. If, for example, I announce, 'I have a headache,' there is no difficulty in construing what I 'say,' but there may be great difficulty in construing implications like 'I desire sympathy' or 'I have a right not to engage in distasteful work.' Such implications may belong to my verbal meaning, or they may not belong. This is usually the area where the interpreter needs a guiding principle.

It is often said that implications must be determined by referring to the context of the utterance, which, for ordinary statements like 'I have a headache,' means the concrete situation in which the utterance occurs. In the case of written texts, however, context generally means verbal context: the explicit meanings which sur-

round the problematical passage. But these explicit meanings alone
do not exhaust what we mean by context when we educe implications. The surrounding explicit meanings provide us with a sense of
the whole meaning, and it is from this sense of the whole that we
decide what the problematical passage implies. We do not ask
simply, 'Does this implication belong with these other explicit
meanings?' but rather, 'Does this implication belong with these
other meanings *within a particular sort of total meaning*?' For example,
we cannot determine whether 'root' belongs with or implies 'bark'
unless we know that the total meaning is 'tree' and not 'grass.' The
ground for educing implications is a sense of the whole meaning,
and this is an indispensable aspect of what we mean by context.

Previously I defined the whole meaning of an utterance as the
author's verbal intention. Does this mean that the principle for
admitting or excluding implications must be to ask, 'Did the author
have in mind such an implication?' If that is the principle, all hope
for objective interpretation must be abandoned, since in most cases
it is impossible (even for the author himself) to determine precisely
what he was thinking of at the time or times he composed his text.
But this is clearly not the correct principle. When I say, 'I have a
headache,' I may indeed imply, 'I would like some sympathy,' and
yet I might not have been explicitly conscious of such an implication.
The first step, then, in discovering a principle for admitting and
excluding implications is to perceive the fundamental distinction
between the author's verbal intention and the meanings of which he
was explicitly conscious. Here again, Husserl's rejection of psycholog-
ism is useful. The author's verbal intention (his total verbal meaning) may be likened to my 'intention' of a box. Normally, when I
perceive a box, I am explicitly conscious of only three sides, and yet
I assert with full confidence (although I might be wrong) that I
'intend' a box, an object with *six* sides. Those three unseen sides
belong to my 'intention' in precisely the same way that the unconscious implications of an utterance belong to the author's
intention. They belong to the intention taken as a whole.

Most, if not all, meaning experiences or intentions are occasions
in which the whole meaning is not explicitly present to consciousness. But how are we to define the manner in which these unconscious
meanings are implicitly present? In Husserl's analysis, they are
present in the form of a 'horizon,' which may be defined as a system
of typical expectations and probabilities.[15] 'Horizon' is thus an
essential aspect of what we usually call context. It is an inexplicit
sense of the whole, derived from the explicit meanings present to
consciousness. Thus, my view of three surfaces, presented in a

familiar and typically box-like way, has a horizon of typical continuations; or, to put it another way, my 'intention' of a whole box defines the horizon for my view of three visible sides. The same sort of relationship holds between the explicit and implicit meanings in a verbal intention. The explicit meanings are components in a total meaning which is bounded by a horizon. Of the manifold typical continuations within this horizon the author is not and cannot be explicitly conscious, nor would it be a particularly significant task to determine just which components of his meaning the author *was* thinking of. But it is of the utmost importance to determine the horizon which defines the author's intention as a whole, for it is only with reference to this horizon, or sense of the whole, that the interpreter may distinguish those implications which are typical and proper components of the meaning from those which are not.

The interpreter's aim, then, is to posit the author's horizon and carefully exclude his own accidental associations. A word like 'vegetable,' for example, had a meaning horizon in Marvell's language which is evidently somewhat different from the horizon it has in contemporary English. This is the linguistic horizon of the word, and it strictly bounds its possible implications. But all of these possible implications do not necessarily belong within the horizon of the particular utterance. What the word implies in the particular usage must be determined by asking, 'Which implications are typical components of the whole meaning under consideration?' By analogy, when three surfaces are presented to me in a special way, I must know the typical continuations of the surfaces. If I have never encountered a box before, I might think that the unseen surfaces were concave or irregular, or I might simply think there are other sides but have no idea what they are like. The probability that I am right in the way I educe implications depends upon my familiarity with the type of meaning I consider.

That is the reason, of course, that the genre concept is so important in textual study. By classifying the text as belonging to a particular genre, the interpreter automatically posits a general horizon for its meaning. The genre provides a sense of the whole, a notion of typical meaning components. Thus, before we interpret a text, we often classify it as casual conversation, lyric poem, military command, scientific prose, occasional verse, novel, epic, and so on. In a similar way, I have to classify the object I see as a box, a sphere, a tree, and so on before I can deduce the character of its unseen or inexplicit components. But these generic classifications are simply preliminary indications. They give only a rough notion of the horizon for a particular meaning. The aim of interpretation is to specify the horizon as far as possible. Thus, the object I see is not simply a box but a cigarette carton, and not simply that but a carton for a particular brand of cigarettes. If a paint mixer or dyer wants to specify a particular patch of color, he is not content to call it blue; he calls it Williamsburg Blue. The example of a color patch is paradigmatic for all particular verbal meanings. They are not simply *kinds* of meanings, nor are they single meanings corresponding to individual intentional acts (Williamsburg Blue is not simply an individual patch of color); they are *typical* meanings, particular yet reproducible, and the typical *components* of such meanings are similarly specific. The interpreter's job is to specify the text's horizon as far as he is able, and this means, ultimately, that he must familiarize himself with the typical meanings of the author's mental and experiential world.

The importance of the horizon concept is that it defines in principle the norms and limits which bound the meaning represented by the text. But, at the same time, the concept frees the interpreter from the constricting and impossible task of discovering what the author was explicitly thinking of. Thus, by defining textual meaning as the author's meaning, the interpreter does not, as it is so often argued, impoverish meaning; he simply excludes what does not belong to it. For example, if I say, 'My car ran out of gas,' I imply, typically, 'The engine stopped running.' Whether I also imply 'Life is ironical' depends on the generality of my intention. Some linguistic utterances, many literary works among them, have an extremely broad horizon which at some points may touch the boundaries of man's intellectual cosmos. But whether this is the case is not a matter for a priori discussion; the decision must be based on a knowledgeable inference as to the particular intention being considered.

Within the horizon of a text's meaning, however, the process of explication is unlimited. In this respect Dryden was right; no text is ever fully explicated. For example, if I undertook to interpret my 'intention' of a box, I could make explicit unlimited implications which I did not notice in my original intention. I could educe not only the three unseen sides, but also the fact that the surfaces of the box contain twenty-four right angles, that the area of two adjoining sides is less than half the total surface area, and so on. And if someone asked me whether such meanings were implicit in my intention of a box, I must answer affirmatively. In the case of linguistic meanings, where the horizon defines a much more complex intentional object, such determinations are far more difficult to make. But the probability of an interpreter's inference may be judged by two criteria alone—the accuracy with which he has sensed the horizon of the whole and the typicality of such a meaning within such a whole. Insofar as the inference meets these criteria, it is truly an explication of textual meaning. It simply renders explicit that which was, consciously or unconsciously, in the author's intention.

The horizon which grounds and sanctions inferences about textual meaning is the 'inner horizon' of the text. It is permanent and self-identical. Beyond this inner horizon any meaning has an 'outer horizon'; that is to say, any meaning has relationships to other meanings; it is always a component in larger realms. This outer horizon is the domain of criticism. But this outer horizon is not only unlimited, it is also changing since the world itself changes. In general, criticism stakes out only a portion of this outer horizon as its peculiar object. Thus, for example, Eliot partitioned off that aspect of the text's outer horizon which is defined by the simultaneous order of literary texts. The simultaneous order at a given point in time is therefore the inner horizon of the meaning Eliot is investigating, and this inner horizon is just as definite, atemporal, and objective as the inner horizon which bounds textual meaning. However, the critic, like the interpreter, must construe correctly the components of his inner horizon, and one major component is textual meaning itself. The critic must first accurately interpret the text. He need not perform a detailed explication, but he needs to achieve (and validate) that clear and specific sense of the whole meaning which makes detailed explication possible.

Determinateness of Textual Meaning

In the previous section I defined textual meaning as the verbal intention of the author, and this argues implicitly that hermeneutics must stress a reconstruction of the author's aims and attitudes in order to evolve guides and norms for construing the meaning of his text. It is frequently argued, however, that textual meaning has nothing to do with the author's mind but only with his verbal achievement, that the object of interpretation is not the author but his text. This plausible argument assumes, of course, that the text automatically has a meaning simply because it represents an unalterable sequence of words. It assumes that the meaning of a word sequence is directly imposed by the public norms of language, that the text as a 'piece of language' is a public object whose character is defined by public norms.[16] This view is in one respect sound, since textual meaning must conform to public norms if it is in any sense to be verbal (i.e. sharable) meaning; on no account may the interpreter permit his probing into the author's mind to raise private associations (experience) to the level of public implications (content).

However, this basically sound argument remains one-sided, for even though verbal meaning must conform to public linguistic norms (these are highly tolerant, of course), no mere sequence of words can represent an actual verbal meaning with reference to public norms alone. Referred to these alone, the text's meaning remains indeterminate. This is true even of the simplest declarative sentence like 'My car ran out of gas' (did my Pullman dash from a cloud of Argon?). The fact that no one would radically misinterpret such a sentence simply indicates that its frequency is high enough to give its usual meaning the apparent status of an immediate given. But this apparent immediacy obscures a complex process of adjudications among meaning possibilities. Under the public norms of language alone no such adjudications can occur, since the array of possibilities presents a face of blank indifference. The array of possibilities only begins to become a more selective system of *probabilities* when, instead of confronting merely a word sequence, we also posit a speaker who very likely means something. Then and only then does the most usual sense of the word sequence become the most probable or 'obvious' sense. The point holds true a fortiori, of course, when we confront less obvious word sequences like those found in poetry. A careful exposition of this point may be found in the first volume of Cassirer's *Philosophy of Symbolic Forms*, which is largely devoted to a demonstration that verbal meaning arises from the 'reciprocal determination' of public linguistic possibilities and subjective specifications of those possibilities.[17] Just as language constitutes and colors subjectivity, so does subjectivity color language. The author's or speaker's subjective act is formally necessary to verbal meaning, and any theory which tries to dispense with the author as specifier of meaning by asserting that textual meaning is purely objectively determined finds itself chasing will-o'-the-wisps. The burden of this section is, then, an attack on the view that a text is a 'piece of language' and a defense of the notion that a text represents the determinate verbal meaning of an author.

One of the consequences arising from the view that a text is a piece of language—a purely public object—is the impossibility of defining in principle the nature of a correct interpretation. This is the same impasse which results from the theory that a text leads a life of its own, and, indeed, the two notions are corollaries since any 'piece of language' must have a changing meaning when the changing public norms of language are viewed as the only ones which determine the sense of the text. It is therefore not surprising to find that Wellek subscribes implicitly to the text-as-language theory. The text is viewed as representing not a determinate meaning, but rather a system of meaning potentials specified not by a meaner but by the vital potency of language itself. Wellek acutely perceives the danger of the view:

> Thus the system of norms is growing and changing and will remain, in some sense, always incompletely and imperfectly realized. But this dynamic conception does not mean mere subjectivism and relativism. All the different points of view are by no means equally right. It will always be possible to determine which point of view grasps the subject most thoroughly and deeply. A hierarchy of viewpoints, a criticism of the grasp of norms, is implied in the concept of the adequacy of interpretation.[18]

The danger of the view is, of course, precisely that it opens the door to subjectivism and relativism, since linguistic norms may be invoked to support any verbally possible meaning. Furthermore, it is not clear how one may criticize a grasp of norms which will not stand still.

Wellek's brief comment on the problem involved in defining and testing correctness in interpretation is representative of a widespread conviction among literary critics that the most correct interpretation is the most 'inclusive' one. Indeed, the view is so widely accepted that Wellek did not need to defend his version of it (which he calls 'Perspectivism') at length. The notion behind the theory is reflected by such phrases as 'always incompletely and imperfectly realized' and 'grasps the subject most thoroughly.' This notion is simply that no single interpretation can exhaust the rich system of meaning potentialities represented by the text. Hence, every plausible reading which remains within public linguistic norms is a correct reading so far as it goes, but each reading is inevitably partial since it cannot realize all the potentialities of the text. The guiding principle in criticism, therefore, is that of the inclusive interpretation. The most 'adequate' construction is the one which gives the fullest coherent account of all the text's potential meanings.[19]

Inclusivism is desirable as a position which induces a readiness to consider the results of others, but, aside from promoting an estimable tolerance, it has little theoretical value. Although its aim is to reconcile different plausible readings in an ideal, comprehensive interpretation, it cannot, in fact, either reconcile different readings or choose between them. As a normative ideal, or principle of correctness, it is useless. This point may be illustrated by citing two expert readings of a well-known poem by Wordsworth. I shall first quote the poem and then quote excerpts from two published exegeses to demonstrate the kind of impasse which inclusivism always provokes when it attempts to reconcile interpretations and, incidentally, to demonstrate the very kind of interpretive problem which calls for a guiding principle:

> A slumber did my spirit seal;
>   I had no human fears:
> She seemed a thing that could not feel
>   The touch of earthly years.
>
> No motion has she now, no force;
>   She neither hears nor sees;
> Rolled round in earth's diurnal course,
>   With rocks, and stones, and trees.

Here are excerpts from two commentaries on the final lines of the poem; the first is by Cleanth Brooks, the second by F.W.Bateson:

> [The poet] attempts to suggest something of the lover's agonized shock at the loved one's present lack of motion—of his response to her utter and horrible inertness. . . . Part of the effect, of course, resides in the fact that a dead lifelessness is suggested more sharply by an object's being whirled about by something else than by an image of the object in repose. But there are other matters which are at work here: the sense of the girl's falling back into the clutter of things, companioned by things chained like a tree to one particular spot, or by things completely inanimate like rocks and stones. . . . [She] is caught up helplessly into the empty whirl of the earth which measures and makes time. She is touched by and held by earthly time in its most powerful and horrible image.

> The final impression the poem leaves is not of two contrasting moods, but of a single mood mounting to a climax in the pantheistic magnificence of the last two lines. . . . The vague living-Lucy of this poem is opposed to the grander dead-Lucy who has become involved in the sublime processes of nature. We put the poem down satisfied, because its last two lines succeed in effecting a reconciliation between the two philosophies or social attitudes. Lucy is actually more alive now that she is dead, because she is now part of the life of Nature, and not just a human 'thing.'[20]

If we grant, as I think we must, that both the cited interpretations are permitted by the text, the problem for the inclusivist is to reconcile the two readings.

Three modes of reconciliation are available to the inclusivist: (1) Brooks' reading includes Bateson's; it shows that any affirmative suggestions in the poem are negated by the bitterly ironical portrayal of the inert girl being whirled around by what Bateson calls the 'sublime processes of Nature.' (2) Bateson's reading includes Brooks'; the ironic contrast between the active, seemingly immortal girl and the passive, inert, dead girl is overcome by a final unqualified affirmation of immortality. (3) Each of the readings is partially right, but they must be fused to supplement one another. The very fact that the critics differ suggests that the meaning is essentially ambiguous. The emotion expressed is ambivalent and comprises both bitter regret and affirmation. The third mode of reconciliation is the one most often employed and is probably, in this case, the most satisfactory. A fourth type of resolution, which would insist that Brooks is right and Bateson wrong (or vice versa), is not available to the inclusivist, since the text, as language, renders both readings plausible.

Close examination, however, reveals that none of the three modes of argument manages to reconcile or fuse the two different readings. Mode 1, for example, insists that Brooks' reading comprehends Bateson's, but although it is conceivable that Brooks implies all the meanings which Bateson has perceived, Brooks also implies a pattern of emphasis which cannot be reconciled with Bateson's reading. While Bateson construes a primary emphasis on life and affirmation, Brooks emphasizes deadness and inertness. No amount of manipulation can reconcile these divergent emphases, since one pattern of emphasis irrevocably excludes other patterns, and, since emphasis is always crucial to meaning, the two constructions of meaning rigorously exclude one another. Precisely the same strictures hold, of course, for the argument that Bateson's reading comprehends that of Brooks. Nor can mode 3 escape with impunity. Although it seems to preserve a stress both on negation and on affirmation, thereby coalescing the two readings, it actually excludes both readings and labels them not simply partial, but wrong. For if the poem gives equal stress to bitter irony and to affirmation, then any construction which places a primary stress on either meaning is simply incorrect.

The general principle implied by my analysis is very simple. The submeanings of a text are not blocks which can be brought together additively. Since verbal (and any other) meaning is a *structure* of component meanings, interpretation has not done its job when it simply enumerates what the component meanings are. The interpreter must also determine their probable structure and particularly their structure of emphases. Relative emphasis is not only crucial to meaning (perhaps it is the most crucial and problematical element of all), it is also highly restrictive; it excludes alternatives. It may be asserted as a general rule that whenever a reader confronts two interpretations which impose different emphases on similar meaning components, at least one of the interpretations must be wrong. They cannot be reconciled.

By insisting that verbal meaning always exhibits a determinate structure of emphases, I do not, however, imply that a poem or any other text must be unambiguous. It is perfectly possible, for example, that Wordsworth's poem ambiguously implies both bitter irony and positive affirmation. Such complex emotions are commonly expressed in poetry, but if that is the kind of meaning the text represents, Brooks and Bateson would be wrong to emphasize one emotion at the expense of the other. Ambiguity or, for that matter, vagueness is not the same as indeterminateness. This is the crux of the issue. To say that verbal meaning is determinate is not to exclude complexities of meaning but only to insist that a text's meaning is what it is and not a hundred other things. Taken in this sense, a vague or ambiguous text is just as determinate as a logical proposition; it means what it means and nothing else. This is true even if one argues that a text could display shifting emphases like those magic squares which first seem to jut out and then to jut in. With texts of this character (if any exist), one need only say that the emphases shift and must not, therefore, be construed statically. Any static construction would simply be wrong. The fundamental flaw in the 'theory of the most inclusive interpretation' is that it overlooks the problem of emphasis. Since different patterns of emphasis exclude one another, inclusivism is neither a genuine norm nor an adequate guiding principle for establishing an interpretation.

Aside from the fact that inclusivism cannot do its appointed job, there are more fundamental reasons for rejecting it and all other interpretive ideals based on the conception that a text represents a system of meaning possibilities. No one would deny that for the interpreter the text is at first the source of numerous possible interpretations. The very nature of language is such that a particular sequence of words can represent several different meanings (that is why public norms alone are insufficient in textual interpretation). But to say that a text *might* represent several structures of meaning does not imply that it does in fact represent all the meanings which a particular word sequence can legally convey. Is there not an obvious distinction between what a text might mean and what it does mean? According to accepted linguistic theory, it is far more accurate to say that a written composition is not a mere locus of verbal possibilities, but a record (made possible by the invention of writing) of a verbal actuality. The interpreter's job is to reconstruct a determinate actual meaning, not a mere system of possibilities. Indeed, if the text represented a system of possibilities, interpretation would be impossible, since no actual reading could correspond to a mere system of possibilities. Furthermore, if the text is conceived to represent all the *actual* structures of meaning permissible within the public norms of language, then no single construction (with its exclusivist pattern of emphases) could be correct, and any legitimate construction would be just as incorrect as any other. When a text is conceived as a piece of language, a familiar and all too common anarchy follows. But, aside from its unfortunate consequences, the theory contradicts a widely accepted principle in linguistics. I refer to Saussure's distinction between *langue* and *parole*.

Saussure defined *langue* as the system of linguistic possibilities shared by a speech community at a given point in time.[21] The system of possibilities contains two distinguishable levels. The first consists of habits, engrams, prohibitions, and the like derived from past linguistic usage; these are the 'virtualities' of the *langue*. Based on these virtualities, there are, in addition, sharable meaning possibilities which have never before been actualized; these are the 'potentialities.' The two types of meaning possibilities taken together constitute the *langue* which the speech community draws upon. But this system of possibilities must be distinguished from the actual verbal utterances of individuals who draw upon it. These actual utterances are called *paroles*; they are uses of language and actualize some (but never all) of the meaning possibilities constituting the *langue*.

Saussure's distinction pinpoints the issue: does a text represent a segment of *langue* (as modern theorists hold) or a *parole*? A simple test suffices to provide the answer. If the text is composed of sentences, it represents *parole*, which is to say, the determinate verbal meaning of a member of the speech community. *Langue* contains words and sentence-forming principles, but it contains no sentences. It may be represented in writing only by isolated words in disconnection (*Wörter* as opposed to *Worte*). A *parole*, on the other hand, is always composed of sentences, an assertion corroborated by the firmly established principle that the sentence is the fundamental unit of speech.[22] Of course, there are numerous elliptical and one-word sentences, but wherever it can be correctly inferred that a text represents sentences and not simply isolated words, it may also be inferred that the text represents *parole*, which is to say, actual, determinate verbal meaning.

The point is nicely illustrated in a dictionary definition. The letters in boldface at the head of the definition represent the word as *langue*, with all its rich meaning possibilities. But under one of the sub-headings, in an illustrative sentence, those same letters represent the word as *parole*, as a particular, selective actualization from *langue*. In yet another illustrative sentence, under another subheading, the very same word represents a different selective actualization. Of course, many sentences, especially those found in poetry, actualize far more possibilities than illustrative sentences in a dictionary. Any pun, for example, realizes simultaneously at least two divergent meaning possibilities. But the pun is nevertheless an actualization from *langue* and not a mere system of meaning possibilities.

The *langue-parole* distinction, besides affirming the determinateness of textual meaning, also clarifies the special problems posed by revised and interpolated texts. With a revised text, composed over a long period of time (*Faust*, for example), how are we to construe the unrevised portions? Should we assume that they still mean what they meant originally or that they took on a new meaning when the rest of the text was altered or expanded? With compiled or inter-polated texts, like many books of the Bible, should we assume that sentences from varied provenances retain their original meanings or that these heterogeneous elements have become integral components of a new total meaning? In terms of Saussure's distinction, the question becomes: should we consider the text to represent a compilation of divers *paroles* or a new unitary *parole* 'respoken' by the new author or editor? I submit that there can be no definitive answer to the question, except in relation to a specific scholarly or aesthetic purpose, for in reality the question is not, 'How are we to interpret the text?' but, '*Which* text are we to interpret?' Is it to be the heterogeneous compilation of past *paroles*, each to be separately considered, or the new, homogeneous *parole*? Both may be repre-sented by the written score. The only problem is to choose, and having chosen, rigorously to refrain from confusing or in any way identifying the two quite different and separate 'texts' with one another. Without solving any concrete problems, then, Saussure's distinction nevertheless confirms the critic's right in most cases to regard his text as representing a single *parole*.

Another problem which Saussure's distinction clarifies is that posed by the bungled text, where the author aimed to convey a meaning which his words do not convey to others in the speech community. One sometimes confronts the problem in a freshman essay. In such a case, the question is, does the text mean what the author wanted it to mean or does it mean what the speech community at large takes it to mean? Much attention has been devoted to this problem ever since the publication in 1946 of Wimsatt's and

Beardsley's essay on 'The Intentional Fallacy.' In that essay the position was taken (albeit modified by certain qualifications) that the text, being public, means what the speech community takes it to mean. This position is, in an ethical sense, right (and language, being social, has a strong ethical aspect): if the author has bungled so badly that his utterance will be misconstrued, then it serves him right when people misunderstand him. However, put in linguistic terms, the position becomes unsatisfactory. It implies that the meaning represented by the text is not the *parole* of an author, but rather the *parole* of the speech community. But since only individuals utter *paroles*, a *parole* of the speech community is a non-existent, or what the Germans call an *Unding*. A text can represent only the *parole* of a speaker or author, which is another way of saying that meaning requires a meaner.

However, it is not necessary that an author's text represent the *parole* he desired to convey. It is frequently the case, when an author has bungled, that his text represents no *parole* at all. Indeed, there are but two alternatives: either the text represents the author's verbal meaning or it represents no determinate verbal meaning at all. Sometimes, of course, it is impossible to detect that the author has bungled, and in that case, even though his text does not represent verbal meaning, we shall on misconstruing the text as though it did, and no one will be the wiser. But with most bungles we are aware of a disjunction between the author's words and his probable meaning. Eliot, for example, chided Poe for saying 'My most immemorial year,' when Poe 'meant' his most *memorable* year.[23] We all agree that Poe did not mean what speakers of English generally mean by the word 'immemorial'—and so the word cannot have the usual meaning. (An author cannot mean what he does not mean.) The only question, then, is: does the word mean more or less what we convey by 'never to be forgotten' or does it mean nothing at all? Has Poe so violated linguistic norms that we must deny his utterance verbal meaning or content?

The question probably cannot be answered by fiat, but since Poe's meaning is generally understood, and since the single criterion for verbal meaning is communicability, I am inclined to describe Poe's meaning as verbal.[24] I tend to side with the Poes and Malaprops of the world, for the norms of language remain far more tolerant than dictionaries and critics like Eliot suggest. On the other hand, every member of the speech community, and especially the critic, has a duty to avoid and condemn sloppiness and needless ambiguity in the use of language, simply in order to preserve the effectiveness of the *langue* itself. Moreover, there must be a dividing line between verbal meanings and those meanings which we half-divine by a supra-linguistic exercise of imagination. There must be a dividing line between Poe's successful disregard of normal usage and the incommunicable word sequences of a bad freshman essay. However, that dividing line is not between the author's meaning and the reader's, but rather between the author's *parole* and no *parole* at all.

Of course, theoretical principles cannot directly solve the interpreter's problem. It is one thing to insist that a text represents the determinate verbal meaning of an author, but it is quite another to discover what the meaning is. The very same text could represent numerous different *paroles*, as any ironic sentence discloses ('That's a *bright* idea?' or 'That's a bright *idea!*'). But it should be of some practical consequence for the interpreter to know that he does have a precisely defined task, namely, to discover the author's meaning. It is therefore not only sound but necessary for the interpreter to inquire, 'What in all probability did the author mean? Is the pattern of emphases I construe the author's pattern?' But it is both incorrect and futile to inquire, 'What does the language of the text say?' That question can have no determinate answer.

Verification

Since the meaning represented by a text is that of another, the interpreter can never be certain that his reading is correct. He knows furthermore that the norms of *langue* by themselves are far too broad to specify the particular meanings and emphases represented by the text, that these particular meanings were specified by particular kinds of subjective acts on the part of the author, and that these acts, as such, remain inaccessible.[25] A less self-critical reader, on the other hand, approaches solipsism if he assumes that the text represents a perspicuous meaning simply because it represents an unalterable sequence of words. For if this perspicuous meaning is not verified in some way, it will simply be the interpreter's own meaning, exhibiting the connotations and emphases which he himself imposes. Of course, the reader must realize verbal meaning by his own subjective acts (no one can do that for him), but if he remembers that his job is to construe the author's meaning, he will attempt to exclude his own predispositions and to impose those of the author. However, no one can establish another's meaning with certainty. The interpreter's goal is simply this—to show that a given reading is more probable than others. In hermeneutics, verification is a process of establishing relative probabilities.

To establish a reading as probable it is first necessary to show, with reference to the norms of language, that it is possible. This is the criterion of *legitimacy*: the reading must be permissible within the public norms of the *langue* in which the text was composed. The second criterion is that of *correspondence*: the reading must account for each linguistic component in the text. Whenever a reading arbitrarily ignores linguistic components or inadequately accounts for them, the reading may be presumed improbable. The third criterion is that of *generic appropriateness*: if the text follows the conventions of a scientific essay, for example, it is inappropriate to construe the kind of allusive meaning found in casual conversation.[26] When these three preliminary criteria have been satisfied, there remains a fourth criterion which gives significance to all the rest, the criterion of plausibility or *coherence*. The three preliminary norms usually permit several readings, and this is by definition the case when a text is problematical. Faced with alternatives, the interpreter chooses the reading which best meets the criterion of coherence. Indeed, even when the text is not problematical, coherence remains the decisive criterion, since the meaning is 'obvious' only because it 'makes sense.' I wish, therefore, to focus attention on the criterion of coherence and shall take for granted the demands of legitimacy, correspondence, and generic appropriateness. I shall try to show that verification by the criterion of coherence, and ultimately, therefore, verification in general, implies a reconstruction of relevant aspects in the author's outlook. My point may be summarized in the paradox that objectivity in textual interpretation requires explicit reference to the speaker's subjectivity.

The paradox reflects the peculiar nature of coherence, which is not an absolute but a dependent quality. The laws of coherence are variable; they depend upon the nature of the total meaning under consideration. Two meanings ('dark' and 'bright,' for example) which cohere in one context may not cohere in another.[27] 'Dark with excessive bright' makes excellent sense in *Paradise Lost*, but if a reader found the phrase in a textbook on plant pathology, he would assume that he confronted a misprint for 'dark with excessive blight.' Coherence depends on the context, and it is helpful to recall our definition of context: it is a sense of the whole meaning, constituted of explicit partial meanings plus a horizon of expectations and probabilities. One meaning coheres with another because it is typical or probable with reference to the whole (coherence is thus the first cousin of implication). The criterion of coherence can be invoked only with reference to a particular context, and this context may be inferred only by positing the author's horizon, his disposition toward a particular type of meaning. This conclusion requires elaboration.

The fact that coherence is a dependent quality leads to an unavoidable circularity in the process of interpretation. The interpreter posits meanings for the words and word sequences he confronts, and, at the same time, he has to posit a whole meaning or context in reference to which the submeanings cohere with one another. The procedure is thoroughly circular; the context is derived from the submeanings and the submeanings are specified and rendered coherent with reference to the context. This circularity makes it very difficult to convince a reader to alter his construction, as every teacher knows. Many a self-willed student continues to insist that his reading is just as plausible as his instructor's, and, very often, the student is justified; his reading does make good sense. Often, the only thing at fault with the student's reading is that it is probably wrong, not that it is incoherent. The student persists in his opinion precisely because his construction *is* coherent and self-sustaining. In such a case he is wrong because he has misconstrued the context or sense of the whole. In this respect, the student's hardheadedness is not different from that of all self-convinced interpreters. Our readings are too plausible to be relinquished. If we have a distorted sense of the text's whole meaning, the harder we look at it the more certainly we shall find our distorted construction confirmed.

Since the quality of coherence depends upon the context inferred, there is no absolute standard of coherence by which we can adjudicate between different coherent readings. Verification by coherence implies therefore a verification of the grounds on which the reading is coherent. *It is necessary to establish that the context invoked is the most probable context.* Only then, in relation to an established context, can we judge that one reading is more coherent than another. Ultimately, therefore, we have to posit the most probable horizon for the text, and it is possible to do this only if we posit the author's typical outlook, the typical associations and expectations which form in part the context of his utterance. This is not only the one way we can test the relative coherence of a reading, but it is also the only way to avoid pure circularity in making sense of the text.

An essential task in the process of verification is, therefore, a deliberate reconstruction of the author's subjective stance to the extent that this stance is relevant to the text at hand.[28] The importance of such psychological reconstruction may be exemplified in adjudicating between different readings of Wordsworth's *A Slumber Did My Spirit Seal.* The interpretations of Brooks and Bateson, different as they are, remain equally coherent and self-sustaining. The implications which Brooks construes cohere beautifully with the explicit meanings of the poem within the context which Brooks adumbrates. The same may be said of Bateson's reading. The best way to show that one reading is more plausible and coherent than the other is to show that one context is more probable than the other. The problem of adjudicating between Bateson and Brooks is therefore, implicitly, the problem every interpreter must face when he tries to verify his reading. He must establish the most probable context.

Now when the *homme moyen sensuel* confronts bereavement such as that which Wordsworth's poem explicitly presents, he adumbrates, typically, a horizon including sorrow and inconsolability. These are for him components in the very meaning of bereavement. Sorrow and inconsolability cannot fail to be associated with death when the loved one, formerly so active and alive, is imagined as lying in the earth, helpless, dumb, inert, insentient. And since there is no hint of life in Heaven but only of bodily death, the comforts of Christianity lie beyond the poem's horizon. Affirmations too deep for tears, like those Bateson insists on, simply do not cohere with the poem's explicit meanings; they do not belong to the context. Brooks' reading, therefore, with its emphasis on inconsolability and bitter irony, is clearly justified not only by the text but by reference to universal human attitudes and feelings.

However, the trouble with such a reading is apparent to most Wordsworthians. The poet is not an *homme moyen sensuel*; his characteristic attitudes are somewhat pantheistic. Instead of regarding rocks and stones and trees merely as inert objects, he probably regarded them in 1799 as deeply alive, as part of the immortal life of nature. Physical death he felt to be a return to the source of life, a new kind of participation in nature's 'revolving immortality.' From everything we know of Wordsworth's typical attitudes during the period in which he composed the poem, inconsolability and bitter irony do not belong in its horizon. I think, however, that Bateson overstates his case and that he fails to emphasize properly the negative implications in the poem ('No motion has she now, no force'). He overlooks the poet's reticence, his distinct unwillingness to express any unqualified evaluation of his experience. Bateson, I would say, has not paid enough attention to the criterion of correspondence. Nevertheless, in spite of this, and in spite of the apparent implausibility of Bateson's reading, it remains, I think, somewhat more probable than that of Brooks. His procedure is also more objective. Even if he had botched his job thoroughly and had produced a less probable reading than that of Brooks, his method would remain fundamentally sound. Instead of projecting his own attitudes (Bateson is presumably not a pantheist) and instead of positing a 'universal matrix' of human attitudes (there is none), he has tried to reconstruct the author's probable attitudes so far as these are relevant in specifying the poem's meaning. It is still possible, of course, that Brooks is right and Bateson wrong. A poet's typical attitudes do not always apply to a particular poem, although Wordsworth is, in a given period, more consistent than most poets. Be that as it may, we shall never be certain what any writer means, and since Bateson grounds his interpretation in a conscious construction of the poet's outlook, his reading must be deemed the more probable one until the uncovering of some presently unknown data makes a different construction of the poet's stance appear more valid.

Bateson's procedure is appropriate to all texts, including anonymous ones. On the surface, it would seem impossible to invoke the author's probable outlook when the author remains unknown, but in this limiting case the interpreter simply makes his psychological reconstruction on the basis of fewer data. Even with anonymous texts it is crucial to posit not simply some author or other, but a particular subjective stance in reference to which the construed context is rendered probable. That is why it is important to date anonymous texts. The interpreter needs all the clues he can muster with regard not only to the text's *langue* and genre, but also to the cultural and personal attitudes the author might be expected to bring to bear in specifying his verbal meanings. In this sense, all texts, including anonymous ones, are 'attributed.' The objective interpreter simply tries to makes his attribution explicit, so that the grounds for his reading are frankly acknowledged. This opens the way to progressive accuracy in interpretation, since it is possible then to test the assumptions behind a reading as well as the coherence of the reading itself.

The fact that anonymous texts may be successfully interpreted does not, however, lead to the conclusion that all texts should be treated as anonymous ones, that they should, so to say, speak for themselves. I have already argued that no text speaks for itself and that every construed text is necessarily attributed. These points suggest strongly that it is unsound to insist on deriving all inferences from the text itself. When we date an anonymous text, for example, we apply knowledge gained from a wide variety of sources which we correlate with data derived from the text. This extrinsic data is not, however, read into the text. On the contrary, it is used to verify that which we read out of it. The extrinsic information has ultimately a purely verificative function.

The same thing is true of information relating to the author's subjective stance. No matter what the source of this information may be, whether it be the text alone or the text in conjunction with other data, this information is extrinsic to verbal meaning as such. Strictly speaking, the author's subjective stance is not part of his verbal meaning even when he explicitly discusses his feelings and attitudes. This is Husserl's point again. The intentional object represented by a text is different from the intentional acts which realize it. When the interpreter posits the author's stance he sympathetically reenacts the author's intentional acts, but although this imaginative act is necessary for realizing meaning, it must be distinguished from meaning as such. In no sense does the text represent the author's subjective stance: the interpreter simply adopts a stance in order to make sense of the text, and, if he is self-critical, he tries to verify his interpretation by showing his adopted stance to be, in all probability, the author's.

Of course, the text at hand is the safest source of clues to the author's outlook, since men do adopt different attitudes on different occasions. However, even though the text itself should be the primary source of clues and must always be the final authority, the interpreter should make an effort to go beyond his text wherever possible, since this is the only way he can avoid a vicious circularity. The harder one looks at a text from an incorrect stance, the more convincing the incorrect construction becomes. Inferences about the author's stance are sometimes difficult to make even when all relevant data are brought to bear, and it is self-defeating to make the inferential process more difficult than it need be. Since these inferences are ultimately extrinsic, there is no virtue in deriving them from the text alone. One must not confuse the result of a construction (the interpreter's understanding of the text's *Sinn*) with the *process* of construction or with a validation of that process. The *Sinn* must be represented by and limited by the text alone, but the processes of construction and validation involve psychological reconstruction and should therefore be based on all the data available.

Not only the criterion of coherence but all the other criteria used in verifying interpretations must be applied with reference to a psychological reconstruction. The criterion of legitimacy, for example, must be related to a speaking subject, since it is the author's *langue*, as an internal possession, and not the interpreter's which defines the range of meaning possibilities a text can represent. The criterion of correspondence has force only because we presume that the author meant something by each of the linguistic components he employed, and the criterion of generic appropriateness is relevant only so far as generic conventions are possessed and accepted by the author. The fact that these criteria all refer ultimately to a psychological construction is hardly surprising when we recall that to verify a text is simply to establish that the author probably meant what we construe his text to mean. The interpreter's primary task is to reproduce in himself the author's 'logic,' his attitudes, his cultural givens, in short, his world. Even though the process of verification is highly complex and difficult, the ultimate verificative principle is very simple—the imaginative reconstruction of the speaking subject.[29]

The speaking subject is not, however, identical with the subjectivity of the author as an actual historical person; it corresponds, rather, to a very limited and special aspect of the author's total subjectivity; it is, so to speak, that 'part' of the author which specifies or determines verbal meaning.[30] This distinction is quite apparent in the case of a lie. When I wish to deceive, my secret awareness that I am lying is irrelevant to the verbal meaning of my utterance. The only correct interpretation of my lie is, paradoxically, to view it as being a true statement, since this is the only correct construction of my verbal intention. Indeed, it is only when my listener has *understood* my meaning (presented as true) that he can *judge* it to be a lie. Since I adopted a truth-telling stance, the verbal meaning of my utterance would be precisely the same, whether I was deliberately lying or suffering from the erroneous conviction that my statement was true. In other words, an author may adopt a stance which differs from his deepest attitudes in the same way that an interpreter must almost always adopt a stance different from his own.[31] But for the process of interpretation, the author's private experiences are irrelevant. The only relevant aspect of subjectivity is that which determines verbal meaning or, in Husserl's terms, content.

In a sense all poets are, of course, liars, and to some extent all speakers are, but the deliberate lie, spoken to deceive, is a borderline case. In most verbal utterances, the speaker's public stance is not totally foreign to his private attitudes. Even in those cases where the speaker deliberately assumes a role, this mimetic stance is usually not the final determinant of his meaning. In a play, for example, the total meaning of an utterance is not the intentional object of the dramatic character; that meaning is simply a component in the more complex intention of the dramatist. The speaker himself is spoken. The best description of these receding levels of subjectivity was provided by the scholastic philosophers in their distinction between 'first intention,' 'second intention,' and so on. Irony, for example, always entails a comprehension of two contrasting stances (intentional levels) by a third and final complex intention. The speaking subject may be defined as the final and most comprehensive level of awareness determinative of verbal meaning. In the case of a lie, the speaking subject assumes that he tells the truth, while the actual subject retains a private awareness of his deception. Similarly, many speakers retain in their isolated privacy a self-conscious awareness of their verbal meaning, an awareness which may agree or disagree, approve or disapprove, but which does not participate in determining their verbal meaning. To interpretation, this level of awareness is as irrelevant as it is inaccessible. In construing and verifying verbal meaning, only the speaking subject counts.

A separate exposition would be required to discuss the problems of psychological reconstruction. I have here simply tried to forestall the current objections to extrinsic biographical and historical information by pointing, on the one hand, to the exigencies of verification and, on the other, to the distinction between a speaking subject and a 'biographical' person. I shall be satisfied if this part of my discussion, incomplete as it must be, will help revive the half-forgotten truism that interpretation is the construction of *another's* meaning. A slight shift in the way we speak about texts would be highly salutary. It is natural to speak not of what a text says, but of what an author means, and this more natural locution is the more accurate one. Furthermore, to speak in this way implies a readiness (not notably apparent in recent criticism) to put forth a whole-hearted and self-critical effort at the primary level of criticism—the level of understanding.

FRANK CIOFFI

Intention and Interpretation in Criticism

If we adapt Wittgenstein's characterisation of philosophy: 'putting into order our notions as to what can be said about the world,' we have a programme for aesthetics: 'putting into order our notions as to what can be said about works of art.'

One of the tasks of such a programme would be to elucidate the relation in which biographical data about an author, particularly of the kind loosely known as knowledge of his intentions, stand to those issues we call matters of interpretation. I.e., the relation between questions like these:

Whether it is Goethe who is referred to in the first line of the first canto of *In Memoriam*. Whether it is the poet who is speaking in the concluding lines of *Ode on a Grecian Urn*. Whether Pope is 'screaming with malignant fury' in his character of Sporus. Whether Hamlet in his famous soliloquy is contemplating suicide or assassination. Whether Milton's Satan in his speech in Book IV beginning 'League with thee I seek' may be wholly or partly sincere. Whether the governess who tells the story in James' *Turn of the Screw*, is a neurotic case of sex-repression and the ghosts not real ghosts but hallucinations. Whether Wordsworth's *Ode: Intimations of Immortality* is 'a conscious farewell to his art, a dirge sung over his departing powers' or is a 'dedication to new powers'; and whether the 'timely utterance' referred to in that poem is *My Heart Leaps Up* or *Resolution and Independence*. Whether we are meant to reflect that Othello becomes jealous very quickly on very little provocation. Whether the Moses of Michelangelo is about to hurl the tablets of the law to the ground or has just overcome an impulse to do so. Whether Shakespeare's Sonnet 73 contains an allusion to despoilt and abandoned monasteries. Whether the image which floats before Yeats' mind in *Among School Children*, 'hollow of cheek,' is of an old woman or of one beautiful in a *quattrocento* way. Whether the metaphors in Othello's soliloquy which begins 'Steep me in poverty to the very lips' are deliberately inappropriate so as to suggest the disorder of Othello's mind. Whether Ford Madox Ford's novel *Parade's End* is a trilogy or a tetralogy. Whether on reading the line 'in spite of that we call this Friday good' from *East Coker* we are to think of Robinson Crusoe's friend. Whether Gertrude's marriage to Claudius was incestuous.

Whether Othello was black or brown. Whether Pipit in Eliot's *A Cooking Egg* is young or old, of the same social status as the speaker or not and whether the connotations of the expression 'penny-world' in that poem are sordid or tender. Whether in *The Mystery of Edwin Drood* Dickens has deepened his analysis of Victorian society to include Imperialism; and whether John Jasper in that novel is a member of the Indian sect of Thugs. Whether we should identify with Strether in *The Ambassadors* and whether the Ververs in *The Golden Bowl* are unqualifiedly admirable.

And statements like these:

That Eliot associates the Hanged Man, a member of the traditional tarot pack, with the Hanged God of Frazer and with the hooded figure in the passage of the disciples to Emmaus. That Hopkins said: The Sonnet on Purcell means this: 1–4 I hope Purcell is not damned for being a protestant because I love his genius, etc. 'Low lays him' means 'lays him low,' 'listed is enlisted' etc., etc. That Wordsworth wrote *Resolution and Independence* while engaged on the first part of the Immortality Ode. That Henry James in 1895 had his faith in himself shaken by the failure of his plays. That Donne's *A Valediction: Forbidding Mourning* was addressed to his wife. That James was conversant enough with English ways to know that no headmaster would have expelled a boy belonging to a county family without grave reasons. That A. E. Housman vehemently repudiated the view that his poem *1887* contained a gibe at the Queen. That Swift was philanthropic and well-loved by his friends. That Maude Gonne was an old woman when Yeats wrote *Among School Children*. That Keats in his letters uses the word 'beauty' to mean something much more subtle than is ordinarily meant by it. That Eliot meant the lines 'to Carthage then I came, burning, burning, burning . . .' to evoke the presence of St Augustine and the Buddha, of Western and Eastern Asceticism. That Abraham Cowley had had very little to do with women. That ruined monasteries were a not uncommon sight in 1585. That Henry James meant his later novels to illustrate his father's metaphysical system. That Conrad in *The Arrow of Gold* presents an unrealistic and sentimentalised portrait of a woman. That Wordsworth nowhere in his work uses the word 'glory' to refer to his creative powers. That Eliot told someone that Richards in his account of *A Cooking Egg* was 'barking up the wrong tree.' That Tennyson shortly before his death told an American gentleman that he was referring to Goethe when he wrote 'of him who sings to one clear harp in divers tones.' That there were no industrial mills when Blake wrote *Jerusalem*. That in the book of *Exodus* Moses shattered the tablets of the law. That Dickens wrote a letter at the time of the Sepoy mutiny advocating the extermination of the Indian people.

In this paper I have assembled and invented examples of arguments which use biographical claims to resolve questions of interpretation and confronted them with a meta-critical dogma to the effect that there exists an operation variously known as analysing or explicating or appealing to the text and that criticism should confine itself to this, in particular eschewing biographical enquiries.

By now any of you who are at all interested in this topic must have had the phrase 'the intentional fallacy' occur to you. This phrase owes its currency to a widely anthologised and often-alluded to paper of that title by two Americans, Wimsatt and Beardsley. I want now to try to bring what they say in it into relation with the issue I have raised.

o   o   o

The first statement of their thesis runs: '. . . the design or intention of the author is neither available nor desirable as a standard for judging the success of a literary work of art.' These words don't really mean what they say. They don't mean that an artist may have intended to create a masterpiece but for all that have failed to do so; for the authors go on to say of their thesis that it entails 'many specific truths about inspiration, authenticity, biography, literary history and scholarship,' etc., and none of these specific truths follows from the truism that knowledge of an artist's intentions cannot provide us with criteria for judging of his success. The charitable conviction that they mean more than this is borne out by a later statement of the thesis; this time to the effect that it is a thesis about the *meaning* of a work of art that they are concerned to advance: that certain ways of establishing this meaning are legitimate whereas others are not. So, presumably, what they intended to say is: 'the design or intention of an author is neither available nor desirable as a standard for judging the meaning of a literary work of art.' But no argument can profitably be conducted in these terms. For if a discrepancy should come to light between a reader's interpretation of a work and the interpretation of the author or his contemporaries, no way of determining which of these could be properly described as *the* meaning of the work could be produced.

What an author meant, by a poem, say, what his contempories took him to mean, what the common reader makes of it and what makes the best poem of it are usually concomitant and allow us to speak of *the* meaning without equivocation. If when confronted by instances in which this concomitance breaks down we appeal to only one of the ordinarily coincident features as if we had a settled convention behind us, the question becomes intractable. If the question is expressed instead as 'How should this poem be read?' it at least becomes clearer what the issues are. So the thesis becomes, 'The design or intention of an author is neither available nor desirable as a standard for judging how a work of literature should be read.' But does any criticism of literature consist of the provision of standards by which you may judge how the work should be read? One of the pieces of criticism which the authors have provided in their paper as an illustration of how it should be done concerns Eliot's *The Love Song of J. Alfred Prufrock*. They say that when Prufrock asks, 'would it have been worth while . . . to have squeezed the universe into a ball,' 'his words take half their sadness and irony from certain energetic and passionate lines of Marvell's *To His Coy Mistress*.' This may be true and it may be helpful but nothing in it answers to the description of providing a standard by which the work may be read. What they have done or have tried to do is to produce in the reader a more adequate response to Eliot's lines by reminding him of Marvell's. If we bring their thesis in line with their practice it becomes: 'The design or intention of the author is neither available nor desirable as a means of influencing a reader's response to a literary work.' But since they give us an example of what they consider as irrelevant to criticism the fact that Coleridge read Purchas, Bartram, Milton and Bruce and this is not a fact about either his design or his intention it is obvious that they mean something rather wider than this, something which the expression 'biographical data' would be a closer approximation to. This gives us 'biographical data about an author, particularly concerning his artistic intentions is not desirable [I omit 'available' as probably just a sign of nervousness] as a means of influencing a reader's response to a literary work.'

What any general thesis about the relevance of intention to interpretation overlooks is the heterogeneity of the contexts in which questions of interpretation arise. This heterogeneity makes it impossible to give a general answer to the question of what the relevance of intention to interpretation is. There are cases in which we have an interpretation which satisfies us but which we feel depends on certain facts being the case. It may involve an allusion and we may wish to be reassured that the author was in a position to make the allusion. In this case biographical facts act as a kind of sieve which exclude certain possibilities. Then there is the case where we are puzzled, perhaps by an allusion we don't understand, perhaps by syntax, and reference to the author's intention, though it does not guarantee a favourable response, may at least relieve this perplexity and make one possible. There are cases in which we suspect irony but the text is equivocal, and cases where we aren't sure what view the author wishes us to take of the situation he places before us. Then there are the most interesting cases, those in which the text seems unmistakably to call for a certain interpretation and this is found satisfying, but in which we learn with surprise that it has been explicitly repudiated by the author. Even within the same kind of context the author's intention will vary in relevance depending on the kind of question involved; whether it concerns the meaning of a word or the tone of a passage, the view to be taken of a character or a situation or the general moral of an entire work.

Why did Wimsatt and Beardsley think they had a general answer to the question of deciding what the response to a work of literature should be? This is what they say:

> There is a difference between internal and external evidence for the meaning of a poem, and the paradox is only verbal and superficial that what is (1) internal is also public. It is discovered through the semantics and syntax of a poem, through our habitual knowledge of the language, through grammars, dictionaries and all the literature which is a source of dictionaries, in general through all that makes a language and culture; while what is (2) external is private or idiosyncratic; not a part of the work as a linguistic fact; it consists of revelations (in journals, for example, or letters, or reported conversations) about how or why the poet wrote the poem. To what lady while sitting on what lawn, or at the death of what friend or brother. There is (3) an intermediate kind of evidence about the character of the author or about private or semi-private meanings attached to words or topics by an author or by a coterie of which he is a member. The meaning of words is the history of words, and the biography of an author, his use of a word, and the associations which the word had for him are part of the word's history and meaning. But the three types of evidence, especially (2) and (3) shade into one another so subtly that it is not always easy to draw a line between examples, and hence arises the difficulty for criticism.

It is not clear from this account what the authors mean to exclude as illicit sources of interpretive data. Once the author's character and the private associations a word may have for him are admitted among these, along with all that makes a language and a culture, what is there left to commit fallacies with? Were it not that their illustrations give a much clearer impression of their attitude than their attempts at explicit formulation of it do, and show it to be much more restrictive, they could be suspected of advancing one of those enchanted theses which possess the magical power of transforming themselves into truisms at the touch of a counter-example. They say of a line in Eliot's *The Love Song of J. Alfred Prufrock*: 'I have heard the mermaids singing each to each' that it bears some resemblance to a line of Donne's: 'Teach me to heare Mermaides singing' so that the question arises whether Eliot's line contains an allusion to Donne's. They go on to say that there are two radically different ways of answering this question. The way of poetic exegesis and the way of biographical enquiry, and the latter would not be a critical enquiry and would have nothing to do with the poem. The method of poetic exegesis consists of asking whether it would make any sense if Donne's mermaids were being alluded to. The biographical approach would be to ask Eliot what he thought at the time he wrote it, whether he had Donne's mermaids in mind. The answer to this question would be critically irrelevant. It is not surprising that their example bears them out since it was hand-chosen, as it were. To expose its tendentiousness we need only take an example in which it was felt that a literary allusion would enhance the value of the lines. Let us take their own example of Marvell's *To His Coy Mistress*, familiarity with which they maintain enhances the value of certain lines of Eliot's. If we take the case of someone not familiar with Marvell's *To His Coy Mistress*, then the biographical claim that Eliot alludes to it in Prufrock would enhance its value for them. If on the other hand they merely applied the test of poetic exegesis and in-corporated the allusion to Marvell's *To His Coy Mistress* into the poem without knowing whather Eliot was alluding to it, it is doubtful whether their appreciation would survive the discovery that he was not. If a critical remark is one which has the power to modify our apprehension of a work, then biographical remarks can be critical. They can serve the eliminative function of showing that certain interpretations of a work are based on mistaken beliefs about the author's state of knowledge.

o o o

We can illustrate this eliminative function of biographical data by taking the very case on which Wimsatt and Beardsley based their arguments as to its irrelevance. They quote a quatrain from John Donne's *A Valediction: Forbidding Mourning*:

Moving of th' earth brings harmes and feares,
Men reckon what it did and meant,
But trepidation of the spheares,
Though greater farre, is innocent.

They then go on to criticise an interpretation of this quatrain which basing itself on the biographical fact that Donne was intensely interested in the new astronomy and its theological repercussions sees in the phrase 'Moving of the earth' an allusion to the recently discovered motion of the earth round the sun. Wimsatt and Beardsley show the unlikelihood of this, not by disputing the well-authenticated facts concerning Donne's interest in astronomy, which would be to use a biographical method, but through an analysis of the text. They maintain that whereas the fear which is produced by the motion of the earth is a metaphysical, intellectual one, the fear which Donne is attempting to discourage is of the emotional kind which an earth-quake is more likely to produce and that this accords better with the 'tear-floods' and 'sigh-tempests' of the poem's second stanza than the earth's motion. Let us concede that the authors have made it very plausible that Donne was alluding not to the heliocentric theory of the earth's motion but to earthquakes. The gratuitousness of the con-clusion which they draw from this becomes apparent if we ask the following question: have they established that Donne was not referring to the motion of the earth round the sun as persuasively as our belief in Donne's ignorance of the heliocentric theory would establish it? Wouldn't this 'external' fact outweigh all their 'internal' ones?

At this point someone who finds my question unrhetorical is thinking to himself 'dark satanic mills.' It is true that the knowledge that the poem that prefaces Blake's *Milton* is not an expression of the Fabian sentiments it has been usually taken as being has not caused the traditional interpretation to be abandoned. I suggest that what we have in this case is something in the nature of a spontaneous adaptation of Blake's poem. It is unlike what we ordinarily consider an adaptation in not being conscious (initially at any rate) and not involving any physical change in the work adapted. Does the fact that this was possible in the case of Blake's lyric reflect adversely on it as poem? Does the fact that the melody of *God Save the Queen* could be fitted with new words and become the national anthem of a republican nation reflect on it? The combination of resolution and exaltation which characterises Blake's poem carries over into its adaptation; it functions like a melody. We should see cases like that of *Jerusalem* as continuous with more deliberate cases of adaptation. When Pistol tells *French* audiences that his 'rendezvous is quite cut off,' his Doll lies dying of Maladie of *Naples*.[1] Does anything follow as to the relevance or irrelevance of an author's intentions? Then neither does it in the case of *Jerusalem*. It would only follow if the discovery that a work was an adaptation made no difference to us. There is one sort of literature in which adaptation is a matter of indifference: jokes. Wilkes becomes Disraeli and Disraeli becomes Birkenhead. The two Jews become two Irishmen or two Chinese.

CIOFFI

But then, we speak of the author of a poem but not of the author of a joke. I am saying: we don't stand in the same relation to Blake's lyric after changing our conviction as to what he meant to convey as we did before. If the case were one in which the discrepancy between the author's interpretation and the reader's were one as to the very emotions expressed and not just the accompanying imagery our attitude would be very different. Frank Harris read A. E. Housman's poem *1887* as an anti-imperialist gibe and the expression 'God Save the Queen' which recurs in it as a sarcastic jeer until Housman revealed otherwise. Thereafter he naturally found it difficult to do so in spite of his conviction both as to the superiority of his interpretation and its greater consonance with Housman's general outlook. ('How was I to know that someone steeped in a savage disgust of life could take pleasure in outcheapening Kipling at his cheapest?')

The following examples should make it clear how inept Wimsatt's and Beardsley's characterisation of the role of biographical data in critical discourse is. An example which seems to support their account is Leavis' reaction to John Middleton Murry's attempt to give the word 'beauty' in the concluding couplet of Keats' *Ode on a Grecian Urn* a less limiting sense based on the use Keats made of the word in his letters.

> To show from the letters that 'beauty' became for Keats a very subtle and embracing concept and that in his use the term takes on meanings that it could not possibly have for the uninitiated is gratuitous and irrelevant. However his use of the word may have developed as he matured, 'beauty' is the term he used and in calling what seemed to him the supreme thing in life 'beauty' he expresses a given bent—the bent everywhere manifest in the quality of his verse, in its loveliness . . . and that 'beauty' in the *Ode on a Grecian Urn* expresses this bent is plain, that it should is the essence of the poem, and there is nothing in the poem to suggest otherwise.

This may sound as if a general principle akin to Wimsatt's and Beardsley's is being employed, but that this is not so Leavis' practice elsewhere shows. For example,

> Hopkins' *Henry Purcell* is a curious special case, there can be few readers who have not found it strangely expressive and few who could have elucidated it without extraneous help. It is not independent of the explanatory note by Hopkins that Bridges prints. Yet when one approaches it with the note fresh in mind, the intended meaning seems to be sufficiently in the poem to allay at any rate the dissatisfaction caused by baffled understanding.

We must not be misled by the expression 'a curious special case.' Leavis' dealings with *The Waste Land* make it clear that the only question which arises in connexion with notes or other extraneous aids to understanding is not one of their legitimacy but of their efficacy. For example, Leavis says of *The Waste Land* that it 'sometimes depends on external support in ways that can hardly be justified . . . for instance, the end of the third section "The Fire Sermon." . . . No amount of reading of the *Confessions* or *Buddhism in Translation* will give these few words power to evoke the kind of presence that seems necessary to the poem.' Of another passage he writes: 'it leaves too much to Miss Weston; repeated recourse to *Ritual and Romance* will not invest it with the virtues it would assume.' On the other hand, of Eliot's note on *Tiresias*, Leavis remarks, 'if Mr Eliot's readers have a right to a grievance, it is that he has not given this note more salience.' 'Power to evoke,' 'invest with virtues,' these are not the idioms in which the probative value of statements is weighed.

Wimsatt and Beardsley are aware of the problem posed them by Eliot's notes to *The Waste Land* and make the suggestion that the notes should be considered as part of the poem. They thus become internal evidence, and may be consulted with a good conscience. Does it follow that since the effectiveness of certain lines in *Prufrock* depends on familiarity with Marvell's *Coy Mistress*, Marvell's poem should be considered part of Eliot's, or does this not follow because whereas we are expected to be familiar with Marvell's poem, familiarity with the contents of Eliot's notes is not expected of us? Then is this what the distinction between external and internal evidence comes to; the difference between what we can and can't be expected to know?, and how is it decided what we can be expected to know? Leavis has said of Quentin Anderson's book on Henry James, 'thanks to the light shed by Mr Anderson, we can see in the peculiar impressiveness of Mrs Lowder of the *Wings of the Dove* a triumph of morality art.' Is Mr Anderson's book also to be considered part of James' *Wings of the Dove* then?

No amount of tinkering can save Wimsatt and Beardsley's distinction between internal and external evidence. It isn't just that it's made in the wrong place, but that it is misconceived from the start. A reader's response to a work will vary with what he *knows*; one of the things which he knows and with which his responses will vary is what the author had in mind, or what he intended. The distinction between what different people know of an author before reading his work or what the same person knows on successive occasions can't be a logical one. When is a remark a critical remark about the poem and when a biographical one about the author? The difficulty in obeying the injunction to ignore the biographical facts and cultivate the critical ones is that you can't know which is which until after you have read the work in the light of them.

The assumption which stultifies their exposition is the conception of critical argument as the production and evaluation of evidence. They say that there are two kinds of evidence: that provided by poetic exegesis and that provided by biographical enquiry. But the examples they give of poetic exegesis seem not to be evidence but conclusions or judgments. For example, that the lines from *Prufrock* take half their sadness and irony from lines in a poem of Marvell's, or that the mermaids in *Prufrock* derive no benefit from a reminiscence of the mermaids in Donne. We could construe these statements as evidence, only by taking them as biographical statements about Wimsatt and Beardsley, but so taken they would stand in the same relation to critical judgment as biographical statements about Eliot. If a critical remark fails to confirm or consolidate or transform a reader's interpretation of a work it will then become for him just evidence of something or other, perhaps the critic's obtuseness. Biographical remarks are no more prone to this fate than any others.

o o o

In the sixth stanza of Yeats' *Among School Children* there occur the lines:

Plato thought nature but a spume that plays
Upon a ghostly paradigm of things;
Solider Aristotle played the taws
Upon the bottom of a king of kings.

Many editions give the first word of the third line 'solider' as 'soldier.' This is due to a compositor's error, a transposition of two letters which went unnoticed because by a fluke instead of producing gibberish, it produced the English word 'soldier.'

The American critic Delmore Schwartz was thus led to advance his well-known interpretation to the effect that the expression 'soldier Aristotle' alludes to a legend that Aristotle accompanied Alexander on his military expedition to India. Since there is obviously a contrast intended between the unworldliness of Plato and the down-to-earthness of Aristotle, Schwartz' military interpretation accords well with the rest of the poem. But in spite of this, now that we know of the error wouldn't we insist on the restoration of the lines as Yeats wrote them and regard the view that there is a military allusion in the lines as a mistake? It might be objected that this is not to the point because the case here is one of a discrepancy between what the author *wrote* and what we made of it and not between what he *meant* and what we made of it.

64

But can this distinction be upheld? Can't we imagine cases where the words were homophones? In such a case the only distinction between what an author wrote and a mistaken reading would be what he meant. In fact, we needn't imagine such a case. Hopkins' note on his poem *Henry Purcell* provides us with one: 'One thing disquiets me: I *meant* "fair fall" to mean "fair (fortune be) fall": it has since struck me that perhaps "fair" is an adjective proper and in the predicate and can only be used in cases like "fair fall the day," that is "may the day fall, turn out fair." My lines will yield a sense that way indeed, but I never meant it so.' Is the possible meaning mentioned but rejected by Hopkins any more tenable than 'soldier Aristotle'?

There is thus no doubt that there are cases in which knowledge of an author's avowed intention in respect of his work exercises a coercive influence on our apprehension of it. The question now arises: When doesn't it? My answer is, 'When the issue is of a complexity comparable to that which would cause us to discount his avowed intention in respect of something not a work of literature.' To put it another way, we tend to think that there are cases where we over-ride the author's intention and persist in an interpretation which he has rejected but where what we are really doing could less misleadingly be described as favouring one criterion of intention as against another. If we establish the existence of a discrepancy between the interpretation we give to a work of art, and that of the author, we haven't shown that the work has a meaning independent of what the author intends because what the author intends will now be the interpretation given to the work by us and his own statement as to its meaning an aberration. The notion of the author's intention is logically tied to the interpretation we give to his work. It's not just that our language works this way; but that our minds do. Confronted with a choice between saying that an effect so complex could have come about by accident and that the author was mistaken we would opt for the latter. The work will be considered more conclusive evidence of his intention than his own statements. The colour flows back.

Edmund Wilson's dealings with Henry James' *The Turn of the Screw* bring this out clearly. *The Turn of the Screw* was generally considered a superior ghost story until Wilson popularised the view that the ghosts were figments of the narrator's imagination and the work a study in thwarted Anglo-Saxon spinsterdom. He thought he had discovered that the text was skilfully ambiguous so as never unequivocally to imply the ghosts' objective existence. He was able to interpret some passages in James' preface to the book to similar

effect. The publication of James' notebooks some years later, however, made it clear that James' conscious intention was to produce a
ghost story. At the same time Wilson came to admit that the text
itself was not completely reconcilable with his thesis that the ghosts
were hallucinatory. Nevertheless, Wilson continued to insist that it
was not a straightforward ghost story, but a study in the neurotic
effects of repressed sexuality. His arguments for this provide an
excellent example of what I have called the colour flowing back.
Instead of simply enjoying a gratuitous effect for its own sake,
Wilson convinces himself, on the basis of certain biographical facts
about James, that at the time the book was written, his faith in himself had been shaken and that 'in *The Turn of the Screw*, not merely is
the governess self-deceived, but that James is self-deceived about
her. The doubt that some readers feel as to the soundness of the
governess' story are the reflection of doubts communicated unconsciously by James himself.'

The real interest of this kind of example is that it brings out quite
clearly what otherwise is not so apparent; that there is an implicit
biographical reference in our response to literature. It is, if you like,
part of our concept of literature. It is only when it is missing that we
notice that it was always there.

I want now to deal with some notorious ostensible counter-
examples. This is the fifth stanza of Yeats' *Among School Children*:

What young mother a shape upon her lap
Honey of generation had betrayed,
And that must sleep, shriek, struggle to escape
As recollection or the drug decide,
Would think her son, did she but see that shape
With sixty or more winters on its head,
Compensation for the pang of his birth,
Or the uncertainty of his setting forth?

There is an accompanying note to this poem which indicates that the
phrase 'honey of generation' is taken from an essay of Porphyry's
and that Yeats has arbitrarily used it to refer to 'the drug that
destroys the recollection of pre-natal freedom.' It is then, the shape
upon the mother's lap, the child, which has been betrayed by being
born. John Wain has put forward a reading according to which it is
the mother who has been betrayed, and 'honey of generation' is an
allusion to the sexual pleasure which accompanies conception, and
the desire for which has betrayed her. Doesn't this example show
the irrelevance of intention? Not necessarily. It could be interpreted
as a case where we take the poem as better evidence of what the poet
intended than his own explicit remarks on the subject. To persist in

an interpretation in spite of an author's explicit disavowal of it is not necessarily to show an indifference to the author's intention. For we may feel that he was mistaken as to what his intention was. A case which comes to mind is Goldsmith's withdrawal of the gloss he offered on the word 'slow' in the first line of his poem, *The Traveller*, 'Remote, unfriended, melancholy, *slow*.' Goldsmith said it meant 'tardiness of locomotion' until contradicted by Johnson. 'No sir. You do not mean tardiness of locomotion. You mean that sluggishness of mind that comes upon a man in solitude.'

Though it might be true, as Wimsatt and Beardsley say, that critical enquiries are not settled like bets, neither need questions of intention be. I can't resort here to the argument I used in the case of Donne's *Valediction* and ask you to imagine what your attitude to Wain's interpretation would be if you were convinced that Yeats was ignorant of the fact on which it is based, since this fact, that sexual pleasure is an incentive to procreation, is not such as can be overlooked. Nevertheless, I want to maintain that we don't, if we accept Wain's interpretation, think it an accident that it should be possible to read the text as he does, but we feel that the ambiguity which makes it possible was the result of a connection in Yeats' mind between the expression 'honey of generation' and sexual pleasure. (In fact this can be demonstrated.)

In order to convince you that an implicit biographical inference is at work even in Wain's interpretation, I want you to imagine the case altered in some important respects. Imagine that the reading according to which it is the mother who is betrayed, was also that of Yeats, and that there was no footnote referring to Porphyry's essay, of which Yeats was completely ignorant, but that a reader familiar with it and sharing its views on pre-natal existence, insisted on taking the expression 'honey of generation' as an allusion to the drug which destroys the recollection of pre-natal freedom and, therefore, to the infant, and not the mother, as betrayed. Wouldn't our attitude to this interpretation be quite different from our attitude to Wain's? Wouldn't we feel it perverse? And since it can't be the text which makes it perverse but only the facts about Yeats as we have imagined them, doesn't our implicit biographical or intentionalistic approach to literature emerge quite clearly here?

Of course, there are cases where the pleasure we take in literature doesn't depend on this implicit biographical reference. Literature, as Wittgenstein probably said, is a motley. Nursery rhymes come to mind as the most notable example. But in general we do make such a reference. Eliot's attitude towards a line of Cyril Tourneur's illustrates this reluctance to take pleasure in what is accidental and unintended. The line is: 'The poor benefit of a bewildering minute,' which is given as 'The poor benefit of a bewitching minute' in the texts both of Churton Collins and of Nicoll who mention no alternative reading. Eliot comments: '*it is a pity* if they be right for "bewildering" is much the richer word here.' It has been argued that if the folio text of *Henry V* was right and Theobald's lovely guess wrong so that Shakespeare made the dying Falstaff allude to a painting rather than babble of green fields most of us would persist in reading the traditional and incorrect version. We probably would but it would worry us; and if 'a babbled of green fields' wasn't even Theobald's guess but a transcriber's or printer's unthinking error, it would worry us even more. The suspicion that a poetic effect is an accident is fatal to the enjoyment which literature characteristically offers. If the faces on Mount Rushmore were the effect of the action of wind and rain, our relation to them would be very different.

o o o

In the course of their criticism of the interpretation of Donne's poem which saw in it an allusion to the revolution of the earth round the sun Wimsatt and Beardsley remark, 'But the text itself remains to be dealt with . . .'!

Where understanding fails, says Goethe, there immediately comes a word to take its place. In this case the word is 'text.' Let us appeal to the text. But what is the text? These critics talk of the text of a poem as if it had an outline as neat and definite as the page on which it is printed. If you remind yourself of how questions about what is 'in the text' are settled you will see that they involve a great deal which is not 'in the text.' Though there are many occasions on which we can make the distinction in an immediately intelligible and non-tendentious way, where an interpretative issue has already arisen, the use of a distinction between internal, licit considerations, and external, illicit ones is just a form of question-begging.

What are we to say of attempts to support an interpretation by citing other works of the author? For example, Leavis on Conrad's *Heart of Darkness*: 'If any reader of that tale felt that the irony permitted a doubt regarding Conrad's attitude towards the Intended, the presentment of Rita (in *The Arrow of Gold*) should settle it.' Isn't this illicit? Isn't the common authorship of several works a biographical fact?

What of the use of previous drafts of a work for critical purposes? Leavis in commenting on Hopkins' *Spelt from Sybil's Leaves* is able to enforce his point that 'Hopkins' positives waver and change places and he is left in terrible doubt' by showing that in a previous draft of the poem the word-order in the phrase 'black, white; right, wrong' was conventionally symmetrical 'black, white; wrong, right.' The only doubt which might arise in connexion with Leavis' point is whether the word-order may have been altered to avoid a rhyme, but this is equally intentionalistic.

Marius Bewley supports his interpretation of James' *The Turn of the Screw* by pointing out that when James collected his stories for the definitive edition he put it in the same volume as one called *The Liar*.

Even if the anti-intentionalist thesis were qualified to accommodate all these there would still be a fundamental objection to it.

You must all have had the experience while reading of having the words suddenly undergo a radical transformation as you realised you had missed the end of a quotation, say, and mistaken the speaker. The more familiar the speakers the greater the transformation when you realised your mistake. Doesn't this illustrate the importance of implicit biographical assumptions in interpreting what we read? Here's an illustration: In Rudyard Kipling's *Loot* occur the lines:

An' if you treat a nigger to a dose of cleanin'-rod
'E's like to show you everything he owns.

Hugh Kingsmill has quoted these lines as an example of Kipling's brutality and even Kipling's biographer, Edward Shanks, is embarrassed by them. Edmund Wilson, on the other hand, in his well-known essay on Kipling, says this about them: 'Kipling was interested in the soldier for his own sake, and made some effort to present his life as it seemed to the soldier himself. The poem called *Loot*, for example, which appears to celebrate a reprehensible practice is in reality perfectly legitimate because it simply describes one of the features of the soldier's experience in India. There is no moral one way or the other.' T. S. Eliot takes a similar line in his introduction to his selection of Kipling's verse.

How is this issue to be decided? By an appeal to the text? Isn't it rather our sense of Kipling which will determine the side we come down on? A sense built up not only from the other tales but from his autobiography and other sources as well? Don't these throw a 'field of force' round the work? If it had been written by someone else wouldn't this make a difference to our apprehension of it? Isn't this like the case described by Wittgenstein in the *Philosophical Investigations*? 'I see a picture which represents a smiling face. What do I do if I take the smile now as a kind one, now as a malicious one? Don't I often imagine it with a spatial and temporal context which is one either of kindness or of malice? Thus I might supply the picture with the fancy that the smiler was smiling down at a child at play, or again on the suffering of an enemy.'

The difference of opinion between F. R. Leavis and Marius Bewley over James' *What Maisie Knew* is an excellent illustration of an interpretation depending on 'the fiction I surround it with.' Unfortunately it is too long to quote, but the gist of it is that Bewley finds the atmosphere of the book one of horror and its theme the meaning and significance of evil, whereas Leavis can detect no horror and sees it as an extraordinarily high-spirited comedy reminiscent of the early part of *David Copperfield*. Bewley in attempting to locate the source of their difference says that it has its 'origin in areas not readily open to literary-critical persuasion' and 'that the way one senses the presence of evil and horror in the novel may be due to one's conception of them outside the novel.'

There is one aspect of our response to a work of literature to which biographical data seem to have particular relevance and that is our conviction as to an author's sincerity. It is certain that there are cases where biographical considerations are genuinely relevant and equally certain that there are cases where they are intrusions which we feel we ought not to allow to condition our response. But it is difficult to know where the line should be drawn. I suppose that we would all consider Beethoven's inability to get on with Scott's *Kenilworth* because 'This man writes for money' as eccentric, though the decline in Trollope's reputation which followed his revelation as to his methods of composition and his business-like attitude towards his writing, show it is not rare. Perhaps these responses should be considered more as moral gestures, like refusing to hear Gieseking perform, rather than as aesthetic responses.

A good example of a response which is genuinely critical but which we would all consider misplaced is Johnson's criticism of Abraham Cowley's *The Mistress*:

> But the basis of all excellence is truth: he that professes love ought to feel its power. Petrarch was a real lover and Laura doubtless deserved his tenderness. Of Cowley we are told by Barnes, who had means enough of information, that whatever he may talk of his own inflammability, and the variety of characters by which his heart was divided, he in reality was in love but once, and then never had resolution to tell his passion!
> This consideration cannot but abate in some measure the reader's esteem for the work. . . .

Another, perhaps slightly less conclusive example is provided by Johnson's remarks on Cowley's poem on the death of Hervey . . .

> but when he wishes to make us weep he forgets to weep himself, and diverts his sorrow by imagining how his crown of bays, if he had it would *crackle* in the *fire*. It is the odd fate of

this thought to be the worse for being true. The bay leaf crackles remarkably as it burns, as therefore this property was not assigned to it by chance, the mind must be thought sufficiently at ease that could attend to such minuteness of physiology.

It might be argued that Johnson has indicated a source of dissatisfaction *in* the poem, the bay leaves image. But it is what this enabled him to infer about something *outside* the poem concerning Cowley which abated his esteem. If he could have been convinced that Cowley was ignorant of the propensity of bay leaves to crackle remarkably and the felicity of his image therefore fortuitous, Johnson would presumably have liked the poem better. But it would be a mistake to think Johnson simply absurd here. Suppose that the poem in question were Bishop King's *Exequy* and the biographical fact that he was never married and therefore never bereaved. Some of us would decide it didn't matter, some that it did and some would oscillate. This is an example of the more general dilemma which arises when an empirical concomitance on which we habitually depend and so regular that it has influenced the build of our concepts, disintegrates. Van Meegeren's *Disciples at Emmaus*, the poems of Ern Malley, Macpherson's *Ossian*, Chatterton's *Rowley*, all point the same moral.

D. W. Harding raised a related issue in a vivid form some years ago. He wrote:

We think of it (a work of art) as being a human product, as implicitly sanctioning and developing interests and ideals and attitudes of our own. That being so it does become disconcerting to find that for the author it satisfied certain impulses which we ourselves are glad not to possess, or which if we do possess we think better left unsatisfied. The same thing goes on in social intercourse of a simpler kind than literature. We enjoy the *bon mot* with which our friend disposes of a charlatan, but if we know that he is incidentally working off irrelevant spite against either the charlatan or the world in general the flavour of the remark is spoilt. The *bon mot* is as good as ever regarded as something impersonal, but as a human product it no longer gives us pure satisfaction—an element of distaste or regret comes in and makes our state of mind more complex. Many people find this more complex attitude extremely difficult to maintain . . . especially because in most actual cases the neurotic flaw can be detected in the work itself.

But once in possession of biographical data it is difficult to be sure what is 'in the work itself.' Leavis has suggested it is a pity much is known of Pope's life since the expression of spite, envy, venom and malice so often found in his work is a consequence of the distorting effect of this knowledge.

What I have called 'putting a field of force round a work,' surrounding it with a web of associations, may be effective even when it doesn't deserve to be. But this kind of suggestibility is a risk all critical remarks run and not merely biographical ones. Would anyone have found the last few lines of Bishop King's *Exequy* productive of an effect of terror if Eliot had not said so? And would Eliot himself if he had not first come across them in Poe's *The Assignation*? It is the fact that we can speak of criticism which is effective but mistaken which makes the analogy with argument so tempting for there too we speak of conclusions seeming to follow but not following; so it seems that we can have specious criticism in the same sense in which we have specious argument. But this is an illusion. You don't show that a response to a work of literature is inadequate or inappropriate in the way that you show that the conclusion of an argument has been wrongly drawn.

Wittgenstein has some remarks in Part Two of the *Investigations*, which shed light on the nature of the intractability which characterises so much critical argument and make its prevalence less surprising. His remarks though concerned with the question of the genuineness of an expression of feeling have a more general application. He contrasts our judgments about sincerity with those about colour. 'I am sure, *sure* that he is pretending: but some third person is not. Can I always convince him? And if not, is there some error in his reasoning or observations?' Though there are those whose judgment is better in such matters and rules for determining this, these do not form a system and only experienced people can apply them. There are consequences which distinguish correct from incorrect judgment, but these are of a diffuse kind and like the rules incapable of general formulation . . . 'only in scattered cases can one arrive at a correct and fruitful judgment.' It is not surprising, then, that 'the game often ends with one person relishing what another does not.'

Conclusion

What I have been saying is this: a conviction that a poet stands in a certain relation to his words conditions our response to them. That this should be so seems to me part of the 'physiognomy' of literature (as Wittgenstein might have put it). We are not ordinarily aware of this as these convictions tend to be held in solution in 'the work itself.' It is only in exceptional circumstance that we crystallise them out as explicit beliefs and become aware of the role they play. Why should anyone wish to deny this? Because it is then only a step to the production of phantasy-theses like Wimsatt's and Beardsley's, 'What is said about a poem is subject to the same scrutiny as any statement in linguistics or in the general science of psychology.'

This in its turn has its source in the determination to tidy up the activity of reading and to reduce what it involves to a neat, logically homogenous set of considerations such as guarantee a readily communicable rationale. The idea of a work of literature as 'a linguistic fact' or an 'integrated symbol' is comparable to the notions of 'a concept' in philosophy or 'behaviour' in psychology in being the manifestation of an irresistible demand for discrete, coherent and enduring objects of investigation. But, 'Literature is a motley.'

EMILIO ROMA III

The Scope of the Intentional Fallacy

One of the more controversial articles published in the philosophy of criticism during the past twenty-five years is 'The Intentional Fallacy' by W. K. Wimsatt, Jr. and Monroe Beardsley. Scholars from a variety of disciplines have expended a lot of energy in attacking and defending the Wimsatt–Beardsley position. Their efforts fall mainly into two classes. Either they have been exploratory with respect to the nature of the concept 'intention', but *so* exploratory as to present no tangible discovery;[1] or they have merely been occasions to air the author's own views, views which take sides, but views which in the end only serve to define what positions may be taken without really convincing anyone whether one position is clearly better than the other(s).[2] This dilemma is really rather odd because in a certain sense it is pitifully easy to understand what the intentional fallacy amounts to. There is a kind of minimal meaning to it, and I suspect that introductory students in courses in Aesthetics and Criticism have little difficulty in understanding it. 'Difficulties' seem to arise primarily in connection with its implications and general scope within the totality of criticism. However, it would be wrong to conclude that these difficulties have nothing to do with the intentional fallacy. They do. And the reason is this: the *way* in which one argues for, that is, establishes, the intentional fallacy has much to do with its implications and general scope within the realm of criticism.

There are several ways in which Wimsatt and Beardsley argue for it in their article, but the one that appears to have attracted the most attention depends upon a distinction between 'inside' and 'outside' the poem. In the argument, this distinction receives support from a leading principle, namely, 'Poetry is a feat of style by which a complex of meaning is handled all at once.' Both the distinction and the principle have implications that I believe to be misleading. However, the ways in which Wimsatt and Beardsley argue in their article are not the only ways. In his book, *Aesthetics: Problems in the Philosophy of Criticism*, Beardsley uses the distinctions of the earlier article, but in his section entitled 'Meaning in Literature' offers yet another way of establishing the intentional fallacy. His argument here depends upon a logical distinction between the questions 'What does the *speaker* mean?' and 'What does the sentence mean?'[3] At least, this is the way he states the distinction, and I will go into it further later. In this paper, I will discuss these ways of approaching the intentional fallacy, showing what is to be disparaged in the one and appreciated in the other, and, I hope, say something important about the scope of this fallacy which has bearing on the area of reasons in literary criticism.

Toward the beginning of their article, Wimsatt and Beardsley set forth 'a series of propositions' which they take to be 'axiomatic.' The second and the third state respectively the distinction and the principle mentioned above. Here is the relevant part of the third:

> 3. 'A poem should not mean but be.' A poem can *be* only through its *meaning*—since its medium is words—yet it *is*, simply *is*, in the sense that we have no excuse for inquiring what part is intended or meant. Poetry is a feat of style by which a complex of meaning is handled all at once.

There is no argument offered for the truth of this proposition, and at present I am not interested in what sort of argument might be offered. Suffice it to say that it functions in the context of their article in two ways. It establishes an area that we may loosely call 'aesthetic inquiry', as differentiated from historical, sociological or psychological inquiry, and it provides a foundation for the 'inside-outside' distinction. These two functions are not really separate, though one may treat them as if they were, and I will do just this, considering the first in what immediately follows.

One may have a number of different motives for asking, 'What does the poem mean?' or 'What does this passage (image, metaphor) mean?' Although it would be wrong to severely categorize the interests and purposes of professional scholars, one is surely justified in noting differences among them, and with this in mind, one may imagine that a biographer or historian might be interested to know that the poem or some passage in it was intended to serve as a stimulus for the overthrow of existent political institutions, whereas a psychologist could conceivably be interested to discover that the very same passage is indicative of some sort of emotional disorder in either the poet himself or some segment of his society. Both the historian and psychologist may pursue their inquiry further; the historian, by conducting more extensive research into the political order of the period and drawing more extensive conclusions about the meaning of the poem within the context of his research; the psychologist, by proceeding in much the same fashion as the historian, except with a different set of documents, and hence a different context. In each of these cases, a context is established which is greater in scope than the poem. That is, the poem is viewed in relation to political upheaval or mental stability. It derives *its* significance or meaning from the significance or meaning of the subject matter to which it is referred.

But if Wimsatt and Beardsley are correct in supposing that 'Poetry is a feat of style by which a complex of meaning is handled all at once,' then the literary critic *need not*[4] conduct his inquiry by referring the poem to another subject matter. The context of his inquiry may simply be the poem itself, even though the nature of existent political institutions and the emotional disorder of the poet may figure into it. Thus, the initial function of the axiom we have been considering is to establish the *possibility* of engaging in a certain kind of inquiry which we may loosely call 'aesthetic' or 'literary' criticism. But this axiom has another function; it supports a distinction that I mentioned above. This distinction is contained in one of their other axioms, and here are its relevant parts:

> 2. One must ask how a critic expects to get an answer to the question about intention. How is he to find out what the poet tried to do? If the poet succeeded in doing it, then the *poem itself* shows what he was trying to do. And if the poet did not succeed, then the poem is not adequate evidence, and the critic must go *outside* the poem—for evidence of an intention that did not become effective *in the poem*. [My italics. E.R.]

Now, this axiom, unlike the other, is not a simple statement or declaration of principle. It is argumentative, and the argument requires clarification. Imagine the following situation: a critic, burdened about the meaning of a passage in some poem, is prompted to ask, 'What do you suppose the poet meant by that?' He receives this reply from Wimsatt and Beardsley, 'If the poet succeeded in doing what he meant to do, then you can tell what he meant from the poem itself.' Offhand, one may suppose that some other reasonable replies to the critic's question might have been, 'You can find out in the poet's journal,' 'Look in the collection of letters that he wrote his brother,' 'Why don't you ask him?' Wimsatt and Beardsley do not make it clear why these other replies are not to be considered, and since it may be assumed that part of the force of the intentional fallacy depends upon the exclusion of these replies, one may fruitfully inquire into the rationale underlying the restrictiveness of their own answer, and assume it to lie in a clarification of the argument presented in their axiom.

It is obviously true that if the poet succeeded in doing what he intended, then his intention may be correctly inferred from the poem itself. It is equally true that if he did not succeed, then the possibilities of correctly inferring his intention from the poem itself become greatly decreased. But in this latter case, there is no reason for the critic who is interested in the meaning of the poem to seek out the poet's intention, since 'it did not become effective in the poem.' Hence, the only time a knowledge of the poet's intention will matter is when he succeeds. But if he succeeds, one can tell his intention from the poem itself; one need not go *outside* of the poem. On this interpretation, the intentional fallacy seems to have something to do with going *outside* of the poem, i.e., to the poet's journal, letters, etc. At least, Leslie A. Fiedler places this interpretation upon it in an article of his.[5] In one place, he discusses a book called *Reading Poems*. He points out that in this book, the poems are not printed in chronological order and the names of the authors are not attached. All of this is presumably done to prevent the student from bringing irrelevant information to his reading of the poems. But Fiedler points out that,

> . . . the good teacher is himself aware to begin with of the contexts, social and biographical, of a large number of the pieces. Frankly, that is why they make sense to him; and even when he admonishes the young to 'stay *inside*' the poems, he is bootlegging from 'outside' . . .[6]

One of the main points of Fiedler's article is that 'bootlegging from outside' is not to be despised if the information bootlegged is 'connected' with what is inside the poem.[7] But one may seriously doubt that Wimsatt and Beardsley would disagree with this aspect of Fiedler's position. In fact, the intentional fallacy, properly understood, derives its relevance and import from a desire to *connect* 'inside' and 'outside'. This point may be brought out by considering both of the Wimsatt-Beardsley axioms, and reinterpreting the latter in terms of the former.

The rationale for staying 'inside' of the poem, for going to 'the poem itself,' is derived from the axiom that establishes a context for literary criticism. If 'poetry is a feat of style by which a complex of meaning *is handled all at once* [my italics],' then the meaning of any given passage cannot be separated from the meaning of the whole. The whole is the poem itself, as differentiated from journals, letters, and autobiographies, and if it is the poem that one is concerned with, then *its* meaning is not *necessarily* to be found in journals, letters, and such; these references may be used as sources for interpretation, but they can never be used as a testing ground.

> The use of biographical information need not involve intentionalism, because while it may be evidence of what the author intended, it may also be evidence of the meaning of his words and the dramatic character of his utterance.[8]

But if it is evidence of the meaning of his words or the dramatic character of his utterance, then the poem will tell us this, and not the source that we used.

Even if this rendering of the intentional fallacy has an intuitively unassailable character about it, it is not difficult to see that the axiom upon which it is based is open to attack. And Fiedler attacks it:

> The notion that a work of art is, or should be, absolutely self-contained, a discrete set of mutually inter-related references, needs only to be stated clearly to seem the *reductio ad absurdum* which it is.[9]

We never do get to see the *reductio*, and this is probably because the notion which supposedly reduces itself to absurdity when clarified is never clarified. But even if the notion were clarified, and even if it did reduce itself to absurdity, it would still be possible to give a statement of the intentional fallacy which would be logically unassailable. In order to see that this is the case, one need only state Fiedler's basic principle which is roughly, if not exactly, given the context of his article, contrary to the Wimsatt–Beardsley principle. Here it is:

> It is impossible to draw a line between the work the poet writes and the work he lives, between the life he lives, and the life he writes. And the agile critic, therefore, must be prepared to move constantly back and forth between life and poem, not in a point-less circle, but in a meaningful spiraling toward the absolute point.[10]

But if 'it is impossible to draw a line between the work the poet writes and the work he lives,' why does Fiedler insist so vehemently on *connecting* the two? Obviously, because not every event, not every motive, not every intention of the poet's life is relevant to any given poem that he writes. If this is true, and it may hardly be doubted, then we can always distinguish between statements about motive and intention and statements about the poem. According to Beardsley,[11] 'We can ask two questions: (1) What does the *speaker* mean? (2) What does the sentence mean?' Within the domain of criticism proper, the following two statements may be distinguished: 'The poet intended his poem to mean X', and 'The poem means X'. I know of no one who has insisted that a poet cannot fail in doing what he intended, and hence, I know of no one who has maintained that the above distinction cannot be made. And if the above distinction *can* be made, then it alone is sufficient to establish the intentional fallacy. It will always be fallacious to conduct criticism in such a way that arguments like the following occur: 'The poem means X *because* the poet said in his journal that he intended it to mean X.' But perhaps it is not altogether clear why the above distinction cannot be denied. Still further, it might seem strange to the reader that the intentional fallacy on this way of stating it turns out to be a fallacy to which Fiedler could assent. For, if Fiedler recognizes the need to *connect* the poet's life with his work, then implicitly he recognizes that statements about the poet's life which concern intent and motivation are logically distinct from statements about the poem. At least he would recognize this in some sense, though it is not at all clear in what sense. One may seriously wonder then, whether there is an area of disagreement between the Wimsatt–Beardsley thesis and Fiedler's position. I think there is, and it has to do with the general scope of the intentional fallacy within the area of reasons in literary criticism. In fact, it has to do with the very nature of the intentional fallacy.

The dispute is roughly this: Fiedler wants to argue that one must connect the poet's life with his poem. He explicitly points out[12] that much bad criticism has come from the failure to connect life and work. Thus far, we could take him to be saying that if the critic is going to use material from the poet's life, he must connect it with the poem. Wimsatt and Beardsley would applaud this sentiment. But this is not all that Fiedler is saying. What he wishes to insist on most of all is that a critic will get at the meaning of a poem *if and only if he does connect* it with the poet's life. That is, he not only should make the connection *if he just happens* to use material from the poet's life; rather he *must* use this material, and if he wishes to be a good critic, he should make the connection. Now, it is precisely this aspect of Fiedler's position that would most probably draw a negative reaction from the Wimsatt–Beardsley camp. It may even be suggested that the position itself is *an instance* of the crime of intentionalism.

Perhaps, it is. No doubt, the best way of deciding whether it is would be to present a thorough examination of Fiedler's entire thesis, an undertaking which far surpasses the scope of this paper. However, there is yet another way, which while being somewhat inconclusive with respect to the finer points of the Fiedler thesis, will at least tend to clarify the nature and scope of the intentional fallacy. Any statement of the Fiedler thesis involves at least one necessary condition, which has to do with the sorts of reasons that may be offered in support of interpretations. The one condition is that the following reasons, or reasons much like them, count for or against interpretations: (1) the poet and his literarily inclined contemporaries would not have read the poem that way; (2) the poet and his contemporaries would not have taken that word (or passage) to mean that.[13] This is a minimal requirement of Fiedler's position, and if the intentional fallacy rules out these reasons, we will have shown that Fiedler's position commits this fallacy. Of course, if it does not rule out these reasons, this will not show that Fiedler's position is consistent with it, since it may be inconsistent with other aspects of his thesis. But, in this paper, it is not Fiedler with whom I am concerned, but rather the nature and scope of the intentional fallacy. I strongly suspect that many people believe that it excludes reasons like the ones I have mentioned, and the most probable reason that they do consists in the assumption that the intentional fallacy implies that no critical arguments of relevance can take place 'outside' of the poem. It may even be that Wimsatt and Beardsley believe this, though if they do, their belief is inconsistent with the only plausible interpretation that may be placed upon certain of the principles contained in their article.

'The meaning of words is the history of words,' say Wimsatt and Beardsley, 'and the biography of an author, his use of a word, and the associations which the word had for *him*, are part of the word's history and meaning.'[14] This statement is the philosophical basis for a sustained argument, the main purpose of which is to establish that words, and hence poetry, have meaning independently of a poet's having to *intend* meaning into them. Obviously, this conclusion is sound in some sense, but it is important to know what that sense is, since certain implications may be drawn from it which seem to be quite unsound. The prime target for examination is the following statement: 'The meaning of words is the history of words.' It is not clear what this statement means. Accordingly, I will start with what I take to be some fairly certain observations; the more problematic ones will be set aside until later.

It is fairly certain that, among other things, this statement may be taken to mean that the meaning of a word is established through usage. People use words, and they use them at certain times, in certain places and situations: in conducting business, in political discussions, in creating and criticizing poetry, and in numerous other contexts. Business is conducted and poetry written in Italy, Sweden, China, and other places which are more or less determinate, and always at a specific time: 350 BC, 1300 AD, and so on. For the time being, I will speak as if the notion of time, place and context have no logical relation at all, even though it is obvious that the notion of context is explained to some extent in many *possible* accounts of the other two. These rather vague preliminary observations give some rationale to the following tentative conclusion: words, at least in part, acquire their meanings from use within fairly determinate contexts at certain times and places. One element of the preceding sentence requires emphasis, namely, the phrase *'at least in part'*. Surely, it would be wrong to suppose that all one need do in order to add a new word to our language is utter a sound in some context, at some place and time.

I may say, ' "prophablia" are graceful,' here, now, within this context, without thereby elevating the sound 'prophablia' to the status of a word. It may very well be true that there is a sense in which 'prophablia' is meaningful. One may understand it to function as an example in this context; an example intended to establish that sounds do not become words by being used at certain times and places, within some context. But it would be strange, if not perverse, to suppose that 'prophablia *means* 'a sound which does not become a word by being used at certain times and places, within some context'.[15] Obviously, Wimsatt and Beardsley do not want their statement—'the meaning of words is the history of words'—to mean, 'A sound becomes a word, that is, acquires a meaning, by being used in some place and context at some time'.

It is probably true that their statement is not meant to be of the kind that admits of the sort of criticism brought out above. That is, they are not primarily denying views of language that are in agreement with traditional accounts of Plato's conception of Universals. They are not trying to answer the question, 'How does a word (any word) get a meaning?', but rather another question, 'How might one go about discovering the meaning of some word?' The sort of question about words that they have in mind may be answered in much the same way that they would answer a question about the meaning of a poem.

> . . . it is discovered through the semantics and syntax of a poem, through our habitual knowledge of the language, through grammars, dictionaries, in general through all that makes a language and culture.[16]

This way of approaching the problem coincides with the more abstract 'the meaning of words is the history of words.' That is, the meaning of a word may be discovered 'through all that makes a language and culture': in dictionaries, grammars, and generally, in all and any contexts in which the word appears.

If one wants to know what some word or passage in a poem means, he need not suppose its meaning to lie in a secret mentalistic sort of entity called 'the poet's intention.' Some poems are difficult to comprehend, but this is never because of a secret mental-stuff that stands behind the poem and intends a meaning into it. After all, the poet uses words, casts them as metaphors, images and so on, but he *does* use words—not sounds—and they have a meaning independently of his having used them, even though it is true that he might modify their meanings by using them in the way he does. Wimsatt and Beardsley may have a conventionalistic view of language, or they may, though this is debatable, have the view usually attributed to Plato. It does not matter. On either view, they may consistently make the observations which I have attributed to them.

Now, all of the observations made thus far must be considered in a situation where their relevance may easily be grasped. Such a situation generally is the context of literary criticism; specifically, it is the context of *dispute* or *argument* within literary criticism. Essentially, arguments about interpretation concern relevance. Everyone knows that words like 'plausibility', 'relevance', 'meaning', and 'workability' are relational in character. There is no such thing as a word, metaphor or image which has meaning, yet does not have meaning to anyone. Similarly, there are no interpretations or readings of poetry which are relevant, but not relevant to someone. In fact, if this were not in some sense true, there probably would not be any arguments about relevance or meaning. After all, disputes within the domain of criticism cannot *always* be attributed to insensitivity, ignorance, obsessiveness or insanity. If a man is not a charlatan or joker, it is not unreasonable to assume that the interpretation or reading that he gives a poem is plausible and relevant *to him*. But, of course, his reading may not be relevant *for us*, and the words he discusses may not have the same meaning *to us* that they do to him. At this point, we may want to tell him that he is wrong.

Someone may now wish to argue that we can never do much more than point out that he is 'wrong to us'; there is 'no disputing about taste.' This problem need not concern us here, because no one, so far as I know, has ever argued that the intentional fallacy implies that there is no disputing about taste, that no one can question another's interpretation. Even on contemporary views of criticism, which tends to be anti-reasons, there is at least *one* reason which counts for and against interpretations, namely, the reading fails because it does not account for certain significant passages in the poem, and hence does not bring out the *richness* of the poem. This reason is essentially evaluative, and at the same time, it does not go 'outside' of the poem. Evaluative reasons are closely connected with stylistic or formal considerations, and these considerations determine the meaning of the poetic utterance. This is precisely what Wimsatt and Beardsley mean when they say that 'Poetry is a feat of style by which a complex of meaning is handled all at once.' Hence, the intentional fallacy surely does *not* imply that no arguments can take place in criticism. 'Internal' arguments, so-called, can have objective validity.

But what of 'external' arguments, arguments that take place 'outside' the poem? On the basis of some of the earlier conclusions about the meanings of words, it is tempting to present the following argument. Words do not get their meanings *simply* by being used at some time, in some place and context, and consequently, they do not *simply* get their meanings from being used in some poem, either. Therefore, arguments about the meanings of words in a poem can take place 'outside' of the poem. Unfortunately, this argument will not work; at least, not right now. It would be rejected on the grounds that the only meaning which counts for the critical viewpoint, given the fact that the poet can modify 'conventional' meanings,[17] is the meaning *in* the poem. And the meaning *in* the poem is governed by formal considerations. This rejection is consistent with, indeed, grounded in, Wimsatt's and Beardsley's leading principle. Suppose we let the rejection 'ride' for the moment; rather than a frontal assault on its validity, it might be better to see what it involves.

Does it imply that we are *prohibited* from saying that the meaning *in* a poem is in *any way governed* by the conventional meanings of words? If so, this seems to imply that the meanings of the words in a poem are derived solely from its formal nature, which, presumably establishes the context of the poem. But, this is the sort of view that we rejected earlier, and since it is so patently false, one is forced to conclude that the position under examination does not depend upon it. Perhaps, it is the phrase 'in the poem' that needs to be understood. What is *in* the poem and what is 'outside' of it? A poem, after all, is not a spatial entity. It is not the case that I find myself unhappily 'outside' when I catch myself gazing at the white margin on the right-hand side of the page. And surely I am not 'inside' simply because my attention is directed at type print in the middle of the page.

The 'inside-outside' distinction is really a distinction of relevancy and irrelevancy, and insofar as it is, it involves some commitment to the nature of relevancy in criticism. What makes some statements about a poem relevant and others irrelevant? How is the decision made? Obviously, the sorts of reasons that count in critical disputes have something to do with this question. The position under examination accepts evaluative reasons as relevant; they are 'internal'. Suppose we endorse this view. What follows for the critical procedure? No doubt, it follows that the critic must show concern for style, for the formal elements of a poem. But how is this related to the meanings of words, and entire passages composed, at least partly, of words? Does the critic show concern for the meaning of this or that word? I do not think that it follows from this view that the critic *ought not* to consider these things. All that follows is that he ought to consider these aspects of the poem in relation to formal aspects. But ought he not also to consider the formal aspects in relation to the others? If 'poetry is a feat of style by which a complex of meaning is handled all at once,' why should the emphasis be placed upon the 'feat of style' rather than the 'complex of meaning'? When the 'inside-outside' distinction is made out in terms of relevance, there does not appear to be any reason for admitting 'stylistic' reasons as relevant and denying this significance to other sorts of reasons. There is not more reason for supposing that one is 'inside' the poem when he discusses formal elements only, than there is for supposing that he is 'outside' of the poem when his attention is strictly confined to 'content' elements. Both kinds of elements are relevant to aesthetic meaning, and this means that there are at least two ways in which one can be 'wrong' about a poem. One *can* be 'wrong' because he does not know the meaning of a word or passage, and the failure here need not consist in his being wrong about the style, or in his neglect to connect meaning and style. Still further, there is no connection to be made unless he, in some sense, knows what the words mean.[18]

In any case, this idea of 'making a connection' is misleading. The ultimate connection (or lack of one) is made by the poem (or in one's experience of it). Criticism is a second-order discipline. It does not create the poetic utterance; rather, it makes statements about it, and there statements may be relevant or irrelevant. If there really are problems about relevance in the interpretation of poetry, and not just pseudo-problems that may be swept away with a deft piece of philosophical analysis, then one is simply deceiving himself in supposing that these problems are solved by the dictum, 'Style determines relevance.' For, if one can be wrong about a word, perhaps he can be wrong about an image, and this might make him wrong about the style.

What may be concluded from this discussion? Have we somehow proven that arguments which are relevant to the meaning of a poem may take place 'outside' of it? In the light of what has been said, it is difficult to understand what this would mean. For example, what are we to understand by arguments which take place 'inside' of the poem? But perhaps, all that is being said is that a person can be wrong about the meaning of some word, and that it is possible to establish what the word does mean without consulting the poem. Someone might now argue that we can proceed in this way only if the meaning we do agree upon is relevant to the meaning of the poem or some passage in it. Granted that the meaning a word has 'conventionally' may be altered, and perhaps radically by its poetic setting, it still does not follow that the meaning it has in its poetic setting is not governed by its 'conventional' meaning. It is just wrong to argue that the word gets its meaning from the style alone. And, it is simply irrelevant to say that it is the meaning it has in its poetic setting which really counts, because *it is precisely this meaning that we are trying to get at.*

Thus, arguments about the meaning of a word which determine what we are going to take a word to mean in a poem can legitimately take place; and they concern reasons that may be counted as relevant or irrelevant for the interpretation that might be given to a poem. However, this does not yet show that it counts against an interpretation to point out that the poet and his literarily inclined contemporaries would never have taken some word or passage to mean what some problematic interpretation takes them to mean. It is questionable what Wimsatt and Beardsley would say about the relevance of this reason. At least, it is questionable on the basis of their article. In a footnote to their statement that 'the meaning of words is the history of words,' they maintain that 'the history of words *after* a poem is written may contribute meanings which *if relevant* [my italics] to the original pattern should not be ruled out by a scruple about intention.'[19] I don't have any scruples about intention, but . . . if relevant to what? Their answer: 'to the original pattern.' Again, style is treated as though it had nothing whatsoever to do with content. What are we going to say about the style *after* we have changed our mind about the meanings of some of the words, and hence some of the images, metaphors, and less indirect passages? Will our statements irrevocably remain the same? No argument will be presented to the contrary because I cannot imagine what the position which would defend such a view would be like.

It is a plain and simple fact that words have meanings independently of a poet's using them. It is equally as plain that their 'conventional' meaning partially determines their poetic meaning. To the extent that this is true, the critical context of the poem is larger than it is usually understood to be by people who like to talk about the 'poem itself' or its 'insides'. Wimsatt and Beardsley are substantially correct, given the critical enterprise, in saying that 'the meaning of words is the history of words,' even though this statement must remain only partially analyzed in this paper. And, even if their statement should not be taken to mean that sounds become words merely by being used in fairly determinate contexts, places and times, one ought not be persuaded to remove all emphasis from the word '*history*'. After all, anachronisms are not only caused by a failure to cope with stylistic subtlety. On the basis of all of these considerations, one is surely justified in concluding that the way the poet and his contemporaries understood a word or passage is relevant evidence for making *a decision about the meaning of* a poetic utterance. I do not say that this is *always* relevant evidence.

What then may we conclude about the intentional fallacy? I think it is still fallacious for a critic to insist that a given passage means what he claims it does because the poet said that it meant (or he intended it to mean) this in his journal. There is no way in which my argument is inconsistent with this statement of the intentional fallacy. When it comes to the meaning of words, poets do not create them any more than poems. When it comes to the relevance of interpretations, poets have no claim to omniscience. Even if they could claim omniscience, they would have to claim omnipotence, too. For, they would need both in order to be assured of an infallible execution of intent. Essentially, the intentional fallacy represents no more than Fiedler's 'failure to connect'; it is the formal statement of the demand for a connection.

E.D.HIRSCH, Jr

In Defense of the Author

It has been said of Boehme that his books are
like a picnic to which the author brings the words
and the reader the meaning. The remark may
have been intended as a sneer at Boehme, but it
is an exact description of all works of literary art
without exception.

NORTHROP FRYE

Banishment of the Author

It is a task for the historian of culture to explain why there has been
in the past four decades a heavy and largely victorious assault on the
sensible belief that a text means what its author meant. In the earliest
and most decisive wave of the attack (launched by Eliot, Pound, and
their associates) the battleground was literary: the proposition that
textual meaning is independent of the author's control was associated
with the literary doctrine that the best poetry is impersonal, objective,
and autonomous; that it leads an afterlife of its own, totally cut off
from the life of its author.[1] This programmatic notion of what poetry
should be became subtly indentified with a notion of what all poetry
and indeed all forms of literature necessarily must be. It was not
simply desirable that literature should detach itself from the subjective realm of the author's personal thoughts and feelings; it was,
rather, an indubitable fact that all written language remains independent of that subjective realm. At a slightly later period, and for
different reasons, this same notion of semantic autonomy was advanced by Heidegger and his followers.[2] The idea also has been
advocated by writers who believe with Jung that individual expressions may quite unwittingly express archetypal, communal meanings.
In some branches of linguistics, particularly in so-called information
theory, the semantic autonomy of language has been a working
assumption. The theory has found another home in the work of non-
Jungians who have interested themselves (as Eliot did earlier) in
symbolism, though Cassirer, whose name is sometimes invoked by
such writers, did not believe in the semantic autonomy of language.[3]
As I said, it is the job of the cultural historian to explain why this
doctrine should have gained currency in recent times, but it is the

theorist's job to determine how far the theory of semantic autonomy deserves acceptance.

Literary scholars have often contended that the theory of authorial irrelevance was entirely beneficial to literary criticism and scholarship because it shifted the focus of discussion from the author to his work. Made confident by the theory, the modern critic has faithfully and closely examined the text to ferret out its independent meaning instead of its supposed significance to the author's life. That this shift toward exegesis has been desirable most critics would agree, whether or not they adhere to the theory of semantic autonomy. But the theory accompanied the exegetical movement for historical not logical reasons, since no logical necessity compels a critic to banish an author in order to analyze his text. Nevertheless, through its historical association with close exegesis, the theory has liberated much subtlety and intelligence. Unfortunately, it has also frequently encouraged willful arbitrariness and extravagance in academic criticism and has been one very important cause of the prevailing skepticism which calls into doubt the possibility of objectively valid interpretation. These disadvantages would be tolerable, of course, if the theory were true. In intellectual affairs skepticism is preferable to illusion. The disadvantages of the theory could not have been easily predicted in the exciting days when the old order of academic criticism was being overthrown. At that time such naïvetés as the positivistic biases of literary history, the casting about for influences and other causal patterns, and the post-romantic fascination with the habits, feelings, and experiences surrounding the act of composition were very justly brought under attack. It became increasingly obvious that the theoretical foundations of the old criticism were weak and inadequate. It cannot be said, therefore, that the theory of authorial irrelevance was inferior to the theories or quasi-theories it replaced, nor can it be doubted that the immediate effect of banishing the author was wholly beneficial and invigorating. Now, at a distance of several decades, the difficulties that attend the theory of semantic autonomy have clearly emerged and are responsible for that uneasiness which persists in the academies, although the theory has long been victorious.

That this state of academic skepticism and disarray results largely from the theory of authorial irrelevance is, I think, a fact of our recent intellectual history. For, once the author had been ruthlessly banished as the determiner of his text's meaning, it very gradually appeared that no adequate principle existed for judging the validity of an interpretation. By an inner necessity the study of 'what a text says' became the study of what it says to an individual critic. It became fashionable to talk about a critic's 'reading' of a text, and this word began to appear in the titles of scholarly works. The word seemed to imply that if the author had been banished, the critic still remained, and his new, original, urbane, ingenious, or relevant 'reading' carried its own interest.

What had not been noticed in the earliest enthusiasm for going back to 'what the text says' was that the text had to represent *somebody's* meaning—if not the author's, then the critic's. It is true that a theory was erected under which the meaning of the text was equated with everything it could plausibly be taken to mean. The theory of semantic autonomy forced itself into such unsatisfactory, ad hoc formulations because in its zeal to banish the author it ignored the fact that meaning is an affair of consciousness not of words. Almost any word sequence can, under the conventions of language, legitimately represent more than one complex of meaning.[4] A word sequence means nothing in particular until somebody either means something by it or understands something from it. There is no magic land of meanings outside human consciousness. Whenever meaning is connected to words, a person is making the connection, and the particular meanings he lends to them are never the only legitimate ones under the norms and conventions of his language.

One proof that the conventions of language can sponsor different meanings from the same sequence of words resides in the fact that interpreters can and do disagree. When these disagreements occur, how are they to be resolved? Under the theory of semantic autonomy they cannot be resolved, since the meaning is not what the author meant, but 'what the poem means to different sensitive readers.'[5] One interpretation is as valid as another, so long as it is 'sensitive' or 'plausible.' Yet the teacher of literature who adheres to Eliot's theory is also by profession the preserver of a heritage and the conveyor of knowledge. On what ground does he claim that his 'reading' is more valid than that of any pupil? On no very firm ground. This impasse is a principal cause of the loss of bearings sometimes felt though not often confessed by academic critics.

One ad hoc theory that has been advanced to circumvent this chaotic democracy of 'readings' deserves special mention here because it involves the problem of value, a problem that preoccupies some modern literary theorists. The most valid reading of a text is the 'best' reading.[6] But even if we assumed that a critic did have access to the divine criteria by which he could determine the best reading, he would still be left with two equally compelling normative ideals— the best meaning and the author's meaning. Moreover, if the best meaning were not the author's, then it would have to be the critic's

—in which case the critic would be the author of the best meaning. Whenever meaning is attached to a sequence of words it is impossible to escape an author.

Thus, when critics deliberately banished the original author, they themselves usurped his place, and this led unerringly to some of our present-day theoretical confusions. Where before there had been but one author, there now arose a multiplicity of them, each carrying as much authority as the next. To banish the original author as the determiner of meaning was to reject the only compelling normative principle that could lend validity to an interpretation. On the other hand, it might be the case that there does not really exist a viable normative ideal that governs the interpretations of texts. This would follow if any of the various arguments brought against the author were to hold. For if the meaning of a text is not the author's, then no interpretation can possibly correspond to *the* meaning of the text, since the text can have no determinate or determinable meaning. If a theorist wants to save the ideal of validity he has to save the author as well, and, in the present-day context, his first task will be to show that the prevailing arguments against the author are questionable and vulnerable.

'The Meaning of a Text Changes—Even for the Author'

A doctrine widely accepted at the present time is that the meaning of a text changes.[7] According to the radical historicistic view, textual meaning changes from era to era; according to the psychologistic view, it changes from reading to reading. Since the putative changes of meaning experienced by the author himself must be limited to a rather brief historical span, only the psychologistic view need concern us here. Of course, if any theory of semantic mutability were true, it would legitimately banish the author's meaning as a normative principle in interpretation, for if textual meaning could change in any respect there could be no principle for distinguishing a valid interpretation from a false one. But that is yet another problem that will be dealt with in a suitable place.[8] Here I need not discuss the general (and insoluble) normative problems that would be raised by a meaning which could change, but only the conditions that have caused critics to accuse authors of such fickleness.

Everyone who has written knows that his opinion of his own work changes and that his responses to his own text vary from reading to reading. Frequently an author may realize that he no longer agrees with his earlier meaning or expression and will revise his text. Our problem, of course, has nothing to do with revision or even with the fact that an author may explain his meaning differently at different times, since the authors are sometimes inept explainers of their meanings, as Plato observed. Even the puzzling case of the author who no longer understands his own text at all is irrelevant to our problem, since his predicament is due to the fact that an author, like anyone else, can forget what he meant. We all know that sometimes a person remembers correctly and sometimes not, and that sometimes a person recognizes his mistakes of memory and corrects them. None of this has any theoretical interest whatever.

When critics assert that the author's understanding of his text changes, they refer to the experience that everybody has when he re-reads his own work. His response to it is different. This is a phenomenon that certainly does have theoretical importance—though not of the sort sometimes allotted to it. The phenomenon of changing authorial responses is important because it illustrates the difference between textual meaning and what is loosely termed a 'response' to the text.

Probably the most extreme examples of this phenomenon are cases of authorial self-repudiation, such as Arnold's public attack on his masterpiece, *Empedocles on Etna*, or Schelling's rejection of all the philosophy he had written before 1809. In these case there cannot be the slightest doubt that the author's later response to his work was quite different from his original response. Instead of seeming beautiful, profound, or brilliant, the work seemed misguided, trivial, and false, and its meaning was no longer one that the author wished to convey. However, these examples do not show that the meaning of the work had changed, but precisely the opposite. If the work's meaning had changed (instead of the author himself and his attitudes), then the author would not have needed to repudiate his meaning and could have spared himself the discomfort of a public recantation. No doubt the *significance* of the work to the author had changed a great deal, but its meaning had not changed at all.

This is the crux of the matter in all those cases of authorial mutability with which I am familiar. It is not the meaning of the text which changes, but its significance to the author. This distinction is too often ignored. *Meaning* is that which is represented by a text; it is what the author meant by his use of a particular sign sequence; it is what the signs represent. *Significance*, on the other hand, names a relationship between that meaning and a person, or a conception, or a situation, or indeed anything imaginable. Authors, who like everyone else change their attitudes, feelings, opinions, and value criteria in the course of time, will obviously in the course of time tend to view their own work in different contexts. Clearly what changes for them is not the meaning of the work, but rather their relationship to that meaning. Significance always implies a relationship, and one constant, unchanging pole of that relationship is what the text means. Failure to consider this simple and essential distinction has been the source of enormous confusion in hermeneutic theory.

If we really believed that the meaning of a text had changed for its author, there could be only one way that we could know it: he would have to tell us. How else could we know that his understanding had changed—understanding being a silent and private phenomenon? Even if an author reported that his understanding of his meaning had changed, we should not be put off by the implausibility of the statement but should follow out its implications in a spirit of calm inquiry. The author would have to report something like this: 'By these words I meant so and so, but now I observe that I really meant something different,' or, 'By these words I meant so and so, but I insist that from now on they shall mean something different.' Such an event is unlikely because authors who feel this way usually undertake a revision of their text in order to convey their new meaning more effectively. Nevertheless, it is an event that *could* occur, and its very possibility shows once again that the same sequence of linguistic signs can represent more than one complex of meaning.

Yet, even though the author has indeed changed his mind about the meaning he wants to convey by his words, he has not managed to change his earlier meaning. This is very easily proved by his own report. He could report a change in his understanding only if he were able to compare his earlier construction of his meaning with his later construction. That is the only way he could know that there is a difference: he holds both meanings before his mind and rejects the earlier one. But his earlier meaning is not thereby changed in any way. Such a report from an author would simply force a choice on the interpreter, who would have to decide which of the author's two meanings he is going to concern himself with. He would have to decide which 'text' he wanted to interpret at the moment. The critic is destined to fall into puzzlement if he confuses one text with the other or if he assumes that the author's will is entirely irrelevant to his task.

This example is, as I said, quite improbable. I do not know of a single instance where an author has been so eccentric as to report without any intention to deceive that he now means by his text what he did not mean. (Deliberate lies are, of course, another matter; they have no more theoretical interest than failures of memory.) I was forced into this improbable example by the improbability of the original thesis, namely that an author's meaning changes for himself. What the example showed on the contrary was that an author's original meaning *cannot* change—even for himself, though it can certainly be repudiated. When critics speak of changes in meaning, they are usually referring to changes in significance. Such changes are, of course, predictable and inevitable, and since the primary object of criticism, as distinct from interpretation, is significance, I shall have more to say about this distinction later, particularly in Chapter 4. For the moment, enough has been said to show that the author's revaluation of his text's significance does not change its meaning and, further, that arguments which rely on such examples are not effective weapons for attacking either the stability or the normative authority of the author's original meaning.

'It Does Not Matter what an Author Means— Only what his Text Says'

As I pointed out in the first section, this central tenet in the doctrine of semantic autonomy is crucial to the problem of validity. If the tenet were true, then any reading of a text would be 'valid,' since any reading would correspond to what the text 'says'—for that reader. It is useless to introduce normative concepts like 'sensitive,' 'plausible,' 'rich,' and 'interesting,' since what the text 'says' might not, after all, be any of those things. Validity of interpretation is not the same as inventiveness of interpretation. Validity implies the correspondence of an interpretation to a meaning which is represented by the text, and none of the above criteria for discriminating among interpretations would apply to a text which is dull, simple, insensitive, implausible, or uninteresting. Such a text might not be worth interpreting, but a criterion of validity which cannot cope with such a text is not worth crediting.

The proponents of semantic autonomy in England and America can almost always be relied on to point to the example of T. S. Eliot, who more than once refused to comment on the meanings of his own texts. Eliot's refusals were based on his view that the author has no control over the words he has loosed upon the world and no special privileges as an interpreter of them. It would have been quite inconsistent with this view if Eliot had complained when someone misinterpreted his writings, and, so far as I know, Eliot with stoical consistency never did complain. But Eliot never went so far as to assert that he did not mean anything in particular by his writings. Presumably he did mean something by them, and it is a permissible task to attempt to discover what he meant. Such a task has a determinate object and therefore could be accomplished correctly or incorrectly. However, the task of finding out what a text says has no determinate object, since the text can say different things to different readers. One reading is as valid or invalid as another. However, the decisive objection to the theory of semantic autonomy is not that it inconveniently fails to provide an adequate criterion of validity. The decisive objection must be sought within the theory itself and in the faultiness of the arguments used to support it.

One now-famous argument is based on the distinction between a mere intention to do something and the concrete accomplishment of that intention. The author's desire to communicate a particular meaning is not necessarily the same as his success in doing so. Since his actual performance is presented in his text, any special attempt to divine his intention would falsely equate his private wish with his public accomplishment. Textual meaning is a public affair. The wide dissemination of this argument and its acceptance as an axiom of recent literary criticism can be traced to the influence of a vigorous essay, 'The Intentional Fallacy,' written by W. K. Wimsatt and Monroe Beardsley and first published in 1946. The critic of the arguments in that essay is faced with the problem of distinguishing between the essay itself and the popular use that has been made of it, for what is widely taken for granted as established truth was not argued and could not have been successfully argued in the essay. Although Wimsatt and Beardsey carefully distinguished between three types of intentional evidence, acknowledging that two of them are proper and admissible, their careful distinctions and qualifications have now vanished in the popular version which consists in the false and facile dogma that what an author intended is irrelevant to the meaning of his text.

The best way to indicate what is fallacious in this popular version is to discuss first the dimension in which it is perfectly valid—evaluation. It would be absurd to evaluate the stylistic felicity of a text without distinguishing between the author's intention to convey a meaning and, on the other hand, his effectiveness in conveying it. It would be similarly absurd to judge the profundity of a treatise on morality without distinguishing between the author's intention to be profound and his success in being so. Evaluation is constantly distinguishing between intention and accomplishment. Take this example: A poet intends in a four-line poem to convey a sense of desolation, but what he manages to convey to some readers is a sense that the sea is wet, to others that twilight is approaching. Obviously his intention to convey desolation is not identical with his stylistic effectiveness in doing so, and the anti-intentionalists quite justly point this out. But the intentional fallacy is properly applicable *only* to artistic success and to other normative criteria like profundity, consistency, and so on. The anti-intentionalist quite properly defends the right and duty of the critic to judge freely on his own criteria and to expose discrepancies between wish and deed. However, the intentional fallacy has no proper application whatever to verbal meaning. In the above example the only universally valid meaning of the poem is the sense of desolation. If the critic has not understood that point, he will not even reach an accurate judgement—namely, that the meaning was ineptly expressed and perhaps was not worth expressing in the first place.

Beneath the so-called intentional fallacy and, more generally, the doctrine of semantic autonomy lies an assumption which if true would at least render plausible the view that the meaning of a text is independent of its author's intention. I refer to the concept of a public consensus. If a poet intended his poem to convey desolation, and if to every competent reader his poem conveyed only a sense that twilight is approaching, then such public unanimity would make a very strong case (in this particular instance) for the practical irrelevance of the author's intention. But when has such unanimity occurred? If it existed generally, there would not be any problems of interpretation.

The myth of the public consensus has been decisive in gaining wide acceptance for the doctrine that the author's intention is irrelevant to what the text says. That myth permits the confident belief that the 'saying' of the text is a public fact firmly governed by public norms. But if this public meaning exists, why is it that we, who are the public, disagree? Is there one group of us that constitutes the true public, while the rest are heretics and outsiders? By what standard is it judged that a correct insight into public norms is lacking in all those readers who are (except for the text at hand) competent readers of texts? The idea of a public meaning sponsored not by the authors intention but by a public consensus is based upon a fundamental error of observation and logic. It is an empirical fact that the consensus does not exist, and it is a logical error to erect a stable normative concept (i.e. *the* public meaning) out of an unstable descriptive one. The public meaning of a text is nothing more or less than those meanings which the public happens to construe from the text. Any meaning which two or more members of the public construe is ipso facto within the public norms that govern language and its interpretation. Vox populi: vox populi.

If a text means what it says, then it means nothing in particular. Its saying has no determinate existence but must be the saying of the author or a reader. The text does not exist even as a sequence of words until it is construed; until then, it is merely a sequence of signs. For sometimes words can have homonyms (just as, by analogy, entire texts can), and sometimes the same word can be quite a different word. For example, when we read in Wordsworth's *Intimations Ode* the phrase 'most worthy to be blessed,' are we to understand 'most' as a superlative or merely an intensifier like 'very'? Even on this primitive level, signs can be variously construed, and until they are construed the text 'says' nothing at all.

'The Author's Meaning is Inaccessible'

Since we are all different from the author, we cannot reproduce his intended meaning in ourselves, and even if by some accident we could, we still would not be certain that we had done so. Why concern ourselves, therefore, with an inherently impossible task when we can better employ our energies in useful occupations such as making the text relevant to our present concerns or judging its conformity to high standards of excellence? The goal of reproducing an inaccessible and private past is to be dismissed as a futile enterprise. Of course, it is essential to understand some of the public facts of language and history in order not to miss allusions or mistake the contemporary senses of words, but these preliminary tasks remain squarely in the public domain and do not concern a private world beyond the reach of written language.

Before touching on the key issue in this argument—namely, that the author's intended meaning cannot be known—I would like to make an observation about the subsidiary argument respecting the public and private dimensions of textual meaning. According to this argument, it would be a mistake to confuse a public fact—namely, language—with a private fact—namely, the author's mind. But I have never encountered an interpretation that inferred truly private meanings from a text. An interpreter might, of course, infer meanings which according to our judgment could not possibly under any circumstances be implied by the author's words, but in that case we would reject the interpretation not because it is private but because it is probably wrong. That meaning, we say, cannot be implied by those words. If our skepticism were shared by all readers of the interpretation, then it would be reasonable to say that the interpretation is private. However, it is a rare interpretation that does not have at least a few adherents, and if it has any at all, then the meaning is not private; it is at worst improbable.

Whenever an interpretation manages to convince another person, that in itself proves beyond doubt that the author's words *can* publicly imply such a meaning. Since the interpreted meaning *was* conveyed to another person, indeed to at least two other persons, the only significant interpretive question is, 'Did the author really intend that public meaning by his word?' To object that such a meaning is highly personal and ought not to have been intended is a legitimate aesthetic or moral judgment, but is irrelevant to the question of meaning. That meaning—if the author did mean it—has proved itself to be public, and if the interpreter manages to do his job convincingly, the meaning can become available to a very large public. It is simply a self-contradiction for a member of the public to say, 'Yes, I see that the author did mean that, but it is a private not a public meaning.'

The impulse that underlies this self-contradictory sort of argument is a sound insight that deserves to be couched in terms more suitable than 'public' and 'private.' The issue is first of all a moral and aesthetic one. It is proper to demand of authors that they show consideration for their readers, that they use their linguistic inheritance with some regard for the generality of men and not just for a chosen few. Yet many new usages are bound to elude the generality of men until readers become habituated to them. The risk of resorting to semi-private implications—available at first only to a few—is very often worth taking, particularly if the new usage does finally become widely understood. The language expands by virtue of such risky innovations. However, the soundest objection to so-called private meanings does not relate to moral and aesthetic judgment but to the practice of interpretation. Those interpreters who look for personal implications in such formalized utterances as poems very often disregard genre conventions and limitations of which the author was very well aware. When an author composes a poem, he usually intends it as an utterance whose implications are not obscurely autobiographical. There may be exceptions to this rule of thumb, and poetic kinds are too various to warrant any unqualified generalizations about the conventions of poetry and the intentions of authors, but too many interpreters in the past have sought autobiographical meanings where none were meant. Such interpreters have been insensitive to the proprieties observed by the author and to his intentions. The fallacy in such interpretations is not that the inferred meanings are private, but that they are probably not the author's meanings. Whether a meaning is autobiographical is a neutral and by itself irrelevant issue in interpretation. The only thing that counts is whether the interpretation is probably right.

The genuine distinction between public and private meaning resides in the first part of the argument, where it is asserted that the author's intended meaning cannot be known. Since we cannot get inside the author's head, it is useless to fret about an intention that cannot be observed, and equally useless to try to reproduce a private meaning experience that cannot be reproduced. Now the assertion that the author's meaning cannot be reproduced presupposes the same psychologistic theory of meaning which underlies the notion that an author's meaning changes even for himself. Not even the author can reproduce his original meaning because nothing can bring back his original meaning experience. But as I suggested, the irreproducibility of meaning experiences is not the same as the irreproducibility of meaning. The psychologistic identification of textual meaning with a meaning experience is inadmissible. Meaning experiences *are* private, but they are not meanings.

The most important argument to consider here is the one which states that the author's intended meaning cannot be *certainly* known. This argument cannot be successfully met because it is self-evidently true. I can never know another person's intended meaning with certainty because I cannot get inside his head to compare the meaning he intends with the meaning I understand, and only by such direct comparison could I be certain that his meaning and my own are identical. But this obvious fact should not be allowed to sanction the overly hasty conclusion that the author's intended meaning is inaccessible and is therefore a useless object of interpretation. It is a logical mistake to confuse the impossibility of certainty in understanding with the impossibility of understanding. It is a similar, though more subtle, mistake to identify knowledge with certainty. A good many disciplines do not pretend to certainty, and the more sophisticated the methodology of the discipline, the less likely that its goal will be defined as certainty of knowledge. Since genuine certainty in interpretation is impossible, the aim of the discipline must be to reach a consensus, on the basis of what is known, that correct understanding has *probably* been achieved. The issue is not whether certainty is accessible to the interpreter but whether the author's intended meaning is accessible to him. Is correct understanding possible? That is the question raised by the thesis under examination.

Most of us would answer that the author's meaning is only partially accessible to an interpreter. We cannot know all the meanings the author entertained when he wrote down his text, as we infer from two familiar kinds of evidence. Whenever I speak I am usually attending to ('have in mind') meanings that are outside my subject of discourse. Furthermore, I am always aware that the meanings I can convey through discourse are more limited than the meanings I can entertain. I cannot, for example, adequately convey through words many of my visual perceptions—though these perceptions are meanings, which is to say, objects of consciousness. It is altogether likely that no text can ever convey all the meanings an author had in mind as he wrote.

But this obvious fact is not decisive. Why should anyone with common sense wish to equate an author's textual meaning with all the meanings he happened to entertain when he wrote? Some of these he had no intention of conveying by his words. Any author knows that written verbal utterances can convey only verbal meanings—that is to say, meanings which can be conveyed to others by the words he uses. The interpretation of texts is concerned exclusively with sharable meanings, and not everything I am thinking of when I write can be shared with others by means of my words. Conversely, many of my sharable meanings are meanings which I am not directly thinking of at all. They are so-called unconscious meanings. It betrays a totally inadequate conception of verbal meaning to equate it with what the author 'has in mind.' The only question that can relevantly be at issue is whether the *verbal* meaning which an author intends is accessible to the interpreter of his text.

Most authors believe in the accessibility of their verbal meaning, for otherwise most of them would not write. However, no one could unanswerably defend this universal faith. Neither the author nor the interpreter can ever be certain that communication has occurred or that it can occur. But again, certainty is not the point at issue. It is far more likely that an author and an interpreter can entertain identical meanings than that they cannot. The faith that speakers have in the possibility of communication has been built up in the very process of learning a language, particularly in those instances when the actions of the interpreter have confirmed to the author that he has been understood. These primitive confirmations are the foundation for our faith in far less primitive modes of communication. The inaccessibility of verbal meaning is a doctrine that experience suggests to be false, though neither experience nor argument can prove its falsity. But since the skeptical doctrine of inaccessibility is highly improbable, it should be rejected as a working assumption of interpretation.

Of course, it is quite reasonable to take a skeptical position that is less sweeping than the thesis under examination: certain texts might, because of their character or age, represent authorial meanings which are now inaccessible. No one would, I think, deny this reasonable form of skepticism. However, similar versions of such skepticism are far less acceptable, particularly in those theories which deny the accessibility of the author's meaning whenever the text descends from an earlier cultural era or whenever the text happens to be literary. These views are endemic respectively to radical historicism and to the theory that literary texts are ontologically distinct from non-literary ones. Both of these theories are challenged in subsequent chapters. However, even if these theories were acceptable, they could not uphold the thesis that an author's verbal meaning is inaccessible, for that is an empirical generalization which neither theory nor experience can decisively confirm or deny. Nevertheless, with a high degree of probability, that generalization is false, and it is impossible and quite unnecessary to go beyond this conclusion.

'The Author often does not Know What he Means'

Ever since Plato's Socrates talked to the poets and asked them with quite unsatisfactory results to explain 'some or the most elaborate passages in their own writings,' it has been a commonplace that an author often does not really know what he means.[9] Kant insisted that not even Plato knew what he meant, and that he, Kant, could understand some of Plato's writings better than Plato did himself.[10] Such examples of authorial ignorance are, no doubt, among the most damaging weapons in the attack on the author. If it can be shown (as it apparently can) that in some cases the author does not really know what he means, then it seems to follow that the author's meaning cannot constitute a general principle or norm for determining the meaning of a text, and it is precisely such a general normative principle that is required in defining the concept of validity.

Not all cases of authorial ignorance are of the same type. Plato, for instance, no doubt knew very well what he meant by his theory of Ideas, but it may have been, as Kant believed, that the theory of Ideas had different and more general implications than those Plato enunciated in his dialogues. Though Kant called this a case of understanding the author better than the author understood himself, his phrasing was inexact, for it was not Plato's meaning that Kant understood better than Plato, but rather the subject matter that Plato was attempting to analyze. The notion that Kant's understanding of the Ideas was superior to Plato's implies that there is a subject matter to which Plato's meaning was inadequate. If we do not make this distinction between subject matter and meaning, we have no basis for judging that Kant's understanding is better than Plato's. Kant's statement would have been more precise if he had said that he understood the Ideas better than Plato, not that he understood Plato's meaning better than Plato. If we do not make and preserve the distinction between a man's meaning and his subject matter, we cannot distinguish between true and false, better and worse meanings.

This example illustrates one of the two main types of authorial ignorance. It has greatest importance in those genres of writing that aspire to tell the truth about a particular subject matter. The other principal type of authorial ignorance pertains not to the subject matter but to the author's meaning itself, and can be illustrated whenever casual conversation is subjected to stylistic analysis:

'Did you know that those last two sentences of yours had parallel constructions which emphasized their similarity of meaning?'

'No! How clever of me! I suppose I really did want to emphasize the similarity, though I wasn't aware of that, and I had no idea I was using rhetorical devices to do it.'

What this example illustrates is that there are usually components of an author's intended meaning that he is not conscious of. It is precisely here, where an interpreter makes these intended but unconscious meanings explicit, that he can rightfully claim to understand the author better than the author himself. But here again a clarification is required. The interpreter's right to such a claim exists only when he carefully avoids confusing meaning with subject matter, as in the example of Plato and Kant. The interpreter may believe that he is drawing out implications that are 'necessary' accompaniments to the author's meaning, but such necessary accompaniments are rarely unavoidable components of someone's *meaning*. They become necessary associations only within a given *subject matter*.[11] For example, although the concept 'two' necessarily implies a whole array of concepts including those of succession, integer, set, and so on, these may not be implied in a given usage of the word, since that usage could be inadequate or misconceived with respect to the subject matter in which 'two' falls. Only within that subject matter does there subsist necessity of implication. Thus, by claiming to perceive implications of which the author was not conscious, we may sometimes distort and falsify the meaning of which he was conscious, which is not 'better understanding' but simply misunderstanding of the author's meaning.

But let us assume that such misunderstanding has been avoided and that the interpreter really has made explicit certain aspects of an author's undoubted meaning of which the author was unconscious — as in stylistic analysis of casual conversation. The further question then arises: How can an author mean something he did not mean? The answer to that question is simple. It is not possible to mean what one does not mean, though it is very possible to mean what one is not conscious of meaning. That is the entire issue in the argument based on authorial ignorance. That a man may not be conscious of all that he means is no more remarkable than that he may not be conscious of all that he does. There is a difference between meaning and consciousness of meaning, and since meaning is an affair of consciousness, one can say more precisely that there is a difference between consciousness and self-consciousness. Indeed, when an author's meaning is complicated, he cannot possibly at a given moment be paying attention to all its complexities. But the distinction between attended and unattended meanings is not the same as the distinction between what an author means and what he does not mean. No example of the author's ignorance with respect to his meaning could legitimately show that his intended meaning and the meaning of his text are two different things.

Other varieties of authorial ignorance are therefore of little theoretical interest. When Plato observed that poets could not *explain* what they meant, he intimated that poets were ineffectual, weak-minded, and vague—particularly with respect to their 'most elaborate passages.' But he would not have contended that a vague, uncertain, cloudy, and pretentious meaning is not a meaning, or that it is not the poet's meaning.[12] Even when a poet declares that his poem means whatever it is taken to mean (as in the case of some modern writers who believe in the current theory of public meaning and authorial irrelevance), then, no doubt, his poem may not mean anything in particular. Yet even in such a limiting case it is still the author who 'determines' the meaning.

One final illustration of authorial ignorance, a favorite among literary critics, is based on an examination of an author's early drafts, which often indicate that what the author apparently intended when he began writing is frequently quite different from what work means. Such examples show how considerations of style, genre, and local texture may play a larger part in his final meaning than that played by his original intention, but these interesting observations have hardly any theoretical significance. If a poet in his first draft means something different than he means in his last, it does not imply that somebody other than the poet is doing the meaning. If the poet capitalizes on a local effect which he had not originally intended, so much the better if it makes a better poem. All this surely does not imply that an author does not mean what he means, or that his text does not mean what he intends to convey.

If there is a single moral to the analyses of this chapter, it is that meaning is an affair of consciousness and not of physical signs or things. Consciousness is, in turn, an affair of persons, and in textual interpretation the persons involved are an author and a reader. The meanings that are actualized by the reader are either shared with the author or belong to the reader alone. While this statement of the issue may affront our deeply ingrained sense that language carries its own autonomous meanings, it in no way calls into question the power of language. On the contrary, it takes for granted that all meaning communicated by texts is to some extent language-bound, that no textual meaning can transcend the meaning possibilities and the control of the language in which it is expressed. What has been denied here is that linguistic signs can somehow speak their own meaning—a mystical idea that has never been persuasively defended.

F.E.SPARSHOTT
Criticism and Performance

HAVING disposed of the final cause, we have now only to deal with the efficient cause of criticism and, since criticism is essentially criticism of something, with the object of criticism, the performance criticized. System requires us first to take up the efficient cause, but the momentum of our discussion suggests that we reverse the order; for we have just uncovered an ambiguity always latent in the concept of performance that we can no longer ignore. Granted that criticism and performance are correlatives, that to be a critique is to be an appraisal of a performance and to be a performance is to be a fit object for a critique, we have still to determine whether the nature of the critique determines what the performance is or whether the nature of the performance determines what sort of critique is fitting. There are indications in our previous discussions that would support either view.

It seems obvious on the face of it that performances control critiques: what it is fitting for me to say about what you have done depends on what it was you were doing. Ultimately we shall not be able to get round that blunt truth. But the course of our discussion had rather favoured the opposite view. We said that to be a performance was simply to be taken as a performance of such and such a kind: that performances are constituted by the isolating action of the attention. But such isolation is just what critics do, singling out for their notice only some features of what is done, and among these features attending more to some than to others. Thus the idea of literature is an invention of literary critics, and presumably poets poetize as birds sing until the critical intelligence crystallizes out their song. This is, however, an unbearably paradoxical thesis. It entails that the development of an art will be determined not by what its practitioners do but by what its critics say, and it is hard to conceive of a history of an art written on this basis. It suggests, too, that critics cannot mistake performances of one kind for performances of another kind; whereas it seems plain that such mistakes are not only possible but common. And surely it is possible, as we have seen, to mistake something for a performance that is not a performance at all, whether or not the appraisal of the supposed performance is a sound appraisal of what the performance would have been. Finally, to make the performance something constituted by criticism seems to reduce it to the content rather than the object of criticism, and one feels that a critique should be directed upon something that is not merely other than but independent of itself.

We seem to have reached an impasse. We cannot say that what performance has been performed is a matter of brute fact, since we have seen that not all that goes on in the area defining a performance is part of the performance. The bassoonist's hiccups showed that. But now it seems that we cannot allow the critic to decide the question either. Who, then, is to decide? The most likely candidate is the performer. After all, he starts the whole business: without him there is no performance, what he does is the performance, the critic cannot criticize until he has performed. But the objections to this position are well known. How do we know what the performer's decision is? If by looking at his performance, we are back where we started. If we ask him, either he will answer as a critic, a possibility we have just spurned, or by telling us what he intended. But his intentions are no use to us: if he did what he intended to do, his intentions will be realized in his work and we did not need to ask him; if he failed to do what he intended to do, his intentions are irrelevant to our interest in his actual performance. Besides, a man's view of his intentions is likely to change in the course of his work and in retrospect; he may work better than he knows; and, in short, his 'intentions' as invoked in this context seem to be mere retrojections in time of his performance, rather than the other way round. And of course in most cases the artist is not there to be asked, and this does not faze critics. It is when a critic tells us of an artist's intentions in sculpting what later turns out to be a piece of driftwood that we realize most sharply the delusive character of the appeal to intentions.

The case against statements of intent as infallible guides to interpretation is watertight, but we cannot get rid of the performer so easily. It seems perfectly obvious that, provided that the performer knows what he is doing, his statements of what he is up to will at the very least be the most valuable clues we could possibly have; and we may concede that performers normally do know what they are doing. If you are puzzled by what someone is doing, asking him what he is trying to do is such an obvious step that no smart argument could possibly talk us into thinking it foolish. But the proviso that the performer should 'know what he is doing' is necessary, and seems to undermine our case. For the phrase is ambiguous. It may mean that he should be acting consciously, but in that sense is here irrelevant. It may mean that he should be acting skilfully, but in that sense does not have the required consequence: a man may be acting most

expertly, doing a most craftsmanlike job, and yet have only the haziest
notion of the nature of his performance, its aesthetic implications and
social import and so on, for his skill may be all in his hand. To carry
the required consequence the proviso must be taken as meaning the
same as 'provided that he knows what his performance is', and this
reduces our claim to the merest and most useless tautology. The relevance of the artist's statement of his intentions indeed remains. But
it now becomes simply the fact—incontestable, one would have
thought, but often contested—that artists know their own work
much more intimately than anyone else is likely to, and for some time
after its first presentation are the only people who know much about
it. The performer retains this position until someone else has had the
time and inclination to submit his performance to similarly careful
scrutiny. His privileged position is thus simply that of a singularly
well-informed critic.

The extent of the privilege that the performer's special information
gives him is questionable. Let us suppose that a man writes an autobiographical novel. The nature of the performance may depend on
the special relation between narrated and actual incident; but this
relation is known only to the author. Must we than take the author's
word for the precise nature of the performance? Or, to take a simpler
case: a poet may write what appears to be an ode to his mistress, but
is in fact an ode to his pet dog. Of course, if one knows that, the
poem is changed, and may be much improved by an irony that then
becomes noticeable; but no one would know if the author did not
tell them. But then, if the author has not included in his work anything from which the special relationship could be recognized, can
we really say that it is part of his performance? Probably many sincerely intended love lyrics could be improved by reading them as if
they were meant for dogs. One is inclined to say that if the special
relationship is like that of the portrait, in that the reference outside
the work itself to bitch or biography was accessible to the work's
primary public, the reference in all its complexity may be held to be
part of the performance, but not otherwise; it is not enough that the
performer should privately intend it and perhaps not even that he
should afterwards claim it. But the considerations that would incline
us to say so are ones that have not yet come into our purview; we
return to them in a moment. Let us first take the simpler case of declarations of intent that accompany and even form part of the performance, such as the introductory remarks to this essay that I am
writing. How far do they control the way in which the performance
is to be taken? In what circumstances is one justified in ignoring
them? Surely in some cases at least they are to be taken simply as

106

part of the performance, part of 'the act' as we say; but in what cases? This question at least is answered by the existence of a literary convention that nowadays distinguishes the preface to a work or the title of a picture from the introduction to the work or words painted into the picture. But even so such directive remarks may sometimes be ignored. For example, if they are mere pleas designed to soften criticism, they are better ignored; and if they have no bearing on what is actually done it is plain that the actual accomplishment is decisive. But if they single out one among possible ways of taking what is done they are presumably authoritative, even if we then choose to thicken or muddy the texture by admitting the excluded readings in Empsonian ambiguity. Surely it must be presumptively true that the performance is a more or less successful version of what the performer meant it to be, as it is certainly what he has made it to be, and an occasional (or even quite frequent) falsification of this presumption would not suffice to invalidate it as the only possible basis for understanding.

The current objections to making the performer's intention the basis of interpretation, which we summarized above, rest on a misunderstanding both of what a performance is and of what an explanation in terms of intention is. Thus, although they are unanswerable, they do not call for an answer: against a certain kind of exegesis they are unquestionably valid, but do not touch at all the sorts of explanation that we should wish to defend. They maintain, essentially, that the appeal to intentions turns away from the phenomenon itself to something else, the performer's frame of mind, which is merely one of the causal antecedents of the phenomenon. But this is to speak as though the performance were one phenomenon and the performer quite another. We have ourselves been guilty of a version of this error when we wrote just now of 'the artist's knowledge of his work', as though a performer were a bystander at his own performance, differing from other bystanders only in that he has a closer view of it. But of course he is not the spectator of his performance but the performer of it: he does not have knowledge about it, even in the unmediated way in which one has knowledge of one's own private aches and pains, but, as Mr Melden has laboured to make plain in his *Free Action*, he knows it in and through doing it.

The conventional attack on 'the intentional fallacy', as formulated by Mr Beardsley in his *Aesthetics*, proposes the fork just mentioned. The object of criticism is the aesthetic object, a complex percept; whatever is no part of this percept is something other than the aesthetic object and therefore irrelevant to criticism. The performer's intention is no part of the percept, but part of its cause, and thus extraneous. But this fork depends on our taking the performance as an aesthetic object rather than a work of art, as if it were a natural object and not a performance at all. And one cannot, does not, and should not, take performances so. How can one possibly, in reading a poem or looking at a picture, ignore the fact that it is the product of a human agency; and what could one gain by doing so? As Miss Gardner has remarked in *The Business of Criticism*, even those critics who in their explications make the limited pretence of ignoring the historical and biographical background of their texts are able to do so only because that background is so thoroughly familiar to them that they do not have to think about it; and what the alarming protocols in Richards's *Practical Criticism* prove is mostly that that is a silly way to read poetry. It is silly because, like those tests in which people are challenged to tell butter from margarine while blindfold, it supposes that perceptual situations remain unchanged when abstracted from their normal living context.

If criticizing with reference to the performer's 'intentions' is not adducing psychic causes, no more is it misconstruing a part-whole relation as a means-end relation: it cannot be reduced to analysis of the percept as percept, because to be a performance is not to be a percept, any more than it is to be the effect of a cause. In referring to the means that the performer took to achieve the end proposed one analyses the performance strictly as a performance, something done by someone who is up to something humanly intelligible. Intentions are not antecedent states of mind, although antecedent thought may be involved: to state an intention is to specify a state of affairs to be achieved, in the light of which the action performed can be seen to fit into its human context. In the case of performances, the intention must be taken to be the complete performance itself, the situation brought about conceived as intended; to interpret a performance in terms of intentions is thus nothing more than to interpret it as structured for understanding and hence for appreciation, as part of the world of human interaction. Thus to understand a performance is, as Collingwood said of the understanding of historical events, to re-think what was done rather than to describe what took place, to bring oneself and others to see how what was done made sense as the thing to do in the circumstances. The difference between historical and critical explanation would be that the 'circumstances' for the critic are not a historical situation confronting the agent but simply the performance itself that is to be performed, presenting a 'problem' that may not be antecedent to its 'solution'. The difficulty in explaining what is meant here is that the kind of understanding that is meant is too pervasively familiar to be explained in simpler terms. All that one has to do is to resist the temptation to reduce it to a causal explanation of the kind appropriate to the natural sciences. But this temptation is for some people overwhelmingly strong: they cannot stop themselves imagining that by 're-thinking' one means reconstructing psychic antecedents. They are perfectly correct in thinking that the 'intention' invoked is, as we said above, nothing but the retrojected shadow of what was in fact done; what they fail to notice is that the retrojection is absolutely necessary, since it amounts, not to a postulation of an unobservable psychic entity, but simply to the reconstruction of the performance itself in terms that make its nature as performance clear. All that these people need to do is in fact to embark on an explanation of a historical event or a criticism of a performance, and take a good look at what they in fact do. In fact, they themselves tend to give the game away by using the word 'interpretation' for critical explanation; for we have seen that only signs can be interpreted, and not natural objects or occurrences as such.

The concept of performance, we have throughout insisted, is an isolating concept; criticism must be based on isolation. But what is isolated is not a mere percept but, precisely, a performance, with its implied performer and act of performing. The difficulty that has been felt about the appeal to intentions is that such an appeal must be incompatible with critical isolation; but it is not. Performance is, after all, activity. Nor do performances lack context. Since whatever is performed is performed by someone for someone, a context is not only necessarily present but necessarily implied. The critic does not jettison the context; rather, he holds it in suspension. The difficulty of criticism is precisely that a performance is communication and action as well as isolated percept; the person who cannot hold these aspects together in his mind is just a bad critic. We do not have to choose between them, nor do the arguments that compel us to recognize one aspect compel us to reject the others.

The position we have now reached is, no doubt, intellectually dismaying. As always when one tries to get something relating to human activity just right, we have been reduced to babbling. This is because one can only avoid babbling by restricting oneself to what can be clearly stated, and whatever can be clearly stated is a simplification. What we have to do, however, is not to commit ourselves to incompatible simplifications, but to resist any: to keep a steady hold on the complex reality from which the simplifications abstract. Unfortunately this form of spiritual exercise is no help to us in our present situation, in which we are confronted with the simplifying question: what is it that determines what has been performed? Certainly, we can now say, it is the performer's intention after all, but what good is that? For the interpretation by intention now appears to be no more than the interpretation of the performance that makes the best sense of the performance as something that could conceivably be intended to be performed. In other words, the performer's *statement* of what he intended, even when available, is not authoritative. No doubt it is true that the performer knows his performance in the very performing of it and not as a spectator; but this special knowledge may be just the knowledge 'in the hand' that we spoke of earlier, and what the performer says he meant to do is at best only indirectly related to such knowledge. As with actions in general, the performer's declaration does indeed have a privileged position, but it is not a pre-emptive one. Allowing for, accepting, discounting, taking *cum grano* and otherwise coping with people's statements about what they would be at is something we do all the time: it makes up one of the major skills of our practical life, and it is quite absurd to suppose that it might be reduced to any codified form.

No one accepts, in any case, that a performer is the sole qualified critic or exegete of his own work. But what, then, does decide what has been performed? Surely we can at least say that what may properly be said to have been performed is strictly limited by what has in fact taken place, no matter how various the abstractions that may be made from it and the interpretations and constructions that may be put upon it. Just so, however many versions there may be of what anyone has done, however many different actions he may legitimately be said to have performed, only some accounts are possible, and an infinite number are ruled out by the blunt fact that he did nothing of the kind. No sophistication about alternative accounts of actions should delude us into forgetting for one moment that if at three o'clock this afternoon I am swimming in Lake Erie I cannot at the same moment be making an illegal left turn off Bloor Street.

We seem at this point to have been brought back to one of the classical termini of epistemological inquiry: to the recognition of an extra-judgemental somewhat that, though it does not prescribe any particular judgement or form of judgement, is none the less such that only some forms of judgement are possible, and such, moreover, that when a given form has been codified into a language, some judgements in that codified form are definitively true and others definitively false. So in the area of our present concern, what the artificer has made is such that, however various the interpretations that may be put upon it, only some will fit; and in terms of the various possible interpretations only some judgements will be tenable.

The positive yield of our discussion of the concept of intention suggests that it may be possible to go beyond the common epistemological minimum. Surely, as M. Gilson has argued, what the performer has brought about, the *opus operatum*, determines rather strictly what the performance is, and the more highly wrought it is the stricter the control will be. A performer has performed what he has performed: that is, he has done what he has succeeded in doing. It follows that whatever yields the most favourable judgement on his work qualifies as the correct interpretation. And this, whatever one thinks of it as affecting the performer's rights over his own work, does correspond to a familiar and quite reliable critical rule-of-thumb: always seek the best case that can be made out for a work, or you may overlook an important factor in its structure.

The position just laid down requires two qualifications, which may turn out to be the same. One is, that an interpretation may be favourable only at the price of being incomplete, of leaving out of account a great deal of what is there and is prima facie part of the performance. The demand for a favourable interpretation is not a call for whitewash. Our critical rule-of-thumb actually showed this, because the point of seeking a favourable interpretation was to make sure of a comprehensive one. Thus the requirement of comprehensiveness takes precedence over that of favourability; but it does not eliminate it, for without the requirement of favourability that of comprehensiveness is meaningless. The second qualification, if it is really different, is that of two alternative interpretations the one that would represent the greater achievement is to be preferred. Prima facie, we recall, what has been achieved is different from what has been performed; but, despite that, in practice the two qualifications may turn out to be the same, because it is conceivable that among performances the magnitude of achievement can be assessed otherwise than by comprehensiveness only if the performances are so different that they could not in any case be related to the same pre-judgemental phenomena.

Judgements as to what has been performed on a given occasion will still remain open to question, for two reasons. On the one hand, it can never be shown that the most exhaustive, comprehensive, and integrated account of a performance that has yet been given (or implied) is the most comprehensive possible: hitherto unnoticed or disregarded aspects that might change our whole opinion of its nature may always remain to be discovered. It is even possible that an alternative and radically different account of it, hitherto quite unsuspected, might one day be offered. On the other hand, one always risks 'reading into' a performance a significance that is not there, or at least supposing oneself to have detected a design or a nuance that no one else can see even after it is pointed out to them. Who can tell for certain the exact point where completing a *Gestalt* passes over into extrapolating a Hercules from a heel? Yet it is obvious that these doubts do not always arise, and that when they do arise they can often be allayed. If I can get no one else to see in a performance what I see, it is most likely not there; and it is most likely that what many have scrutinized will retain few important secrets. At most times and in most cases there is a general consensus as to the nature of any given performance in its broad outlines, and beyond that we should not expect to go.

Serious disagreements among competent persons about the nature of performances, especially when the judges are of different cultural backgrounds and epochs, are likely to reflect different views on the magnitudes of different kinds of achievement. What is successfully present in the performance may be discounted as constituting an achievement of little interest to the critic, who prefers to dwell on what is accidentally present, less systematically or carefully worked out and less regarded in the performer's milieu but assigned by the alien critic to a higher level of attainment. As to the legitimacy of such alien reversals we need take no sides beyond remarking that, on the one hand, it is absurd to treat anything as being what it is not and was never meant to be; whereas, on the other hand, it is equally absurd to demand that any age should allow the standards and interests of another age to take precedence over its own. No doubt the plain man or the plain aesthete will take the alien performance as if it emanated from a performer of his own cultural milieu, the pure scholar will seek to reconstruct its own milieu, and the scholarly connoisseur will allow his scholarship and his local taste to fertilize each other; and critics of different schools and different inclinations will adjust their conflicting fidelities as they think proper and in the light of such knowledge and insight as they have.

Complete understanding, complete description, and the definitive structure of a performance, we have already ruled out as mirages. The decisive factor here is one that may be illustrated from the familiar facts of the use of languages. Anyone who attends carefully to the speech of those around him cannot but notice that each person uses language in his own unique way: the contexts in which he uses a word, and the words he uses in a given sort of context, will in their fine detail be unique to him. We must thus say that each person means a subtly different thing from what anyone else means by many of the words he uses; and presumably the vagaries of his usage will govern his typical expectations, he will initially tend to take people as meaning something more like what he would mean than they actually do. And yet we do understand what other people say, adapting to these variations of usage without effort and without even being conscious of them, and with few mistakes; and in so doing we do not in the smallest degree modify, much less abandon, the pattern of our own usage. In short, human intercourse consists largely of making sense of people in their own terms while at the same time thinking about them in one's own terms, and the interpretation of performances departs from this norm only quantitatively, to the extent that a performance as such is calculated to make public sense in a way in which a private life or even a private conversation is not. Critical theory has often been betrayed into unnecessary simplifications and falsifications by failing to take note of the subtle balance of sympathy and detachment that people always show in understanding one another.

It is clear from the foregoing that no definitive account of what any given performance is can be given: very often there is no problem, but wherever a problem does arise it admits of no one determinate solution. None the less, a formal and schematic account can be given of what determines what performance has been given. The account is very simple, and was in fact implicit in our initial formulation of the concept of performance. Given a restricted context of performing, a performance is constituted out of all and only those actions and products that cohere into a unity; anything not thus cohering is no part of the performance. So now the answer to what the performance is, is that it is that unity to which the least possible of what prima facie forms part of the performance by contextual inclusion is irrelevant. This formulation, forced on us by the momentum of our account and by the apparent failure of alternatives, is of course no novelty, but the commonest requirement of interpretation. And in the light of it we can see that the common critical insistence on coherent complexity as the necessary condition of artistic success is no mere arbitrary fancy, nor a favouring (as is sometimes unkindly alleged) of what lends itself best to prolonged critical discussion, but a mere following out of the implications of performance as such and of the system of critical interpretation least likely to lead to misunderstanding and error.

The formal solution of the problem of what decides does not make decision easy, nor does it answer the question of who decides. It only specifies what sort of question we are faced with. Who then does decide what coheres and what fails to cohere, what connexions are real, what illusory, what important, and what nugatory? Not the performer, we said; and not the critic either, for to interpret is not the same as to decide between interpretations. The answer is, of course, that no one decides, since there are no critical courts of last appeal; or, if one prefers, that everyone decides, the public in that some interpretations win acceptance and others do not, and each individual in that he makes his own decisions in accepting and rejecting. The question 'Who decides?' is undermined by the rejoinder 'What decision is there to make?' Formally, however, given that there may be competing interpretations, we are driven to postulating an extra, higher-level, super-critical type of judgement that determines both what a performance is and what criticism is appropriate to it. But the postulation of such higher-level judgements does not involve the postulation of higher-order beings (super-critics) to make them; nor does it make such judgements authoritative. The difference is simply one of logical level, and the higher-level judgement has no greater claim to certainty, and requires no higher competence, than the lower one. To say that a critique is irrelevant or mistaken is certainly to say that the performance was of a certain kind and has been criticized as being of another kind; but to say such things is merely to pass a judgement whose warrant is not necessarily any better or any worse than that of the critique against which it is directed.

It now appears that judgements as to what performance has been performed may have the status not of critical interpretations but of meta-critical judgements purporting to determine what critiques are relevant and what are not. But all our old questions reappear on this meta-critical level. Are we to say that, granted that there are no decisions to be taken and no courts to appeal to, no such judgements are better than any other; or that their alleged merits are merely a function of their acceptance? Surely this won't do. Some criticisms are obviously inappropriate, obviously miss the point. It will be objected that this 'obviousness' is merely subjective: it cannot have been obvious to the critic himself that he was wrong. But against this objection three points have some weight. One is, that some people really do seem to be stupider, less perceptive, than others. The second is that some people are less familiar than others with certain types of activity, and through inexperience may not be in a position to tell what is going on. The third, which seems to me conclusive, is that the contention that some critiques are better than others was not confined to critiques sincerely made, and it is surely possible for an ingenious person to invent criticisms that are deliberately wide of the mark and that neither he nor anyone else could hold to be relevant. And if such critiques can be produced in jest presumably they can be produced in earnest, for sincerity is no guarantee of infallibility. Even if most judgements of relevance are contestable, and even endlessly debatable, surely not all are. And in fact there is on most performances at most times a rough critical consensus, which is surely not to be despised altogether. Personal bias, eccentricity, obsession, and blind-spottedness are sad but familiar and ineluctable facts, and the most usual reason for inability to get others to share one's vision is, as we have remarked before, that what one would show them is not there to be seen.

W. K. WIMSATT

Genesis : A Fallacy Revisited

It would appear that literary studies, and especially theoretical studies, are subject to endless metamorphic cycles, and if they sometimes make progress, they can also suffer regress. Why not? Poems are, on one view, more or less imperfectly recorded acts of personal agents, and in literary study they are open to boundless speculation by further persons, whose activity, though sometimes partly scientific and historical, is always driven by an aim of individual intelligence. There is no theoretical or critical term set up for the purpose of clarifying or recommending a given perspective which is not suscept-ible of being seen and used in an opposite light. There is no rational and methodological concept, no attempted translucent universal, which is not capable of being transformed, and very quickly, into an opaque historical gimmick—as if some poems could be 'beautiful' in some special Platonic sense (after a certain date), or as if symbolism had begun to appear in poetry about the time of Baudelaire or Mallarmé, just as blood began to circulate in human bodies about the time of William Harvey or dreams to have significance about the time of Freud. These reflections, verging on the melancholy, occur as I survey some recent writings on the critical problem of the artist's life story, his inspirations and his intentions, in relation to his work of art.[1]

Whatever the truth in this debate, or the preferred side (if there is one, and I still think there is), it must be evident that there are two antithetically opposed sides, and probably always will be, correspon-ding to two aspects of literature and to two kinds of persons who come to the study of literature. To speak broadly and to avoid the simplicity of one-word labels (or to defer the economy of such labels), let us say that an art work is something which emerges from the private, individual, dynamic, and intentionalistic realm of its maker's mind and personality; it is in a sense (and this is especially true of the verbal work of art) made of intentions or intentionalistic material. But at the same time, in the moment it emerges, it enters a public and in a certain clear sense an objective realm; it claims and gets attention from an audience; it invites and receives discussion, about its meaning and value, in an idiom of inter-subjectivity and conceptualization. If the art work has emerged at all from the artist's private world, it has emerged into some kind of universal world. The artist was not merely *trying* to do something worthy of notice in that world. He has done it. Artistic activity has produced a valued result. Some critics will wish to talk about just that result. Other critics, however, will not. These will be the critics who entertain an antithetic drive toward viewing the art work as mainly a token of its source, a manifestation of something behind it, that is, the consciousness or personality of the artist (or perhaps of the society in which he lived, or of himself as representative of that society). These critics, wishing to throb in unison with the mind of the artist, will wish to know all about that individual artist and as much as possible about his historic context. At the very least, they will wish to know not only the poem in question, but also all his other poems, his essays, letters, and diaries, his thoughts and feelings,[2] and not only those which occurred before the poem and might in any sense have caused it, but (in the more recent idiom) all those which came after it at any time and are thus a part of the whole personality of which the poem is an expression, the system of contexts of which it is a part.[3]

It was against a background of triumphantly prevalent genetic studies in various modes, and in an effort to give assistance in what seemed a badly needed program to rescue poems from the morass of their origins, that my friend Monroe Beardsley and I published in a *Dictionary of World Literature* (1944) an article entitled 'Intention' and then, in response to a critique of that article, a further development of our argument in the *Sewanee Review* (1946), an essay entitled 'The Intentional Fallacy.' Mr Beardsley followed these articles thirteen years later with some very lucid pages in his volume entitled *Aesthetics* (1958). It seemed to me then, and it still seems, that Mr Beardsley and I succeeded in formulating a clear, reasonable, and viable statement of the thesis that the intention of a literary artist qua intention is neither a valid ground for arguing the presence of a quality or a meaning in a given instance of his literary work nor a valid criterion for judging the value of that work. 'The objective critic's first question, when he is confronted with a new aesthetic object,' says Mr Beardsley in 1958, 'is not, What is this supposed to be? but, What have we got here?'

As I have already noted, however, literary students who love the poem's genesis have no trouble in answering such arguments and returning to that luxuriant pasture. It is enough to assert that biography has such and such joys of discovery and communion, and thus biography *is* relevant to the study of the poem.[4] Or to say that the poet's life itself, or even the style of face he wears, is a work of art parallel to his produced art works, and hence the poet's life *is* a thing of great interest to the literary student.[5] Or that the intention of the artist, revealed in the title of a work or some similar adjacent index, is often a clue which the artist himself seems to feel it prudent to supply to his public, or which the given viewer of a work finds it very helpful to notice, and hence the intention of the artist *is* sometimes 'relevant' to the work.[6] One may even add that in some instances, like that of Mr Beardsley's invention, the 'cruller-shaped object of polished teak' said by the sculptor to symbolize 'Human Destiny,' the plight of the artist who wishes to convey that meaning will indeed be hopeless unless we grant him the privilege of telling us what he wishes. And therefore his intention is indeed relevant and valid.[7] Or, a critic may prefer to talk, not about the meaning of a poem, but about his own 'responses' to it, which may be 'conditioned' by his knowledge of the author's intentions, as these create a kind of 'field of force round the work' or a 'web of associations.' If Housman says that he meant no irony at all, that, it would appear, will settle the question for this critic. If Eliot were to testify that he had never heard of Andrew Marvell, that too would settle a question. Such a critic's responses might apparently also be conditioned by his knowing what Leavis thinks about a problem—though what this may be, in the given instance, seems unhappily in doubt.[8]

The argument about intention is then, in a sense, hopelessly circular and reentering. There is no way to keep the simpler kinds of intention-hunters from jumping on the vehicle of literary inquiry, and nobody I suppose really wishes the power to legislate anything against them. But at the precise level of abstraction and definition at which Mr Beardsley and I argued the question, I do not see that any notable revision is required, or even any very emphatic repetition. Let me try to make a useful reentry into the debate by first noticing a few related, parallel, or complementary terms and focuses of recent literary criticism, perhaps some of them obstructions to a right view of literary 'intention.'

o o o

The idea of poetic 'impersonality' is, I believe, in the thinking of many students a close adjunct to, or required condition for, the kind of criticism which hopes to escape the 'intentional fallacy.' Much difficulty seems to arise here, however, and this has probably been promoted to a large extent by the writings early and late of a poet-critic who did as much as any other single authority to establish in English studies of the mid-century a climate favorable to objective inquiry— T. S. Eliot, of course. In a review of his posthumously collected essays, *To Criticize the Critic*, I have already discussed this matter in the perspective of his later career.[9] It will be sufficient here to look back for a moment at his seminal essay 'Tradition and the Individual Talent' (published during the fall and early winter of 1919 in the last two numbers of *The Egoist, An Individualist Review*). This celebrated early essay, despite its forceful suggestiveness, the smoothness and fullness of its definition of the poet's impersonality (or perhaps inevitably in achieving these qualities), was a highly ambiguous statement. Therein, no doubt, consisted something of its pregnancy. In this essay Eliot as poet and critic is saying two things about three ideas (man, poet, and poem) and saying them simultaneously. He is saying that a poet ought to depersonalize his raw experience, transcend the immediacy of the suffering man. At the same time, he is saying that the reader ought to read the poem impersonally, as an achieved expression, not personally, with attendant inquiries into the sufferings, the motives, the confusions of the man behind the poem. The idea 'poet' as Eliot employs it in this essay is sometimes the antithesis of 'man' and sometimes the antithesis of 'poem.' 'The more perfect the artist, the more completely separate in him will be the man who suffers and the mind which creates.' 'Honest criticism and sensitive appreciation are directed not upon the poet but upon the poetry.' The two meanings are inextricably interwoven in Eliot's rich and memorable sentences. But they are not one meaning, nor does either one entail the other. Eliot, at moments much later in his career, could be very clear about one half of his doctrine. 'I prefer not to define, or to test, poetry by means of speculations about its origins; you cannot find a sure test for poetry, a test by which you may distinguish between poetry and mere good verse, by reference to its putative antecedents in the mind of the poet.'[10] But his injunction against peeping into the poet's activity, if it is valid at all, must be equally valid whether that activity itself is, in the poet's own consciousness, personal or impersonal. In fact, the critical lesson is that from the poem itself we cannot really tell, and so far as we are critics interested in the poem itself, we do not care. Despite his double doctrine of impersonality, the notion of the poet has always been, for Eliot, deeply centered in that personal suffering man himself. 'It is not in his personal emotions . . . that the poet is in any way remarkable or interesting. His particular emotions may be simple, crude, or flat.' Poetry is an 'escape' from personality. Yes, but of course 'only those who have personality and emotions know what it means to want to escape from these things.'[11]

The dubious notion of the poet's impersonal personality, deriving so pervasively in modern America criticism from the ideas of Eliot, has also been colored no doubt by Yeatsian occultist notions of the 'self' and the 'anti-self' or 'mask' (the latter either 'true' or 'false').[12]

Which is the poet in a given poem expressing? His real self? A true mask? A false mask? A fascinating question—and a safe one, so long as the inquirer is aware that the area of of his inquiry is at the moment biography, perhaps a very refined version of this art, but still biography. Perhaps it will be sufficient to say here, without a long excursion, that the thesis that biographical evidence does not establish meaning *in* poems is not the equivalent of a thesis that poems cannot contribute their own kind of meaning, and a very rich and subtle kind, to the writing of biography.[13] For whatever does get into a poem presumably is put there by the poet and reflects *something* in the poet's personality and life. It is for the biographer, in his particular insight and skill, to say what is reflected and in what relation to other things in the poet's life. Nowadays we are increasingly promised, or shown, the inner life of the author mainly on the evidence of the dialectic sequence of his works.[14] If anybody wishes to challenge this as sound biographical method (I at least have no specific wish to do so), it ought to be clear that he does not do so on the same principle as that on which a critic may refuse to decide the meaning or value of a poem on external auctorial testimony or other biographical evidence. Affirmation of a cause and affirmation of an effect are different in their entailments. If a poet sees red, he may well either write or not write a red poem. If he writes a red poem, it would seem to be a sound enough inference, though in some instances little more than a truism, that he has in some sense seen red.

o o o

Patrick Cruttwell, in a richly illustrated and nicely modulated essay of 1959, 'Makers and Persons,'[15] discriminates four degrees of 'distance' between a 'maker' (poet) and the 'person' (man in whom the maker perforce quarries his stuff): (1) the degree or way of 'simple transcript' (genuine or partly faked—Boswell, Pepys, Rousseau, Byron in letters and journals, Montaigne); (2) the 'masked' way— 'the making of a self which pretends not to be, but encourages the reader to think it is,' the real person of the writer (Sterne-Shandy-Yorick, Conrad-Marlow); (3) the way of 'mythologized' self-presentation—'transportation of the person into symbolic figures, references' (The master of this obscure and mysterious way is Eliot); (4) the 'dramatized' way—here 'the distance is greatest between maker and person' (clearest in actual stage drama—the Greeks, Shakespeare, 'the ages of great drama'). After presenting these distinctions, Mr Cruttwell traces, very interestingly and I believe correctly, the rise of the modern cult of personality, the author as 'exhibitionist,' from about the time of Boswell's *Johnson* (1791) through episodes in the career of Byron and in Victorian literary biography. Modern poets themselves have sometimes protested against the invasion of their privacy—in vain, and wrongly. The floodgates of the personal interest, once opened, cannot be forced back. Art betrays its creators, and properly. They betray themselves, once the public and the literary scholars have been put on the right track. In a closing short section on problems for contemporary critics, Mr Cruttwell argues that it is time for critics to overcome any anti-biographical inhibitions which may have been induced by the ideas of 'Eliot, Richards, Leavis and the Scrutineers' or by the 'New Criticism' in America. Let the critics now permit themselves a renewed and healthy release in the satisfaction of the 'curiosity' which poems must in fact surely arouse in them. Who is the critic, after all, who can say that his responses to poetry *are* pure? After we 'have enjoyed' and have been 'impressed' by a writer, by Wordsworth in his Lucy poems, for instance, then we undertake the 'microscopic investigation.' We want to know about Wordsworth's 'incestuous feelings for Dorothy' and what he 'intended' Lucy to 'stand for.' So, in spite of Mr Cruttwell's effort to establish a *critical* direction for his essay, the argument swings round in fact to postcritical interests, moving *from* the recognized and presumably understood poem toward the 'putative antecedents.' Mr Cruttwell has earlier noted that a certain 'degeneration' in Sterne's management of his Tristram and Yorick masks may be explained by a parallel in Sterne's life. 'His failure to hold his masks was a symptom of his person's insincerity and weakness. . . . He slid from one pose to the next, from bawdy to sobstuff and back again, not through choice but through weakness' (p. 491). But Mr Cruttwell can also have his argument the opposite way, on a later page (503), where he argues that Byron aspiring to escape from his true personality in *Childe Harold* wrote untruthfully and badly, but when he abandoned his aspiration to purity and simply 'wrote out out his mood as it came to him' in the 'shameless self-parading of *Don Juan*,' he 'wrote at his best.' The lesson of these two examples seems to be that the biographically oriented critic will find a correspondence between life and work an explanation of either goodness or badness in the work, as he happens to find the work itself good or bad. On another page (494), Mr Cruttwell expatiates upon the futility of trying to find Eliot's personal or secret motive in the epigraph from Marston prefixed to *Burbank with a Baedeker*. Mr Cruttwell is severe on Eliot for his two-faced stance of impersonal secretiveness yet constant invitation to the reader to speculate about personal reasons (in the absence of clear public ones). I think there is some justice in the complaint. I have dwelt long on Mr Cruttwell's essay, however, not only because it seems to me probably the richest and most informative in the recent resurgence of biographically oriented 'critical' arguments, but because in its own ambivalence or thwarted struggle to arrive at a 'critical' direction, it is in fact a larger rewriting of Eliot's original and seminally confused essay of 1919.

o   o   o

A kind of critical metamorphosis to which I alluded in my opening paragraph is well illustrated in the recent history of the very useful term 'persona' in American criticism. This term seems to have gained currency during the mid-century because it was a convenient way of referring to something *in the poem* which could be thought of as a counterpart of the *im*personality which was supposed either to reside in the author or, more accurately, to be a perspective adopted by the critic. This economical employment of the term 'persona' (along with certain related or nearly equivalent terms such as 'fiction,' 'ethos,' 'mask,' or 'muse') might be illustrated near its zenith in Maynard Mack's essay of 1951, 'The Muse of Satire,'[16] distinguishing three 'voices' (the *vir bonus*, the *ingénu*, and the heroic public defender) in the persona or speaker of Pope's formal verse satire. All three of these voices were to be taken *by a critic* dramatically, not biographically, rhetorically, not historically. Something like a sheer reversal from that kind of critical use of persona to a convenient reconfusion of questions about criticism and questions about biography may be witnessed in a very richly variegated essay of 1963 by Irvin Ehrenpreis, entitled 'Personae.'[17] An expression of grave concern that certain nameless 'scholars' have been doing the wrong thing with persona (making it a 'distinguishing property' or special kind of merit in Augustan poetry, rather than the universal and 'inescapable part of language and communication' that it actually is) leads Mr Ehrenpreis, not, as one might at first hope, to a purified image of the scholar-critic, but very quickly into an opposite sort of thing, an exceedingly dense involvement of poet and poem as man and mask, reality and 'rhetorical pose.' 'One could never reveal the whole truth about oneself, even supposing that one knew it.' 'If there is any meaning in the concept of persona or mask, it must imply a difference between appearance and reality.'

Like Mr Cruttwell, whom we have cited above, and like most writers on W. B. Yeats, Mr Ehrenpreis reminds us forcefully that, whatever the relation of persona to author, it is not a simple one either of likeness or of difference. Other recent writers, Maynard Mack in the essay already cited, and notably Wayne Booth in *The Rhetoric of Fiction* (1961),[18] have been stressing a somewhat different, if parallel, truth—that the relation of persona, internally, to other parts or aspects of the work, need not be simple. Persona is not in fact a sufficient conception for the *de*personalization of the poetic object as the critic attends to it. It is not as if the persona is always the simple focus for the expression of everything in the poem. Sometimes he betrays himself in contrast to some cooler or saner perspective. This is the kind of thing that happens obviously in a monodrama like Browning's *Soliloquy of a Spanish Cloister*, a miniature of the situation in a full-scale play or novel, where numerous personae contend within the ambit of an encircling and managing intelligence. Browning's *Soliloquy* is a steady sequence of not very delicate little antithetic jolts. '*Ave, Virgo!* Gr-r-r—you swine!' The ironies of Swift are a more plenary instance of such internal cunning. Mr Ehrenpreis observes that in *A Modest Proposal* there are not two, but three mentalities of 'styles'—that of the initially prominent 'sensible projector' of the proposal, that of the 'monster' looming behind him, and that of a directly speaking, bitter denunciator, all three of these, as we should expect in this essay, said to be styles of the author's own voice. (Here perhaps it is worth adding that while projector and monster are aspects of the same persona, the denouncer is part of a perspective, or, if one wishes, he is a second person, who has already manipulated the projector so as to reveal him as a monster.) But what I am trying to get back to here is the direction of argument. From the work to the author (when one wishes to be biographical) is not the same as from the author (outside the work) to the work. These directions remain opposites no matter how numerous and complicated a set of deflectors or baffles we set up between the two termini.

The fact is that we can, if we wish, learn with relative certainty from biographical evidence that some personae are close to or identical with the author and some are much different from him. Nobody would confuse the persona of Browning's *Soliloquy of a Spanish Cloister* with Browning himself. But almost everybody rushes to confuse the persona of Gray's *Elegy in a Country Churchyard* with Gray himself. In fact it can be shown on quite convincing biographical evidence that the melancholy poet who is the anonymous speaker of that poem is very close to the melancholy poet Thomas Gray—'me I; il Pensoroso.' Nor is that correspondence, in biographical terms, an accident. The *Elegy* does seem to come out of the historic person Thomas Gray much more directly than many other poems come out of their authors. Nevertheless, the *Elegy* is not *about* the historic person Gray. The self-contemplative speaker remains anonymous. The poem itself, if it were anonymous, would be intact.

What, however, if the poem does happen to be a poem *about* that historic person the author, about himself, his friends, and his enemies ? If the author of the *Epistle to Arbuthnot,* says Ehrenpreis, 'were not the great poet of his age, if his relations with his parents were not well known to have been as he testifies, if Atticus and Sporus did not belong to public life, the force of the poem would dwindle' (p. 32). Yet with increase of information, let us notice, comes complexity— and doubt. The canny persona of Pope's satire bears scarcely the same simple relation to the gardener of Twickenham as the melancholy churchyard speaker seems to bear to the pensive fellow of the Cambridge college. Three distinct voices are assigned by Mr Mack to that satiric persona. In what variously shaded relations to the man who is both behind the poem and the subject of the poem may be difficult to say. Pope could be scheming and mean, as well as friendly and noble. The main evidence for his piety to his father is in the poem. Perhaps we do not inquire too rigorously whether he was in fact so righteous, charitable, and simple as the poem would make him. If he was not, still 'his make-up of being so is in itself a piece of greatness; and not to enjoy it is a piece of stupidity.'[19] Perhaps we enjoy it the more for its being in part make-up. And we sense that this is so, or may well be so, in large part from internal evidence, from the perspective or management of the whole witty poem.

In accepting this kind of biographical claim, let us notice that it is a particular kind of claim, not of intention but of subject matter. Pope's sincerity or insincerity, his virtue or his meanness, his character and intention, as generators of the poem or as criteria of its merit, do not really come into question. The poet and his friends and enemies are present in the poem as historic figures, and furthermore as well-established historic figures in precisely the roles they play in the poem. Milton's sonnets 17, 22, and 23 and his other allusions to his blindness provide similar, easy, and unimpeachable examples. Here we enter the problem of the universality and significance of the protagonist—the stature of Samson the agonist compared to that of Hobson the carrier. Aristotle understood that it gives a certain kind of advantage if the man is important. After Milton and Pope, the world became increasingly convinced of the importance of every man. Still it is not true, it never has been true, that the simple meanings or wishes of any man, even of any important man, can generate or guarantee a significant poetic symbol.[20]

o o o

'It is not illusory appearances,' says Ehrenpreis, 'that the real person sets before us: it is the visible effluences, aspects, reflections—however indirect, of an inner being that cannot be defined apart from them. In order to understand any literary work, we must view it as a transaction between us and that inner being' (p. 31). 'Only as a relationship between a real speaker and a real listener can meaning exist' (p. 37). Some years earlier, Father Walter Ong, in one of the best essays on the 'personalist approach' that I know, *The Jinnee in the Well-Wrought Urn*, had written:

> Man's deepest orientation is personal. . . . Each work or art that bids for attention in an act of contemplation is a surrogate for a person. In proportion as the work of art is capable of being taken in full seriousness, it moves further and further along an asymptote to the curve of personality.[21]

Perhaps it does. Yet the argument against intentional reading need not suppose, and does not suppose, that the monkeys in the British Museum will in the foreseeable future, or in any future at all, type out *Paradise Lost*.[22] 'The words of a poem come out of a head, not out of a hat,' as we quoted long ago from E. E. Stoll. James Thorpe has recently demonstrated how much some literary works actually owe to editors and other agents of transmission and even to such chance activity as that of a compositor, who may by mistake introduce a word that conceivably is better than the author's. Mr Thorpe's philosophy of textual criticism says, however, that we should restore the author's own word, and I say the same thing, though perhaps more simply on grounds of plain convenience than he wishes to. He believes that to accept the compositor's happy slip would be to put the aesthetic object not in the realm of 'art' (intended or designed work), but in that of the now popularly received object made by 'chance' (a spilled can of paint, words selected by throwing dice, sounds of traffic recorded at a busy intersection).[23] But it is possible and, as he shows, frequently is the fact that a designed work is the design of more than one head. A second completes the work of the first. In this instance, it would be ourselves, the editors, who, in assessing and adopting the accidental intrusion, were the very junior collaborators in the original author's designed and intended work.

In our frequent focus on the history of modern literature as outlined by Mr Cruttwell, with its heavy personal underpainting, its vigorous cult of personal authentication, let us not forget the massive foundations of the world's literature—the Book of Genesis, the *Iliad*, the *Odyssey*, the works of Virgil, Dante, Chaucer, Shakespeare —which survive for us either anonymously or with the merest wisps or shadows of biography attached. These works, it is to be assumed, no less than those of Milton, Johnson, Byron, Keats, Yeats, or Joyce, speak to us with the 'inner being' of 'real speakers,' as 'surrogates' for persons.

It may promote clarity if at this point we try to map the structure of the argument we are engaged in according to the following types of statement which are our subject matter:

1. Historical, biographical: Thomas Gray was a melancholy poet, and he planned or meant or was likely to mean certain things.

2. Historical, poetic: The speaker of Gray's *Elegy* is a melancholy poet; he uses certain words and images and means certain things.

3. Methodological, explicitly evaluative: The resemblance, or correspondence, between the poet Gray and either the speaker or the perspective of the *Elegy* makes it a good poem or shows that it is good.

4. Methodological, interpretive: The character, mind, or habitual meanings of the poet Gray are a valid guide (or the best guide) to the meaning of the *Elegy*.

This arrangement introduces one distinction on which I have so far not laid any emphasis, that between statements of type 3 and those of type 4. Statements of type 3 (the explicitly evaluative) are more ambitious than those of type 4 (the simply interpretive), but I use this order because those of type 3 are on the whole less plausible, and I wish to dispose of them first. In our articles of 1944 and 1946 Mr Beardsley and I did not labor this distinction. In his *Aesthetics* of 1958 Mr Beardsley has separated the two issues very cleanly, in fact by a space of 428 pages, with I think, considerable increase of clarity for the whole discussion. At the same time, it is my own view (and this will emerge more clearly as I go on) that an argument about instances of type 4 (the interpretive) will very often, or even characteristically, bring in considerations of value.

o o o

Let me proceed to notice and comment upon certain graded instances of argument, first some relating to statements of type 3 (a, b, c), then some relating to type 4 (a, b, c, d, e, f). There is some value in a chart or a guided tour of a field of argument even when the cartographer or guide has to confess that he looks on many of the stopping points as only of historic interest. The point of maximum live concern for our debate, and the one toward which I am working, let me confess in advance, is 4f.

(3a) The poet wrote his poem with the aim of making money, of winning a prize, of pleasing a mistress, of impressing an employer or patron—or for some opposite or more ideal sort of reason. His work was either a 'free' work in Kant's sense, or not free. 'He achieved a result commensurate with such aims. Therefore. . . .' Such reasonings concern what some writers on our problem take pains to distinguish as secondary or ulterior intentions of the artist. We ought to be able to see these as obviously outside any real critical question. In like manner, we should find no trouble in putting to one side the common artistic aim of creating a masterpiece—or perhaps of not creating a masterpiece, but just of turning out a potboiler—or of having a 'lark.'[24] 'He intended only to appeal to popular sentiment; therefore we should not. . . .' (Or, to translate this kind of motive into the key of interpretive argument and thus get it out of the way: 'We know that he thought of this as his masterpiece; therefore it. . . .')

(3b) The poem is or says what the poet himself was or thought or felt; it is hence good—or bad. We have been close to this framing of the argument in our whole discussion of persona. We have seen both kinds of conclusion (bad, for Sterne; good, for Byron) in Mr Cruttwell's essay. This form of the argument runs very readily into talk about 'sincerity' and 'inspiration' and 'authenticity,' topics which Mr Beardsley and I noted with some care in our essay of 1946. In his *Aesthetics* (p. 457) he lists 'expression,' 'sincerity,' and 'intention' together, under the general head of the 'genetic,' but, rightly I believe, he sees 'intention' as focusing most or all of what can be handled with any precision in this area.[25]

(3c) The poet had a specific aim or plan in mind; he managed (whether inspirationally or rationally) to carry this out in the poem; thus he is a successful artist; his work is good art. This is the 'Spingarn-Croce-Carlyle-Goethe' theory named by H. L. Mencken. We alluded to this theory in our article of 1944, and it was defended by Ananda K. Coomaraswamy in his critique of that article.[26] A successfully planned and executed murder was for Mr Coomaraswamy no less a work of art than a poem or painting. Mr Beardsley makes the helpful suggestion that here we may indeed be likely to assign a kind of merit, but it should be understood as referring to the artist himself (who was 'skillful' enough to do what he aimed at doing) rather than to the work—which may be murder, a robbery, a libel, a silly lampoon. It would scarcely be feasible to illustrate all the kinds of evidence (or supposed evidence) that may be adduced for an author's plan outside his poem. I do not know how many kinds there may be, each no doubt with somewhat special problems. Let me adduce a single example, representative I believe, if in part synthetic. Edgar Allan Poe's *Philosophy of Composition* professes to tell us how he proceeded in writing *The Raven*—a poem of a certain ideal length, presenting the most melancholy, moving, and poetic subject conceivable, the death of a beautiful woman, and making use of the most effective poetic device conceivable, a certain simple and sonorous refrain, repeated in various applications. There can be little question that *The Raven* does manifest Poe's professed intentions so far as they are specific and can be made manifest. But to argue (as some proponents of 'intention' have seemed in general to argue) that, because we can here prove that the artist achieved his intentions, we know that *The Raven* is a good work of art would seem a fairly obvious kind of fatuity. A critical enterprise that would more seriously recommend itself would surely be the inquiry whether the proposed subject and technique were actually the most poetic conceivable. One kind of objection to such an argument from Poe's intention (or one explanation for giving it up) might be to say that Poe's *Philosophy of Composition* is not a valid guide to his intention in the poem because it is an ex post facto invention and a tongue-in-cheek tour de force. Perhaps so. But here we catch ourselves moving from intention to intention—when does the witness mean what he says?—and we may be left with the generally not very satisfactory principle that an external statement of intention by an author has to be examined to see if it was written before the poem or after. So externality is invested with externality, and testimonies written before the poem might well have suffered by change of intention while the poem was being written.

Another sort of argument in favor of intention as a criterion of value might say: Well, what is meant is precisely the fullness of the executed plan as seen in the poem itself. We can see the author's *skill* precisely in this. To which we might retort: Yes, precisely. We see a value of fullness, richness, design in the poem itself. *From this* we infer an artist and a skillful artist, and not the other way round. We do not compare the poem with any blueprint of the author's mind.

o o o

Let us turn then and consider some phases of the intentionalistic argument relating to statements of type 4 in our plan, those of interpretation—the author's mind outside the poem as a key to his meaning inside the poem.

(4a) A few of the recent writers on the term 'intention' have pointed out, as indeed Mr Beardsley and I were careful to point out in 1944, that interpretations apparently based upon an author's 'intention' often in fact refer to an intention as it is found in, or inferred from, the work itself.[27] Obviously the argument about intention (or about the author's intention outside the work) is not directed against such instances—unless in an incidental and general plea for clarity in the use of critical terms. Such arguments may extend to *conflicts* of intention, or shifts of design, in a given work. They may give rise to such notions as that of a 'secret meaning' (or even an unconscious meaning) to be distinguished from an 'overt meaning.' 'Milton was of the Devil's party without knowing it.' That is, Milton's *Paradise Lost*, in spite of certain contrary indications in it, on the whole makes Satan a hero. This argument can be enlarged by appeals to Milton's own rebellious personality, his political and religious prose writings. Yet it can be carried on too, and sufficiently, within the poem itself. Actually the poem itself seems to be the chief or only evidence which Blake, the author of the assertion just quoted, has in mind. Another classic instance is Tolstoy's judgment that Chekhov, in his story *Darling*, while trying to ridicule the womanliness of a woman, succeeded (like Balaam trying to curse the Israelites) only in pronouncing a blessing. Tolstoy had behind him a tradition of Russian book-reviewing which looked for covert and risky political meanings in nineteenth-century fiction.

(4b) In another variation of the same interpretive argument, the author's intention is sometimes said to have at least an 'advisory' force.[28] This seems hardly a claim that ought to be debated. No doubt the author is likely to be a good guide. Yet it cannot be that on principle he is an infallible guide. As a commentator on his own works he enjoys no prescriptive, or creative, rights. If he says there is red in his poem, we will look carefully in the expectation of *finding* it.[29]

(4c) A somewhat similar sounding, but actually different, argument says that the intention of the artist (as learned in titles of works, epigraphs, and the like) may sometimes be said to fill in certain details or aspects of a work actually missing from the work but presumably needed for its understanding and appreciation.[30] In our article of 1946, Mr Beardsley and I discussed something like this under the head of the modern poet's penchant for esoteric allusion, and we suggested that titles, epigraphs, and notes such as T. S. Eliot wrote for *The Waste Land*, were in fact loosely attached parts of poems or annexes of half-assimilated materials. As such they seemed to raise some questions about the achieved integrity of the poems. The notes to *The Waste Land* are not a manifest virtue, rather something we accept and submit to being teased by, in view of the probable depths of the poem itself, and latterly in view of Eliot's reputation.[31] Taken literally, the argument seems to imply some deficiency in the work of art itself, some need of adjunct or aid. On the assumption that the work of art is on the whole, or basically, worthwhile, nobody would wish to rule out such help—any more than to deny a crutch to a lame man, or an extra stone to a sagging arch. Only note that the crutch must fit the man; the stone must fit the arch, and in fact the stone becomes part of the arch. These analogies seem closer to what is meant by such special invocations of artist's intentions than, say, the use of a strong glass to see a miniature painting or a strong light in a gallery. The glass and the light can find only what is already there.[32]

Certain external aids or annexes to poems, we have just assumed, do fit or are appropriate to the poems in question. More broadly, however, if we are to think of poems as having any built-in character or structure of their own at all, then the inquiry must run the risk of encountering inappropriately offered annexes, false clues, mistaken efforts of the energetic historian.

(4d) Certainly there are features of gross material or of structure in art works which not only do not call for the artist's intention to help their interpretation but will even strongly defy contradictory indications. If the artist makes a statue of granite, then it is granite, and an affidavit that he thought he was working in marble or intended to work in marble or would rather have worked in marble will not make any difference.[33] The same principle will hold if the artist writes in English but happens to think he is writing in French. Or if he defies some code of classic rules, though he happens to think he is observing them, or vice versa. The former, or conservative, self-deception may be illustrated in Corneille's retospective defense of *Le Cid*. The general principle for literary criticism was put precisely by Samuel Johnson in his *Preface to Shakespeare*: 'Whether Shakespeare knew the unities and rejected them by design, or deviated from them by happy ignorance, it is, I think, impossible to decide and useless to inquire.'[34]

(4e) Problems of local semantics may be more difficult. But even here, the more explicit the conflicting auctorial testimony, the more likely it is to seem comic in the degree of its externality and irrelevance. A member of the London Literary Club, Anthony Chamier, better known as a statesman than as a litterateur, once asked Oliver Goldsmith 'What he meant by *slow*, the last word in the first line of *The Traveller*, "Remote, unfriended, melancholy, slow." Did he mean tardiness of locomotion? Goldsmith, who would say something without consideration, answered "Yes." ' But Samuel Johnson happened to be present and cut in, 'No, Sir; you do not mean tardiness of locomotion; you mean, that sluggishness of mind which comes upon a man in solitude.' 'Chamier believed then' that Johnson 'had written the line as much as if he had seen' Johnson write it.[35] It is worth adding that one editor of Goldsmith, Austin Dobson, has observed, 'It is quite possible that Goldsmith meant no more than he said.'[36] But an earlier commentator, John Forster, says: 'Who can doubt that he also meant slowness of motion? The first point of the picture is *that*. The poet is moving slowly, his tardiness of gait measuring the heaviness of heart, the pensive spirit, the melancholy

of which it is the outward expression and sign.'[37] The point of the
present exposition is that Goldsmith, though undoubtedly in some
sense closer to the generative intention of his own poem than the
others, is not in virtue of that fact a better critic or interpreter. If
Forster seems better than Dobson and better even than Johnson in
this instance, the grounds of his judgment and ours must lie in the
observable force and relevance of the word 'slow' in the *context* of
the first line of Goldsmith's pensive travelogue.

Mr Beardsley has cited the nearly parallel instance of A.E.
Housman's angry attempt to deny the irony at expense of state and
church manifest in his poem for Queen Victoria's fiftieth anniversary.
'Get you the sons your fathers got, And God will save the Queen.'
Here a statement made in retrospect and under provocation, a kind
of profession of loyalty to a soverign, stands in sharp contradiction
not only to the cunning details of the poem in question but to the
well-known skeptical and cynical cast of the poet's canon.

The two instances just adduced may seem a parody of the intentionalistic argument, but they are no more than a fair parody of that
argument as often formulated. Simple, even extreme, examples have
the advantage of revealing and clarifying principles.

A classic instance of an author's serious intention, antecedent to
and simultaneous with the writing, yet doomed to defeat, is
Chekhov's desire (revealed in his letters) to have his *Seagull* and
Cherry Orchard produced as comedies—resulting only in Stanislavsky's successful and now well-established interpretation of them
as tragedies—or at least as very cloudy 'dramas.'[38]

(4f) But let us now refine (or complicate) the argument a little
with an example from the other end of a scale of explicitness in
auctorial testimony—where no single explicit statement is adduced,
but where the author's life and canon or some parts of them are
urged as a surrounding and controlling context for the poem or
some details of it. In our article of 1946, Mr Beardsley and I wrote:
'The meaning of words is the history of words, and the biography of
an author, his use of a word, and the associations which the word
has for *him*, are part of the word's history and meaning.' But a critic
who is habitually concerned with this kind of evidence, we added,
will in the long run produce a far different sort of comment from that
of the critic who is mainly concerned with the public linguistic and
cultural elements of the poem.

We are now seeking a maximum or crucial instance where a poet's
private or personal and habitual meaning (as inferred from external
documents) clearly clashes with what he managed to realize in the
public materials (linguistic and cultural) of his poem. Such instances

are no doubt difficult to find, because poets by and large do manage to say what they mean. There is a sense in which, even when their words are 'peculiar' or catachrestic, poets remain the 'servants' of their language rather than its 'masters.'[39] In order to show a clear instance of the sort of conflict we are interested in, it may be necessary for the expositor himself to drive both sides of an interpretive difference, the intentionalistic and the non-intentionalistic—and thus perhaps to expose himself to the opportunism of the captious. But the following may serve at least to define the issue. The materials are well known, but not the interpretive problem as I shall urge it. William Blake wrote in a sketchbook:

An ancient Proverb

Remove away that blackning church
Remove away that marriage hearse
Remove away that man of blood
You'll quite remove the ancient curse[40]

These lines remained in the sketchbook, where they deserved to remain. They are a raw expression of certain soreheaded antinomian attitudes which are beyond doubt a part of Blake's biography at the period when he was writing the *Songs of Experience*. Blake also wrote in the same sketchbook a draft for his 'song' *London*, which he worked over with much struggle, adding only as an afterthought, in several successive versions, the last black stanza.

> I wander thro' each charter'd street,
> Near where the charter'd Thames does flow,
> And mark in every face I meet
> Marks of weakness, marks of woe.
>
> In every cry of every Man,
> In every Infant's cry of fear,
> In every voice, in every ban,
> The mind-forg'd manacles I hear:
>
> How the Chimney-sweeper's cry
> Every black'ning Church appalls;
> And the hapless Soldier's sigh
> Runs in blood down Palace walls.
>
> But most, thro' midnight streets I hear
> How the youthful Harlot's curse
> Blasts the new-born Infant's tear,
> And blights with plagues the Marriage hearse.[41]

The concluding phrase repeats that of the second line of the *Ancient Proverb* and creates a crux on which I wish to focus. This dark city

poem is about human 'weakness' and 'woe' as they may be observed
in certain (uncertain) visual and auditory betrayals ('marks' and
'cries') and in certain (uncertain) imputed human causes (charters,
bans, mind-forged manacles). The word 'ban' as it is used in the
second stanza of the poem no doubt includes many kinds of legal or
official yells, proclamations, summonses, prohibitions, curses—no
doubt even marriage bans. At this point let us consult one of the best
informed and most soberly reliable of recent Blake critics.

> The one thing needful in achieving this transformation [of the
> human spirit] is the removal of the mind-forged manacles of the
> institutional tyrannies—marriage, the church, and the king.
>
> 'Every ban' . . . is a multiple clank of the awful trinity of
> king, priest, and marriage.
>
> It is the marriage hearse that breeds youthful (and thus po-
> tentially innocent) harlots, by creating the necessity for prostitu-
> tion. If there were no marriage, there would be no ungratified
> desires, and therefore no harlots. Thus it is ultimately the mar-
> riage hearse itself and not the youthful harlot which breeds the
> pestilence that blights the marriage hearse.[42]

Mr E. D. Hirsch, as I have said, is well informed about Blake and
reliable, and I believe he gives us an accurate reading of a sort of
intention which Blake probably did entertain, a phase at least of
Blake's habitual mind as it may be supposed to stand at some distance
behind the poem. Mr Hirsch gives us a good and learned instance
of the new cryptography in Blake reading. 'If there were no marriage,
theℓe would be no ungratified desires, and therefore no harlots.' One
thing, however, which perhaps he does not notice, or perhaps does
not worry about, is that these ideas are silly. (Why wouldn't there be
many ungratified desires, as many at least as there were losers in stag
combats, or wooers rejected, or pursuers eluded, or matings frustra-
ted? and *many* harlots? and *many* whore-masters?) An admirer of
Blake the poet might well be content to leave these ideas, if he could,
on a back shelf in the doctrinaire part of Blake's mind. What if we
actually do find them or manage to put them in the poem? Won't
this make the poem silly? And, since interpretation and evaluation
are at the very least closely related, won't we be in danger of reading
the poem as a pretty bad poem? And isn't this poem, in fact, supposed
to be a masterpiece, 'one of the best city poems ever written?' Isn't it,
in fact, a masterpiece? It will be worthwhile to look closely at the
difference between the last stanza of the engraved poem *London* and
the crude second line of *An ancient Proverb*, which stayed in the
sketchbook. Blake's struggle with *London* was in part a struggle to
make the last line of the last stanza viable. The tough fact was that

the word 'marriage' in the history of English usage and culture was
not the name of an evil. ('Let me not to the marriage of true minds
admit impediments.') It was the name of a sacred institution and a
first principle of stability for nearly every important value in a whole
religiously and ethically oriented civilization and culture. The ex-
plosive force of the two violently juxtaposed terms at the end of the
last line of *London* is a poetic fact. But this was not to be achieved by
the easy way of simple supposition or assertion (though that may be
a rationale which very well suits the aims of the biographical critic
or cryptographer). Here the angry conscience of William Blake the
doctrinaire prophet and activist clashed violently with the more tact-
ful and skillful conscience of William Blake the poet, master and ser-
vant of the English language.[43] The latter conscience, apparently
after a hard struggle, won and (perhaps without Blake's being fully
aware of what happened—who knows?) saved him from engraving
a poem with a lame, perhaps even silly and ruinous, last line. Let us
imagine that some inquisitor of school curricula, reading Mr Hirsch's
gloss on *London*, were to file a protest against corrupting the minds
of schoolchildren by the required study of this depraved poem. One
sort of answer, from the defenders of the English curriculum, might
be that it was good for children to hear all views and to be exposed
to a liberal assault upon the mores in which home, church, and state
were trying to educate them. But another answer that surely would
not be long delayed would be to the effect that Blake's *London* in fact
says no such thing. True, the English teacher or the school principal
would say, the poem stresses charters and mind-forged manacles, but
circumstances, real and symbolic (the cry of sweeps, the decay of
churches, the blood of soldiers), are adduced to give specific topical
color to the imputations. We are dealing with very concretely colored
instances. And in the last stanza it is potently suggested that there is
a very real and evil antecedent cause why the marriage bed turns to
a hearse. For an initiate reading of the last stanza, consult the career
of an eighteenth-century Londoner like James Boswell or Charles
Hanbury Williams.

In sum, a critic who says that the 'poem' means that 'if there were
no marriage, there would be no ungratified desires,' ought to show
that this meaning actually operates in the poem or is generated by it
—and is not merely a concealed or balked idea entertained by the
author as revolutionary person. I myself think the poem is better than
that meaning, and to judge from the contexts where the poem has
often appeared and from earlier critiques, it would seem that most
readers have also thought so.

Yet even these [blackened churches and blood-stained palace

walls] are less terrible than the hideous perversion of the fairest joy on earth, voiced in the midnight cry of the young harlot. Love itself and the beauty of marriage and birth are stained by this most cruel misery of all.[44]

I have set up this discussion of the poem as a frame of reference within which a student may be able to see the direction in which his own mind moves in search of evidence for the meaning and value of a poem. When he can really see the difference between the directions and the results, than let him decide.

Mr Hirsch's method of reading *London* is not an isolated instance, though his clarity in realizing what he is doing and his frankness in admitting it may be unusual. A new mode in historical studies, which I would describe as a kind of attempted Vista-Vision intentionalism, searches reasons for inferring an author's intention not only in the whole canon of his own works and life record, early and late, but in motifs selected from anywhere in the intellectual ambient of his era. Let me cite a remarkable instance of this new mode in Paul de Man's essay of 1956, 'Keats and Hölderlin.'[45] Here, with the pursuit of the poet as philosopher-hero in full cry and the method of theme and analogy rampant, we bring Keats' *Endymion* into line with his own later *Hyperion* and with Hölderlin's novel *Hyperion* by the simple if eloquently disguised method of arguing that throughout the poem Keats failed to say what he meant. His interest in another kind of meaning was just too much for him. Keats should have been writing, or he wished to be writing, about a very serious subject, the 'eccentric road' of man's repetitive search for recovery of 'unity of being.' But he wrote actually about love (erotic love). 'No wonder it becomes difficult to keep apart the passages in which love is an actual experience, among others, from those in which it is a symbol for something else. But only at the expense of this effort [i.e. violence] can *Endymion* be given a thematic coherence which Keats' *Hyperion* amply substantiates' (p. 36). We proceed to a reading of *Endymion* which makes its point only at the expense of finding the imagery 'incongruous,' 'confusing,' 'bizarre,' 'stifled,' 'awkward' (pp. 37–38)—in short, utterly ineffectual (or inexpressive) and hence unpoetic. This is Keats' *Endymion*. 'A thing of beauty is a joy for ever.'

o o o

Some of our critics have argued that Mr Beardsley and I have examined the term 'intention' in too restricted and too simply mentalistic a sense (intention in the mind of the artist); at the same time they have adduced statements by us that show that we do not in fact object to certain broader invocations of 'intention' (in effect, 'intention' as present and verifiable 'intent' in works of art themselves).

And they have praised other writers, or themselves, for taking the term 'intention' in a broader (or at least other) and more 'generous' sense.[46] One writer has pointed out that we selected an example which showed what we meant and tended to support our argument, and thus he considers our example 'tendentious.'[47] It is difficult to see how such arguments are better than obscurantist devices of one-upmanship. We took 'intention' in a specific or limited sense, because it was just the difference between this sense and the broader (or other) sense that we believed to be often obscured in critical argument, with consequent concealed dilution of, or escape from, objective criticism. At the same time, we tried to make the idea of 'intention' a focal point (and I still believe it was a well-chosen focal point) for a cluster of genetically oriented ideas (inspiration, expression, authenticity, sincerity, purpose, and the like). What might seem at first glance a merely verbal and ambiguous cluster turns out on acquaintance to be a dynamic pattern that is well treated with as much unity of vision as possible. It is my opinion that as criteria for criticism these ideas stand or fall together.

Both in our essay of 1946 and in our earlier dictionary article, Mr Beardsley and I argued 'that the design or intention of the author is neither available nor desirable as a standard for judging the success of a work of literary art.' A recent writer on the same theme has accused Mr Beardsley of having, in 1958, weakened this thesis by asserting merely that the 'specific intention' of the artist outside the work is 'practically never available'—thus, it would appear, making the question only empirical and forfeiting its 'theoretical' and 'philosophical' status.[48] What we meant in 1946, and what in effect I think we managed to say, was that the closest one could ever get to the artist's intending or meaning mind, outside his work, would be still short of his *effective* intention or *operative* mind as it appears in the work itself and can be read from the work. Such is the concrete and fully answerable character of words as aesthetic medium.[49] The intention outside the poem is always subject to the corroboration of the poem itself. No better evidence, in the nature of things, can be adduced than the poem itself. This observation seems to me less needed in meeting the directly evaluative form of the argument (see above, pp. 207–10) than in meeting the interpretive form which we have just been considering. The statement in our essay of 1946 should certainly have read: 'The design or intention of the author is neither available nor desirable as a standard for judging either the meaning or the value of a work of literary art.'

We have never said that the way of the objective critic could be smooth, easy, or perfect. Still we have tried to delineate one of the principles by which this critic will have to discipline his efforts unless he wishes to surrender to the flux, the gossip, the muddle and the 'motley' for which philosophers like Dr Cioffi, Professor Aldridge, and Mr Cruttwell seem so earnestly to yearn.

It is true that verbal compositions do not subsist metaphysically, by or in themselves, as visual words on paper. The difference between 'inside' the poem and 'outside' the poem (to which some of our critics object[50]) is not like the difference between the printed words and the margin of the page. But neither are verbal compositions merely passing acts or moments of the human spirit, sounds heard then or now but not again. The words have their peculiar existence in their meaning, and that derives from and is determined by their context or their history. The study of poems in their public contexts of language and culture sees them in a spread-out and universalized relation to those contexts. It is a study of pattern and ideal and is the only study which is capable of discriminating between the cogently organized artistic structure (both concrete and universal) and the mere particularities of personal moments, accidental and nonce meanings. What kind of unity or entity is the most valid object of literary study ? Roughly, there are three possible answers : the Age, the Author, the Work. Various kinds of interest in race, milieu, and moment (so familiar to academic literary criticism for more than two centuries) come under the first head. Studies of literary genre come here when they get out of hand, and also the more extreme instances of deference to the historical audience.[51] One kind of ultimate metaphysician in favor of the author may be found in Benedetto Croce, who hardly believes in the literary work at all, certainly not in works of any length, but sees the whole duty of the critic as the pursuit of the 'poetical motive,' the 'poetic personality' which he can find anthologically here and there in writers like Goethe, Corneille, and Dante. A newer sort of canonical historicist, as we have seen, makes the idolatrous assumption that a given author's mind or vision during his whole career is necessarily a coherent whole or a dialectic development, as good an entity as, or better than, any one of his works. For the objective critic of literary works, an author has as much unity as he can demonstrate in any given work or in a part of a work. The whole for which the critic looks is the coherently expressive structure, large or small. The poet's canon and life are 'the most essential part of the content of the poem'[52] only to the extent that the poet is talking to himself. The words which the poet writes in a given passage depend for their meaning in one sense on the personal context and the author's intention (his word as *parole*), but they depend also, in a sense more important to the critic, on the wider context of the language (his words as *langue*) and culture.[53] Otherwise they would never, here and now, there and then, make sense to anybody but the author himself. Authors characteristically graduate from earlier, naïve stages and write masterpieces. Characteristically also they write later weaker works. To appreciate *Lear* and *Hamlet* it is not necessary to take into account *A Comedy of Errors* or *Timon of Athens* (or such parts of the latter as Shakespeare wrote) or even *The Tempest*. The search for the author's generative intention as context of the poem is a search for a temporal moment which must, as the author and the poem live on, recede and ever recede into the forgotten, as all moments do. Poems, on this theory of their meaning, must always steadily grow less and less correctly known and knowable; they must dwindle in meaning and being toward a vanishing point. The best known and most valuable poem must be that written but a moment ago—and its best or only possible audience must be the author. But poems we know are not really like that. The most self-assured authors publish their works and hang upon public recognition. Shakespeare has more meaning and value now than he had in his own day. There is a sense in which even Homer, though we construe his language with pain and are not sure how many persons he was. has more meaning and is more valuable today than ever before.

MORSE PECKHAM

The Intentional? Fallacy?

Nowadays in literary academic circles one hears with increasing frequency such remarks as, 'The New Criticism is a dead issue,' or 'The New Critics have had their day; it's all over with.' However, a more accurate statement of the current condition is that the tenets of the New Criticism have so deeply entered current teaching, scholarship, and criticism that, if the issues are dead, it is only because the New Critical solution to those issues has completely triumphed. Certainly, the more sophisticated undergraduate and graduate students I have recently encountered now take as self-evident attitudes which only a generation ago were heatedly argued against by what used to be called the old-fashioned biographical critic. Of the various bits of critical jargon which were once, at any rate, worth fighting about, perhaps the most commonly encountered is the 'intentional fallacy.'

The first of two famous articles by Professor Monroe C. Beardsley, then at Yale, now of the Swarthmore Philosophy Department, and Professor W. K. Wimsatt, Jr., of the Yale English Department, 'The Intentional Fallacy,' was published in the *Sewanee Review*, Vol. LIV (Summer, 1946). At the time that journal was one of the most distinguished and conspicuous places to publish any discussion of literary criticism or any performance of it, and the phrase entered the language of criticism with the utmost rapidity. A good many regarded that essay, and still regard it, as the clincher for the validity of the New Criticism. It has been reprinted several times in anthologies of criticism and aesthetics, and in 1954 it was collected with its companion, 'The Affective Fallacy,' in Wimsatt's *The Verbal Icon*, published by the University of Kentucky Press. As such things go, it is now a generation old and a critical classic.

Everybody knows, of course, what the phrase means, or at least what he thinks it means; but I daresay a good many people might be a little puzzled if they actually read the essay, for I know from diligent inquiry that a great many who use the term have never read the paper from which it comes. However, Professor E. D. Hirsch is one critic who has read it recently, and it is instructive to observe what he says about it in his recent book *Validity in Interpretation* (New Haven, 1967).

The critic of the arguments in that essay is faced with the problem of distinguishing between the essay itself and the popular use that has been made of it, for what is widely taken for granted as established truth was not argued in that essay and could not have been successfully argued in the essay. Although Wimsatt and Beardsley carefully distinguished between three types of intentional evidence, acknowledging that two of them are proper and admissible, their careful distinctions and qualifications have now vanished in the popular version which consists in the false and facile dogma that what an author intended is irrelevant to the meaning of his text (p. 11).

I admire Hirsch's book, but it has serious weaknesses, and this discussion of the intentional fallacy is among its least convincing sections. He has excellently expressed what he calls 'the popular version' in the title of the section in which the discussion occurs, 'It Does Not Matter What an Author Means.' The question is, is there any justification in the original essay for this 'popular version' ?

To begin with, I must say that I do not find 'The Intentional Fallacy' either clear, well argued, or coherent. Indeed many of the authors' fundamental propositions are not argued at all. They are merely asserted, by fiat. The essay's success can only be accounted for by the fact that its dogmatisms were uttered in a situation in which a great many people were prepared to accept them without argument. If the 'popular version' has indeed been mistaken, it is perhaps because the mere title was enough for a good many critics, teachers, and students; it said all they wanted to have said; it summed up the doctrine of the New Criticism in a brilliant phrase which also gave fairly precise directions for the kind of verbal response one should make to a poem in interpreting it. Actually, the essay is rather careless, and so is Hirsch's account of it. For example, he asserts that the authors 'carefully distinguished between three types of intentional evidence.' It is not nit-picking to point out that the authors do *not* distinguish between three types of intentional evidence. Rather, they distinguish between three types of 'internal and external evidence for the meaning of a poem,' and they assert that one of these types, the biographical, which they call external, private, and idiosyncratic, 'need not involve intentionalism,' but that it usually has, to the distortion of poetic interpretation. That is, when Hirsch writes 'three types of intentional evidence,' he has ascribed 'intentional' to three types of evidence which Beardsley and Wimsatt specifically said were not intentional evidence.

This shows not only that Hirsch was so over-eager to prove that it is correct to talk about intention that he missed the Beardsley-

Wimsatt point but also that the essay is easily misunderstood, or at least that it needs to be read with great care. There is, moreover, another reason for bringing up Hirsch. His book is, I believe, going to be widely read and will have a very great influence. It is undeniably an important work. No doubt his version of the Beardsley-Wimsatt essay will be pretty generally accepted as authoritative. Without wishing, therefore, to impugn the value of his work, I think it is of some importance to determine whether or not what Hirsch calls the false and facile popular version of 'The Intentional Fallacy' has any justification in the essay itself, and this will serve also to begin an attack on what is a very vexing problem.

Professor Hirsch has subsumed the notion that 'what an author intended is irrelevent to the meaning of his text' under the doctrine of 'semantic autonomy.' It is a good phrase, and I shall adopt it. Beardsley and Wimsatt exemplify it when they write that 'the design or intention of the author is neither available nor desirable as a standard for judging the success of a work of literary art.' (For 'work of literary art' I shall henceforth use the term 'poem.') Thus their primary interest is in evaluation, not in interpretation; but their argument amounts to the proposition that intention is irrelevant to evaluation because it is irrelevant to interpretation. At several points in the essay this assumption of the irrelevance of intention comes out very strongly. For example, 'In this respect poetry differs from practical messages, which are successful if and only if we correctly infer the intention.' Thus it is evident that, according to Beardsley and Wimsatt, the semantic functions of poetry are to be distinguished from those of ordinary language. Again, poetry (. . . is detached from the author at birth and goes about the world beyond his power to intend about it or control it). The poem belongs to the public. It is embodied in language, the peculiar possession of the public.' This last would seem to indicate that poetry is not, after all, distinguishable from ordinary language, until we note that the 'poem is embodied in language.' This certainly seems to indicate that it is other than language. Further, if practical messages require that we infer the intention it would seem that practical messages are not beyond the power of their utterers to intend about them or control them. Moreover, our authors say in a note, 'And the history of words *after* a poem is written may contribute meanings which if relevant to the original pattern should not be ruled out by a scruple about intention.' From other statements we glean that 'pattern' here means 'pattern of meanings,' for 'Poetry is a feat of style by which a complex of meaning is handled all at once.' It would certainly be strange for practical messages—in which the authors include such kinds of discourse as science—to be open to new semantic functions. This note, then, seems coherent with the doctrine of semantic autonomy. Finally, at the end of the essay they write that to ask Eliot what *Prufrock* means 'would not be a critical inquiry.' To ask a poet what he meant would be 'consulting the oracle,' a superstitious act, presumably. At any rate, it cannot settle a critical inquiry having to do with exegesis.

All this, then, is coherent with the first quotation, which asserts that for practical messages it is legitimate to inquire for the author's intention. It is evident that we do indeed have here an instance of semantic autonomy and that the notion that this famous essay is an exemplification of that doctrine is correct. Hirsch is mistaken in thinking that the doctrine of Beardsley and Wimsatt is different from the popular version. By Hirsch's standards they stand condemned of the 'false and facile dogma that what an author intended is irrelevant to the meaning of his text.' The popular version is, after all, the correct one.

It is not difficult to refute the doctrine of semantic autonomy. It can be put in the form of asserting that poetry has unique semantic functions, different from those of all other kinds of linguistic utterance. It is evident that, in its radical form, this is not an historical or cultural statement: it does not mean, for example, that in a given cultural epoch poets are, as it were, assigned a class of message that they and they alone are privileged to deliver. No, the poem is embodied in language; presumably, then, either in practical messages something nonpoetic is embodied, and this gives poetry semantic autonomy, or it means that the mode of embodiment is unique, or at least different from the mode of embodiment to be found in practical messages, which is ordinarily taken to mean all nonpoetic messages. In this kind of criticism, as in the essay under consideration, the distinction is ordinarily confused, and perhaps it is unimportant; nevertheless, it is a distinction worth noting for what follows. In either case, however, the consequence is that the critic is privileged, or perhaps required, to employ a special kind of interpretation, called in this essay poetic 'exegesis.' That is, since poetry has semantic autonomy, there is a corresponding interpretive autonomy. Whether or not this kind of interpretation differs from the interpretational modalities used to interpret all other kinds of discourse depends upon the demonstration that there is a distinction between the two. But that in turn depends upon a basis for the interpretation, namely a general theory of interpretation. But such a general theory of interpretation does not exist. There is, therefore, at the present time no way of demonstrating either interpretive autonomy or semantic autonomy for poetry.

Futhermore, if the language of semantic autonomy differs from ordinary language, it would seem to follow that the language of interpretive autonomy differs from the language of ordinary interpretation. It is the objectors to the New Criticism and to semantic autonomy who claim that the New Critics offer not interpretation but another poem. The latter have always vehemently denied this, thus asserting that the validity of interpretive autonomy is not different from the validity, whatever it may be, of any mode of interpretation. Our authors give an example of this. In objecting to a scholarly interpretation of a metaphor by Donne, they assert that, 'To make the geocentric and heliocentric antithesis the core of the metaphor is to disregard the English language, to prefer private evidence to public, external to internal.' One of their points is that 'moving of the earth' is antithetical to 'trepidation of the spheres,' not parallel, as their target, Charles Coffin, would have it. Assuming that Coffin is wrong, as I too think he is, it is impossible to use this disagreement for their theoretical purposes. Coffin may have been carried away by his learning and may have violated common sense in making this mistake; but it is only a mistake. 'Moving of the earth' can be explained in terms of the Copernican hypothesis, even though it may be wrong to do so here. Galileo is said to have said that, after all, the earth does move, though he was speaking Italian; and it seems quite fantastic to maintain that the geocentric and heliocentric theories are private evidence. The point of all this is that in arguing against Coffin, Beardsley and Wimsatt use the same kind of language that he does, the same kind of evidence, public knowledge, and the same kind of interpretive mode. To assert that a man has failed is not to assert that his method is in error, though Beardsley and Wimsatt seem to think so.

There are other ways of showing the impossibility of the doctrine of semantic autonomy, but is it much more instructive to examine and if possible to understand what kind of doctrine it is. It is probable that today Professor Beardsley would consider the proposition that a poem is embodied in language as exceedingly incautious, and it is possible that Professor Wimsatt would feel the same way, but we may be grateful for the statement, for it tells us a good deal. The notion of something suprasensible being embodied in something sensible—for both written and spoken words are phenomenal and sensible—has an irresistibly transcendental ring about it. One could say that all they mean by this is that something originally in the mind of the poet is now embodied in language, but their own position, of course, forbids them to take this way out: it would throw them back on intentionalism. Now, anyone familiar with Christian doctrine can recognize the embodiment thesis as structurally identical with the theory of transubstantiation. Since, however, these days very few are familiar with the thesis of transubstantiation, including a good many professing and practicing Christians, it may be well to define it. It is the thesis that in the celebration of the mass the substance of the bread and the wine become changed to the body and the blood of Christ, though their accidents, such as taste, color, smell, and so on, remain the same. Thus the consecrated bread and wine belong, after this metamorphosis, to a unique category of physical substances.

The structural analogy to the doctrine of the semantic autonomy of poetry is remarkable. A suprasensible quality, poetry, is embodied in a sensible quality, language, and the result is a unique category of language, which requires a unique kind of interpretation. Carlstadt asserted that the bread and wine could not possibly be put into a unique category of physical substances, and that the Lord's Supper was a commemorative rite. Zwingli adopted this thesis, but Luther developed the theory of consubstantiation; the substance and accidents are not changed but a quality is added, as heat is added to an iron bar. In terms of the structural analogy proposed this changes little or nothing; the doctrine of semantic autonomy asserts also that a suprasensible quality is added to a sensible quality. It is noteworthy that the clear-sighted Erasmus felt that the Zwinglian position was irrefutable, but preferred the old doctrine for the sake of peace.

The argument that Carlstadt originated and Zwingli and Oecolampadius and their followers accepted was in fact an instance of semantic analysis, and quite an elegant one. The argument centered on the word 'is' in such Gospel passages as that found in Matt. 26: 26–28. 'And as they were eating, Jesus took bread and blessed it, and brake it, and gave it to the disciples, and said, Take, eat; this is my body. And he took the cup, and gave thanks and gave it to them, saying, Drink ye all of it; for this is my blood of the new testament, which is shed for many for the remission of sins.' The new position claimed that in such phrases as 'this is my body' and 'this is my blood' the word 'is' should properly be interpreted as 'is a sign of,' rather than, as in the orthodox interpretation, 'has become in a unique mode.' Using the language that is here under question, the reformers were claiming that it was the intention of Jesus that his act should not be so interpreted, while the orthodox claimed that Jesus' intention was as they had defined it. This analysis suggests that to call upon 'intention' is a way of explaining and justifying an interpretation rather than a way of using knowledge of intention to control an interpretation. The possibility arises that Beardsley and Wimsatt, in distinguishing language that requires inference of intention from language that does not, have failed to make a sufficiently exacting analysis of the term 'intention.'

To this possibility I shall return. At the moment I would only remark that for the phrase 'the doctrine of semantic autonomy' it would be reasonable to substitute 'the doctrine of semantic real presence.' This is a metaphor, of course, but that does not necessarily mean that it is a falsification of the semantic state of affairs we find here. Whether theologically correct or not, the reformers were claiming that the orthodox were indulging in bad thinking because the doctrine of transubstantiation was an example of ascribing to the sign of something the attributes of the thing itself. In this case, since the thing itself has ceased to exist—the episode of the last supper having had an historical existence—the body and blood said to be in the bread and wine as a consequence of transubstantiation have no existence. The reformers' denial of transubstantiation amounted to the assertion that the orthodox had made a logical error and had hypostatized or reified the nonexistent referent of a pair of words. Likewise, by the doctrine of semantic real presence, as applied in the assertion that a poem is embodied in language, Beardsley and Wimsatt have hypostatized the term 'poem.' Having done so, and having decided that poetry has certain attributes and not others, they then ascribed those attributes to a category of utterances. Thus the doctrines of transubstantiation and of semantic autonomy are instances of the same kind of thinking, or, to be a bit more precise, of semantic behaviour. Consequently it is a justifiable metaphor to call the doctrine of semantic autonomy the doctrine of semantic real presence.

What kind of thinking is it ? In magic we can see the same semantic behavior at work, or at least in certain kinds. Take the old standby, the wax image to which you give your enemy's name and which you stick full of pins and knives. Here again we have the sign, the ascription to the sign of the attributes of the thing signified, and behaving accordingly, that is, placing it in a special category of physical substances, or, as in semantic autonomy, verbal signs. On the whole this kind of magic seems intellectually more respectable than does semantic autonomy. After all, the waxen sign is a sign of something, a living enemy, not a sign of a reified verbal sign, poetry. Now it is also worth noting that the practitioner of magic cannot be refuted. Either his enemy dies, in which case he killed him by stabbing his waxen sign, or his enemy lives, in which case he made a mistake in magical technique. If he lives longer than his enemy, and continues his magical technique, he is bound, sooner or later, to have proof that his magic is efficacious. Likewise, any conclusion arrived at by the doctrine of semantic autonomy cannot be refuted. The easiest way to grasp this is to remind oneself of how frequently one sees it asserted that all interpretations of a poem are equally valid, the criterion being 'interesting,' rather than 'true' or more or less 'adequate.'

Structurally, then, transubstantiation and semantic autonomy are instances of magic. Consequently, the doctrine of semantic autonomy in poetry may be justly called the magical theory of poetry. It is, however, useful to consider all three as examples of the same kind of semiotic behavior and look for a more general statement of that. I think it may be found in the theory of immanent meaning, which is undoubtedly the universal theory, a theory which we are only beginning to see through. It is simply the thesis that words mean, or, alternatively, have meaning. Even so sophisticated a philosophical position as logical positivism accepted this position, as the famous attempt to distinguish between metaphysical or emotional statements and empirical statements witnesses. The former were said to be meaningless, and the latter to have meaning, or to be meaningful. Meaning was said to be immanent in the latter, but not in the former. The inadequacy of this position comes out when we glance at the word 'reference.' Words are said to have reference. But when I say, 'Look at the ceiling,' you look at the ceiling, the sentence does not.

It is not difficult to see how the notion of immanent reference should arise. When I generate an overt utterance, and tell you to look at the ceiling, you perform an act of reference, but you do it in response to my instructions. It is a verbal shorthand, therefore, to say that I have referred to the ceiling. But since my utterance is, among its other semantic functions, a sign of me, by another similar slip the act of reference is imputed to the utterance. Or it can go from your reference to the utterance to me, and by 'it' I mean the chain of ascribing to the sign of something the attributes of that which it signifies. Thus you have attributed your attribute of reference first to me and then to the utterance, or first to the utterance and then to me.

Human beings, then, refer; words do not. Words are signs to which, on interpretation, we respond by various modes of behavior, verbal and nonverbal. The meaning of a bit of language is the behavior which is consequent upon responding to it. Therefore, *any* response to a discourse is *a* meaning of that discourse. That is why an interpretation arrived at on the basis of semantic autonomy cannot be invalidated. However, language is a matter of conventions. Thus the correct meaning of an utterance is the consequent behavior which, for whatever reasons, is considered appropriate in the situation in which the utterance is generated. For example, if I say, 'There is no God,' and my respondent says, 'That is a meaningless utterance,' the response amounts to a claim that it is impossible that there should exist a situation in which any response at all could be appropriate, except for this response.

Let me sum up this position dogmatically, though not without leaning a bit on authority. Forty years ago Grace Andrus de Laguna, of Bryn Mawr College, published her *Speech: Its Function and Development*, a work which, long neglected, has been reissued and is being given serious attention. Her basic proposition is that both the animal cry and speech 'perform the same fundamental function of *coördinating the activities of the members of the group.*' To put it another way, all that the generator of an utterance can do is present a set of instructions for behavior, either his own or another's; and all the responder to an utterance can do is to follow those instructions, or not follow them. That is, if he knows how to interpret those instructions he can if he so decides, behave in accordance with what in that situation is the conventionalized appropriate responsible behavior. I tell you to look at the ceiling; you look at the floor. You have obeyed only part of my instructions. I tell you to look at the ceiling; you fold your arms and glare at me. Have you disobeyed all of my instructions ? Not at all. Any linguistic utterance is first of all an instruction to respond. That response to an instruction is so deeply built into your biological equipment that you cannot possibly avoid it. We may discern, then, three kinds of response to any utterance: inappropriate response, partially appropriate response, appropriate response. These are the meanings of an utterance.

At first glance it may seem that I am about to assert that the doctrine of semantic autonomy opens the way to justifying any inappropriate response. Not at all, and for these reasons. The error of immanent meaning is, for the vast majority of human interactions, not an error at all, or rather is an error of not the slightest importance. When we say, 'This is the real meaning of that utterance,' we are simply responding to the conventions of appropriateness for the situation in which we respond to the utterance. Obviously, then, uncertainty about meaning arises when the conventions are unknown, are imperfectly known, or are disregarded. But why should they ever be disregarded? Once the magical theory of language has taken root, as it has in all living humans who have progressed through infancy, any utterance becomes a sign the response to which entails conforming one's behaviour to a set of conventions appropriate to a situation. Thus, in any sign response there are two ingredients, the sign and the conventionalized behavior patterns. By the magical theory of language, or immanent meaning, we ascribe to the sign the attributes of those behaviors. Thus, in responding to a sign we neglect the complementary circumstance that we are responding to a sign and its situation. To put it another way, the sign on which we focus is but one of many situational signs; it is but one in a constellation of signs. Since all signs are polysemous, that is, since all signs can be, theoretically, responded to by all possible behaviors, the only limit being the conventions we have learned, the sign on which we focus loses its compelling and unitary function to the degree to which we neglect the other signs in the situational constellation of signs. Without trying to trace the history of human semiotic evolution, it is sufficient to point out that the written language preserves an utterance long after the situation in which it was uttered has ceased to exist; this is what Zwingli and his reformers were trying to do, restore the situation in which Jesus' statements about the bread and the wine originally took place and determine their semantic function, that is, the appropriate behavior in response to his words according to the conventions of that situation. Conversely, human beings have the power of imagination, the capacity to create strings of verbal signs to which neither nonverbal response is possible nor nonverbal or verbal response is possible. From that it is but a step to a kind of discourse to which nonverbal overt response is possible but not appropriate. And from there it is but another step to discourse to which overt nonverbal response is currently unknown but for which its situational constellation instructs us to attempt to discover appropriate and overt nonverbal response, as with a scientific theory, with its concomitant situational and conventional instruction to devise an experiment to confirm or disconfirm it.

Thus there are numerous situations in human affairs in which the constellation of supporting situational signs is missing, are conventionally in part disregarded, never existed, or are unconsciously responded to. And here by 'unconscious' I mean all signs not focused on, or, more precisely, all signs the attributes of which have been ascribed to another sign or other signs. To respond to a situation thoroughly means to focus in turn on all the signs in that situation, determine whether or not they are appropriate, and to reascribe to each sign its appropriate attributes. Thus, if we go into a chapel to pray and to experience emotional relief as a consequence, a thorough examination of the situation will show that the emotional relief experienced is a consequence of responding not only to the prayer but also to all the religious signs of the setting in which we have played the suppliant's role. Consequently, I do not assert that the use of the doctrine of immanent meaning, or magical meaning, or semantic real presence, or semantic autonomy in interpreting poetry opens the way to any inappropriate response. It is not quite trivial to point out that any interpretive response is, for poetry, frequently, though not always, appropriate. (Some would assert that it is never appropriate.) Nor is it at all trivial to point out that the semantic autonomist focuses on only a very limited number of verbal signs. Even when in theory he claims that a proper interpretation must necessarily provide a unitary explanation for all terms in the poem, in practice he neglects a great many. Furthermore, his interpretation of a good many words such as articles, prepositions, and conjunctions usually conforms to the conventions of interpretation for those terms. In fact, he is usually so taken with the free-wheeling possibilities for novel interpretations of nouns and verbs, with lesser attention to adjectives and adverbs, that he suffers from a singular paucity of seeing alternative possibilities for the lesser words as well as for syntactical relations. This is not surprising. A theory of immanent meaning inevitably leads to the neglect of the situational sign constellation, to, as it were, the neglect of focusing on focusing; the consequence is a compulsive ascription of attributes from what is signified to the sign focused on.

At this point something of a digression may illuminate what I am trying to say and provide a bit of relief from these dreadful abstractions. Professor Hirsch begins his *Validity in Interpretation* with a quotation from Northrop Frye, the source of which, unfortunately, he does not give us. It goes as follows: 'It has been said of Boehme that his books are like a picnic to which the author brings the words and the reader the meaning. The remark may have been intended as a sneer at Boehme, but it is an exact description of all works of literary art without exception.' It is clear that this statement enrages Professor Hirsch. It enrages me, too; but I do not think that his reply to it is adequate. And his reply, alas, is his book. Certainly, Hirsch was well advised to pick Northrop Frye as his point of departure, for the *Anatomy of Criticism* terminated the theoretical development of the New Criticism, which to be sure was never very powerful. In that book Frye took the doctrine of semantic real presence to its absolute limits: all poems mean the same thing. After that one either decided that the central doctrine of the New Criticism was absurd, as Hirsch probably did; or one concluded that it was now so well protected, so thoroughly proved, that it was not longer arguable and was self-evident. Even if one did not agree with Frye on the thing that all poems mean, he provided a theoretical carte-blanche to make one's own thing that all poems mean.

However, Professor Hirsch has unfortunately attacked Frye and semantic autonomy from an outmoded position, and I fear that his book, for all its many excellencies, will not have the salutary effect I am sure he hoped for, and that I hoped for when I started reading it. For the unfortunate fact is that Frye is right, as far as he goes. He merely does not go far enough. Hirsch's whole effort is to prove that the author brings the meaning as well as the words, and he does as much with this thesis as, I think, is possible, or at least worthwhile. However, Frye's statement is correct if divested of the theory of semantic autonomy and rewritten as follows: 'It has been said of Boehme that his books are like a picnic to which the author brings the words and the reader the meaning. The remark may have been intended as a sneer at Boehme, but it is an exact description of *all linguistic utterances without exception.*'

Everything said here about the human response to signs points to one fact: the response to a sign requires on the responder's part a decision. To be sure, this statement may seem to need some qualification, and perhaps does. The rapidity of most responses to verbal and nonverbal signs alike certainly seems to indicate that the decision is immediate; that is, if by decision we mean those sign responses in which there is observable hesitation, as well as those in which alternatives are so fully explored that years may elapse before the response actually occurs, then it would indeed seem that the use of 'decision' to refer to apparently immediate responses is inaccurate. I think the point is arguable, but until we understand a great deal more than we do about brain physiology, there is little value in arguing it. It is enough to say that a sign which involves the responder in uncertainty requires a decision if it is to be responded to, and that any utterance encountered in a situation other than the one in which it was originally generated offers the possibility of uncertainty and hence decision, unless, as with the bread and the wine, it has been, according to Zwingli, made part of a new situational sign constellation. This explains why Beardsley and Wimsatt can assert that meanings that emerge after a poem is written should not be ruled out by a scruple of intention. Thus, though I do not know if the position has any theological respectability or has ever even appeared in the history of theology, it would be possible to say that what Jesus meant in his remarks to the apostles is irrelevant; and I rather suspect that Newman's idea of the growth of Christian doctrine entails just this, the explanation being that though the Apostles would not have interpreted the remarks as the theory of transubstantiation does, that theory was implicit in Christian doctrine from the moment of its revelation. Thus it is not surprising that Professor Beardsley in his *Aesthetics*, published in 1958, should say that a semantic definition of literature is that 'a literary work is a discourse in which an important part of the meaning is implicit' (p. 126). Such is the necessary consequence of any magical use of the theory of immanent meaning. And indeed Hirsch's discussion of 'implicit' is not one of his happier passages. In fact, with his fundamental notion that meaning is expression in language of a willed intention on the part of an utterer, it is evident that Hirsch also is working from a doctrine of immanent meaning. Thus, for all his efforts—and many of them are admirable and useful—he cannot dispose of the doctrine of semantic autonomy with complete and unequivocal success. This is what I mean when I assert that his book will not have the salutary effect he hopes for.

Poems that as teachers and students and critics we attempt to interpret do not fall in the same category as transubstantiation; an alternative semantic function has not been conventionalized in an historically emergent situation. We ask what the poem means. That is sufficient evidence for our purpose that uncertainty is present, and that a decision must be made. The poems we deal with were uttered in the past; the situations in which they were uttered are no longer existent. What are we to do ? We must make a decision about what is the appropriate verbal response. On what grounds are such decisions properly made ? That vast question I do not propose to answer here. My interest here is only to question the function of asking questions about the intention of the poet, and also to question the strategy of denying that such questions are in order when we interpret a poem.

Let us return to the point at which we started, the Beardsley-Wimsatt proposal that for one category of discourse it is improper to ask questions about intention, but for another category we must 'correctly infer the intention.' It would seem, therefore, that there are such things as correct intentional statements, and that it is possible to locate something properly called 'intention.' What is the status, then, of statements about intention ? As we have seen, all a statement can do is give instructions for responsive behavior. What we call a referential statement—whether it be a book or a word—gives instructions for locating a phenomenal configuration. But it is not so easy as that. All signs are categorial. Thus a referential statement instructs us to locate a category of configurations. To instruct us to infer correctly the intention of the speaker of a particular utterance is to instruct us to locate a specific member of a category. Language, then, apparently can be specific in this qualified sense. But it must be observed that specificity is achieved, and a categorial member located, only because that particular member shares attributes with other members of the same category. Further, it is possible to tell one member from another only if the instructional statement includes other categorial instructions. Here the good old game of fish, flesh, or fowl is helpful, as is the recently deceased 'What's My Line ?' The person or persons having to guess the correct word proceed, within certain rules, by piling up categories the partially shared attributes of which gradually eliminate all but one specific term. In locating nonverbal specificities we proceed in the same way. On the other hand, interlocking categories need not be included in the instruction if the respondent is previously trained to do the locating without such instructions. If I say to someone in a room, 'Bring me the chair,' he would be at a loss to know which one I meant. However, if my instructions were to bring me the chair which is the darkest in color, the interlocking categories of chair, color, and shade would make it possible to respond appropriately to my instructions, even though I myself did not yet know which chair corresponded to these specifications. Likewise, one member of a group can respond correctly to a simple, 'Bring me the chair,' if at some previous time I have instructed him sufficiently in the interlocking categories necessary for his appropriate response.

Beardsley and Wimsatt, then, have instructed us to infer the intention of a speaker. Thus in the situation just outlined an already instructed member of the audience infers that when I say, 'Bring me the chair,' his appropriate response is to take to me the previously designated chair. Now a problem arises, first, if it is the case that in my judgment his response is in fact inappropriate, and that my response to his action is to assert, 'I didn't mean you, blockhead'; and second, if the speaker of the instructions is no longer present in the situation in which the utterance is responded to. The normal test for appropriate behaviour—the response of the speaker of the uttered instructions—is under these conditions impossible. Inference, therefore, is a term used to categorize this last kind of situation, one in which the instructions for response are incomplete and the authoritative judge of appropriateness of response is no longer present. What is the appropriate response in a situation of this sort, one which is characterized by uncertainty about what response is appropriate?

The Beardsley-Wimsatt proposal to infer the intention of a speaker seems at first glance to be a referential statement. It seems to instruct us to locate something, namely an intention. The word 'intention' is like such words as 'will,' 'desire,' 'meaning,' and 'purpose.' They are said to be mental activities; they are supposed to occur in the mind. However, if, as we have seen, all terms are categorial and cannot bear a specific reference to a unique phenomenal configuration, then the status of the mind as such a phenomenal configuration is called in doubt. Indeed, when we ask what the mind is we are often given a list of its attributes, such as will, desire, meaning, purpose, and so on; and these are said to be the mind's contents. But this is nothing but a spatial metaphor, and these terms are but the attributes of the verbal category 'mind.' We may see this from another point of view. Every semiotic response involves interpretation, since we do not respond to a meaning immanent in the sign; and one of the most obvious things in the world is interpretational variability, the easily and constantly observed phenomenon that two people in the identical situation, judging by their overt responses, have interpreted that situation's signs differently. That is, all the word 'interpretation' does is to draw attention to the actuality and possibility of difference of response to a given sign, or, more generally, to difference in sign response. 'Mind,' then, categorizes all responsive activity which exhibits differences in sign response, that is, for reasons suggested earlier, all responsive activity, which is all activity. The word 'mind' then is a category which ascribes to human beings, at least, behavioral differences in the same situation. And words like 'will,' 'desire,' 'meaning,' 'purpose,' and 'intention' are terms which discriminate various sub-categories of behavioral difference. It follows, then, that the Beardsley-Wimsatt proposal to infer the intention of a speaker is not a referential statement; it does not and cannot give us instructions to locate a phenomenal configuration. If they believe it can, they are guilty of that common consequence of the theory of immanent meaning, hypostatization.

What kind of instruction, then, *is* their proposal ? What *would* be an appropriate response ? Some utterances instruct us to locate phenomenal configurations, to be sure; but others instruct us to generate verbal behavior. Such responses are the most mysterious and fascinating that human beings perform. Since language is tied to the world only by behavior, when the response to a generated utterance is only to generate another verbal response, it is not tied to the world at all, or at best only at various points, most frequently at the beginning of a chain of utterances, and, hopefully, at the end. One semantic function of the term 'mind' is precisely to draw attention to this transcendence of the world by language. It is not mind that is metaphysical but language, and it can be said with justice that all language, by itself, is metaphysical. It is not, then, that language is the product of the mind; 'linguistic behavior' is one semantic function of the word 'mind.'

To see what kind of instructions Beardsley and Wimsatt have given us in their proposal that for practical messages we infer the intention it is only necessary to examine the ordinary use of the word 'intention' from this orientation. When in ordinary circumstances, that is, situations in which the speaker of the utterance we are responding to is actually present, we ask the speaker what he meant

when we do not understand the utterance, that is, when we are uncertain as to what verbal or nonverbal response we should offer in
response to his utterance, ordinarily he will give us additional instructions; this is one mode of explanation. 'Bring me the chair!'
'What do you mean?' 'Pick up that chair, which is the darkest color
in the room, and bring it to me!' But instead of answering, 'What do
you mean?' we could elicit the same response, or get the same set of
additional instructions, by asking, 'What do you intend me to do?'
or 'What is your intention?' We will have, then, a general understanding of the term 'intention' if we recognize that it instructs us
how to categorize a certain kind of explanation, one given in response to a demand for additional instructions. But what does intention instruct us to do if the original speaker is not present? This
is a more subtle problem.

Let us imagine that when I ask you to bring me a chair, instead of
asking me what my intention is, you turn to a neighbor and ask him,
'What does he mean? What does he intend me to do? What is his
intention?' Let us assume that the neighbor has privileged information and gives the answer I gave when I was asked. Supposing that
you carry out the instructions, make the appropriate response. When
it comes to judging that appropriateness, which, as we have seen, is
the only way possible to judge whether or not the response is correct,
does the neighbor's statement of intention have as much authority as
mine? Perhaps so, since we defined him as having privileged information, that is, information I gave him. However, if he does not
have the information, but generates his intentional statement from
his interpretation of the situation, including his prior knowledge of
the sort of thing I am likely to say in such situations, does his statement of intention now have as much authority as mine? Again, in
terms of your response, yes; but possibly no, since at first glance it
would seem that I must know my intention better than he could.
Supposing now that you ask me, as you probably feel like doing,
what my intention is in going through all this analytical rigmarole
merely to demolish a position which by my account I have long since
demolished? Presumably my answer—and at the end of this paper
I shall offer an answer—is a report on what I intended to do when I
set out to write this paper. This means, first, that I must have stated
my intention to myself, because 'intention' categorizes a class of
statement, and second, that I consider that I have carried it out, that
I have obeyed those self-directing instructions. Now as it happens in
this particular instance the statement of intention I shall give as my
conclusion was not generated as covert verbal behavior before I
began to write but occurred to me only after the above question

about my intention had occurred to me as a very sensible question to ask.

We may speak of two kinds of intention. One is accessible, a class of instructions or a class of explanations, that is, further instructions. But psychic intention is inaccessible. It happens, whatever it is, between the stimulus and response; it is responsible for those variations in interpretation and behavior which 'mind' in one of its semantic functions categorizes. But in the sense that 'mind' refers to what happens between stimulus and response, it is a word that we use as a bridge to cross an abyss of absolute ignorance. But furthermore, in actual behavior, psychic intention is doubly inaccessible. When we seem to be reporting on psychic intention we are in fact reporting on an historical event; the psychic intention happened before our statement about it, which we take to be a report on it. But, as we all know, historical events are phenomenally no longer existent. Whatever we say about them is not a report but a linguistic construct of a report of an event, and, for psychic intention, an inaccessible event.

Suppose you say to me, 'It is obvious from the tone of your paper that your deliberate intention was to bore me to distraction while confusing me.' Whether I agree with you or disagree, my answer will be, like yours, an explanation of a verbally constructed historical event, not of a phenomenally existent event. That is, both of us have responded to the ongoing situation; we have interpreted that situation; and we have offered an explanation of what is happening in that situation. That is, when you surmise a psychic intention that occurred in the past and I say that I am reporting such a psychic intention, neither of us is doing either of these. We are both making an historical construct in order to provide an explanation for the discourse we are currently encountering. Hence it follows that 'to infer an intention' means to make a linguistic construct of an historical situation so that by responding to the semiotic constellation of that constructed situation we may gain additional instructions for deciding the appropriate verbal response to an utterance to which our initial response was decisional uncertainty. And this is true whether the utterance under consideration was originally uttered two minutes ago or two thousand years ago. The difference is one of relative difficulty, not of kind of behavior. Briefly, an inference of intention is a way of accounting for or explaining the generation of an utterance; it can never be a report. The speaker of an utterance has greater authority than anybody else in his so-called intentional inference only because he is likely to have more information for framing his historical construct, *not* because he generated the utterance.

From this point of view it is not difficult to understand what has happened when you assert that my intention was so-and-so, and I respond, 'I wasn't aware of it, but I guess you're right; indeed, as I think the matter over, I'm sure you are right. What you are saying *was* my unconscious intention.' In such cases I am simply admitting that your responsiveness to the reconstructed situation is superior to mine. The very fact that such chains of linguistic utterance can occur indicates that it is only probable that an utterer has superior authority in generating an intentional explanation; it is never certain; it is, then, always a matter for investigation, never for *a priori* fiat.

It is now possible to see with some clarity, I hope, the kind of error that Beardsley and Wimsatt have made. It is not merely that the doctrine of semantic autonomy is an error; just as important is their error in thinking that it is *ever* possible to locate an historical psychic intention. The inference of intention is an attempt to provide additional instructions for determining our response to the stimulus of a verbal utterance when we are uncertain. Even so fantastic an instance of providing additional instructions for interpreting poetic utterances as the *Anatomy of Criticism* is only that: an attempt to provide additional instructions. The doctrine of semantic autonomy, untenable on other grounds, is also untenable because it attempts to assert by *a priori* fiat that a certain class of additional instructions is, for the interpretation of poetry, inadmissible. But such a distinction is untenable because both semantic autonomous interpretation and so-called intentional interpretation do nothing more than construct a situation in order to derive additional instructions. And the failure of the Beardsley-Wimsatt distinction comes out in several places. It shows up in their attack on Charles Coffin, the interpreter of Donne, in which they confuse a theoretical error with a simple mistake; and again in their denial that the author is an oracle who can settle problems of interpretation. As we have seen, the generator of an utterance only has a pragmatic and probable superior access to information; he is not, by the mere fact of being the author, in a position of superior authority. It emerges in their assertion that 'even a short lyric poem is dramatic, the response of a speaker to a situation. We ought to impute the thoughts and attitudes of the poem immediately to the dramatic *speaker*, and if to the author at all, only by an act of biographical inference'; as we have seen in our analysis of the neighbor's instructions, the author of any statement is always, from the point of view of the responder, a construct. That is, for every statement we always do what Beardsley and Wimsatt say we ought to do only in interpreting poetry. Finally it emerges in their avowed failure to make any sharp distinctions among their three kinds of evidence, and in their nearby statement that 'the use of biographical evidence need not involve intentionalism, because while it may be evidence of what the author intended, it may also be evidence of the meaning of his words and the dramatic character of his utterance.' The fact is that 'evidence of what the author intended' and 'evidence of the meaning of his words and the dramatic character of his utterance' are merely two different sets of verbal instructions for the same kind of verbal behavior.

Thus we may conclude, to put it broadly, that the trouble with 'The Intentional Fallacy' is that its authors are not talking about intention and it is not a fallacy. The doctrine of semantic autonomy, or semantic real presence, or semantic magic, or immanent meaning is untenable; and equally untenable is their attempt to distinguish between two kinds of interpretation. When we interpret poetry, we go through the same behavioral process that we go through when we interpret any utterance. Whether or not we use the word 'intention' in going through that process is not of the slightest importance.

o o o

Finally, let me offer an *ex post facto* statement of *my* intention in going through all this analytical rigmarole. This kind of analysis is, for me at least, very amusing and profitable to write. That it is tedious to read I would not attempt to deny—even for those who have a passionate interest in this kind of verbal analysis, even if that passionate interest has been a result, as mine has been, of a profound dissatisfaction with the confusion into which their training in the study of literature has plunged them. The unhappy fact is that the language of literary criticism is filled with unanalyzed terms, and for the most part it consists merely of pushing around worn-out verbal counters to create pretty new patterns; and this kind of intellectually unsatisfactory and even pointless activity will go on forever unless we put a stop to it. And the only way to stop it that I can see is to engage in the kind of excruciatingly painful, exacting, and wearisome verbal analysis which I have offered here as an example, if not a model, of what we must do. We have indulged ourselves for so long that penance for our sins cannot be anything but humiliating and dreary.

GEORGE WATSON
The Literary Past

Few arts in the English-speaking world today look so thriving and yet so unpretentious as the art of literary history. It is thriving in the plain sense that there is a great deal of it. Discoveries are certainly being made about the literary past, and at great speed. Literary history is demanded, commissioned, published and reprinted as never before. Its lack of pretension, which hardly amounts to a merit, lies in the contrasting circumstance that, in a serious intellectual sense, no one actively concerned with literary studies expects much of it. To expect today, as a European might reasonably have done a century ago, that a great intellectual discovery should be announced in a history of literature is plainly unlikely.

The sharp descent of literary history from the status of a great intellectual discipline to that of a convenient act of popularization can reasonably be dated to the years following the First World War. It is remarkable how suddenly, in the 1920s and after, the critical essay replaced the narrative form of literary history as the staple of literary study. The most influential arbiter of literary judgement in the English-speaking world in this century, T. S. Eliot, effected his revolution almost entirely through the mode of the brief essay, never writing a literary history of anything, mocking delicately at those who did, and willingly abandoning to lesser men the task of making connected sense of his own striking historical intuitions, such as the celebrated 'dissociation of sensibility' among English poets in the seventeenth century. I. A. Richards, who moved two generations to active literary controversy in the wake of Eliot, has chosen to write treatises rather than histories. Other decisive works like William Empson's *Seven Types of Ambiguity* (1930) or his *Structure of Complex Words* (1951) tend to be articulated series of essays rather than continuous narrative studies; and though history does not need to be narrative, it certainly presupposes an active concern with the priorities within the events it describes. *The Oxford History of English Literature*, which began to appear in 1945 as an ambitious attempt to recreate the achievement of the *Cambridge History* (1907–16), clearly suffers from the sudden lack of confidence that had overtaken literary history in the intervening decades; in an attempt to compromise with a sense of uncertainty, perhaps, it has adopted the practice of

---

reducing biographical information on individual authors to foot-notes, as if aware that the case for such information can no longer be assumed. And in 1946 an American journal published an article 'The Intentional Fallacy' by W. K. Wimsatt and Monroe C. Beardsley which formidably summarized the objections of a generation of New Critics, arguing that 'the design or intention of the author is neither available nor desirable as a standard for judging'. The question whether literary history remained a possibility if the study of the author's intention had to be abandoned remained, during the brief heyday of the New Criticism in the 1940s and 1950s, a matter for confused debate. But nobody doubted that the doctrine was somehow or other radically subversive of literary history in the traditional sense.

In this chapter I shall consider whether it could ever be possible, in the light of such familiar objections, to recover the tradition of a confident historiography of literature. Can one ever again write literary history, in the extended sense, that is not demonstrably wrong, in the sense that it is not contradicted by the present state of our knowledge of political and social history, of language, and of literature itself? And if so, could such literary history ever be more than trite, or could it ever again aspire to large and original contributions to human knowledge? Such questions may sound demoralizing. But they are meant at this point of the argument merely to sum up, with some mild exaggeration, the difference between the intellectual climates of the twentieth and the nineteenth centuries, when the composition of intellectual history—Ruskin on modern painters, Sainte-Beuve on the Pléiade and Port-Royal, Burckhardt on the Italian Renaissance, Buckle on the history of civilization, Nietzsche on the origins of tragedy, Frazer in the *Golden Bough*—could without affectation be numbered among the larger achievements of the human mind.

This chapter will take the form of summarizing and refuting some of the principal objections levelled against literary history, not always explicitly, in the present century.

Can Literary History be Original?

Nineteenth-century literary history served the unexceptionable function of showing what was there to be read, and at a period when the great modern literatures were becoming educational subjects on a large scale for the first time. Nobody, it may be supposed, would wish to question that function even now, and it is likely that extended histories of English literature, for instance, will continue to be written and published. But equally, nobody would normally attribute to that function anything greater than an elementary interest. It may be the task of the schoolboy to find out what there is to be read, but it is the task of maturity to read it, so that a history of a literature conceived in these terms can at the best only map a familiar terrain as a guide to the beginner.

This is a comprehensible and familiar view of what literary history can do, but it is based upon a highly exaggerated notion of the degree to which the great modern literatures are known territories. It is perilously easy to suppose that the main tasks of literary history have now been performed. The triviality of many subjects accepted by universities for literary research, and even by publishers as books, is often adduced as evidence here. It is natural to suppose all this to be symptomatic of a subject nearing the point of exhaustion, and common to find scholars engaged in literary research who are ready to sell the pass by claiming to think just that. In a similar way, it is said, the study of physics in the late nineteenth century was thought by many physicists to be nearing completion, with a few loose ends to be accounted for by the end of the century: but the loose ends proved more interesting than anybody could then imagine. And it is possible that literary history today is in a similar condition. Nobody engaged in the serious teaching of English, certainly, could suppose on a full examination of the evidence that all the best subjects have been 'done'; though equally, the teacher may often feel that the questions he finds unanswered are too momentous to be confided to a beginner. There is still no history either of Old or of Middle English which consolidates the achievement of W. P. Ker in the 1890s and after in demonstrating a wide grasp of the intellectual issues involved in the texts and an awareness of their place in a European setting. If English Renaissance drama is amply discussed, its prose is not. It is notable, indeed, that there is no satisfactory history of English prose in any age. The relations between the novel and society have been well, if incompletely, discussed: but novels tell stories, and there is no good study of what it is to tell a story. There is no convincing study of Restoration drama, none of Dryden and his contemporaries as poets, and no connected study of the English eighteenth century which clarifies the relation between its greatest authors and the European Enlightenment. There are good individual studies of the intellectual debts and preoccupations of certain of the English Romantic poets, but no connected history of English romanticism that makes full use of these discoveries. The Victorian novel has received most rewarding attention since the 1940s, but the controversial prose of the Victorians far less; and there is still no work of the first interest on the totality of Victorian poetry. These deficiencies in English literary history are not mentioned here in order to provoke offers of help. Anyone with the capacity to do work like this has the capacity to see without prompting that it needs to be done. But they certainly suggest that English literary history is a study still little advanced beyond the pioneer stage.

The question at issue here is the prospect of a continuing and original study of literary history rather than particular answers to particular questions. If large questions are unanswered, then a prospect of long and vital activity is clearly in view: actually to answer them would be to defeat the argument. And to assert that they need to be answered is not meant to imply that in the present state of knowledge they can be answered. There may be convincing reasons, for the moment, why they cannot. It is easy and even convincing to argue, for example, that the time for a definitive study of Victorian poetry has not yet come: but then it is precisely because it has not yet come that the future of literary history seems in principle to be so well assured. The loss of confidence in the discipline in the first half of the twentieth century, at least in the English-speaking world, may soon come to look like a mere eddy in a flood that no fashion like the New Criticism can stem. It is not credible, after all, that societies as advanced and as leisured as the West should ever lose curiosity about the processes by which their civilizations were formed. And the homeland of a great world literature, such as England, is in no position to set a limit to the interest the world may choose to take in what has now become its lingua franca. If the English do not write English literary history, in a word, then, somebody else will.

Are Poems Historical Acts?

But the nagging doubt about literary history in the present century does, after all, have more than the semblance of an objection of principle and is something more than a mere intellectual fashion. It is based upon a persuasive scepticism about the status of a poem as an historical act. This scepticism needs to be seen in perspective. Nobody has ever doubted that poems were written in the past. But it does not plainly follow that a poem is an historical document in the sense that it derives its chief interest and value from the personality and purpose of its author in the historical conditions under which he wrote. The debate surrounding the 'intentional fallacy' has been concerned with this larger issue—an issue in which 'the poet's intention' is only one of the problems involved. To speak of the intentional fallacy at all was to react against an historical view of literature which, by the 1940s, had been dominant in the West for over a hundred years. And to accept it as a fallacy was to offer a view deeply subversive to literary history, as it was meant to be, since the literary historian is bound to assume a correspondence of some kind between what the poet and his age might reasonably be thought to have in mind, on the one hand, and the true meaning of the poem on the other. When the historian investigates the question whether the figure of Shylock in *The Merchant of Venice* represents an anti-Semitic view, for instance, he regards the question as hardly distinguishable from a question about what Shakespeare and his first audience would have thought of Shylock. If the literary historian is to be told that the play now exists independently of its creator, and that the modern reader or actor is entitled to make what sense he can of it, then he had better gather up his writing materials and go elsewhere. Such an atmosphere is not for him.

In the following discussion, which is offered among other things as a refutation of the claim that intentionalism is a fallacy, I shall deliberately widen the scope of the argument to include issues beyond the intention of the poet himself. This procedure is justifiable to the extent that the issue involved in contemporary controversy is genuinely wider than the protagonists have always fully realized. What is involved here, at its widest extent, is the mementous issue whether literature is primarily to be studied as a purposive activity or not. It was among the greatest achievements of nineteenth-century historiography to emphasize, perhaps even to exaggerate, the sense of purpose out of which a great poem is born. If this process is to be put into reverse, and if literature is now to be regarded as the first audiences for the Homeric poems perhaps regarded the *Iliad*, or as those who listen to pop-songs today regard what they hear—experiences involving curiosity about the performers, it may be supposed, rather than about the creators—then powerful reasons would be needed for supposing that such a reversal would represent a gain to civilized values. For most men who have valued the literary experience in the past century and more, literature is by contrast the supremely purposive activity: 'an objective, a projected result', as Henry James once called it emphatically, adding sententiously: 'it is life that is the unconscious, the agitated, the struggling, floundering cause'.[1]

It was the Victorians themselves who raised the first protests against the prevailing obsession of their age with the pastness of the past. Robert Browning, who was perhaps the first Englishman to consider the issue in print, argued in a preface of 1852 on Shelley that, in the case of 'objective' poets at least, biography may be dispensed with as 'no more necessary to an understanding or enjoyment . . . than is a model or anatomy of some tropical tree to the right tasting of the fruit we are familiar with on the market-stall'. Saintsbury sometimes claimed to believe—in his study of *Dryden* (1881), for example—that only the verbal analysis of poems can be defended in principle, though he practised many other sorts himself. Matthew Arnold spent half a lifetime emphasizing the essential timelessness of great poetry. Oscar Wilde spoke of the work of art as having 'an independent life of its own' which may 'deliver a message far other than that which was put in its lips to say'. Quiller-Couch, in his Cambridge lectures *On the Art of Writing* (1916), held that the greatest literature is always

> seraphically free
> From taint of personality.

E. M. Forster, in an essay of 1925 entitled 'Anonymity', argued that 'a poem is absolute', and that 'all literature tends towards a condition of anonymity. . . . It wants not to be signed'. Like so many campaigns against the Victorians, the campaign against literary history is itself Victorian in its origins. But the real reason for rehearsing these objections, which if placed beside the manifestoes of French '*l'art pour l'art*' and Proust's *Contre Sainte-Beuve* would make a massive dossier, is to emphasize the scope and variety of the campaign rather than its antiquity. And many of these issues are rightly associated, various as they are. If in the following account I attempt to refute the case point by point, it is rather in the hope of marshalling a lucid argument in favour of a new tradition of literary history than out of any inclination to convict others of muddle or equivocation.

First, there is the issue of evaluation by intention. I mention this here only for the sake of completeness, since no one, it may be supposed, has ever seriously held that a poem is good because its author intended it to be so. To deny, against Wimsatt and Beardsley, that an author's intention is properly 'a standard for judging . . . success' is to consider a phrase that opens many issues: but so far as this one is concerned, it would be better to suppose that it had never existed.

The appeal to fulfilled intention, however, is a more serious matter, in the sense that it is a fallacy which is plausible enough to be believed. It is often suggested that a poet has done enough if he fully performs what he set out to do, and often objected that it is improper to demand of the author that he should have written a different book. But it is notable that good critics often demand of an author, and with good reason, that he should have written a different book. And it is not at all obvious that in principle they should not. When Dr Johnson, in his Life of Dryden, complained of *Absalom and Achitophel* that:

> the original structure of the poem was defective; allegories
> drawn to great length will always break; Charles could not run
> continually parallel with David,

he is certainly regretting that Dryden had not written a radically
different poem, and to object that he should accept the poem for
what it is amounts to a demand that he should abdicate his function
altogether. But then to fulfil an intention, in literature as in life, is not
necessarily to behave as one should. If a man sets out to shoot his
mother-in-law, and does so, one may applaud his marksmanship but
not the deed itself.

If these were the only uses to which the determination of authorial
intention were put by critics, it would be easy to agree that intentionalism is a fallacy. But they are not. After all, there is the wide
and distinct issue of the distribution of literature: not just in the way
of mechanical improvements like the invention of printing, but in
matters which affect the literary experience at its deepest roots. It is
of much less than decisive importance that Chaucer did not intend
his poems to be printed, for instance; though the fact that he probably intended his poems to be heard rather than silently perused is a
fact of real interest. To print is to multiply copies, and the world is
evidently right to assume that Chaucer's intentions in the matter are
of little concern now. But a new form of distribution might represent
a more radical change of emphasis than this. Milton is unlikely to
have intended *Samson Agonistes* for the stage; Shakespeare designed
his plays altogether for performance, and is unlikely to have taken
much interest in their publication. Again, nobody supposes such intentions to be decisive upon posterity; but equally, the probability
that *Samson* was written for the study rather than for the stage is a
major fact about *Samson*. Anyone who supposed that Milton was
attempting a theatrical rival to Dryden's *Conquest of Granada*, for example, would probably prove an unreceptive reader of Milton's play.
It is said that Tibetan tea, which is partly composed of rancid butter,
is revolting to Western tastes if considered as tea but acceptable if
considered as soup. When we ask of a poem questions of the order of
'What did the poet intend it for ?'—whether stage or study, whether
court audience or popular—the answer seems in principle likely to
be useful to the extent that it is accurate. This is surely a good question to ask, and anybody who objects at this point that the search for
the author's intention is necessarily a fallacy should be sent about his
business.

It seems likely, too, that the purposive property of literature is
under unnecessary attack at this point. To concede, for instance, that
a good stage-play could be written by someone who is not trying to

write a stage-play at all is not only to concede something vastly improbable in itself. It is also to humiliate the status of literature as a human act. As Wordsworth put it, a poet is a man speaking to men. On the whole, we listen to those who address us in order to discover what they mean. It is also true that, in rare and memorable instances, people say remarkable things without meaning them. But anybody who conducted his social life on the principle that conversation is worth listening to only or mainly for the sake of such instances would be guilty of continuous discourtesy and, still more important, would find himself much the worse for the bargain. Freaks in creation exist: Musset, for example, is said to have written his plays with no thought for the stage, though in fact they succeed there. But freaks are exactly what such cases are.

A further support for the doctrine of the poem as an historical act seems to arise from the study of the literary kinds. This is an extension of the preceding argument concerning the distribution of literature, and one to be distinguished from it only with difficulty. Nobody, in all probability, has ever denied that on the whole a novel is a novel, or an elegy an elegy, because its author intended it to be so. But in the anti-historical atmosphere of the early twentieth century it was possible to protest that, since works usually bear the evidence of the kind to which they belong on their faces, the historical critic had little to contribute by 'going outside the poem'. This view is certainly mistaken. When a reader recognizes a novel to be such, or chooses it because it is such, he is certainly using evidence from outside the work as well as evidence from within. He is recognizing features in the novel he holds in his hand which resemble those in other novels he has read. The uncertainty that overhangs early and unestablished literary forms, such as the novel in early eighteenth-century England, and the hesitating attempts to confer dignity and status upon such forms, as in Fielding's formula of the 'comic epic in prose', are examples of the problems that ignorance or uncertainty concerning the literary kinds can raise. And when the literary historian identifies the lineage of poems whose pedigrees have fallen into oblivion—when he identifies one of *The Canterbury Tales* as a beast-fable, for instance, and another as a romance of courtly love— he is restoring to the consciousness of the reader knowledge of an indispensable kind. But then the achievements of genre-identification seem among the most massive and incontestable triumphs of historical criticism over the past two hundred years. To demonstrate the complex relation between Spenser's *Faerie Queene*, for instance, and the Italian epics which in the sixteenth century dominated the mode of romantic epic throughout Europe, is to restore to the

English poem the status and interest of a masterpiece and rescue it
from the imputation of a work that might otherwise barely survive
as a loose collection of occasional beauties.

If the wider problem of language is considered in the same light,
the historical status of literature grows steadily and inescapably
clearer. It was sometimes objected of historical criticism that it encouraged a chaos of romantic individualism on the part of poets in
their use of language, whereas the fashionable demand in the earlier
years of the century was for continuity, order and 'the tradition'.
Words, it was emphasized by the New Critics and others, need to be
disciplined to fit the norms of language, so that the poem itself might
ideally exist in a void of space or time, a formal object or 'well
wrought urn'. 'The work after being produced must continue to
exist independently of the author's intentions or thoughts about it.
The idiosyncrasies of the author must not be repugnant to the norm'.[2]
But certain celebrated literary effects, after all, *are* repugnant to the
norms of language as established in their age. The obscenities of
Swift are repugnant to the norms of polite language in the Augustan
age, as they were meant to be, and it is just their repugnancy—in
this case, their power to shock—that makes them tell. Some English
poets are well known to have used linguistic devices—Milton's syntax, Dylan Thomas's diction—which deviate from any known use of
language in their age, and the reader is meant to sense that a deviation
or perversion of usage is happening. It is admittedly tempting to
suppose that there must be some limit to the degree of repugnancy
that is admissible in literature; and certainly there is a point beyond
which language can only turn into nonsense. But then nonsense can
be literature too, and sometimes is—a warning that, if there is a limit
to be placed, it may be worth insisting that it should be placed at
some remote point.

In any case, to speak of norms of language is to concede, however
unwittingly, the case for an historical discipline. The poem itself is
not the norm, after all, and in itself it cannot reveal what the norm is.
In order to demonstrate the idiosyncrasies of Milton's syntax in
Paradise Lost, it is of no use to confine the discussion to the poem itself: one must look at other documents by Milton and by his contemporaries. The oddities of Thomas's diction exist only in relation
to mid-twentieth-century usages outside his poems. If we are
anxious to pretend that poems could ever 'exist independently of the
author's intentions', we had better banish all idea of the norm. And
in banishing that, it is easy to see, a great deal of significance must go
too. A reader content to suppose that Milton's language was the
ordinary language of his age would certainly miss much of the signifi-

cance of *Paradise Lost*. To evade in all circumstances the study of the author's intentions, in fact, is at times to evade the meaning of the poem itself.

What does it mean to speak usefully of an author's intentions in his poem ? I emphasize 'usefully', since it is right to concede at once that such discussions need not be useful at all; and doctrines like 'the intentional fallacy' probably represent an exaggerated reaction to this realization, obvious as it is. But then the historian, whether of literature or of anything else, is in no way committed to the view that everything about the past is of equal interest: in fact it is precisely the historian who is expected to show the greatest skill and experience in sorting the important evidence from the insignificant. That is his trade. When we have shown that much skilful and informed speculation about the poets' intention does not help in reading his poems — a charge sometimes levelled against J.L. Lowes' study of Coleridge, *The Road to Xanadu*, for example — nothing decisive has been said or shown against the nature of such enquiries in general. If it sometimes helps, it does not follow that it always helps. Equally, the historical critic need not allow himself to be held committed to the view that his enquiry is utterly limited to the question of what the poet intended. It is notorious that Shakespeare would not understand much modern Shakespearean criticism. But then that, in itself, is hardly an objection to what the critics are doing. Newton, equally, would presumably not understand modern physics. It seems likely that one or the other, if he could return to life, might be trained in understanding and would prove an unusually apt pupil; but to demand of the historical critic that he should in all circumstances limit himself to seeing in a Shakespeare play only as much as the dramatist himself might have seen and in something like the very terms in which he would have seen it is to ask, in large measure, that literary studies should be stopped.

On the other hand, the historical criticism of literature imposes a limit of another and more reasonable kind than this. If it does not forbid elucidation beyond the point where the poet himself might cease to follow the argument, it commonly forbids explanations that run counter to what the poet could have thought or felt. The enlargement of 'intended' to 'thought or felt' is a safety-device in this argument, but an allowable one if it is conceded how much wider than the conscious and articulate intention of the poet the scope of the modern argument about the poet's intention has proved. To set out to show that Shakespeare was something like a Marxist, or that he had a horror of autocracy and the police-state, is to attempt to prove something that runs counter not only to the texts of the plays but, short of the remotest freak of intellectual history, counter to anything an Elizabethan could have believed. When one exclaims 'But Shakespeare *can't* have thought that', the curtain that drops upon the line of argument is a curtain that has good reason to be there.

'Subconscious' Intention

In studying the poet's intention in his poem, is there a useful distinction to be drawn between intentions that are conscious and those that are not? Could there, for that matter, be any question of preferring conscious to subconscious intention, or *vice versa*, on grounds of authenticity? It seems unlikely that there could ever be a single and simple answer to questions of such complexity as these; but in saying that, and in showing that, doctrines of a rasher and more absolute kind would at least have been rendered more difficult to sustain. Literature is not a single substance with a single set of properties: it represents countless systems of language at their greatest extent and diversity. It is far more diverse than ordinary conversation, for example; and yet no one would seriously expect a single and simple answer to the question whether, in listening to the conversation of a friend or acquaintance, one should attribute greater importance to what he consciously means to say, on the one hand, or to what one guesses from his word or gesture to be the secret and unsuspected springs of his behavior. It would depend upon the friend, one would reply, and upon the context of the conversation. An answer as dull and as accurate as this would at least have the merit of dismissing the notion that there is a single correct way in which to interpret language.

It is certainly clear that in literature, as in other uses of language, both concerns are normal. There is nothing exceptional or remote about the activity of psycho-analysing an author as one reads him, or a friend as one listens: though the term 'psycho-analysis' suggests a more formal and regulated activity than any that is commonly involved here. To ask, in reading Byron's *Don Juan*, whether Byron's exhibitionism of style and moral licence does not subconsciously reveal a sense of tragic despair is not in itself to offend against any reasonable canon of judgement. It is an appropriate question, just as it may be appropriate to wonder of an acquaintance who boasts of his sexual prowess whether it is more than a boast. Much intelligent comment on *Wuthering Heights* and *Jane Eyre* plausibly attributes to the novels an interest in feminine sexuality which the Brontë sisters themselves would have been shocked to learn of. Or consider this interpretation of 'Sohrab and Rustum', which exploits the fact that Matthew Arnold's father was a famous headmaster:

However dangerous may be the practice of unraveling unconscious literary symbolism, it is almost impossible not to find
throughout 'Sohrab and Rustum' at least a shadowy personal
significance. The strong son is slain by the mightier father; and
in the end Sohrab draws his father's spear from his own side to
let out his life and end the anguish. We watch Arnold in his later
youth and we must wonder if he is not, in a psychical sense,
doing the same thing.[3]

The example is an unusually pure case of imputing a subconscious
intention to a poet, since there is no external evidence that Arnold
consciously disliked or resented his father. He would almost certainly have been shocked and repelled by this interpretation. In itself,
one need not consider that a decisive objection: indeed there have
been extremes of psycho-analytical criticism which would have considered it confirmatory evidence. But in this controversy, fortunately,
there seems to be no point in the critic taking sides. If the intentions
of the poet are none the less that for being subconscious, there is no
obvious advantage in insisting that subconscious intention is exceptionally significant. The very phrase 'subconscious intention' is
paradoxical enough without exaggerating the paradox to the point
of absurdity.

But equally, it seems clear that conscious and subconscious intentions differ strikingly in their evidences and are usefully, even
inevitably, distinguishable. We might choose to accept, for instance,
with the several careful qualifications offered, the view that in 'Sohrab
and Rustum' Arnold was subconsciously working out a sense of a
fear or hostility of which he was himself unaware. Such a view makes
good sense of the epilogue of the poem, what is more—'But the
majestic river floated on . . .'—and in a way that no other view can
easily do, since the gradual frustration of the great river in its march
to the sea fits nothing in the story of the Persian tragedy of father
against son, but could momentously record Arnold's own sense of
personal failure and inadequacy. But this view, helpful as it is, depends heavily upon understanding the difference between conscious
intentions and other kinds. To suggest that Arnold was knowingly
exploiting in this poem a hostility towards his father of which he was
fully aware would be to offer a distinct, even a radically opposed,
view to the first. That would amount to a very different poem indeed.
It seems clear, in fact, that the critic commonly investigates both
conscious and subconscious intentions in literature, and that when
he performs his function well he tends to be sharply aware of the
difference between them.

Is Intention Prior to Creation?

It is a matter of common experience to anyone who writes that a work rarely, if ever, merely represents the fulfilment of an original intention. A poem is a progressive act. It may arise out of an itch to write a poem. The Trinity manuscript of Milton, for instance, suggests that the young Milton had decided to write an epic before he had settled upon a biblical subject: the ambition to compose a poem of heroic dimensions preceded the ambition to justify the ways of God. It is often observable that the ambition to be a novelist precedes the choice of a subject or plot for any specific novel; and even in those cases where the idea for the novel was genuinely the impulse that set the novelist writing, it is hardly conceivable that the idea should fail to grow and to change under his hand. The fact seems so universal as to be worth elevating into a law. Kleist once spoke of the act of writing as a 'gradual fabrication'; and R. G. Collingwood, in his *Principles of Art* (1938), raised the point to the level of a major distinction between art and mere craft, while admitting that some works of art partake of some of the properties of craft as well:

> The artist has no idea what the experience is which demands expression until he has expressed it. What he wants to say is not present to him as an end towards which means have to be devised; it becomes clear to him only as the poem takes shape in his mind, or the clay in his fingers. (p. 29)

The principle may have been overstated by Collingwood: to suggest that the artist has no idea of what he means until he has said it is perhaps best regarded as a truth exaggerated for rhetorical effect. But creation can be usefully interpreted in this way if Collingwood's terms are moderated and refined beyond the point to which he felt it necessary to go. Composition is not, after all, confined to the period in which the poet holds pen in hand. The process of 'gradual fabrication' has begun long before, perhaps years before; and the finished poem is more likely to represent a point of abandonment than an end of the journey foreseen from the start. But then there is nothing destructive to historical criticism in the view that the poet's intentions are subject to continuing change and revision. Rather the contrary: many poems may be best interpreted by an historical study of a progressive intention. Milton's *Lycidas* is perhaps a classic example, since it begins and ends as pastoral elegy but incongruously includes much else besides. It invites an informed and disciplined speculation about Milton's private ambitions as a poet ('Fame is the spur . . .'), about his view of the condition of the clergy in the 1630s, and about his own religious sensibility and hopes of after-life.

It is entirely plausible to suggest that Milton only discovered the totality of what he meant by *Lycidas* in the act of writing it. But the poem is in no way less Miltonic for that reason. Because a man alters his intention in the course of action, it can hardly be said of him that he is acting other than according to intention.

Schools and Influences

The tradition of nineteenth-century literary history, then, may be considered in better repair than is commonly supposed: it is rather the confident arguments of its opponents in the last century and in this that are in urgent need of help. But even when the arguments for history have been carefully reviewed, and when it has been admitted anew that poems are best studied as human actions in the contexts of their time and place, it is often objected that the tools of traditional literary history are no longer in working use. The study of the great vernacular literatures such as French and English took their rise, almost inevitably, from the formal study of classical texts in the Renaissance, where the task of establishing historical priorities within literary traditions which had already ceased to exist for a millennium and more, or of grouping poets into schools of literature and of tracing literary debts and influences, was already well advanced by the seventeenth century. In England Bacon, in his *Advancement of Learning* (1605), proposed as a task for others an intellectual history of modern civilization in which poetry would play its part; and by the end of the century Rymer had written the first clear example of the history of a literary kind in English, *A Short View of Tragedy* (1693); to be followed almost at once by Dryden's long histories of satire and of epic (1693–7) in the form of extended prefaces to his poetic versions of Juvenal and Virgil. By the mid eighteenth century literary history might be considered an established form in England. It had grown out of two kindred disciples of the preceding age, criticism and literary antiquarianism; so that by the time Johnson and the Warton brothers came upon the scene it had fully digested the implications of Dryden's remarks in his preface to the *Fables* (1700) half a century before:

> Milton was the poetical son of Spenser, and Mr Waller of Fairfax; for we have our lineal descents and clans as well as other families: Spenser more than once insinuates that the soul of Chaucer was transfused into his body; and that he was begotten by him two hundred years after his decease. Milton has acknowledged to me that Spenser was his original . . .

The remark parallels the numerous classical discussions of literary debts and literary traditions in ancient literature based upon the principle of *imitatio veterum*, or the conscious imitation of a poetic forerunner. By the 1750s it is a familiar principle of modern criticism. Thomas Warton's study of the *Faerie Queene* (1754), which included a study of Spenser's literary sources, and Johnson's *Dictionary* of the following year, which based itself heavily upon quotations from the best English authors, show how firmly established the discipline already was. William Warburton, in his edition of Pope (1751), spoke proudly of 'the rise and progress of the several branches of literary science' as being 'one of the most curious parts of the history of the human mind', adding that it was an achievement as such still unrecorded among Englishmen.

These are all studies in similarities. The more sophisticated doctrine of literary history as a species of reaction or counter-influence is more difficult to trace. It is certainly part of the practice of antiquity, if not part of its theory. The relation of Virgil to Homer, or of Lucan to Virgil, is not merely one of learning and imitating: it is also a relationship of repulsion, marked by a determination to '*faire autre chose*',[4] to avoid or invert characters, incidents or turns of style which have exhausted themselves in the existing tradition through mere familiarity. The doctrine of imitation as doing something different, whether radically or subtly so, lies at the root of much literary history and is a necessary assumption of any advanced example of the narration of a tradition such as the history of a literary kind: advanced, since any history content merely to describe one work after another without seeking causal relations between them would be lacking in an essential historical property. It is a familiar truth that we do not know enough about the past fully to explain why it was that what happened actually happened: but it does not follow from this that causal enquiries should not be attempted at all. When theories of imitation as counter-influence, of 'doing something different', were adopted into the discipline of literary history in the late eighteenth century and after, they introduced a new consciousness of the principle of literary causality which has hardly been explored even in outline. How far, it may be asked, can the principle of counter-influence extend before the relationship as a whole ceases to count as significant ? To do something different is not to ignore the tradition, after all: on the contrary, it is to take stock of its potentialities with a cool, or hostile, or perhaps appreciative eye. When Fielding in *Joseph Andrews* resolved to write a novel as little like Richardson's *Pamela* as he could (if one may so exaggerate and simplify his purposes) he none the less wanted and needed to maintain a resemblance clear enough to make his points against Richardson tell. Sterne's parody of many narrative styles shortly afterwards in *Tristram Shandy* presupposes an intimate recollection of the narratives he is parodying. The principle is familiar, and examples could be paralleled many times over. It helps to suggest the range and unexplored possibilities that the practice of literary history, once thought to be a dying art, may still have to offer. Certainly the study of the literary past is in no way limited, as is often assumed, merely to recounting what happened, to showing what is there to be read, to grouping in 'schools' and abstract categories such as romanticism. Such categories, it has often been objected, may harden rapidly into easy formulae for the avoidance of thoughtful and disciplined response. But if literary history has its vulgarities, it has its classic achievements too. The greatest original intelligences of Europe, including Dryden, Voltaire, Johnson, Coleridge and Nietzsche, have at times not disdained to practise it. The objections raised against it in the last hundred years, it is true, have been numerous, fashionable and widely believed, but they cannot be called powerfully argued or easily sustained under critical examination. And there seems to be no good reason to suppose that the study is in the remotest sense an exhausted one. The world has surely been right, in defiance of intellectual fashion, to continue to read literary history and to ask for more. It has writers and readers, tasks to perform and good reasons for performing them. What it strangely seems to lack, in spite of all this, is a sense of its own importance and a will to assert it.

A. J. CLOSE

Don Quixote *and the 'Intentionalist Fallacy'*

A word of explanation should be offered first as to why this venerable
aesthetic problem is being revived once more. I have just completed
a study of the literary criticism of *Don Quixote* since the time of
German Romanticism.[1] Its main conclusion is that this criticism falls
into a 'Romantic' tradition which disconcertingly tries to do two
things simultaneously: (*a*) to recover sympathetically the cultural
context in which the book was written and to interpret it accordingly;
(*b*) to use *Don Quixote* as a peg on which to hang the diverse pre-
occupations (artistic, moral, political and philosophical) of the nineteenth and twentieth centuries. The result is an oddly double-focused
image of the book, in which a subjectively modern viewpoint upon
it conflicts with a scholarly one and also with the scholarly methodology (historical orientation, citation from the text, and so on) used
as means of exegesis. This contradictory dualism seems to derive
from a deeper philosophical confusion as to how one arrives at the
meaning of literary classics. On the one hand it is felt that there is
such a thing as 'the author's view', which must be taken into account
and can only be understood in a determinate cultural context. On
the other hand the critics want to proclaim a right not to be bound
absolutely either by 'the author's view' or by its relevant context.
They base this right on time-honoured and still respectable axioms
about literary art, according to which it is allegedly a fallacy to pursue, or feel limited by, the author's intentions: 'Great works of art
mean more than they literally say'; 'great art transcends the original
intentions of its creator and means something new to every epoch';
'we can never know, and need not concern ourselves with, what the
writer intended.' I believe that these assumptions have a dubious
philosophical basis. This article is an attempt to scotch them. While
it is essentially of a philosophical nature, it has an empirical basis in a
documented insight into the manifold muddles of practical criticism
which the 'anti-intentionalist' clichés can inspire. I have found that
these muddles are duplicated on an abstract level by philosophers
and aestheticians in their treatment of the question of intentions. In
the first part of this article, I propose to identify typical ways in which
one can go wrong by using restricted or inexact senses of 'intention'
as primary models for generalization about the concept; in the

second part to argue that essential features of the language by which we identify intentions outside art are indispensable features of critical discourse, and that consequently the claim that the knowledge of intentions in art is unnecessary or impossible is tantamount to denying the basic pre-conditions of critical language.

Let us take as a basis for a definition of intention the distinctions proposed by Miss Anscombe in her book of that title: (*a*) intentional activity; (*b*) intention with which, or what a man aims at in doing something intentionally; (*c*) expressions of intention for the future.[2] Following Anscombe, we will consider (*b*) as the crucial concept, and take it that when we use (*b*) we imply (*a*). Actions are intentional when they can be interrogated with a certain sense of the question 'Why?' In this sense 'Why?' elicits reasons for acting; and the reasons indicate the purpose towards which the actions are directed.

In talking of intentions we can either allude to something further which a man works towards in performing an action (*e.g.* 'answering the door' in 'putting on slippers'), or else we can cite this further goal as an explanatory description of the action (*e.g.* by describing the man putting on slippers as answering the door). In the first case we conceive of the intention as an objective lying beyond the boundaries of the action; in the second case we locate it within those boundaries, picking out from the details of the performance the end towards which they contribute as means. Of the two concepts the second (*i.e.* intention 'within') is the more common in the language of literary criticism; it corresponds to that use of 'intention' which is analogous to 'meaning'. When we inquire about the intentions of sonnet *X* we are not asking a parallel question to 'What were his intentions in saying that?'—a question by which we typically probe the ulterior goal or hidden motive lying behind the patent meaning of a man's remarks. Rather we are considering the constitutive elements of a way of saying something which is self-sufficiently arresting and whose point is simply its capacity for arresting our interest in that way. Those constitutive elements are sonnet *X*'s 'meaning'; and I take 'meaning' in a sense broad enough to include all the factors which can interest, move or delight us in poetry—metaphor, conceit, rhythm, euphony, thought, etc. Later I shall equate meaning with 'illocutionary force'.

However, the concept of intention 'beyond', which Anscombe has shown to be basic to our use of intention, does enter into the language of literary criticism in fundamental ways. For example, after one has established the intrinsic end or essential point of a performance (intention 'within') one can then visualize the details as means contributing teleologically towards an end. When one gives explanations-by-motives (a point to be illustrated later) one offers explanations of a means-to-end type. So one does too when one visualizes a writer as fulfilling any kind of over-all design, or as furthering such intellectual or aesthetic or temperamental pre-occupations as the criticism of structural stylistics characteristically illuminates. More basically still, there is a whole series of further ends which works of art, considered as complete entities, may properly be said to promote: giving diverse forms of aesthetic pleasure; decoration; ostentation; glorifying God; inspiring piety; instructing; ridiculing *mores*; making propaganda; projecting a view of human nature. For Cervantes *Don Quixote* had the (aesthetic) end of moving the melancholy to laughter and the merry to redoubled laughter; it also had the (socially improving) end of discrediting the chivalric romance. The two ends are inseparably linked. Anscombe says that Aristotle's practical syllogism, corresponding to his notion of practical reasoning and to Anscombe's own series of questions 'Why ?', is the implicit logical structure of our knowledge and explanation of intentions. Practical reasoning starts from a premise which characterizes a state of affairs as desirable; it ends, typically, in an action whose point is shown by the premises. Our exegetical explanations often presuppose that literature can be conceived on this model.

A major source of confusion is to see intention as a 'mental objective', connected with action contingently or causally but not logically. Many aestheticians seem to hold an Aristotelian picture of the mind, according to which 'intending' is akin to Aristotle's 'formal cause' — a prefixed, static, mental norm by which the artisan's physical work (Aristotle's 'efficient cause') is guided, and from which it may well deviate by virtue of the accidents of matter, the vagaries of chance or the artisan's incompetence. For Wimsatt and Beardsley intentions are 'design or plan in the author's mind'.[3] A similar picture of intention is implied by the cliché: 'Surely it's not what the author *intended* to say that counts but what he *said*,' as if what he said was by no means necessarily what he meant to say. The conclusion then reached is: 'Why bother with the blueprint when the product is available for inspection ? If the author fulfilled the blueprint, then the product becomes the perfect manifestation of it; if he did not, then we shall never know what it was like.'

The objections to this view are threefold. First, in equating intention with mental aims it ignores that the practical knowledge which intentional action involves is essentially displayed in *doing*; and that our action can be a fulfilment of intentions, and can thereby display its ultimate intention, even if it fails in this final target or if it deviates from a plan that was originally proposed. In reaching this

view anti-intentionalists have probably been influenced by two considerations: (*a*) the truism that what someone ideally projected
('intended'), but may not have achieved, need not dictate our evaluation of what he did; (*b*) the apparent parallelism between the question whether it is relevant to know intentions in literary art and the
question whether it is relevant to know motives and hoped-for consequences ('intentions') in the adjudication of crime, ethical conduct,
and success or failure in practical affairs. In cases (*a*) and (*b*) we often
say in ordinary language that a man's 'intentions' are irrelevant to,
or need not decisively affect, the judgement of his actions. Here the
metaphors of ordinary language can be misleading. What we do in
such cases is to single out from the whole complex of intentions that
a determinate human act reveals *one* facet of intentionality which
critically interests us, because it might tilt the balance of our judgement, and deem it as wholly irrelevant for certain purposes of evaluation (case *a*), or else as an insufficient mitigating or blameworthy
factor (case *b*). Though we call this facet the agent's 'intentions', we
ought not philosophically to be held to mean, since to mean it would
be nonsense, that it is irrelevant to take into consideration any part
of the complex of a man's intentions in order to know, explain and
judge his actions. For example, if (*a*) the hired cook, out of excess
of ingenuity, spoils the *crêpes flambées* at an important dinner, and if
(*b*) the police squad-car, zealously speeding to the scene of the accident, hits a pedestrian on the way, the ensuing reprimands would
necessarily and properly take into account at least the cook's intention to cook a type of pancake and the squad-car-driver's intention
to speed, whatever professed indifference to 'intentions' the reprimands might contain. To evaluate artefacts and moral actions involves knowing a large part of the agent's intentions, although *how*
large a part, and what proportion of all the motives, calculations,
hopes and ambitions which accompanied the action (and to which
the label 'intentions' can more or less loosely be given), will vary
according to our interests and purposes. Thus even in cases like (*a*)
and (*b*) the logic of our evaluations implies that we see intentions as
tied to their actions and objectives, even if our usage often suggests
otherwise. If this is true for ethics and practical affairs, then it must
a fortiori be true for literature, since the intentions that we assess
here are simply an intrinsic feature of linguistic acts—*i.e.* the meaning of acts of communication—and not a motive or well- or ill-
intentioned consequence which, however illegitimately, we tend conceptually to separate from its action. Therefore any approximate
equivalent to the ethical debate about the relevance of intentions can
surely have no place in literary criticism.

Secondly there are important differences between interpreting literature and judging success or failure in practical affairs. In the latter case we usually reckon with concrete goals or standards (*e.g.* not burning pancakes) against which we can measure performance and concerning which it is natural to envisage agents forming prior mental aims. One result of this is that critics and aestheticians are sometimes beguiled into assuming that to know an artist's intentions is essentially to concern oneself with some tangible further aim of his, particularly of a socially improving kind; and anti-intentionalists have concluded that because such concerns often lead nowhere, so must the pursuit of intentions.[4] Intentions in literature, however, tend not to conform to this simple model; they include such non-tangible 'aims' as the cerebral Jamesian interest in presenting the ambiguous complexities of a moral issue or a Quevedo's delight in the dramatic dissonances of a conceit. Likewise 'success' in literature is usually a satisfactory way of saying something which only becomes apparent when something is said that way. The unreality of the anti-intentionalist view is that it assumes that we normally might or could discuss literature in terms of some preordained target, manifest to writer and critic, which the work either misses or fulfils.

Thirdly the premise that intending is essentially a matter of having a mental, normative picture of one's completed action stands exposed to the difficulties which the later Wittgenstein characterized in his analysis of such concepts as meaning and intending. Since these difficulties are familiar, I shall outline them schematically: (*a*) there is the problem how one's action comes under the control of intention owing to the merely contingent, and not logically inherent, relation of intention to act; (*b*) there is the difficulty of characterizing this mental intention, and the related difficulty that in common experience we often act without any such inward resolve.

The fallacies considered hitherto mainly consist in 'internalizing' intentions, seeing them as a dimension of mental or psychological attitudes which have somehow to be reached 'behind' the literary text. Such a conception is evident in the Wimsatt/Beardsley view that intentions are more or less equivalent to biographical facts about an author—his background-knowledge, emotions, psychology, private life, allusions, and habitual word-associations. This is a common view. The problem of how such items, which are obviously not all equivalent to intentions, may be said to relate to them is typically left unexamined.[5] It is simply assumed that to explore these areas of an author's life is what the recovery of intentions mainly involves. It is further postulated that the intentions discoverable through these biographical data are not necessarily coincidental with that pattern of meaning which makes the best sense of the author's words; and the dilemma which anti-intentionalists then propose to their opponents is either that they have no evidence to work on (when the author has left no spoken or written record of his 'intentions'), or else that his indications are liable to prove arbitrary or misleading.

A salient case of such 'internalization' is the tendency to equate intentions with any kind of motive or psychic factor. Now there is an important area where intentions and motives overlap, where the purposes of action can be redescribed as the desires for the sake of which they are done and vice versa. It could be argued that some motive (*e.g.* dread) can always be found to explain intention (*e.g.* he acted lest . . . out of dread); and that motives and intentions tend to merge or point towards each other. In deciding what shall or shall not qualify as intentions, however, we should have clearly in mind the central paradigm of intentions as being the rationally acknowledgeable purposes of action, including the 'meanings' of linguistic actions. With this paradigm before us we would normally rule out, as not meeting the qualification-requirements of intentions or as not constituting those motives which directly explain and therefore merge with intentions, various species of psychic cause (neuroses, traumas, most subconscious drives, the trigger-mechanisms of literary creation), and various factors which belong to the psychological background of creation and may indeed explain some of the writer's intentions but not those which he has *qua* literary artist (rivalry, the rebuff of patrons, the harrying of creditors, gloom over a mistress's death). Granted these restrictions, some typical anti-intentionalist definitions of intentions must be deemed out of court. Wimsatt and Beardsley partly equate them with 'the way he felt, what made him write'; Kuhns sees the quest for intentions as an inquiry into 'the artist's personal life-problems, life-history, and psychic peculiarities'.[6] Many aestheticians picture intentions as causes of a quasi-mechanical or quasi-biological kind. Northrop Frye, for instance, has compared literature to snowflakes and likened its genesis to a snowflake's cell-formation process.[7] Having painted this misleading picture of what intentions are, these aestheticians then have little trouble in showing that the pursuit of intentions can often be irrelevant. In answer to them one can only endorse Skinner's recent observation that they have scarcely met the central question whether it is pertinent to study the author's intentions *in* writing his work.[8]

In saying all this, I do not mean to rule out the possibility of establishing causal connexions between the author's psychology and what he intentionally creates, nor to deny that biographical or psychological data may sometimes be relevant to illuminating his intentions, nor yet to deny that we may sometimes want to talk of 'half-conscious' or even 'unconscious' intentions.[9] On this last point we should doubtless want to stress that such a use of the concept will inevitably be exceptional and parasitic upon more normal uses of it.

At this point it is relevant to indicate in what ways motives can merge with intentions. 'Explanation-by-motives' represents one important species of exegetical argument. The literary critic often gives an enriched explanation of a literary effect by imaginatively projecting a dimension of beliefs, attitudes and preferences which led the author to create that effect. In the case of *Don Quixote* it matters considerably to know that Cervantes, as a professional writer, was seriously concerned with the problem of making literature of popular entertainment accord with cultured canons of art rather than with the lowest common denominator of vulgar taste. The concern is voiced in *Don Quixote*, Part I, Chapters 47 and 48, in a discussion about fiction and drama, which is the ideological centre-piece of the whole novel. Knowing about this attitude helps one to understand the nature of parody in *Don Quixote* (i.e. its essentially literary or aesthetic bias) and explains why parody should be expended so incisively and profusely on a butt (the romances of chivalry) which might otherwise appear unworthy of extended ridicule. What one does in this piece of critical explanation is to start from an intended effect—parody in *Don Quixote*—and descriptively account for it by reference to the author's outlook and motives, which here can be represented as, or assimilated to, his intentions. The important point is that explanation-by-motives is logically subordinate and posterior to the identification of intended effects, and that the primary evidence for it is manifested in them.

The 'internalization' of intentions tends to falsify the status of authorial declarations of intention in literary criticism by making them appear oracular guides to information which ought properly to be regarded as logically deducible from the literary work itself and from the background of linguistic usage and cultural reference to which it belongs. I certainly have no wish to dispute the value of authorial declarations of intention (whether given directly in forewords, postscripts and marginalia, or indirectly in significant asides by fictitious characters); they provide a basis of sound literary criticism. But it is important not to misrepresent the implications of our dependence upon them. The fact that we are thus dependent, especially in reading old books like *Don Quixote*, or the esoteric forms of modern symbolist poetry, tends to make us overlook the fact that the essential criteria of meaning in literature remain the framework of context, usage and cultural suppositions to which I have just alluded. Even the author's declarations of intention are subordinate to these criteria. That is to say they are subject to exactly the same checks as those by which we judge intentions in the absence of the author's disclosures; and because they are thus checkable we may occasionally wish to reject them.

The belief that the recovery of intentions is impossible or irrelevant in criticism frequently rests on a distinction between Poetry and Prose. Poetry here includes all imaginative literature; Prose includes everything else, the favourite examples being the scientific treatise, the philosophical discourse, and the language of practical needs. Prose is supposed to convey or symbolize meanings which emanate from the utterer's conscious intentions and are pictures or mental propositions about the world: *e.g.* 'The discursive writer writes as an act of conscious will, and that conscious will is set over against the body of things he is describing.'[10] By contrast Poetry's function is 'centripetally directed; it is directed towards putting words together, not towards aligning words with meanings'.[10] Together with these distinctions there goes a medieval division between the faculties of mind alleged to be responsible for these expressive modes, and between the types of audience-response that they elicit. Poetry comes from the subconscious, the imagination, our 'symbolizing' faculties; Prose from discursive reason and the conscious will. Poetry is an 'autonomous symbol' of non-finite significance, an apparatus which each reader can use differently by virtue of its 'endless power of semination' and its capacity 'to open up levels of our interior reality'; Prose exhausts its function once there has occurred an exact coincidence between the pictures in the utterer's and audience's minds.[11]

These widespread assumptions, which have august origins in Romantic and Symbolist aesthetics, present easy targets for Wittgensteinian critical analysis. The whole conception of Poetry gets leverage from an antithetical, and shaky, conception of Prose. Especially dubious are the assumptions that there is *one* generic purpose which all forms of Prose have in common (*i.e.* taking pictures of reality for practical ends), and that Prose serves to communicate intentional representations of reality in the writer's conscious mind to the minds of his readers. Futhermore, the dichotomy faces serious empirical objections. So much of what is deemed proper to Poetry (stylized ceremony of expression, metaphor, symbol, etc.) enters vitally into many aspects of Prose as well, and so many of the families of Poetry overlap with genera of expression which on this view are essentially Prosaic, that the whole antithesis crumbles beneath the weight of exceptions and borderline cases. The dichotomy is a product of our inbuilt philosophical tendency to reach for categorical simplifications; and the attempt to effect such unitary reduction makes as little sense in the case of Poetry or literary art, with its myriad heterogeneous species, as it does in that of Prose.

The Poetry/Prose dichotomy is not a harmlessly abstract cliché. In *Quixote* criticism it has often been invoked as an implicit plea for a mitigation in the adequacy of the evidence that requires to be produced. The most diverse and outlandish meanings—philosophical creeds, moral views, political attitudes—have been ascribed to *Don Quixote* on the strength of the argument: 'Cervantes was an artist, not a philosopher; he therefore speaks with the language of poetic suggestion, not of analytic abstraction.' It is evident that such argument can give free play to a critic's subjective sensibility and inventive ingenuity.

o o o

I now pass to the consideration of two ways in which recent philosophical analyses of the procedures and logic involved in our explanation of intentional action (including communication) can be shown to apply as fundamentally to the language of literary criticism as they do to ordinary language. To these two ways we have already in effect added a third by suggesting that means-to-end explanation (as elicited by Anscombe's series of questions 'Why ?') are basic to literary exegesis. If this can be shown, then the essential axiom of anti-intentionalism—that the explanation of literary art by reference to the author's intentions is unnecessary or irrelevant or impossible—breaks down. It breaks down before the fact that such explanation is a necessary feature of any discussion about literary art and is subject to the same generic norms of correctness or appositeness as those which apply to the identification of intentions in non-artistic discourse. In literary criticism, as elsewhere, the diagnosis of intentions can often be correct, and demonstrably correct. If it were consistently false or problematic, then I suggest that a language of literary criticism would scarcely be conceivable.

Our discovery of intentions, in art as elsewhere, is primarily effected by consideration of what agents *do*. Anscombe has spoken of the motives which make us suppose that we discover them primarily by the interrogation of agents: among other reasons is the fact that for the most part we have no need to ask agents for their intentions, since we know what these are, and only make inquiry in those doubtful cases where we are uncertain. She points out later why it is that men can know each other's intentions without constant mutual interrogation. A good many of the familiar concepts of day-to-day discourse (telephoning, calling, groping, crouching, signing, paying, sending for, hiring . . .) are concepts of human action of an intentional kind. These, and a host of others, pick out from the multifarious details of human behaviour the purposes towards which it is directed. We have these identifying concepts because human purposes interest us (we have no equivalent conceptual armoury for events in the natural world, such as the movement of trees in the wind); and 'enormously complicated tacit conventions' of language enable us to apply them as a matter of course in our reports upon human actions. Thus 'even a child' could say, for example, of a man lying on a bed that he is resting or of a man handing over a bit of paper to a girl that he is paying the bill.[12] What Anscombe is applying here is the Wittgensteinian insight—an insight which has influenced many post-Wittgensteinian philosophers—that the explanation of intentional behaviour, as of linguistic meaning, can be achieved by the setting of an action (or utterance) against a background of human conventions, expectations, practices and procedures, and by redescribing it in terms of the function that it has by its conformation to that wider context. Now this is not the only way of explaining human actions; nor is it the only way of explaining intentions. However, it does, I believe, represent the chief way in which we explain intentions in literary criticism.

How does this mode of explanation apply to utterances in particular, rather than to acts in general? An answer to this question is that, as Austin and others have shown, utterances can be acts. Take the example given by Strawson in his development of Austin's concept of 'illocutionary' action—the policeman saying to the skater: 'The ice over there is very thin.'[13] An essential part of the explanation of this statement would be an identification of its 'illocutionary force': that is, of what the policeman *does* in saying what he says. Beyond its 'locutionary' meaning the statement has in this context the force of a warning. Austin's reason for the distinction between meaning and force, locution and illocution, was that even after one has elucidated grammatically and philologically what the sense of a statement is, questions will still remain as to the dynamic 'use' that the statement has in its context.[14] The way that one determines this 'use' is by reference to conventions of human behaviour—conventions which Austin regarded as being over and above the linguistic conventions of grammar and vocabulary. According to Austin all 'serious' or 'normal' statements in language have some kind of illocutionary force.[15] That force might be called the social or situational function that an utterer performs in saying words with a certain locutionary meaning (warning, entreating, pronouncing, naming, marrying, ordering, complimenting, stating . . .); the function is identified by the conformity of the words to certain more or less institutionalized procedures or conventions (whereby to say, for example, 'I do' in certain contexts is to marry), and is often rendered explicit by the utterance of performative formulae (*e.g.* 'I beg you . . .' before words which perform the act of entreating). The generality of application of Austin's doctrine is one reason why I believe that the concept of illocutionary redescription is applicable to statements in literary criticism. Another reason is that there seems to be an overlap between Austin's concept of contextual 'force' and Anscombe's concept of intentional human action. Basically similar principles of conventionalized redescription appear to be involved in saying of a man lying on a bed: 'He's resting,' as are involved in saying of the imaginary policeman: 'He's warning the skater.' For Austin it is by reference to communal knowledge of convention-governed practices that we identify the force of utterances; for Anscombe it is through our familiarity with human purposive skills, and with the linguistic conventions which identify them, that we can say what other people's intentions are. Anscombe declares that the concepts of human action by which we identify intentions cover most of man's natural history. I take it that literary art, and the explanation of it, fall under that broad head.

These analyses of how we discern the intentions of intentional linguistic activity have the following significance for literary criticism. The demonstration of intentions (in one important sense of that concept) is shown to consist in the determination of an act's logical function in its context, that function in turn being determined by reference to the background of relevant conventions and 'language-games' in which it fits, is learnt, and derives its life. This, rather than by an interview with the agent, is how we normally test the intentionality of actions. In the imaginary example the skater might for a moment be doubtful that the policeman was in fact warning him, and might only decide that to warn was indeed his intention by observing that simultaneously with his utterance he gesticulated and raised his voice. Here the consistent, mutually corroboratory implications of all the signs taken together determine what the utterance meant. Yet obviously gesticulations and shouts do not mean by nature and autonomously; they too, as well as utterances like the policeman's, are conventional signs. Thus the skater's interpretation is (*a*) by reference to the immediate context and (*b*) by tacit reference to a background of conventionalized (or normative) usage and behaviour. The literary critic, in his doubtless more sophisticated way, adopts the skater's exegetical procedure. The basic form of significant propositions in literary criticism corresponds to that 'convention-orientated' redescription of an action by which we identify its point, force or purpose, and hence its intention. Literary criticism, therefore, may be said to boil down to statements of the form: 'He's warning the skater' or: 'He's paying the bill,' although in order to be deemed to correspond to that form they surely need not parade a third-person subject and an active verb in the present indicative. The critic's assertions come under the head of Anscombe's concepts of intentional human action and/or, when they deal with the dynamic 'use' of statements, under that of Austin's doctrine of illocutionary forces. In either case they involve the convention-governed identification of intentions. As these examples indicate, the conventionalized redescription is the form of many key-statements about most aspects of literary art:

(a) *Don Quixote* is a work of comedy (genre-identification). (b) Cervantes often adapts rhetorical techniques of amplification and reduplication for ends of burlesque bathos (analysis of style). (c) Sancho Panza is an illiterate rustic simpleton (character-evaluation). (d) Sancho Panza's comic attributes are essentially those of the foolish funny servants—the *bobos* or *simples*—of sixteenth-century Spanish drama (source-identification). (e) *Don Quixote*, Part I, Chapter 47 sets forth, *via* the comments of the Canon of Toledo, Cervantes's objections to the chivalric romance and his classically-based formula for the ideal prose epic (the gist of a theoretical argument). (f) Don Quixote changes nothing—except Sancho Panza's character (the mutual impact of literary characters). (g) The episode of Mambrino's helmet is a turning-point in the hero's personality, for thereafter he shows a conciliatory tolerance towards viewpoints which contradict his own (psychology and development). (h) Cervantine irony tends to emphasize the surface speciousness, persuasiveness, or grandeur of the utterances of its victims in order to intensify the effect of ironic deflation (narrative techniques). (i) The ethos at the core of *Don Quixote* is thoroughly middle-brow and conventional; not so the amused insight into preposterous eccentricity which it displays (the author's world-view).

While I believe that all the above statements are at least arguably true, I maintain that (a), (b), (c), and (d) are either truisms or demonstrable truths. The fact is significant because it presupposes that one may state truths about the artist's intentions in doing what he does. Before this assertion the extreme forms of anti-intentionalism collapse.

That a number of the above examples are classifiable under Anscombe's concepts of intentional human action would not, I think, be seriously challenged. To say: '*Don Quixote* is a work of comedy' or: 'Sancho Panza is an illiterate rustic simpleton' is to assign the complex of Cervantes's actions in writing his novel or creating the character of Sancho to a certain generic class, and to ascribe to him the intentions characteristic of that class. One does the same when saying of a man lying on a bed: 'He's resting.' However, the assertion that some of the examples belong to the category of illocutionary redescriptions is perhaps more controversial and requires to be made good. In doing so I shall try to clarify the reasons why I call the critic's activity *conventionalized* redescription.

The doctrine of illocutionary forces relates to 'ordinary language'. To show its applicability to literary art I take an example which spans ordinary language and literary art: Churchill's dictum: 'Never in the field of human conflict was so much owed by so many to so few.'

Now on Austin's analysis the illocutionary force of this utterance would be something like 'praising'; and praising is akin to the often encountered literary device of hyperbolic eulogy. We may interject here, for illustration, miscellaneous types of illocutionary force that the literary critic might commonly identify: 'writing in the lyric (grand, tragic, panegyric) mode', 'allegorizing', 'symbolizing', 'narrating', 'parodying', 'introducing a story (or character)', 'resolving a plot', 'using dialogue (asides, soliloquies)'. That is to say, it is as true of statements in literary art as it is of statements in ordinary language that they are subsumable under some category of illocutionary force. To return to Churchill's declaration, it would seem possible to give a finer specification of what kind of praise this is; and to do so would surely not be a departure from illocutionary redescription but rather a refinement upon it. So one would say that the statement is a species of hyperbole in epigrammatic form, and that it is typical of panegyric oratory. Further it has the classic rhetorical aims of persuading and moving. This more detailed account is still convention-dependent; it picks out the conventionally identifiable 'forces' that the statement exhibits; 'asserting', 'arguing', 'defining', 'exaggerating for effect', 'hyperbolically comparing'. In so doing it pinpoints the kinds of comprehension and response that an audience would appropriately register, *e.g.* by taking hyperbole as a partly true expression of admiration rather than as literal fact. However, this exegesis, in order to qualify as good literary criticism, could go still further in placing the Churchillian statement within specific family-groups of an illocutionary kind. The literary critic might proceed thus: 'Churchill extols the grandeur of the pilots' action by the audacious, sweeping inclusiveness of his claim that the nation's indebtedness is without historical precedent, by his authoritative and law-like assessment of the proportions of the debt, and by the deliberate sublimity and grandiose symmetry of his style.' Here one notes the family-resemblances that Churchill's statement bears to various other forms of statement—to panegyric assertions of uniqueness, to law-like definitions, to historical invocations of precedent—and defines its function in terms of all these family-resemblances taken together. Here one encroaches on the area where the illocutionary force that a statement has does not necessarily have an appropriate verb or term for identifying it. Thus 'citing precedents' is a conventionally recognized illocutionary act; 'asserting uniqueness' is not. Yet 'asserting uniqueness' is still an illocutionary force; and this description of Churchill's statement is still convention-dependent in the sense of 'conforming to recognizable norms of classificatory description'. The norms in this case are equivalent to nothing less than the patterns into which speech-situations fall and the labels that we have for identifying them. These situations are so diffuse that one cannot envisage them all falling under descriptive identifying labels (as many functions of rhetoric do); yet they display diverse family-likenesses and are consequently capable of description by a process of analogy and contrast. Such a process, I believe, underlies all literary criticism whether it is concerned with the intentions of individual statements or passages, or with the intentions that are displayed in major parts of a literary work.

What we have achieved by this analysis is an account of the statement's 'meaning'. Here 'meaning' has a fuller sense than either Austin's concept of locutionary meaning or the notion of paraphrase. It is equivalent to 'illocutionary force' (with the comprehension of locutionary meaning being taken for granted) and to what Grice has recently called 'utterer's occasion-meaning'.[16] Suppose that we give a paraphrase of Churchill's statement: 'What he said, in effect, was that the R.A.F. had performed an outstanding feat of arms and that the nation was deeply in its debt.' This paraphrase, or any imaginable equivalent, is obviously a deficient account of the precise communicative functions of the Churchillian statement. It leaves out of the picture the specific complex of illocutionary forces which the statement has; it fails to convey many of the nuances that the words have by being uttered in precisely this way in this context (Grice's 'utterer's occasion-meaning'). Now an exact definition of the statement's communicative functions would have to record these individuating characteristics. In doing so it would resemble good literary criticism—especially by its conformity to the literary critic's typical insistence that his task is not paraphrase or grammatical gloss, but the elucidation of the specifically artistic purposes of literature. If it is accepted that there is an overlap between, on the one hand, 'illocutionary force' and 'utterer's occasion-meaning' and, on the other hand, the full contextual meaning studied by the literary critic, then certain important consequences follow. Both the above-mentioned philosophical concepts have been defined (by Strawson, elaborating on Austin, and by Grice) in terms of the concepts of intention and of the conventionalized identification.[17] What follows is that the full definition of 'meaning' in literature is equivalent to the recovery of intentions. If it is objected that I have been talking primarily of statements, rather than of larger features of literature, I would counter by saying that even generalizations about these larger features ultimately reduce to (implicit) assertions about statements. At the very least it can be claimed that in one basic aspect the critic's work consists of the recovery of intentions.

Further interesting consequences follow—consequences which clarify the central function of literary criticism. This function is often defined (partly as a result of anti-intentionalist doctrine) in ways which float unhappily among the following formulations: 'saying what "the poem" means', 'saying all that it suggestively implies for me, the reader', 'evaluating it'. I would maintain that the critic's task is essentially represented by the first of these formulations. Now according to the way of thinking which believes in the Poetry/Prose dichotomy, it is characteristically the function of Prose to convey meanings (in the traditional sense), these being loosely equated with 'intentions' of the writer, i.e. what he formulates conceptually. It is further implied that the aesthetic functions of statements (Poetry) are an overplus of significance which, though not unintended by the writer, are not fully intended by him, or may exceed his intentions. By this means some of the essential communicative functions of imaginative literature become divorced from the writer's intentions. By my concept of 'meaning' the attachment would be re-effected. The term 'meaning', despite its being taken in an extended sense, is helpful in the context of my argument because it suggests that the aesthetic qualities of statements are integral to the communicative act, that recognition of them is the primary response that the imaginative writer seeks, that such recognition is generically akin to other forms of meaning-identification and follows the same tacit process of conventionalized reference, and that such recognition is tantamount, when correct, to the identification of intentions.

To what extent does my list of exegetical statements about *Don Quixote* correspond to self-consciously formulated declarations of intention on the part of Cervantes ? Since it is clearly a mistake to suppose that intentional action only occurs when preceded by a form of mental incantation ('Here I employ irony . . .') there is no need to represent these statements as transcriptions of events in Cervantes's mind. The question is rather whether he would conceivably have been likely to acknowledge these as his intentions, or whether he did in fact do so. The answer to this is that he either avows explicitly, or almost certainly would have avowed, intentions (a), (c), (d), (e), (f). He would probably have assented to (b), (g) and (h), though he would have been unlikely to arrive at these assertions spontaneously. It is possible that he would have acknowledged (i) provided that one eliminates from it that part which, as in the case of (f), is clever over-statement, and that further part which fuses description with partly derogatory value-judgements on his moral attitudes.

It seems that intentions (b), (g), (h) and (i) present us with a paradox. How can we assert that these propositions represent Cervantes's intentions if he was unlikely to have formulated them himself ? This paradox derives its power to tease from our tendency to regard all intentions either as self-consciously conceptualized, or as capable of becoming so. Intentions (understood as 'meanings') are commonly taken as whatever someone actually formulates; and intentions ('purposes') are equated with whatever someone is capable of formulating about the goals of his action. Now I do not in principle wish to challenge—indeed I strongly support—the view that 'having the concept of the action one is performing' is a necessary condition of being its intentional author, and that the knowledge *of* one's intentions is logically linked with the knowledge that one displays in executing them.[18] Rather I wish to point out that, as authors of intentional actions (particularly linguistic actions), we do not necessarily have very precise or detailed concepts by which to identify the infinite host of conventionalized skills that we imitatively pick up and intentionally use when we learn a language. If we had, then philosophers, grammarians, rhetoricians, literary critics and others would be out of a job. Doubtless we have a unique authority in formulating our linguistic intentions, as we do in our other acts; yet our formulations may be capable of much finer and more expert honing than we ourselves could give. For a critic's description of an author's intentions to be correct it is not necessary that it should have occurred to the latter in very much the same terms, but rather that it should fit as an accurate explanatory grid over what he has written and that one should be capable of envisaging the author assenting to the description once its terms had been made familiar to him.

The linguistic or literary skills which enter into communicative intentions without necessarily being capable of exact formulation by their user include the whole conceptual and stylistic infrastructure of language, and also its emotive and aesthetic features. I refer, for example, to the subtle distinctions implicit in our use of difficult words or concepts; to the emotive function of the stylistic devices in rhetorical statements; to the nuances which are given to meaning by gestures, tones of voice, metaphors, word-rhythms; to the attitude that an occasional essayist might adopt towards his readers (flattery, cajolery, urbanity, button-holing familiarity); to the elements of a writer's 'style' in the sense of outlook or vision (which like style or dispositional traits in personality may go unformulated by the subject). I refer, more specifically, to the cases of irony and parody in *Don Quixote* with their brilliantly varied and subtle uses. Everyone would agree that Cervantes is a master of these techniques, and that these techniques have to be intentional virtually by definition. Yet it is unlikely that Cervantes would have used these concepts, or any equivalent ones, to describe the comedy of *Don Quixote*. It is also improbable that he would have pondered much about the comic devices which these concepts refer to. Though Cervantes was an intelligent critic and theorist of literature, he would neither have been inclined nor (probably) able to indulge in the speculations which propositions (b) and (h) represent. The reason for this is that Renaissance literary criticism did not tend towards a theory, nor towards critical discussion, of the comic. His comments on the humour of *Don Quixote* tend to be on the level of: 'The bystanders were much amused at the lunacies (*disparates*) of Don Quixote and the simple-minded nonsense (*simplezas, necedades*) of his squire'. Thus there are major features of Cervantes's literary art which we would naturally describe as being consciously and deliberately created, which constitute his intentions (whether one takes the term to signify meanings or purposes), but which he would have been unlikely to formulate or conceptualize himself in any way more precise than by such statements as: 'Here I was trying to be funny.' M. Jourdain could speak prose without knowing that he was doing so.

In two articles which set out to define the logical pre-conditions for human communication Grice has discussed meaning in terms of the concept of intention—a concept which is basic to his conceptual scheme.[19] There are, I believe, two reasons why he accords it this basic status: first, human communication uses signs or language as means to ends ('inducing beliefs', 'issuing orders'); second, communication as such only takes place on the basis of mutual recognition, by utterer and audience, of the fact that an utterance is intentionally used as means for securing an intended response. Grice strongly emphasizes this second point, namely that the intended force of utterances (the utterer's 'occasion-meaning') must be grasped *via* the mediation of the audience's recognition that the utterance was made with the intention of applying that determinate force and no other. 'Communication' is not achieved if Mr x leaves in Mr y's room pictures of Mrs y displaying undue familiarity with Mr z; it is only achieved if Mr x draws, under Mr y's gaze, a recognizable diagram depicting the unpalatable truth, and if Mr y appreciates that the diagram has the intended force of a warning.

I believe that Grice's analysis of the prerequisite of intentional communication has important application to literary art, as the following pair of contrasted situations may show. We are at Lady Windermere's tea-party. The butler enters with loaded tray, trips up, and falls flat on his face, causing havoc to the china. Our first impulse, perhaps, is to assist him to his feet and ask if he's all right. Now let us suppose that we are spectators at a farce. The butler enters with loaded tray, etc. If our reaction here is to rush on stage and administer comfort, we shall be making fools of ourselves. The reason is that the butler's entry here is a 'communication' (a communication more elaborate than a joke, but not unlike a joke), intended to 'mean something' (the representation of a funny event) and intended to produce a certain response from the audience. The fact that we do recognize the butler's entry in the second case as a complex kind of statement with a determinate meaning—intended as such and intended to be recognized as such—is evident from the fact that we, the audience, remain rooted in our seats, whether or not we evince the hoped-for further response of laughter.

The recognition that poets, novelists and dramatists intend to arrest our attention, and engage our interest, in certain ways is basic to our response to literature. Hence we describe our suspension of disbelief in reading novels as 'willing'. Hence we have a name—'the interruption of artistic illusion'—for those situations where in the body of a novel or play the artist draws deliberate attention to some part of the subtle interrelation between the spell-binder, the spellbound, and the spell. The interrelation is subtle because, for novelistic or dramatic communication to occur, the public must lucidly recognize it and yet respect the convention by which one agrees to pretend that it is not there. Hence too we find those cases where artistic communication is short-circuited irresistibly funny. The best example is provided by a work of fiction—*Don Quixote*—which is based on the situation of a man taking a fictitious genre so seriously that he madly comes to confuse it with history and tries to enact it in real life. Now it may be objected that I am merely discussing our acknowledgement of the intentionality of literary art with reference to the basic conventions of literature or drama. To know that writers have aesthetic designs upon it is not necessarily to know what these designs are. Of course this is true. Yet I submit that this truth implicitly entails the main point that I wish to establish: that we fundamentally recognize art as intentional and must logically be prepared to represent our specific interpretation of it as a response intended by the artist. In Grice's words, 'a reference to an intended effect of, or response to, the utterance of *x* would provide material for answering the question *what* U meant by uttering *x*'.[20]

I think that we always tacitly conceive of artistic meaning as an *intended* response. The fact that we do so becomes explicitly manifest at certain moments of literary art: those where a passage can have more than one meaning but has a particular meaning by virtue of the fact that some restrictive convention is being operated. Examples are: irony, dramatic irony, parody, allegory or symbolism, and in general any literary mode which we specifically call 'stylized' or 'conventional'. Now in these cases failure to recognize the convention results usually in serious failures of communication. In cases of such failure, actual or potential, it is normal for the literary critic to insist on the intentionality of the use of the convention: *e.g.*: 'Surely you can't take the adulterous love-scene at the *Comices Agricoles* in *Madame Bovary* as being seriously romantic; it's meant ironically.' There is a parallel in *Don Quixote*. Since the early nineteenth century critics have tended to split the hero's delusions into a noble half and a comic half, to assert that his aims are sublime though the means that he employs to further them are absurd. An important reason why this view enjoyed (and enjoys) wide currency is that Don Quixote's practical acts are manifestly farcical (he charges at windmills believing them to be giants), whereas his declaration of chivalric aims *could* with some measure of speciousness be taken as unimpeachably serious. Thus it is not immediately obvious that 'righting wrongs', 'succouring the oppressed', 'serving a lady', 'seeking honourable fame', are ends to be held up to ridicule. It is undoubtedly true that *if* Cervantes regarded Don Quixote's profession of these aims as idealistic declarations in any normal sense of 'idealistic', then he would have been very loath to deride them. Yet he does deride them in his novel for precisely the same reason as he ridicules Don Quixote's acts—because the aims, like the acts, are a madly literal mimicry of the stereotype behaviour of the heroes of chivalric romance. In other words, the aims (like the acts) are presented as parody; and this would have been immediately obvious to the seventeenth-century reader, who would have recognized in Don Quixote's phraseology a direct mimicry of that used by knights-errant in the declaration of *their* aims. Consequently this reader would not have taken Don Quixote as a deranged, but part-sublime, idealist; he would have seen him as a comical lunatic engaged in the highly unnatural business of modelling his every act and utterance, as a self-supposed knight-errant, on the behaviour typical of heroes of fiction. I think that the normal, natural response to the above-described misinterpretation of Don Quixote's declaration of aims would be: 'But surely, don't you see ? It's intended as parody.' In making this assertion we would not be giving a piece of inside information in the absence of which it would be perfectly in order to take Don Quixote's behaviour as something other than parody. The continuation of that response would be to point to the general context of the knight's behaviour, and also to chivalric romances, and then to demonstrate that it makes consistently better sense to interpret Don Quixote's behaviour as parody than in any other way. To discover the intentions of an action we turn to its context. Yet what we are doing in searching for these intentions—and this is the point that I wish to stress here—is looking for an intended response; and it is ultimately to this intentionality that we appeal when we object to a response which misses the point.

If Grice's analysis is admitted as having purchase on literary art, then it follows that this comes under the general category of 'communication' and that the responses which literature seeks are securely anchored in utterer's intentions. By this I do not mean that we find farces, for example, funny just because their creators intend them to be so. Rather I mean that our finding them funny is normally dependent on our prior recognition that they are intended as such. I would also maintain that our evincing amusement is logically bound up with the knowledge by which we know the primary 'intended response'; to know fully what it 'means' is to know that it is good (or bad) comedy. Thus the favourable or unfavourable impact that art makes upon us is not, like Austin's 'perlocutionary' force, a set of causal effects conceptually separable from the identification of illocutionary force, but is part-and-parcel of it. However, the important question of the relationship between understanding and appreciating, knowing and evaluating, is one that this paper cannot investigate.

E.D.HIRSCH, Jr
Three Dimensions of Hermeneutics

How important are the theoretical disagreements that now divide serious students of interpretation? How true is the resigned opinion that our various schools and approaches are like a multitude of warring sects, each with its own uncompromising theology? Is it the destiny of those who practice interpretation never to achieve an ecumenical harmony of theoretical principles? If that is our destiny, so much the worse for theory, which is then only the ideology of a sect, and so much the better for the common sense of a practitioner who disdains theory to get on with his work.

> For modes of faith let graceless zealots fight;
> His can't be wrong, whose life is in the right.

A theorist would be right to reply that the repudiation of theory in favor of common sense implies a theoretical position, and that the commonality of common sense would seem to require a wide measure of theoretical agreement about the nature of a 'sensible' or 'good' interpretation. In my opinion, such implicit agreement is not only possible but already widely extant. The appearance of disagreement, which itself produces so many quarrels, can be traced back to a tendency of interpretive theory to lump together both what interpreters agree on and what in the nature of the case they can never agree on. The distinction in my title between various dimensions of hermeneutics suggests my ecumenical purpose; by separating the separable it may be possible to disclose areas of agreement shared by apparently conflicting theories.

As a first step, I propose that interpretive theories should not lump together the descriptive and the normative aspects of interpretation; that theorists should disengage the descriptive dimension of hermeneutics, which concerns the nature of interpretation, from the normative dimension, which concerns its goals. For the goals of interpretation are determined ultimately by value-preferences, and interpreters do not exhibit more agreement in their values than the generality of people. I know it is usual to argue, as Coleridge did, that certain values and therefore certain interpretive norms are permanently rooted in the nature of literature, that the normative is derived from the descriptive. I know why Coleridge and others have held this view in the history of literary theory; they have desired a permanent and universal sanction for certain evaluative norms of literature, and what more permanent sanction could exist than 'the nature of literature'? By the same reasoning, it is convenient to derive permanent, normative principles of interpretation from 'the nature of interpretation.'

I find the structure of such reasoning entirely circular: good literature is that which conforms to the true nature of literature; good interpretation is that which conforms to the true nature of interpretation. But what is this 'true nature' except a tautological rephrasing of 'good literature' or 'good interpretation'? Are there not numerous examples of bad literature or bad interpretation which do not conform to this true nature? Yet if these bad examples are pieces of literature, if they are instances of interpretation, they must exhibit the true nature of literature or of interpretation. The Coleridgean argument imports the normative into the descriptive from the beginning, by sleight of hand.

Stated bluntly, the nature of interpretation is to construe from a sign-system (for short, 'text') something more than its physical presence. That is, the nature of a text is to mean whatever we construe it to mean. I am aware that theory should try to provide normative criteria for discriminating good from bad, legitimate from illegitimate constructions of a text, but mere theory cannot change the nature of interpretation. Indeed, we need a norm precisely because the nature of a text is to have no meaning except that which an interpreter wills into existence. We, not our texts, are the makers of the meanings we understand, a text being only an occasion for meaning, in itself an ambiguous form devoid of the consciousness where meaning abides. One meaning of a text can have no higher claim than another on the grounds that it derives from the 'nature of interpretation,' for all interpreted meanings are ontologically equal; they are all equally real. When we discriminate between legitimate and illegitimate meanings in *Lycidas*, for example, we cannot claim merely to be describing the nature of Milton's text, for the text compliantly changes its nature from one interpreter to another. This ontological equality of all interpreted meanings shows forth in the fact that hermeneutic theory has sanctioned just about every conceivable norm of legitimacy in interpretation. From this historical fact I infer that interpretive norms are not really derived from theory, and that theory codifies *ex post facto* the interpretive norms we already prefer.

To take a central example from the history of interpretation: by the eighteenth century an impressive victory had been won over certain medieval modes of interpretation, so that by then anachronistic allegorizing seemed to be permanently repudiated. Under the post-medieval view, since Homer and Virgil were not Christian their texts could not legitimately be regarded as Christian allegories. Schleiermacher, in the late eighteenth century, was merely codifying the work of his humanistic predecessors when he stated the following as a universal canon of interpretation: 'Everything in a given text which requires fuller interpretation must be explained and determined exclusively from the linguistic domain common to the author and his original public.'[1] Under this principle, Christian allegorizing of the ancients is deprived of all legitimacy, and the way is thereby opened to an interpretation that is truly historical and scientific.

Or, so it seemed to Schleiermacher. But the humanistic repudiation of anachronisms cannot be upheld on purely cognitive or logical grounds. Under Schleiermacher's canon, no text can legitimately mean at a later time what it could not have meant originally, but logic alone hardly supports this inference. The medieval interpreters were well aware that Homer and Vergil had been pagans who could not consciously have intended or communicated Christian meanings. The exegetes of the Middle Ages implicitly held to another principle which can be stated as follows: 'Everything in a given text which requires fuller interpretation need *not* be explained and determined exclusively from the linguistic domain common to the author and his original public.' Which principle is logically the more compelling, this implicit medieval one, or that of Schleiermacher? The answer is easy. The medieval principle is logically stronger because self-evidently a text can mean anything it has been understood to mean. If an ancient text has been interpreted as a Christian allegory, that is unanswerable proof that it can be so interpreted. Thus, the illegitimacy of anachronistic allegory, implied by Schleiermacher's canon, is deduced neither from empirical fact nor logic. His norm of legitimacy is not, of course, deduced at all; it is chosen. It is based upon a value-preference, and not on theoretical necessity. His preference for original meaning over anachronistic meaning is ultimately an ethical choice. I would confidently generalize from this example to assert that the normative dimension of interpretation is always in the last analysis an ethical dimension.

At this point I shall not digress to take sides in the ethical dispute between the anachronists and the historicists, for I wish to deal with that issue at the end of this essay. But I do pause to observe that the exegetical morality of the medieval allegorizers is not necessarily less admirable than their logic. Indeed, it seems to me that both Schleiermacher and those medieval interpreters repudiated by his canon are following according to their different lights the very same ethical principle. For anachronistic meaning and original meaning have this in common: they are both attempts to achieve legitimacy under the criterion of the 'best meaning.' In the history of interpretation it would seem to be a constant principle that the 'best meaning' is to be considered the most legitimate meaning of a text. The differences arise in defining 'best.' An interpreter of the thirteenth century could argue that Christian allegory is a better meaning than the original, pagan one, while a humanist of the Renaissance could respond that the original meaning in antiquity is superior to any that could be imposed by the graceless culture of the Middle Ages. In the late eighteenth and early nineteenth century Romantics like Schleier-macher could extend the humanist tradition with the argument that the original meaning is always the best meaning no matter what the provenence of the text, because every culture has infinite value in its own right; each culture is a note in the divine symphony, as Herder rhapsodized; or as Ranke preached, every age is immediate to God. Although we no longer shore up our historicism with such quasi-religious conceptions, the romantic ideal of cultural pluralism has continued to be the dominant ethical norm for interpretation during most of the nineteenth and twentieth centuries: it is more com-prehensive and more humanizing to embrace the plurality of cultures than to be imprisoned in our own. We ought therefore to respect original meaning as the best meaning, the most legitimate norm for interpretation. Only recently has historicism turned back upon itself to announce that we *are* imprisoned in our own culture willy-nilly, and we must therefore return to a quasi-medieval conception of interpretation, namely that the best meaning (for that matter any meaning) must be anachronistic whether we like it or not. Under this recent conception, the 'best meaning' reveals itself as a self-conscious, ethical choice as to what is best 'for us today' according to some standard that is compelling in our present historical circum-stances.

If the normative dimension of hermeneutics belongs, as I have argued, to the domain of ethical choice, is it nevertheless possible to discover truly universal principles of the sort Schleiermacher en-visioned, principles that do not depend on the value-preferences of individual interpreters? Is there in hermeneutics an analytical dimension which, in contrast to the normative, is logically deductive, empirically descriptive, and neutral with respect to values and ethical choices? The spirit of the present age inclines us skeptically to assume that such a pretense of objective neutrality would merely be a mask for a particular set of values. Yet if we could manage to find an area of agreement shared by widely different interpretive sects, then the reality of a truly descriptive dimension of hermeneutics would come to seem more plausible. And if the area of theoretical agreement could be gradually enlarged, there might emerge a sense of community in the discipline of interpretation, a sense of belonging to a common enterprise.

○ ○ ○

One example of a purely descriptive theoretical conception, and one that seems to me potentially fruitful is the distinction between meaning and significance. When I first proposed this distinction my motivation was far from neutral; I equated meaning simply with original meaning, and I wished to point up the integrity and permanence of original meaning.[2] This earlier discussion I now regard as being only a special application of a conception that is in principle universal. For the distinction between meaning and significance (and the clarifications it provides) are not limited to instances where meaning is equated with the author's original meaning; it holds as well for any and all instances of 'anachronistic meaning.'[3]

This universality in the distinction is readily seen if meaning is defined *tout court* as that which a text is taken to represent. No normative limitations are imported into the definition, since under it, meaning is simply meaning-for-an-interpreter. Moreover, the definition does not (and did not in my earlier discussion) limit itself merely to a paraphrasable or translatable 'message,' but embraces every aspect of representation, including the typographical and phonemic, which an interpreter construes. My earlier definition of meaning was too narrow and normative only in that it restricted meaning to those constructions where the interpreter is governed by his conception of the author's will. The enlarged definition now comprises constructions where authorial will is partly or totally disregarded.

The important feature of meaning as distinct from significance is that meaning is the determinate representation of a text for an interpreter. An interpreted text is always taken to represent something, but that something can always be related to something else. Significance is meaning-as-related-to-something-else. If an interpreter did not conceive a text's meaning to be *there* as an occasion for contemplation or application, he would have nothing to think or talk about. Its thereness, its self-identity from one moment to the next allows it to be contemplated. Thus, while meaning is a principle of stability in an interpretation, significance embraces a principle of change. Meaning-for-an-interpreter can stay the same although the meaningfulness (significance) of that meaning can change with the changing contexts in which that meaning is applied. An interpreter could, for instance, find the following to be variously meaningful: 'The cat is on the mat,' depending on whether the cat has left the mat, on whether he likes cats, and so on. The point is not that an interpreter must apply meaning to changing contexts, but that he could do so and still be able in every case to construe his text as representing an identical meaning.

Alternative kinds of semantic classification can, of course be made, as the work of Ingarden demonstrates, but I conceive this dual classification to be deeply fundamental and non-arbitrary because of the double-sidedness of speech. An interpreter is always playing two roles simultaneously—as speaker (or re-speaker) of meaning and as listener to meaning. Both moments are necessary, for if the text is not 'spoken' (construed) it cannot be 'heard,' and if it is not heard, it cannot have been, for the interpreter, spoken. Meaning is what an interpreter actualizes from a text; significance is that actual speaking as heard in a chosen and variable context of the interpreter's experiential world.

The main objection to this distinction between a principle of stability and a principle of change has been that it fails to describe what actually takes place in the process of interpretation. It is said that the distinction proposes what is in fact a psychological impossibility. If this were so the objection would be fatal, since empirical truth is the ultimate arbiter of theories in the practical disciplines. But I doubt the empirical validity of the objection, which implies that the interpreter's mind is not divisible, cannot be in two places at once. As I have just suggested, the very foundation of the distinction between meaning and significance is that doubling of the mind which is omnipresent in speech, and is called by linguists '*dédoublement de la personnalité*.'[4] Such doubling is not a matter of doubt among students of literature, who know myriad examples of self-multiplication within the boundaries of individual works. When a writer puts on a mask for ironic effect, as in Swift's *A Modest Proposal*, the interpreter's mind must be in two places at once as he entertains both the perspective of the modest proposer and the perspective of Swift. In every ironic construction we entertain two perspectives at once, and there is not, I think, any rigid limitation on the number of perspectives we can entertain at once. Similarly, when an interpreter emphatically rejects the attitudes of a speaker or writer, he also adopts those attitudes in order to reject them.

I have dwelt on meaning and significance because I believe this purely analytical distinction can help resolve some of the disagreements in hermeneutics, particularly certain disagreements involving the concept of historicity. This concept belongs to a third dimension of hermeneutics—the metaphysical. Adherents to Heidegger's metaphysics take the view that all attempts accurately to reconstruct past meanings are doomed to failure since not just our texts but also our understandings are historical. It is the nature of man to have no permanently defined nature distinct from his historically constituted existence. Whatever we know is decisively accommodated to our own historical world and cannot be known to us apart from that determining context. An interpreter must therefore learn to live with his historical self just as Freud would have him live with his subliminal self, not by trying to negate it, which is impossible, but by consciously making the best of it. Interpreters make the best of our historicity not by reconstructing an alien world from our texts but by interpreting them within our own world and making them speak to us.

o o o

This metaphysical position, skeptical and dogmatic at once, needs to be isolated from the analytical dimension of hermeneutics. No doubt it can be argued that analysis always carries metaphysical implications, and no doubt a shrewd ontologist could deduce metaphysical principles from the analytical distinction between meaning and significance. Yet I would wish to reply that the exercise would be pointless, since the distinction concords with a number of different metaphysical positions. Moreover, I would argue that there is far less danger in ignoring metaphysics than in introducing it prematurely into the practical questions of interpretation. A precocious ascent into the realm of ontology is just what needs to be avoided in the descriptive, analytical side of hermeneutic theory.

It is a notable irony that Heidegger's metaphysics itself depends upon a purely analytical principle taken directly from hermeneutic theory—namely the hermeneutic circle. This principle holds that the process of understanding is necessarily circular, since we cannot know a whole without knowing some of its constituent parts, yet we cannot know the parts as such without knowing the whole which determines their functions. (This principle can be easily grasped by self-consciously construing a sentence.) In *Sein und Zeit*, Heidegger expands the circumference of the hermeneutic circle beyond textual interpretation to embrace all knowing. Everywhere in knowledge the whole is prior to its parts, since the meaningfulness of a part is disclosed only in its relation to or function within a larger whole. The prior sense of the whole which ultimately lends meaning to any person's experience is his spiritual cosmos or *Welt*. But, since a person's *Welt* is always constitutively historical, it follows that any meaning we experience must have been pre-accommodated to our historical world. We cannot escape the fact that our historical world is a pre-given of our experience and is therefore constitutive of any textual interpretation.

This generalized version of the hermeneutic circle seems at first glance to support the position that accurate reconstruction of past meaning is impossible. It is futile to project ourselves into the historical past where our texts arose, since our own present world is already pre-given in our attempted projection. Our reconstruction can never be authentic because we can never exclude our own world through which alone the past was disclosed. Our own present is the pre-given and the foregone conclusion in any historical reconstruction. If Heidegger's version of the hermeneutic circle is correct, it follows that the traditional aims of historical scholarship are largely illusory.

The direct application of this metaphysical argument to textual interpretation seems to me premature on at least two grounds. First, the metaphysical principle says nothing about subtle questions of degree. It argues that some degree of anachronism is necessarily present in any historical reconstruction, but as to whether a particular reconstruction is severely or trivially compromised the principle says nothing. The history of interpretation exhibits remarkable congruities between views of, say, *Hamlet* in the nineteenth and twentieth centuries, and shows remarkable conflicts of interpretation within the confines of either period. Obviously, the pre-given historical world cannot be the decisive factor that accounts in such cases for the similarities between different periods or the unreconcilable differences of interpretation within the same period. A premature recourse to metaphysics in order to explain these anomalies can easily become a facile substitute for serious thought, and historical reconstruction can cease to be even a plausible goal of inquiry. That is not, however, the logical consequence of Heidegger's metaphysics. Under his principles all interpretations are time-bound and anachronistic, both those which attempt accurate reconstruction and those which do not. Yet deliberate reconstructions are different from deliberate anachronisms whether or not we follow Heidegger, and particular reconstruction *may* be fairly accurate even under his principles. It follows that the decision to attempt a reconstruction instead of a vital, present-day interpretation is not, after all, governed by metaphysics. Even if Heidegger is right, the two kinds of attempt are both possible, and the decision to make one kind of attempt rather than the other remains an ethical choice, not a metaphysical necessity.

The second and more important objection to carrying Heidegger's metaphysics directly into the theory of interpretation is that his expanded version of the hermeneutic circle is in crucial respects probably wrong. The principle of the hermeneutic circle does not lead inevitably to dogmatic historical skepticism. If an interpretation is grounded in the interpreter's entire *Welt*, it will no doubt be different from any past meaning, since undoubtedly a person's entire spiritual world will be different from any that existed in the past. Yet it is open to question whether the whole that prestructures meaning must be conceived in this comprehensive way. The very introduction of 'historicity' as a chief characteristic of *Welt* means that a boundary has been drawn, since historicity is not the chief component of a person's spiritual world. It is, rather, a limited domain of shared cultural experience apart from the bigger domain of unshared experience that makes up a person's world. The Heideggerian concept of *Welt* is at times undistinguishable from what used to be called *Zeitgeist*, and is just as problematical as the earlier concept. To limit the circumference of *Welt* (after having insisted upon its expansion) at the vague boundary between shared and private experience is entirely arbitrary.

Nevertheless, a boundary is certainly convenient. For if *Welt* is taken in its entirety, then each person's *Welt* is unique, and accurate understanding of another's meaning becomes impossible. But if I agree to draw a boundary, how do I decide where it should be drawn? I see only one way to avoid arbitrariness in the decision, and it is based on the observation that the *Welt* which actively prestructures an interpretation is always a highly selective sub-cosmos of an interpreter's world. For instance, any person who is now understanding my present discourse must be *excluding* far more of his spiritual world than ever he is bringing to the exercise. Such excluding is indeed logically necessary to any act of interpretation. On logical grounds, De Morgan has brilliantly shown that we cannot interpret discourse without limiting the *Welt* or 'universe' that forms its context, and he coined the phrase 'universe of discourse' to describe this necessary limitation.[5] Since the spiritual universe that actively governs an interpretation is limited and selective, no inherent necessity requires this delimited world to be different from any that existed in the past.

This last objection to Heidegger's dogmatic historical skepticism is, I believe, fatal, but the death struggle will have to take place elsewhere, conducted by professional wrestlers, and not by amateurs like me. The implications of these objections for the theory and practice of interpretation are the matters I wish to stress, and these implications are to my mind bluntly negative on the question whether metaphysics offers anything of practical utility to hermeneutic theory. First, metaphysical speculation has not yet brought to interpretation the power to deduce, *a priori*, significant matters of fact. It does not demonstrate that fairly accurate reconstruction is impossible; it does not, to my mind, even prove that absolutely accurate reconstruction doesn't actually occur, for metaphysics has no power to legislate what is or is not the case in the realm of the possible. It cannot, therefore, help us in specific instances. Second, metaphysics, being by nature universal, applies indiscriminately to all interpretations, both those that attempt historical reconstruction and those that disdain it. Thus, it provides no basis for choice as between various aims of interpretation. Powerless in deciding matters of fact, Heideggerian metaphysics is equally powerless to dictate what ought to be chosen in the realm of values. We can depend neither on metaphysics nor on neutral analysis in order to make decisions about the goals of interpretation. We have to enter the realm of ethics. For, after rejecting ill-founded attempts to derive values and goals from the presumed nature of interpretation, or from the nature of Being, what really remains is ethical persuasion.

o   o   o

In resisting some claims of current 'metaphysical hermeneutics' I must admit to at least one metaphysical assertion: an interpreter is not necessarily so trapped in historicity that he loses his freedom; he is free to choose his aims, and within the context of those aims and the broad conventions of language, he is free to choose his meanings. I therefore understand the current controversy over historicity as a conflict not of abstract theories, but of values. When we are urged to adopt present relevance rather than original meaning as the 'best meaning,' we find ourselves repeating the old pattern of controversy between the medieval allegorists (the Heideggerians of an earlier day) and the later humanists. While this conflict cannot be resolved by mere analysis, its issues can be clarified, and clarification may bring unforeseen agreement.

Sometimes, for instance, the conflict between proponents of original and of anachronistic meaning is shown by analysis to be no conflict at all. These arguments about meaning sometimes originate in a failure to notice that meaning and significance—two different things—are being given the same name. To take a homely and simple example, some time ago, while driving on the New Jersey Turnpike, my wife and I were trying to interpret a sign that kept appearing on the median strip of the highway. It looked like this:

203

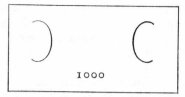

After pondering these hieroglyphics in vain, we began to notice a feature of the Turnpike that was consistently associated with the sign; a few seconds after seeing the sign, we would pass a gap in the median strip wide enough to let a car cross over to the other side of the road. At this gap we found another sign:

FOR OFFICIAL
USE ONLY

The problem was solved. The mysterious sign foretold that a gap would appear in the median strip after 1000 feet. But I was not altogether satisfied with my wife's description of the sign's meaning, namely that 'official cars will be able to turn onto the other side of the road after 1000 feet.'

No one would deny that my wife's interpretation was justified. My only doubt was whether the interpretation described the sign's *meaning*. While it certainly described a significance of the sign to drivers of official cars and other law-abiding personalities, what about its significance to a bank-robber who is trying to elude official cars? Wouldn't he regard the sign as signalling an opportunity to reverse his direction? What about a stranded pedestrian or a theorist? Would they interpret the first sign as meaning something about official cars?

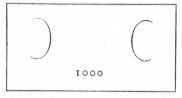

What would happen to the sign's meaning if the authorities decided to take down all the secondary signs that restricted the use of the gaps to official cars? In these imaginary instances, the mysterious sign would still preserve a stable, self-identical meaning, namely that a gap will occur in the median strip after 1000 feet.

I find this example instructive in a number of ways. It suggests, first of all, that meaning cannot exceed or arbitrarily delimit the conventional semantic possibilities of the symbols used. After all, nothing in the original sign restricts the meaning to official cars, although the following sign, for example, undoubtedly would:

Second, even if we wish to determine meaning according to the author's original intention, meaning still operates under the above constraint, because although the original intention was to restrict the sign's application, nothing in the symbol system exhibits that restriction in a communicable way. Third, we can infer from the example that private or coterie symbol-systems lose their restrictiveness as soon as the code becomes known outside the coterie—in this case the closed society of officials on official highway business. Once the secret symbols have been interpreted for me, the sign means the same thing for me (not to-me) as it does to a highway patrolman or to anyone else who has learned the code. (*The Waste Land* was once a coterie poem; now it is understood by high school students.) Fourth, the distinction between the communicable meaning of the highway sign, or any other symbol-system, and its various kinds of significance applies universally to authors and interpreters alike. Thus, while the original intention was no doubt to restrict the sign's application or audience, that does not alter its original communicable meaning, but simply defines its *original significance*, which is quite another matter.

For some time now literary theorists, particularly the New Critics, have attempted to preserve this distinction under a different guise, and have deplored the use of biographical or historical information for restricting textual meaning to its original historical or biographical circumstances. Even if Shakespeare had written *Richard II* to support the rebellion of Essex (which of course he didn't) that wouldn't limit the meaning of the play to its original application. When the followers of Essex brought out the play's significance to their political aims, however, no great violence was done to its original meaning. Nor would any important distortion result from

HIRSCH

documents that showed autobiographical impulses in Shakespeare's portrayal of Richard. Modern applications of Shakespeare's original meaning could be equally innocent of distortive influence. For a self-identical meaning (original or anachronistic, simple or complex) has the great advantage of flexibility; being very sure of itself, of its self-identity, it can enter new worlds and play new roles with confidence.

If one resists confusing meaning and significance one gets the impression that most controversies in interpretation do not really involve a conflict over original meaning versus anachronistic meaning. Usually the debates can be readily transposed into disagreement over the proper *emphases* of an interpretation, over whether it is better to explain original meaning or to bring out some aspect of the significance of meaning, for the interpreter or for present-day readers. The followers of Essex took the second course, without necessarily distorting Shakespeare's meaning. Our imaginary bank-robber on the New Jersey Turnpike would not be distorting the meaning of the highway sign if he decided to disregard its 'official use' and found a special significance for himself. In examples like these, original meaning is tacitly assumed even while original significance is ignored. Whenever interpretive conflicts are concerned only with emphasis in the conduct of a commentary, then they are conflicts about immediate aims and not about meanings. Most interpreters retain a respect for original meaning, and recognition of this might mollify some of our disagreements.

No doubt, what I am saying could never bring together certain extreme controversialists like Roland Barthes and Raymond Picard who have recently acted out the old dilemmas of original versus anachronistic meaning in their polemics over Racine. What can one say by way of reconciliation if Barthes claims to be uninterested in Racine's original meaning, and Picard argues that Racine could not have meant what Barthes construes from the texts? It is difficult for a non-specialist to judge the true facts of this noted case, but I have the impression that the controversy provides an unusually pure modern example of the rival claims between original and anachronistic meaning. Most recent conflicts between ancients like Picard and moderns like Barthes are not so clearly drawn, since most of us would be chagrined to learn that we had made elementary mistakes in construing the language of an early period, and our very embarrassment would indicate that we recognized the co-equal and harmonious claims of original meaning and modern significance, even if Barthes does not. At the same time, most interpreters would reject the opposite excess (even if Picard does not) of ignoring the difference between original meaning and original significance, an oversight that is the occupational vice of antiquarians. With excesses on both sides, Barthes and Picard can serve as a cautionary example, to help avoid a head-on collision between original meaning and anachronistic meaning. That much the analytical dimension of hermeneutics can serve to do.

But the ethical problem is not to be solved quite that simply. Even if some interpretive disagreements turn out to reside in choice of emphasis rather than choice of meaning, still a choice of emphasis is ultimately an ethical choice. Many of us have felt at one time or other a distinct preference for anachronistic over original meaning, although nothing in the analytical or metaphysical dimensions of hermeneutics compels us to choose one over the other. Even textual editors, who owe professional allegiance to the author's original meaning, have been known to waver. Should 'Music when soft voices die' really stand as the first line of Shelley's poem? Should brightness really fall from the 'hair' instead of from the 'air'? The text sometimes seems so much better if we ignore the author's probable intention or what he probably wrote. Every interpreter has a touch of the medieval commentator looking for the best meaning, and every editor has a drop of Bentley's blood. It is not rare that anachronistic meaning on *some* ground or other is undoubtedly the best meaning.

Therefore, let me state what I consider to be a fundamental ethical maxim for interpretation, a maxim that claims no privileged sanction from metaphysics or analysis, but only from general ethical tenets, generally shared. *Unless there is a powerful overriding value in disregarding an author's intention (i.e. original meaning), we who interpret as a vocation should not disregard it.* Mere individual preference would not be such an overriding value, nor would be the mere preferences of many persons. The possible exception is mentioned only because every ethical maxim requires such an escape clause. (Example: unless there is a powerful overriding value in lying, a person should tell the truth. Yet there are times when a lie is ethically better than to tell the truth, so the maxim cannot be an absolute one.) Similarly, one might fudge on original meaning for the sake of young, impressionable children, and so on. But except in these very special cases there is a strong ethical presumption against anachronistic meaning. When we simply use an author's words for our own purposes without respecting his intention, we transgress what Charles Stevenson in another context called 'the ethics of language,' just as we transgress ethical norms when we use another person merely for our own ends. Kant held it to be a foundation of moral action that men should be conceived as ends in themselves, and not as instruments of other men. This imperative is transferable to the words of men because speech is an extension and expression of men in the social domain, and also because when we fail to conjoin a man's intentions to his words we lose the soul of speech, which is to convey meaning and to understand what is intended to be conveyed.

I am not impressed with the view that this ethical imperative of speech, to which we all submit in ordinary discourse, is not applicable to written speech or, in particular, to literary texts. No literary theorist from Coleridge to the present has succeeded in formulating a viable distinction between the nature of ordinary written speech and the nature of literary written speech. For reasons I shall not pause to detail in this place, I believe the distinction can never be successfully formulated, and the futility of attempting the distinction will come to be generally recognized. Moreover, if it is seen that there is no viable distinction between 'literature' and other classifications of written speech, it will also come to be recognized that the ethics of language hold good in all uses of language, oral and written, in poetry as well as in philosophy. All are ethically governed by the intentions of the author. To treat an author's words merely as grist for one's own mill is ethically analogous to using another man merely for one's own purposes. I do not say such ruthlessness of interpretation is never justifiable in principle, but I cannot imagine an occasion where it would be justifiable in the professional practice of interpretation. The peculiarly modern anarchy of every man for himself in matters of interpretation may sound like the ultimate victory of the Protestant spirit. Actually, such anarchy is the direct consequence of transgressing the fundamental ethical norms of speech and its interpretation.

The question I always want to ask critics who dismiss authorial intention as their norm is one that could be transposed into the categorical imperative or simply into the golden rule. I want to ask them this: 'When you write a piece of criticism, do you want me to disregard *your* intention and original meaning? Why do you say to me "That is not what I meant at all; that is not it at all"? Why do you ask me to honor the ethics of language for your writings when you do not honor them for the writings of others?' It was not surprising that M. Barthes was displeased when his intentions were distorted by M. Picard. Few critics fail to show moral indignation when their meaning is distorted in reviews and other interpretations of their interpretations. But their sensitivity is often one-way, and in this they show an inconsistency amounting to a double standard—one for their authors, another for themselves. They are like the tenant farmer whose belief in redistributing everybody's property extended to land, money, horses, chickens, and cows, but, when asked about pigs, said: 'Aw hell, you know I gotta couple of pigs.'

The vocation of interpretation has always carried ethical duties. Recently, we have been reminded by Frederick Crews and others of the responsibilities that devolve on us because interpretation always implies ideology, and is thus never entirely removed from social action. (He who is not with me is against me.) We can add that a professional interpreter has an obligation to shared knowledge as well as to other social values, and that shared knowledge implies a shared norm of interpretation. But aside from these public responsibilities, an interpreter, like any other person, falls under the basic moral imperative of speech, which is to respect an author's intention. That is why, in ethical terms, original meaning is the 'best meaning.'

QUENTIN SKINNER
Motives, Intentions and the Interpretation of Texts

The main question I wish to raise is whether it is possible to lay down any general rules about how to interpret a literary text.[1] This presupposes, however, that one is clear both about what is meant by the process of interpretation and why it is necessary to undertake this process at all. I shall begin, therefore, with the briefest possible consideration of these two issues as a preliminary to my main discussion.

What is 'interpretation'? Professor Aiken has complained that the term is habitually used 'with abominable looseness by critics and philosophers of art.'[2] It does seem to be agreed, however, by most literary theorists that when we attempt to interpret a text, what we are basically trying to do is 'to construe it to mean something.'[3] As Bloomfield puts it, 'if we interpret a work of art, we are seeking its significance.'[4] Two words of caution are perhaps in order here. We must certainly be careful to avoid the vulgarity—which philosophers of art are much more prone to than practising critics—of supposing that we can ever hope to arrive at '*the* correct reading' of a text, such that we may speak of having finally determined its meaning and thereby ruled out any alternative interpretations.[5] And we must be careful not to assume too readily that the business of interpretation need always be entirely a reading process.[6] As long as these caveats are borne in mind, however, there seems no objection to saying that the concept of interpretation can briefly be defined as a matter of 'getting at the message' of a text,[7] and of decoding and making explicit its meaning, in such a way that the best reading, rendering what Hirsch has called the 'best meaning,' can thereby be attained.[8]

Why is this process necessary? Why do we need to consider the business of interpreting the meaning of a text as a special and indispensable technique? Two contrasting types of answer have usually been given. One stresses the interaction between the text and the reader, and sees the need for interpretation in phenomenological terms as a response to the reader's ever-changing sense of what he has read, and his ever-present need 'to fit everything together into a consistent pattern.'[9] The other, more conventional answer stresses that any literary work of any interest will virtually by definition be an object of considerable intrinsic complexity, characteristically employing such devices as irony, allusion and a whole range of symbolic and allegorical effects. The need for interpretation is thus seen in terms of the need to make the given work 'more accessible to the reader.'[10] According to a well-worn metaphor, the point is that we must be prepared to '*go beyond* the plain literal sense' in order to disclose the full meaning of the work.[11] Or according to an even more seductive metaphor, we must be prepared to probe *below the surface* of a text in order to attain a full understanding of its meaning.

This brings me to the main question I wish to consider. If we grant that the main aim of the interpreter must be to establish the *meaning* of a text, and if we grant that the meaning is to be found 'beyond' or 'below' its surface, can we hope to frame any general rules about how this meaning may be recovered? Or are we eventually compelled to adopt what Hirsch has called the 'resigned opinion' that 'our various schools and approaches' are no more than dogmatic theologies, generating a corresponding 'multitude of warring sects.'[12]

There is one general rule of interpretation which can obviously be stated at once, since it amounts to nothing more than a massive truism. It is that 'good critical practice depends above all on close and sensitive reading' of the text itself.[13] There is a powerful recent tradition of critical theory, moreover, which has been concerned to derive from this truism a second general interpretative rule. Stated positively, this is that the critic must focus on the text and *only* the text in the attempt to interpret it. To cite Cleanth Brooks, the rule is that 'the closest possible examination of what the poem says as a poem' is all that the interpreter needs to undertake.[14] Or to quote F. R. Leavis, the claim is that 'the text, duly pondered, will yield its meaning and value to an adequate intelligence and sensibility.'[15] Stated negatively, and in the form in which this claim has usually been debated, the rule is that the critic should not attempt to pay any attention to biographical matters, to questions about the writer's motives and intentions, in arriving at his interpretation of the work.[16] To move away from the text itself to a consideration of these factors is to commit 'the intentional fallacy'; to interpret the text, the critic must concentrate his attention exclusively on the text itself.

My aim in what follows will be to focus on this second suggested interpretative rule and to comment on the nature and cogency of the arguments which have recently been advanced for and against it.

The rule is: the critic should not attempt to pay any attention to a writer's motives and intentions in the attempt to establish the meaning of his works. The first stage in any attempted analysis of this claim must consist of trying to get clearer about the sense of 'meaning' which is at issue here. For there seem to be at least three discriminable senses of the term which have become assimilated together in most existing theoretical discussions about interpreting 'the meaning' of texts.

The first is that to ask about meaning in this context may be equivalent to asking: What do the words mean, or what do certain specific words or sentences mean, in this work? (I shall call this meaning$_1$.) It seems to be meaning$_1$ which Wimsatt and Beardsley mainly have in mind in their classic essay on the alleged intentional fallacy. They speak of explicating 'the semantics and the syntax' of a poem, 'through our habitual knowledge of the language, through grammars, dictionaries' and so on. When they turn to discuss a poem by T.S.Eliot, they concentrate on the need to decode 'the meaning of phrases in the poem,' and in speaking generally about biographical evidence they allow it to be relevant when it provides 'evidence of the meaning of his words.'[17] The second sense is that we may instead be asking: What does this work mean to me? (I shall call this meaning$_2$.) This is the sense which the exponents of the New Criticism usually seem to have in mind when they speak about 'structures of effects' and the need to concentrate on assessing their impact on the reader. The same sense of meaning also seems to underlie the phenomenological approach to literary criticism. When Iser, for example, insists on treating the reading process as a 'realisation' of the text 'accomplished by the reader,' he seems mainly preoccupied with meaning$_2$, especially when he argues that 'one must take into account not only the actual text but also, and in equal measure, the actions involved in responding to that text.'[18] Finally, we may be asking: What does the writer mean by what he says in this work? (I shall call this meaning$_3$.) Sometimes it seems to be this sense of meaning which Wimsatt and Beardsley have in mind. When they speak, for example, of the 'pursuit of full meanings' rendered necessary when a writer has a habit of alluding,[19] they no longer seem to be referring to meaning$_1$, which could scarcely be affected by the specific use of a phrase to allude. It seems they must be referring to meaning$_3$—to what the writer may have meant by making such a use of that particular phrase. Sometimes it is obviously this third sense of meaning which a literary critic has in mind. It is this sense, for example, which seems to underlie both the account which Bloomfield gives of a work of art having 'a meaning of organisation'[20] and the distinction which Hirsch offers between meaning and significance, where 'meaning' is 'defined *tout court* as that which a text is taken to represent.'[21]

I now turn to the nature of the arguments which have been advanced in favour of the claim that a critic should not attempt to pay any attention to a writer's motives and intentions in the attempt to establish 'the meaning' of a text. Two types of argument can be distinguished. One is concerned with the need for purity in critical procedures, and thus with the claim that, even if it may be possible to discover biographical information about a writer, the critic must not allow such information to condition and so contaminate his response to the writer's work. The desire to consider anything other than the information provided by the text itself is thus stigmatised by Wimsatt and Beardsley as a 'romantic fallacy.' The claim, as a recent critic of this outlook has expressed it, is that 'the work of art should provide the data for our understanding, it should be self-explicatory. To call in aid necessary information obtained from biographical or historical sources is a failure of art and criticism.'[22]

The second and main type of argument, however, against any attempt to pay attention to biographical information, derives from two contrasting (indeed incompatible) claims which are habitually made about the concepts of motive and intention themselves. The first is that it is because a writer's motives and intentions stand 'outside' his works, and thus form no part of their structure, that the critic should not attempt to pay any attention to them in attempting to elucidate the meaning of a text. This argument, however, seems to have been mounted in a somewhat confused way. It is necessary to distinguish at least three different reasons which have been given for supposing that it follows from the way in which a writer's motives and intentions stand 'outside' his works that they are irrelevant to their interpretation.

One claim has been that motives and intentions are simply impossible to recover. They are 'private entities to which no one can gain access.'[23] This is the first argument advanced by Wimsatt and Beardsley, who ask 'how a critic expects to get an answer to the question about intention,' and who insist that a knowledge of 'design or intention' is simply not 'available' to the critic.[24] The same commitment seems to underlie both Smith's allegation that 'intention is really unknowable' unless we can discover it 'through the medium of the poem'[25] and Gang's comments on 'our inevitable uncertainty about mental processes.'[26] A Cartesian picture of the mind seems at this point to provide the basis for the anti-intentionalist case.

A second claim has been that while it may after all be possible to recover a writer's motives and intentions, to pay attention to such information will be to provide an undesirable standard for measuring the value of what he writes. Wimsatt and Beardsley shift somewhat inconsistently to this ground at an early stage of their discussion of the intentionalist fallacy, claiming that a knowledge of a writer's intentions is not 'desirable as a standard of judging the success of a work of literary art.'[27] Gang also seems to shift to this position when he claims that 'the problem is how far the author's intention in writing a work is relevant to the critic's *judgment* on it.'[28] And so does Smith, when he argues that a concern about intention 'divides the response' of a reader in an apparently undesirable way.[29]

The third claim has been that while it may always be possible to recover a writer's motives and intentions, it will never be *relevant* to pay attention to this type of information if the aim is simply to establish the meaning of a text. Wimsatt and Beardsley eventually shift to this position, insisting that their concern is simply with 'the meaning of a poem' and that the poet's state of mind is a wholly separate matter.[30] An even stronger statement of the same commitment can be found in Ushenko's *The Dynamics of Art*, where it is claimed that 'the intent of the artist is to be counted as one of the antecedents to the aesthetic effect', and that 'an antecedent is no more relevant to the actual work of art than an aftereffect.'[31]

I now turn to the second (and incompatible) claim which is habitually made in this context about the concepts of intention and motive. The reason, it is said, why the critic should not attempt to pay any special attention to these factors is simply that they are 'inside' the work itself, not separate from it, and thus need no separate consideration. A writer, it is said, will normally achieve what he intends to achieve and will normally intend to achieve what he achieves. It follows that all the information we may need to know about these matters will in effect be contained within the texts themselves, and will be revealed by reading them. It is this argument which Hungerland, in criticising the belief in the intentionalist fallacy, takes to be the main claim of the anti-intentionalist critics. They are claiming that if a writer 'has carried out his intentions successfully, the work itself should show what he was trying to do.'[32] This also seems to be yet another of the grounds on which Wimsatt and Beardsley argue for the irrelevance of intentions to interpretation. They ask how the critic should try 'to find out what the poet tried to do.' And they answer that 'if the poet succeeded in doing it, then the poem itself shows what he was trying to do.'[33] The same view seems to have been adopted by several more recent commentators on the intentionalist fallacy. Smith cites the formula, which he attributes to the influence of Brooks and of Warren, that 'a good poem is one that is successful in fulfilling its intentions.'[34] Gang insists that 'whenever something is plainly and unambiguously said, it hardly makes sense to ask the speaker what he intended his words to signify.'[35] And Hough agrees that 'with a completely successful poem all is achievement, and the question of a separately conceivable intention does not arise.'[36]

I am now in a position to ask whether any of these arguments succeed in establishing, for any of the senses of 'meaning' I have discriminated, that the motives and intentions of a writer can and ought to be ignored in any attempt to interpret the meaning of his works.

The first argument, which derived from the desire to maintain the purity of our critical procedures, appears to rest on a confusion. It may be that a knowledge of a writer's motives and intentions is irrelevant to elucidating 'the meaning' of his works in every sense of 'meaning' I have discriminated. But is does not follow from this that the critic ought to—or will even be able to—ensure that this knowledge plays no role in helping to determine his response to that writer's work. To know a writer's motives and intentions is to know the relationship in which he stands to what he has written. To know about intentions is to know such facts as whether the writer was joking or serious or ironic or in general what speech-act he was performing. To know about motives is to know what prompted those particular speech-acts, quite apart from their character and truth-status as utterances. Now it may well be that to know, say, that a given writer was motivated by envy or resentment tells us nothing about 'the meaning' of his works. But once the critic possesses such knowledge, it can hardly fail to condition his response. The discovery, say, that the work was written not out of envy or resentment, but out of a simple desire to enlighten or amuse, seems certain to engender a new response to the work. This may or may not be desirable, but it seems to some degree inevitable.[37]

I now turn to the various arguments which have been derived from analysing the concepts of motive and intention themselves. The first, to the effect that it is actually impossible to recover such mental acts, seems straightforwardly false. I assert this as obvious, and shall make no attempt to prove it. The second seems to be a misstatement. It would clearly be a mistake to suppose that a knowledge of a writer's motives or intentions could ever supply a standard for judging the merit or success of his works. It certainly will not do, as Cioffi has remarked in a similar context, for a writer to assure a critic that he intended to produce a masterpiece.[38] The third argument, however, seems at least partly correct. I shall concede, that is, that even if it may not be true in the case of a writer's *intentions*, it may well be true in the case of his *motives*, that they may be said to stand 'outside' his works in such a way that their recovery will be irrelevant—for all the senses of 'meaning' I have discriminated —to an understanding of the meaning of his works.

This last claim rests, however, on an implied distinction between a writer's motives and intentions which has not usually been made explicit in the literature on the theory of interpretation, but which my argument now requires me to set out.[39] To speak of a writer's motives seems invariably to be to speak of a condition antecedent to, and contingently connected with, the appearance of his works. But to speak of a writer's intentions may be either to refer to his plan or design to create a certain type of work (his intention to do x) or to refer to and describe an actual work in a certain way (as embodying a particular intention in x-ing.) In the former type of case we seem (as in talking about motives) to be alluding to a contingent antecedent condition of the appearance of the work. In the latter type of case, however, we seem to be alluding to a feature of the work itself, and to be characterizing it in terms of its embodiment of a particular aim or intention, and thus in terms of its having a particular point.[40]

We can conveniently corroborate this claim by borrowing the jargon which the philosophers of language have recently developed in discussing the logical relations between the concepts of intention and meaning. They have concentrated on the fact (following J. L. Austin's classic analysis)[41] that to issue any serious utterance is always to speak not only with a certain meaning but also with what Austin labelled a certain illocutionary force. An agent may, in issuing a given (meaningful) utterance, also succeed in performing such illocutionary acts as promising, warning and so on. Austin's usual way of putting the point was that to gain 'uptake' of the illocutionary force of a serious utterance will be equivalent to understanding what the agent was *doing in* issuing that particular utterance. But an equivalent way of putting the same point, which is crucial to my present argument, would be to say that an understanding of the illocutionary act being performed by an agent in issuing a given utterance will be equivalent to an understanding of that agent's primary *intentions* in issuing that particular utterance.[42]

The significance for my present argument of this distinction between motives and intentions, with the isolation of the idea of an intention *in* speaking or writing with a particular force, lies of course in the implication that an agent's motives *for* writing (though not his intentions *in* writing) can indeed be said to stand 'outside' his works, and in a contingent relationship to them, in such a way that their recovery does seem to be irrelevant to the determination of the meaning of the works.

If we now turn, moreover, to the second (and incompatible)

claim which has usually been advanced by literary theorists about the concepts of motive and intention, it may seem that we are already committed to saying that this conclusion holds good for the concept of intention as well. I have sought to show that we may speak of a writer's intentions *in* writing, and of these intentions as being in some sense 'inside' his works, rather than 'outside' and contingently connected with their appearance. The contention of the other argument I have cited, however, is precisely that it is because a writer's intentions are 'inside' his works, and not separate from them, that the critic does not need to pay any special attention to their recovery in his attempt to interpret the meaning of any given work.

This claim, however, seems to rest on conflating two different sorts of question we may wish to ask about a writer's intentions in his works. We may revert to the jargon currently used by the philosophers of language in order to make this point. On the one hand, we may wish to ask about the perlocutionary intentions embodied in a work.[43] We may wish, that is, to consider whether the work may have been intended to achieve a certain effect or response—such as 'to make you sad,'[44] or to persuade you to adopt a particular view, and so on. But on the other hand we may wish, as I have suggested, to ask about a writer's illocutionary intentions as a means of characterising his work. We may wish, that is, to ask not just about whether a given writer achieved what he intended and intended to achieve what he achieved, but rather about just *what* he may have been intending to do *in* writing what he wrote.

This brings me to my central contention about the relations between a writer's intentions and the meaning of his works. On the one hand, I shall concede that a writer's perlocutionary intentions (what he may have intended to do *by* writing in a certain way) do not need to be further considered. They do not seem to need any separate study, since the question whether a given work was intended by its author, say, to induce sadness does seem to be capable of being settled (if at all) only by considering the work itself and such clues about its intended effects as may be contained within it. And the question whether it makes sense to impute such intentions to a given writer on a given occasion does not seem to be a question about the meaning of his works so much as about the success or failure of the work's structure of effects. On the other hand, I now wish to argue that in the case of a writer's illocutionary intentions (what he may have been intending to do simply *in* writing in a certain way) their recovery does require a separate form of study, which it will in fact be essential to undertake if the critic's aim is to understand 'the meaning' of the writer's corresponding works.

It now becomes essential, however, if this central contention is to be established, to revert to the three senses of 'meaning' which I began by discriminating, in order to establish the way in which the particular sense of intentionality I have now isolated is in fact relevant to understanding 'the meaning' of a given writer's works.

If we turn first to meaning₁, it must be conceded that an understanding of a writer's intentions in writing scarcely seems relevant to this sense of 'the meaning' of what he writes. To say this is not to take sides on the immense and immensely difficult question whether our statements about the ('timeless') meaning of words and sentences may not ultimately be reducible to statements about *someone's* intentions.[45] It is only to assert the truism that questions about what the words and sentences I use mean cannot be equivalent to questions about my intentions in using them. If we turn next to meaning₂, it must again be conceded that an understanding of a writer's intentions in writing scarcely seems relevant to this sense of 'the meaning' of what he writes. It is clear, that is, that the question of what a given work of literary art may mean to a given reader can be settled quite independently of any consideration of what its creator may have intended. But if we turn to meaning₃, it seems possible to establish the closest possible connection between a writer's intentions and the meaning of what he writes. For it seems that a knowledge of the writer's intentions in writing, in the sense I have sought to isolate, is not merely relevant to, but is actually *equivalent* to, a knowledge of the meaning₃ of what he writes. The stages by which this conclusion can be reached will by now be clear. To gain 'uptake' of these intentions is equivalent to understanding the nature and range of the illocutionary acts which the writer may have been performing in writing in this particular way. It is to be able, as I have suggested, to characterize what the writer may have been doing—to be able to say that he must have been intending, for example, to attack or defend a particular line of argument, to criticize or contribute to a particular tradition of discourse, and so on. But to be able to characterize a work in such a way, in terms of its intended illocutionary force, is equivalent to understanding what the writer may have *meant by* writing in that particular way. It is equivalently to be able, that is, to say that he must have *meant* the work *as* an attack on or a defence of, as a criticism of or a contribution to, some particular attitude or line or argument, and so on. And so the equivalence between these intentions in writing, and the meaning₃ of what is written, is established. For as I have already indicated, to know what a writer meant by a particular work[46] *is* to know what his primary intentions were in writing it.

I wish finally to protect the thesis I have now advanced from two possible misinterpretations. I have argued that we need to know what a writer may have meant by what he wrote, and need (equivalently) to know his intentions in writing, in order to interpret the meaning₃ of his works. This must first be distinguished, however, from the much stronger claim which is often advanced to the effect that the recovery of these intentions, and the decoding of the 'original meaning' intended by the writer himself,' must form the whole of the interpreter's task. It has often been argued that 'the final criterion of correctness' in interpretation can only be provided by studying the original context in which the work was written.[47] I have not been concerned, however, to lend support to this very strong version of what Bateson has called 'the discipline of contextual reading.' I see no impropriety in speaking of a work having a meaning for me which the writer could not have intended. Nor does my thesis conflict with this possibility. I have been concerned only with the converse point that whatever a writer is *doing in* writing what he writes must be relevant to interpretation, and thus with the claim that *amongst* the interpreter's tasks must be the recovery of the writer's intentions *in* writing what he writes.

This thesis must also be distinguished from the claim that if we are concerned with a writer's intentions in this way, we must be prepared to accept any statements the writer himself may make about his own intentions as a final authority on the question of what he was doing in a particular work.[48] It is true that any agent is obviously in a privileged position when characterising his own intentions and actions. It follows that it must always be dangerous, and ought perhaps to be unusual, for a critic to override a writer's own explicit statements on this point. I see no difficulty in principle, however, about reconciling the claim that we need to be able to characterize a writer's intentions in order to interpret the meaning₃ of his works with the claim that it may sometimes be appropriate to discount his own statements about them. This is not to say we have lost interest in gaining a correct statement about his intentions in our attempt to interpret his work.[49] It is only to make the (perhaps rather dramatic, but certainly conceivable) charge that the writer himself may have been self-deceiving about recognizing his intentions, or incompetent at stating them. And this seems perennially possible in the case of any complex human action.

I have argued for a general hermeneutic rule which contradicts the one general rule proposed by the New Critics: that the recovery of a writer's (illocutionary) intentions must be treated as a necessary condition of being able to interpret the meaning₃ of his works. This in turn suggests a further question about rules of interpretation, which I wish finally to consider: is it possible to state any general rules about how to recover such intentions? There are of course notorious conceptual difficulties involved in the understanding of other people's intentions. I wish to suggest, however, that without eliding these difficulties, at least two such general rules can in fact be framed.

My first suggested rule is: focus not just on the text to be interpreted but on the prevailing conventions governing the treatment of the issues or themes with which the text is concerned. This rule derives from the fact that any writer must standardly be engaged in an intended act of communication. It follows that whatever intentions a given writer may have, they must be conventional intentions in the strong sense that they must be recognizable *as* intentions to uphold some particular position in argument, to contribute in a particular way to the treatment of some particular theme, and so on. It follows in turn that to understand what any given writer may have been *doing in* using some particular concept or argument, we need first of all to grasp the nature and range of things that could recognizably have been done by using that particular concept, in the treatment of that particular theme, at that particular time.

This rule can be applied as a critical as well as an heuristic device, in order to test the plausibility of ascribing any particular intention to a writer in a particular work. It is true that any example of the application of this rule to a work of literature is liable either to look very crude or to be very complicated. It can readily be illustrated, however, by considering a simple example from the history of philosophy. Consider the debate about whether some of the English legal theorists of the seventeenth-century may be said to have intended to articulate a doctrine of the judicial review of statute.[50] I am arguing in effect that these writers will have been limited, in their intentions in writing, by the range of intentions they could have expected to be able to communicate, and thus by whatever stock of concepts, and whatever criteria for applying them, were generally available. It follows that the question whether the seventeenth-century lawyers were adumbrating a doctrine which was later to become politically important, or whether there is merely a random similarity of terminology, may be settled by settling the question whether the concept of judicial review was a part of the stock of concepts available, in its later and popularised sense, to the audiences for whom the seventeenth-century lawyers were writing. If it was not (as I believe can be shown to be the case) then the question loses virtually any meaning, to say nothing of plausibility.

My other suggested rule is: focus on the writer's mental world, the world of his empirical beliefs. This rule derives from the logical connection between our capacity to ascribe intentions to agents and our knowledge of their beliefs. This rule can also be applied critically as well as serving as an heuristic device. Again, a literary example would necessarily be very complex, so consider another example from the history of philosophy. C.B.Macpherson has recently attempted to interpret John Locke's *Two Treatises of Government* by ascribing a particular intention to Locke in writing: the intention to defend the rationality of unlimited capital accumulation.[51] If this is what Locke was *doing in* writing that work, his mental world must have included at least the following beliefs: that his society was in fact becoming devoted to unlimited capital accumulation; that this was an activity crucially in need of ideological justification; and that it was appropriate for him to devote himself to accomplishing precisely this task. It is a remarkable fact about Macpherson's account that no attempt is made to show that Locke did hold all or any of these beliefs. It has recently been shown, moreover, that there is a good deal of evidence to indicate that Locke did not in fact hold the third of these beliefs, while there is no evidence to show that he held the first two of them.[52] (The first is in any case very doubtfully true.) But if Locke did not in fact hold these beliefs (and perhaps could not in principle have held them), then he could not have had the intention *in* writing which Macpherson's account ascribes to him. It is in this way that this second suggested rule (like the first) has a critical as well as an heuristic point.

I have thus sought to set out two stages to my criticism of the New Critics' attitude towards the idea of general hermeneutic rules. I have tried first of all to argue that in order to be able to interpret the meaning of a text, it *is* necessary to consider factors other than the text itself. I have now tried to suggest just *what* other factors need to be taken into consideration. I have thus been concerned to shift the emphasis of the discussion off the idea of the text as an autonomous object, and on to the idea of the text as an object linked to its creator, and thus on to the discussion of what its creator may have been doing in creating it.

GRAHAM HOUGH

An Eighth Type of Ambiguity

Long long ago when the world was young and literary criticism had
just been invented we learnt from William Empson that a poem
might mean more than one thing at the same time, and that far from
being a defect this is likely to be a merit. This idea was not wholly
new. Earlier patristic writers had employed it in the interpretation
of Scripture, and it was already familiar that one literal sense and
three spiritual senses could be contained in the same discourse. But
Scripture being divinely inspired was a special case, and it was
doubtful whether merely human authors could be credited with the
same power of plurisignification. Some of them certainly claimed
it—Dante, for example. Allegorical writing presented a second
meaning behind the surface narrative, and in the Renaissance much
heroic poetry not professedly allegorical was credited with similar
concealed meanings which it was the business of commentators to
unveil. But the concept of multiple meaning did not establish itself
widely in the interpretation of poetry in general. It was Empson's
Seven Types of Ambiguity that led critics and exegetes to see multiple
and simultaneous meaning as part of the normal procedure of
poetry; and it would be hard to exaggerate the consequences of this
for later critical thinking. Neo-classic criticism had worked towards
the idea of a single ascertainable meaning, presumed to be what the
author had intended to put in. Romantic criticism appealed to an
unbounded ocean of inspiration. Post-Empsonian criticism has been
possessed by the idea of layer upon layer of implicit meanings, some
of them not at all obvious, whose intentional status remains un-
defined. And the large body of discussion that is by now assembled
in this area can be seen as directly or indirectly the consequence of
Empson's work.

This has indeed become a central theme in much modern criticism
—that a literary text is a complex entity composed of different meanings, presented not as alternatives and not successively, but mutually
interacting and simultaneous. It is difficult to ascribe some of these
implicit meanings to the 'intention' of the author in any simple sense,
and a secondary discussion has therefore grown up about the place
of the author's intention in establishing the meaning of a text. Some
ambiguities (Empson's second type) arise from a genuine doubt

about the meaning which a particular passage can properly be said to bear. Two alternative meanings seem to be possible and instead of deciding for one or the other we accept both and resolve them in a kind of Hegelian synthesis which is the poem itself. Most ambiguities, however, take a different form. The text seems to have a plain sense about which there is no prima facie doubt, but a number of secondary suggestions can be seen to cluster round this plain sense, modifying and enriching it in various ways. The plain sense can most plausibly be described as 'what the author intended'; the status of the associated suggestions is less certain. Empson is not much interested in this question. As a follower of Richards he approaches interpretation chiefly from the point of view of the reader, and his ambiguities are generally seen as possible reactions in the reader's mind. When he does come near to stating a principle it is the traditional communicative one—that the reaction of the reader is or should be that which the author intended him to have. Yet the actual terms of his discussion allow a good deal of room for other possibilities. He admits a problem about how far the poet is conscious of his own activity. Some ambiguities are of the nature of Freudian slips, the product of unconscious forces. (I will avoid the solecism 'unconscious intention'.) There are others that Empson himself I think would describe as gifts of the language—possibilities of multiple meaning that are built into the lexicon and syntax of English, as of other natural languages. This situation evidently leaves many questions open. An ambiguity which is part of the language can be consciously exploited by the author, passively accepted, or not noticed at all. Can we, in a particular text, distinguish between these states of affairs? How would we set about doing it? If we can distinguish, what difference would it make to interpretation? What is the status for interpretation of an 'unconscious' suggestion, picked up by a reader but not intended by the author? What are we to think of a text of acknowledged literary merit which conveys to most readers a sense that the author would certainly have repudiated? An ingenious or eccentric or specially gifted reader can find a host of implied meanings in an apparently simple text. But how many of them are really there, and are those which are really there always and only those that the author intended?

In this paper I want to suggest that behind Empson's seven types of ambiguity there lurks an eighth—ambiguity between intended and achieved meaning. I shall illustrate some of its effects, and I hope to show that a recognition of its presence is an important part of the interpretation of literary texts. If I am right, it is wrong to fall into the intentional fallacy (which in its extremer forms is indeed a fallacy), but it is equally wrong to relapse into the misplaced scepticism of its opponents. It is in the interplay between intended and unintended that interpretation finds most work to be done. Since I am adding yet another item to the long series of articles on meaning and intention in literature I shall have to begin with a few remarks on the present state of play in this controversy.

The modern discussion of intention in a literary context begins with Wimsatt and Beardsley's article 'The Intentional Fallacy' (*Sewanee Review*, 1946).[1] This critical monument has by now disintegrated, as a result of its own internal contradictions, of direct assaults upon it,[2] and of more philosophical consideration of meaning and intention in a non-literary context. But the ruined site remains, haunted by the memory of an ill-defined New Critical doctrine that the intention of the author (which sometimes means his biography, sometimes his plan of work) is irrelevant (or unavailable, or both) to the interpretation (or evaluation) of a work of literature. This blunderbuss utterance could be, indeed has been, analysed into a variety of propositions, some plainly untrue, some true but on the verge of being truisms, and some doubtful. A typical literary-critical doctrine, in fact. In spite of contradictions and inconsistencies its operational purport is, however, tolerably clear— we are not to ask questions about what the author intended, but only questions about what the words mean. This injunction has been opposed in various ways. The principal philosophical reinforcements that have been brought in by the opposition are to be found in G. E. M. Anscombe's *Intention* (1963) and A. L. Austin's *How to Do Things with Words* (1962): and the most recent and direct form of rejoinder derived from these sources says that to ask questions about what the words mean *is* precisely to ask questions about the author's intentions. I will give two examples. A. J. Close (1972)[3] cites a number of 'time-honoured and still respectable axioms about literary art, according to which it is a fallacy to pursue, or feel limited by, the author's intentions: "Great works of art mean more than they literally say"; "great art transcends the original intentions of its creator and means something new to every epoch"; "we can never know, and need not concern ourselves with, what the writer intended".' He believes that these assumptions have a dubious philosophical basis, and his article is an attempt to scotch them. He concludes that 'the responses which literature seeks are securely anchored in the utterer's intentions.' Quentin Skinner, in an article (1972)[4] which sums up and adds to previous work of his own, comes to a similar conclusion—'that a knowledge of the writer's intentions in writing [in a particular sense of intention which he has isolated] is not merely relevant to, but is actually *equivalent* to, a knowledge of the meaning of what he writes'.

I do not wish at this point to question these conclusions, but to indicate the route by which they have been reached. It is by way of Austin's doctrine of illocutionary acts. This can be summarized as follows. To make any utterance is to perform a locutionary act, and to perform a locutionary act is also and *eo ipso* to perform an *illocutionary* act, i.e. to use the locution in some special way—asking or answering a question, giving information, a warning or an assurance, announcing a verdict or giving a description, etc. There are many possible illocutionary acts, and the class is not clearly defined. The essential part of both Close's and Skinner's argument is that to interpret a literary text is to identify correctly the illocutionary acts performed by the author in writing it. Illocutionary acts are intentional, so in interpreting a text we are recovering the author's intentions.

Skinner is a historian of political thought and uses non-literary examples; Close is more concerned with prose than poetry; but both in the articles cited are explicitly discussing the interpretation of literary texts. It is curious therefore that they both pass over the fact that Austin specifically *excepts* literary, fictional and poetic usage from the general course of his argument.[5]

> Surely the words must be spoken 'seriously'. . . . I must not be joking, for example, nor writing a poem.

> A performative utterance will, for example, be *in a peculiar way* hollow or void if said by an actor on the stage, or if introduced in a poem, or spoken in soliloquy. . . . Language in such circumstances is in special ways—intelligibly—used not seriously, but in ways *parasitic* upon its normal use—ways which fall under the doctrine of *etiolations* of language.

> We must bear in mind the possibility of 'etiolation' as it occurs when we use speech in acting, fiction and poetry, quotation and recitation.

> Let us be quite clear that the expression 'use of language' can cover other matters even more diverse than the illocutionary and perlocutionary acts. For example, we may speak of the 'use of language' *for* something, e.g. for joking; and we may use 'in' in a way different from the illocutionary 'in', as when we say 'in saying "p" I was joking' or 'acting a part' or 'writing poetry'; or again we may speak of 'a poetical use of language' as distinct from 'the use of language in poetry'. These references to 'use of

language' have nothing to do with the illocutionary act. For example, if I say 'Go and catch a falling star', it may be quite clear what both the meaning and the force of my utterance is, but still wholly unresolved which of these other kinds of things I may be doing.[6]

Perhaps Close and Skinner skip these bits out of embarrassment, for the equation of poetry with joking, and the description of literary language as an etiolation, are embarrassingly inadequate. All the same they are important; they call attention to something that is true—that utterances in poems and fictions are not on the same level as those in ordinary life; and Austin's summary relegation of literary language is not perhaps the bland Philistinism that it appears, but just a quick way of limiting his argument. However, if we are concerned with literary interpretation we cannot so limit the argument. We are bound to inquire further into the 'parasitic uses of language', the 'etiolations' which are 'not serious', not the 'full normal use'.

An obvious thing to say here (and Austin actually does say it) is that an apparently illocutionary act in poetry is not really so; it is only the mimesis of an illocutionary act. 'Go and catch a falling star' is not really a command, only the imitation of a command. Does this make any difference to interpretation? It does. If we attempt to recover the illocutionary act of the author, as Close and Skinner tell us to, we do not find him uttering a command, we find him writing a poem. From Austin's point of view that is a special, 'etiolated' use of language; and the literary exegete has to content himself with this dusty answer.

But of course, within the fiction or the poem any illocutionary act can occur that could occur outside it; questions are asked, information is given, verdicts are pronounced, and all the rest. But these are not the acts of the author; they are imitated acts, of fictional characters, devised and combined by the author to form *his own illocutionary act*, which is the whole poem. But can anything as complex as a whole poem constitute an illocutionary act in Austin's sense? If so, it ought to be possible to say what it is doing—asking questions, warning, admonishing, describing, or what not.

The trouble with philosophical or quasi-philosophical arguments like those of Close and Skinner is that even if they are sound (I believe they are partly sound) they are so abbreviated and schematized as to be very unlike the actual process of literary interpretation. They leave out some of the real decisions that have to be made. *How much* of the text is to be taken as constituting an illocutionary act? 'Go and catch a falling star' looks like a command. In its context it is one of a series of commands to do impossible things, and at the end comes a command to find out how honesty can be advanced in the world. The implication is that this is equally impossible. We can identify the illocutionary act performed by this stanza as 'satirizing the falsity and corruption of the world'. The apparent series of commands are a rhetorical device directed towards another end, which has nothing to do with commanding.

But this is only the first stanza of the poem. The second gives a similar set of injunctions to impossible quests, and concludes that it is equally impossible to find a woman who is both true and fair. The illocutionary act here is 'satirizing women'; and this is continued, by a trope which we need not now consider, into the third and last stanza. It appears then that the illocutionary act performed by the whole poem is this one—'satirizing women'—and that the first stanza about the fate of honesty in the world is only a generalizing prologue to the specific message which is about the honesty of women.

We have now identified the illocutionary act performed by the poem, which is what Close and Skinner say we ought to be doing. It would surely be absurd to present this meagre platitude as anything like an interpretation of the poem. Perhaps we have not gone far enough. Perhaps we have relied too exclusively on the text, without inquiring from other sources what intentions could have gone or were likely to have gone into the writing of the poem. One answer to this kind of question presents itself very obviously: satire on the inconstancy of women is a vulgar and time-honoured theme in medieval and renaissance literature. Helen Gardner quotes Nashe in this connection:[7] 'Democritus accounted a fair chaste woman a miracle of miracles, a degree of immortality, a crowne of tryumph, because shee is so harde to be founde.' Professor Gardner also remarks that the listing of impossibilities is a well-known device in classical poetry, 'usually going with oaths of fidelity in the formula "sooner will . . ." ', and cites Propertius, II, XV, 29–36 and Ovid, *Tristia*, I, viii, 1–10. Since Donne's impossibilities pointedly do not go with an oath of fidelity it appears that he is executing a calculated variant on a well-known theme. In the light of this information the intention behind the poem is not so much 'satirizing women' as 'writing an ingeniously novel poem on a conventional but still fashionable theme'. The two are quite different. The intention to satirize women (because you are indignant at women's frailty) is not at all the same thing as the intention to write a clever poem satirizing women (because you enjoy the literary ingenuity of the performance). Probably as in most such cases both intentions are present in some quite undeterminable proportion. But what has become of the trim outlines of the illocutionary act? They have dissolved, in a complex of fused and inseparable intentions.

I conclude therefore that to identify the illocutionary act performed by a text or part of a text is sometimes impossible, sometimes possible, desirable where possible, but always insufficient as an interpretation of the text. It is insufficient because it is schematic and generalized. To satirize women is the intention of many poems; to identify this intention cannot tell us much about this particular poem.

Let us return then to the text, or for the sake of a manageable brevity to part of it, the first stanza.

> Goe, and catche a falling star
> Get with child a mandrake roote,
> Tell me, where all past yeares are,
> Or who cleft the Divels foot,
> Teach me to heare Mermaides singing,
> Or to keep off envies stinging,
>   And finde
>   What winde
> Serves to advance an honest minde.

We can indeed recover the illocutionary act performed by this utterance. We can identify the intention in writing it—to satirize the falsity and corruption of the world. But this is not to interpret the stanza. To interpret the stanza is to account as fully as possible for the unique satisfaction it brings. The satisfaction is a function of meaning—of meaning in the fullest possible sense; not only lexical and syntactical meaning, but connotative meaning, associated suggestions, rhythmical and auditory effects. These partial meanings cannot all be identified with certainty, and the way they interact must be even less certain. So there can be no final or demonstrably best reading. The individual commentator must just do the best he can. I will now do something in this direction, and if it turns out to be not very much it will at least go beyond the identification of illocutionary acts.

There is no difficulty in recovering the intended meaning in a general way—to satirize the falsity of the world. Of course we want to know this; but it is only a diagram. The achieved meaning does not contradict the intentional diagram, but it is something far more complex. The complexity here resides chiefly in the detail of the imagery from which the whole is built up. We have a catalogue of impossibilities. The first is, 'Goe, and catche a falling star'—do something impossible, catch and possess an object of haunting beauty that is by nature evanescent and unseizable. The second 'Get with child a mandrake root'—an equally impossible enterprise, but now one that is sinister and dubious. A mandrake root looks like a human being but is not; to copulate with it would be against nature. It is soporific, aphrodisiac and a fertility charm. It is also perilous, for it is supposed to shriek on being pulled from the ground, and whoever hears the shriek will die. We are in the region of perverse and dangerous sexuality. 'Tell me where all past yeares are'—i.e. find out the secrets of time, memory and survival, satisfy the insatiate metaphysical curiosity. 'Or who cleft the Divels foot'—a trivial impossibility derived from popular superstition, and casting a backward gleam of contempt on the more serious and emotionally charged impossibilities that have preceded it. Yet not all magical and mythical beliefs are contemptible—'Teach me to heare Mermaides singing'; there are no mermaids, or they don't sing, but it would be delightful if there were. It would be delightful if there were, but the world as we know it is full of vain wishes, so teach me 'to keep off envies stinging'—equally impossible, for in such a world we must long for what we have not. And then, if you can perform all these impossible feats you can perhaps perform the most impossible of all—'finde/What winde/Serves to advance an honest minde'. But you cannot do any of these things, so you cannot do that either. There is no way to advance an honest mind, just as there is no mermaids' song; and if there were it would only be a 'winde', which notoriously bloweth where it listeth, ungraspable and uncontrollable.

The common reflection on the fate of honesty in the world arrives already transfigured, because it has been realized in a picture of the world as an honest man feels it. He feels it with *Sehnsucht*, with horror and dread, with intellectual curiosity, with contempt for some of its unreal beliefs, with tenderness for others, with a dour moral realism. A mind as open, various and curious as that is not likely to get far on the narrow road of advancement.

That was a way of putting it—not very satisfactory; a periphrastic study in a worn-out critical fashion. The object of the exercise was to show how small a part of the meaning of the text is accounted for by its general intention—the intention to satirize the falsity of the world. The life is in the detail; and the cumulative effect of the detail is something different, even contrary, to the primarily identifiable intention. The achieved effect is not one of bitterness and disappointment, but of energy, curiosity, intellectual and emotional life, even if enclosed within a recognition of limits and frustrations. This is partly a matter of temperament—Donne's own diffused but ever-present energy and spirit. It is partly the ethos of a class and an age. For one of Donne's class, in his time, it was the part of a man to face the disappointments of life with wit and high spirits. But this is not an 'illocutionary act', unless a man can be said to act simply by being true to himself and the culture he belongs to.

Now I think it is quite impossible to regard the detailed imagery of this passage as 'intended' in the same sense as the general illocutionary act of satirizing or the general rhetorical organization was intended. They were intended, of course, in the minimal sense that Donne wrote them down, presumably while awake and in possession of his faculties. But if he were asked what his intention was in writing 'Go and catch a falling star' the appropriate reply would have been 'I intended to give an example of an impossible action'. And so with the mandrake, mermaids, and the rest. I do not believe that the other considerations I have advanced about these images ever reached the level of conscious intention. Such images come from we know not where—from miscellaneous reading, from a common cultural stock, from private unconscious associations. They are suggested by the exigencies of a rhyme or an accidental occurrence in the outer world. Since they are afterwards written down and put in print they are of course ratified by the conscious will: but if we are on that account to describe them as intentional I think we are stretching the concept of intention, or at any rate using it in a different sense from that employed when we said that the intention of the whole passage was to satirize. To describe the interpretation of poetry as the recovery of the author's intentions is to make the writing of poetry something like the working out of chess problems—moving a certain number of pieces that have fixed powers, with due forethought. Actually it is much more like playing tennis—reacting to unpredictable situations with unpremeditated moves, which may be abortive but may achieve an aptness and accomplishment that is absolutely unforeseeable until it happens; all done, however, within the framework of an intention—to win the game according to the rules. I see now that I am virtually paraphrasing one of the pronouncements that Close wants to scotch—'great art transcends the original intentions of its creator'.

Philosophical writers on literary theory are much afraid of ghosts. They cling to the idea of recoverable authorial intention because they fear that if they let it go they will be lost in a wilderness haunted by the whole disreputable retinue from the magician's house, and the Zeitgeist, the Dialectic, the Nine Muses, the Genius of the Language, the Mind of Europe or even the Holy Spirit itself might be upon them at any moment. I on the contrary wish to maintain that such forces as these do contribute to the composition of poetry, and I will now try to put this contention in more respectable language.

To deny the position of the extreme intentionalists does not entail adopting the old anti-intentionalist doctrine—that we must rely solely on the words on the page to reveal meaning. On the contrary, just because forces other than the intention of the author have contributed to the meaning of the poem it is important to know as much as we can about them. I applaud the two procedural rules suggested by Skinner at the end of his article: 1. 'Focus not just on the text but on the prevailing conventions governing the treatment of the issues or themes with which the text is concerned.' (Indeed I did just that, just now, in considering the prevalence of satires on women in Donne's culture, and of catalogues of impossibilities in literature accessible to him.) 2. 'Focus on the writer's mental world, the world of his empirical beliefs.' (I did that, mildly, in suggesting that Donne thought there were no mermaids.) But it must be added that with literary texts (different in this respect from the historical documents with which Skinner is mostly concerned) such considerations can give no better than probable answers, and sometimes not even that. A certain convention exists, a poet employs it; but this can tell us nothing about the intention with which he employs it—whether merely as a rhetorical device, a framework for a poem, or as an expression of conviction. As for empirical beliefs—a writer on law or government can be presumed to write consistently in accordance with his empirical beliefs. But this is just what a poet does not do. He entertains beliefs about whose empirical status he is doubtful; he makes use of ideas that he knows to be empirically false. Characteristically the poet moves in a sort of half-world where questions of empirical belief are not allowed to arise. This was particularly likely to happen with Donne (or Sir Thomas Browne), living in a culture where the new philosophy had put all in doubt, where old quasi-magical beliefs flourished side by side with new scientific ones, and old magical beliefs could still claim some sort of scientific status (see *Pseudodoxia Epidemica, passim*). There is no knowing what Donne really believed about mandrakes or mermaids; though as it happens it is clear enough in the text we are considering that he is using popular beliefs about them as examples of impossibilities. Better instances would be found in the passages about spheres and intelligences or the corporeal potentialities of angels, where it is quite unclear whether the ideas are used merely as metaphors or as analogies having real scientific foundations. The conclusion to be drawn is that answers to questions about what the poet empirically believed will not necessarily yield answers to questions about what he is doing in a poem.

Skinner's object in suggesting his rules is to lead us back to the author's intentions. They may do so; they are in general useful principles; but in my view they may lead somewhere else. Or of course they may simply fail. The information they provide may be irrelevant, as we have just seen. (The poet describes the moon as a crystal globe inhabited by a pure spirit; we apply rule 2 and discover that he knew very well it was made of green cheese. And nothing of interest seems to follow from this.) I wish to argue, however, that there is indeed relevant and useful information obtained by these methods, that it genuinely assists interpretation, but that what it leads back to cannot be reduced simply to the author's intention.

Yet if not the author's, whose? Or if not intentions, what? Must we believe that statements about the meaning of words and sentences are always reducible to statements about someone's intentions? It seems at first that we must. If we found what appeared to be a tomb in a lonely landscape, with the inscription *Et in Arcadia ego*, we could argue as Panofsky[8] does about whether this means 'I too was a shepherd in Arcadia', or 'Death is in Arcadia too'. We could argue about this because we suppose that someone carved the inscription, with one or the other intention. But if we were to discover that the apparent tomb was only a natural outcrop of rock, and the apparent inscription only the result of erosion, the argument would fall to the ground. There are of course natural signs, which have meaning without intention, as when we see smoke and say, 'That means fire'. But words and sentences are not natural signs and cannot be treated as such.

There is, however, a different analogy that can be applied to the behaviour of words and sentences—and applied particularly aptly to highly organized discourse like poetry. It is the analogy of involuntary symptomatic gestures. 'He said he had never been near the cash-box, but I noticed a shifty look in his eye.' 'He said "Of course I don't care for her at all any more" but as he said it his voice broke.' The shifty look and the breaking voice are certainly unintended, but equally certainly meaningful. Analogous effects can occur within language. Indeed the phenomenon of the breaking voice does occur within language, though only of course within spoken language. Something very similar, however, can happen in poetry.

> Out of the day and night
> A joy has taken flight;
> Fresh spring, and summer, and winter hoar,
> Move my faint heart with grief, but with delight
> No more—O, never more.

In the third line there is both a logical and a metrical gap. There ought to be a fourth season and there ought to be a fifth foot. The manuscript is in such a mess (or so I am told, for I have not seen it) that there is no knowing whether Shelley did not finally intend to insert the missing member, and write 'Fresh spring, and summer, *autumn* and winter hoar'. The line as it stands, with autumn missing, has been praised again and again for its rhythmical and suggestive beauty. And we can see why, or partly see why. The whole poem is about loss and absence; and in a key line something that is expected is absent and lost. And the question of intention is left entirely in abeyance. We simply do not know whether Shelley intended it or not. The effect is remarkably like that of an involuntary break in the voice. Many bewildering minutes could be spent with other textual cruces—babbling of green fields, inquiring whether Hamlet's flesh was solid or Aristotle solider. In all these cases scrupulous editors labour to recover the intention of the author, and readers of poetry remain steadfastly indifferent, and simply prefer what they believe to be the best reading. But I will not pursue this line, as it brings in other considerations aside from my purpose. If Shakespeare never intended to write 'a' babbled of green fields', Theobald did. But what stands out from these textual confusions is how completely in the minds of most readers the question of authorial intention tends to disappear.

To return to involuntary symptomatic gestures. The intentionalists are right to maintain that the basic intentional act performed by the author in writing must be correctly identified. They are right too in maintaining that this frequently requires a search for evidence outside the text. Indeed it is precisely in this respect—the determining of the general intention of the poem—that such evidence is most required. Literary conventions, prevailing cultural assumptions, are not contained within the poem, but are necessary to its proper understanding. What could *Lycidas* mean to a reader who knew nothing of the long tradition of the pastoral elegy? A good deal, no doubt, but half its significance would escape him, and some of its most prominent features would remain impenetrably obscure. To that extent, and it is a very considerable extent, it is false that 'if the poet succeeded in doing it, then the poem itself shows what he was trying to do'. We need prior and external evidence about the poet's intentions. But mounted on that basic intentional structure is the whole inspectable surface of the poem in all its varied detail, much of which cannot properly be described as intentional. I am thinking of rhythmical effects, and of specific imagery, and other things besides. The example from Shelley illustrates the first, that from Donne illustrates the second. Let us look for some more. They are to be found particularly among the Empsonian ambiguities where a

primary sense is obvious, its intentionality not doubted, yet other
less obvious senses can be detected in the background. It was these
situations that gave rise to some of the early objections to Empson's
practice: 'But the writer can't possibly have meant *that*.' By now we
know the answer to that kind of objection: quite likely he did not
mean it, but it is there all the same.

I will take a fairly slight and simple example from Empson, as the
more intricate ones would demand a discussion of his whole method,
which is not my purpose now.[9]

> How loved, how honoured once, avails thee not,
> To whom related, or by whom begot;
> A heap of dust is all remains of thee;
> 'Tis all thou art, and all the proud shall be.
> (Pope, *Elegy to the Memory of an Unfortunate Lady*)

> The two parts of the second line make a claim to be alterna-
> tives which is not obviously justified, and this I think implies a
> good deal. If the antithesis is to be serious, *or* must mean 'one of
> her relations was grand but her father was humble', or the other
> way about; thus one could take *how* to mean 'whether much or
> little' (it could mean 'though you were so greatly'), and the last
> line to contrast her with the *proud*, so as to imply that she is
> humble (it could unite her with the *proud*, and deduce the death
> of all of them from the death of one). This obscurity is part of
> the 'Gothic' atmosphere that Pope wanted: 'her birth was high,
> but there was a mysterious stain on it'; or 'her birth was high,
> but not higher than births to which I am accustomed'. Here,
> however, the false antithesis is finding another use, to convey
> the attitude of Pope to the subject. 'How simple, how irrelevant
> to the merits of the unfortunate lady, are such relationships;
> everybody has had both a relation and a father; how little can I
> admire the arrogance of great families on this point; how little,
> too, the snobbery of the reader, who is unlikely to belong to a
> great family; to how many people this subject would be
> extremely fruitful of antitheses; how little fruitful of antitheses
> it seems to an independent soul like mine.' What is important
> about such devices is that they leave it to the reader vaguely to
> invent something, and make him leave it at the back of his mind.

All that could be securely identified as intentional in these lines is
the contrast between the variety of human situations in life and the
uniformity in the indifferent community of death. There are three
possible steps to take about Empson's commentary on them. 1. We
could say that it is all a fantasy, that the implications discovered are

not there. But the obscure antithesis in the second line is certainly there, to some degree disturbing to the overall intention, or additional to it. 2. We could accept Empson's explication, and say that Pope intended all these things. I do not think this at all plausible. It would be quite incompatible with any view of poetry possible to Pope to admit these multiple and partly conflicting implications in a single passage. 3. We could follow Empson and admit the co-presence of these faintly uneasy implications, but also decide that they were not part of Pope's intention in writing. If they were also incompatible with Pope's known social and personal attitudes we should perhaps be asked to believe too much in admitting them. But they are not. They expose very accurately the precarious balance of Pope's relation to the great world. More than that, they expose something that is generally true about the position of the independent man of letters in this age—something a Marxist could use in a thesis about literature as the apanage of the ruling class. Many elements that enter into the meaning of a literary text are of this kind—the result of unrecognized social forces, expressing themselves in syntax and rhetorical arrangement. Others are of a kind that a Freudian would recognize—after a reading of chapter VI of the *Interpretation of Dreams* or *Wit and its Relation to the Unconscious*. Part of the work of an interpreter of literature is to unmask these concealed meanings.

Unmasking, at any rate in popular fiction, is something that is commonly done to villains; and to do it to a work of literature is apt to suggest that something vaguely discreditable is to be revealed. Vulgar Marxists and vulgar Freudians have both often written with this purpose, and in this tone. But it is a crass error to suppose that by revealing a hidden meaning—a meaning that we have reason to suppose was unsuspected by the author—we are devaluing or impoverishing the text. Any written text is to some extent a palimpsest. The manifest layer consists of the illocutionary acts of the author— intentional by definition. We can take these to include or imply his acknowledged beliefs and assumptions. (To warn a skater that the ice is thin implies a belief that our fellow-creatures should not get accidentally drowned.) But any text also includes unrecognized assumptions and beliefs—those that the writer shares so thoroughly with his age as to be unaware of their presence, those that belong to the unexamined background of his personal life. In purely discursive writing unrecognized elements of this kind are accidents and imperfections—though doubtless inevitable imperfections. But the interpreter even of a historical document, who believes himself to be recovering the pure intended communication of the author, cannot afford to neglect them. If he takes the line that the message is what the author intended and all the rest is noise he is going to miss a good deal. The reader of Bacon or Hobbes will rightly note the overt, intentional bracketing out of established religion, by which it is left immune from the critical operations applied to other human activities. But he will also do well to note that the decorous forbearance to religion in Bacon seems really to be practised in the interests of positive science. And he can hardly help noticing that the irrepressible comic irony with which Hobbes approaches religious doctrine reveals an unacknowledged contempt for everything in religion except the institutional shell.

Now in a literary text—and it is here that the interpretation of literary texts becomes a different thing from the interpretation of pure discursive writing—the unacknowledged layers of meaning are not accidents and imperfections. They are an essential part of the totality to be examined. It was Empson's *Seven Types of Ambiguity* that brought this out into the open and made it central in critical activity. But literature and the interpretation of literature have been with us a long time, and there are not many wholly new critical discoveries. The presence of unacknowledged meanings side by side with the acknowledged ones had long been noticed in an accidental and occasional fashion, even within the sanctuary of neo-classicism. It was Dryden who first observed that Milton had made the Devil his hero. Since then *Paradise Lost* has become the classic case in English of a poem that has retained its power and celebrity unbroken, largely through a reading that contradicts the expressed intentions of the author. For Blake, Milton was of the Devil's party without knowing it. For Shelley, Milton 'alleged no superiority of moral virtue to his God over his Devil'. For Empson the poem is good because it shows how bad the God of Christian theology really is, and unwittingly sets up a lofty humanism against him. 'The root of [Milton's] power is that he could accept and express a downright horrible conception of God and yet keep somehow alive underneath it all the breadth and generosity, the welcome to every noble pleasure, which had been prominent in European history before his time.'[10]

This is not the place for a Milton controversy, or even a controversy about how Milton controversies should be conducted, especially since Empson has done it himself. My point is only to take a conspicuous instance of a poem that lives by meanings that its author must have repudiated. Dodging the theological thunderbolts, we can still advance our argument a step further by showing some of the lesser means by which this was brought about. Again and again Milton writes a glowing and magnificent passage on a classical myth, or on the exercise of some noble human faculty by the fallen angels—and then in the interests of his main design retracts it. The myth was false, the virtues exercised in vain. The architect of Pandemonium was celebrated under other names on earth—[11]

> and in Ausonian land
> Men called him Mulciber; and how he fell
> From Heav'n, they fabled, thrown by angry Jove
> Sheer o'er the crystal battlements; from morn
> To noon he fell, from noon to dewy eve,
> A summer's day; and with the setting sun
> Dropt from the zenith like a falling star,
> On Lemnos th'Aegean isle: thus they relate,
> Erring; for he with this rebellious rout
> Fell long before.

The story is false, but we are told so only after we have extracted the greatest possible imaginative pleasure from it. Similarly with the employments of the fallen angels after the departure of Satan for earth. Some practise athletic and military exercises;[12]

> Others more mild,
> Retreated in a silent valley, sing
> With notes angelical to many a harp
> Their own heroic deeds and hapless fall . . .

> In discourse more sweet
> (For eloquence the soul, song charms the sense,)
> Others apart sat on a hill retir'd,
> In thoughts more elevate, and reason'd high
> Of providence, foreknowledge, will, and fate.

It is hard to see how the devils could have been better employed had they still been angels; and the whole passage breathes a tender and elevated respect for these occupations, fit for an Athenian *kaloskagathos* or a Renaissance gentleman. Yet every item of this noble description is dutifully undercut; the military exercises end in 'wild uproar'; though it was ravishingly sweet, 'the song was partial' (i.e. partisan, unjust); the high reasonings are 'vain wisdom all and false philosophy'.

We can see something of how these contrarieties come about. The lines on Mulciber are from Homer (*Iliad*, 1, 589–94); the falling all day long and dropping on Lemnos with the setting sun are quite literally translated, even, if I am not imagining it, with a modulated version of the original rhythm. They bring with them into Milton's grim theological epic the lightness, freedom, passion and generosity of Homer's Olympians. Empson remarks, 'Milton is extremely cool about the matter; one is made to sit pleasantly with him in the shade all day long, needing no further satisfaction; it is delightfully soothing to feel that the devil is all the time falling faster and faster.' But this ease and disengagement gets into Milton's text not from any concern with devils, for the Homeric passage is not about a devil at all, but about a god, who had quarrelled with the king of the gods. He is telling his own story, long afterwards, to show how dangerous it is to fall out with Zeus; and so far from having been cast into an eternity of torment he is back on Olympus, his wrongs forgotten, handing the drinks round and patching up another family quarrel. The manly exercises of the fallen angels have also a classical origin; they are derived from the funeral games in *Iliad* XXIII and *Aeneid* V. These in their turn recall the Olympic and the Pythian games, at which poetic and rhetorical performances occurred. In discussing Satan a little earlier in the book, Milton had said that the damned spirits 'do not lose all their virtue' (II, 482). Their remaining virtues could scarcely be the theological ones, so in presenting them he goes to the great exemplars of civil and humane virtue in the ancient world; and the 'welcome to every noble pleasure' that Empson justly remarks on comes where it is least convenient to the general design.

The palimpsest again: a text written on the scarcely erased lines of an earlier text. And Milton intends what he is doing; it is part of the accepted procedure for a Renaissance syncretist epic. To identify the fallen angels with the gods of the gentiles, and to bring in with them the whole variegated tapestry of pagan mythology, is a necessary part of his plan. But willed, necessary, and intended as it is, it brings with it consequences that were certainly unintended—that the society in hell seems so much better than that in heaven.

This is the phenomenon that modern French critics call 'intertextuality'—the presence in a literary text of earlier texts, some chosen by the author, some forced upon him by his culture, but always bringing with them consequences that go beyond his intention and pass partly out of his control. This is not merely a pretentious way of saying that writers are influenced by other writers, or that literary traditions exist. It is to reveal—or open the possibility of revealing—a structure special to literature: layer upon layer of meaning, invented, inherited or deliberately acquired, held together by an authorial intention, but always retaining a partial autonomy, so that the author's intention remains only one element (the presiding element, but still only one) in a complex federal association.

In Milton's case we can see how many tensions and contrarieties were forced on him. By reason of his personal history he was in no position to be whole-hearted in condemnation of rebellion. But the psychological compulsions are less interesting than those that arise from his material and his poetic form. He is taking as his foundation extremely early mythical material (Genesis), worked up by still early secondary elaboration (scattered passages throughout the Old Testament and the New). This primitive foundation has in its turn been worked on by centuries of philosophical theology—a moral and metaphysical transformation to which it was always exceedingly recalcitrant. And he has chosen to present his myth in the form of a heroic poem—a particular kind of heroic poem (the Tassonian Christian epic) itself an adaptation of an earlier kind (the Homeric) based on still earlier mythical material derived from an entirely different religious and cultural tradition. His own theology is sophisticated and abstract; but he is obliged by his form to embody it in a story of conflict that can be presented only in quasi-personal terms. The evil and cruelty that Empson uncompromisingly exposes in Milton's epic is not, as Empson's argument requires, simply inherent in the Christian scheme. It is partly inherent in it—the doctrine of eternal punishment is a lasting disgrace to the Christian imagination—but it is partly the consequence of presenting what can only be adequately conceived in metaphysical terms as a concrete fable. A fable must have characters who act and speak; 'God the Father argues like a school divine'; and, condemned to the only terms possible to such a persona, makes a very bad case. The Christian humanism to which Milton with the better part of his mind aspired demands a more radical revision of the Christian myth than probably he was prepared to undertake; it certainly demands a more radical revision than was compatible with presenting the myth as an epic narrative. Dryden and Johnson complained that *Paradise Lost* has only two human characters; but they are only technically right, for the angels fallen and unfallen, the Father and the Son, are conceived as human characters. The epic form allows no other possibility. And in human terms—I mean human terms, not the terms of romantic satanism—most of the courage, nobility, and pathos falls to the defeated and the erring innocents, most of the cruelty, implacability, and deceit to divine omnipotence. In the background is another sort of argument altogether; but not one that could be expressed in character and action.

I seem to have been saying that it is in the unintended meanings that most of the value of *Paradise Lost* resides. This is the fault of a limited range of examples; beauty and generosity appear in Eden too, well within the intentional scheme of the whole poem. But enough has been said to show how bewilderingly the intended and the unintended are crossed and interwoven in the intricate fabric of the poem.

We can see now how natural it was for Empson, preoccupied with the actual business of interpretation, to leave the question of intention largely in abeyance. He had to leave a space round it, for it was in this ambiguous space that most of his work was to be done. Neither 'the words on the page' nor 'the intentions of the author' can alone reveal the significance of a work of literature, and no adequate interpretation of a poem has ever been made by the exclusive pursuit of either of these phantoms. We read the words on the page, but we read the gaps between the words too, and we supplement them with a complex of insight and information that come from outside the text. We identify the intention of the author, as clearly as we can; but this is only the starting-point for understanding. A poem is closer to common speech than it is to non-literary discursive writing. In responding to an utterance in face-to-face conversation we listen to the words; we listen also to the tone of voice, the silence between the words; we are aware of the non-linguistic context; we observe facial and manual gestures, the posture of a body, accompanying acts. The full meaning of the utterance is a fusion of all these factors. In reading a poem the face-to-face situation has disappeared; but it is part of the work of poetry, of the language of poetry, to create an equivalent for it. Auditory and rhythmical effects, unpremeditated images, unsolicited associations, do just this; no more willed and intended (and of course no less) than the facial expressions by which we accompany our speech. That is the situation between the poem and the reader; but there are always others present at this encounter—a culture and a history. Looked at in another way, a poem is like an archaeological site. Beneath the baroque church is the medieval crypt, itself constructed on the ruins of a Roman basilica, and a Mithraic temple lies below. We find one text mounted upon another, layer upon layer of meaning, and we are soon led beyond the manifest text with which we started. What we discover in the end is the locus of a civilization, one of those human constructs that are neither intended nor unintended—unless they are both.

The reason why the argument about intention in literature has gone on so long and so inconclusively is that its terms have been misconceived. We have been presented with false alternatives—to explore the complexities of the inspectable text without extraneous aid, or to recover the uninspectable intentions of the author. Each method has claimed to be sufficient and to exclude the other. I hope

I have shown that neither the presented surface of the text nor the inferred intention of the author is a sufficient basis for interpretation, and that so far from being mutually exclusive they are complementary. If this is so there is nothing left to argue about, and the question of literary intention can be permitted to dissolve.

As always, the matters we have been discussing seem remote from the ordinary reading of poetry. But their purpose, it should be remembered, is that what goes on in the ordinary reading of poetry, implicitly and by intuition, should be made articulate and brought fully into the light. For this we need principles and methods. These are the dogmatisms of learning. Those whose profession is learning have no call to be afraid of them; but they had better get their dogmatisms right.

ALASTAIR FOWLER

Intention Floreat

Our endless reasonings about authorial foreknowledge, about meaning and intention in literature, and about the relevance of discussion
of intention in criticism and interpretation, begin to lose themselves
in wandering mazes. But we are less apprehensive of scholasticism
(for here terms are baggy-loose) than of the debate's losing
momentum as it increases in volume, and turning vague. The
meandering laybrinth may not only permit no progress but conceal
no monster. How frustratingly the intentionalists and anti-
intentionalists write at cross purposes: how seldom the lecturers
wait behind to answer objections. We feel impelled to revolutionize
the terms of a problem whose solution has become so intricate that
it eludes our comprehension as easily as its own simplification. We
want to move on, have done. Yet the classic problem of intentionality
moves too, as ineluctable as meaning, as inseparable as human
nature. Criticism at every turn challenges our policy towards
intentionality. The reason for this becomes plain when the stages of
composition and criticism are reviewed.

Change of intention
Intention means different things at different stages of composition.
Without tracking the viewless flight of Pegasus or pursuing the
Muse into the unconscious, we can sometimes distinguish a specific
intention to compose a work, before many of its constituents are
determined. To the author, this fore-idea can seem the work's
purest, most distinctive form. 'It will never be so good as it is now
in my mind—unwritten.' Virginia Woolf may have been mistaken
in several ways about 'this angular shape' in her mind, the 'very
sharply cornered' work that proved to be *The Waves*, not *The Moths*.
But the fact of preliminary intention remains. And many writers
would agree that the pre-existence of the unwritten work has a
special, pristine value. This is what the subsequent writing has to
realize, or it will be less itself. Intention of this preliminary sort is
often thought of as only prior to an act of composition, and therefore extraneous to the work. But fore-idea and writing have a somewhat closer relation than that. The assumption that a work has no
existence until it is fully composed needs to be challenged. Suppose

a writer planned a computer-assisted poem whose lines were to be anagrams of 'Order in variety I see' and whose words would have their letters in alphabetic order. At the stage when he gives his directions to the programmer, he has composed something.

The idea of the work can change a very great deal in the writing. If Austin Dobson 'intended an ode,/And it turned to a sonnet', which form represents his intention? Apparently the intention forms gradually—whether or not it may become malformed—forms and takes form. Among the penetrating *aperçus* usefully scattered in George Watson's *Study of Literature* is this: 'because a man alters his intention in the course of action, it can hardly be said of him that he is acting other than according to intention'. But it continues to be said of literary works, because most theorists regard literary intention as static. Only recently have theories such as Collingwood's emerged, in which the writer searches for the statement that he only discovers he meant in the work.

If composition is a search for meaning, it is natural to consider the 'final' published form of the work as definitive. Surely it is like the final stage of speech, after feedback has modified ideation. However, the matter is not quite so simple. For one thing, the final form may be chosen just because of correspondence to the fore-idea: even such a confirmed anti-intentionalist as Thomas Creeley can speak of the writer's choosing by a process of *recognition*. Again, abandoned early intentions can still, after they are altered, leave traces, unintelligible in terms of the final intention but not irrelevant to criticism. Nor can one say that the chronologically final form always represents the solution of the work's problems. It may reach out to the best partial solution of many; it may only abandon the search. In other words, the status of the published version can be exaggerated. It is what the writer can be held responsible for, morally and artistically. From another point of view, however, it is no more than the last, decisive stage in a long development, like birth in human development; not for all purposes more decisive than the stage of conception, or when independent existence became possible.

Which intention are we concerned with, then? As with writers, so with works we may usually say that intention *floruit*, about the time of publication. But there are problematic cases, some of them important, such as Wordsworth's various *Preludes*. Are critics, if not editors, to follow William Empson in trying to intercept what they believe to be a declining work, at the point just before intention is falsified?

'It is farther agreed', proclaims the Induction to *Bartholomew Fair*, that on publication 'every person here, have his or their freewill of censure . . . the author having now departed with his right'. The author relinquishes his freedom to exercise judgement by altering his work; but others unquestionably take it up. Not whether, but how, their continued fabrication should be conducted is the issue. Intentionalists will wish to understand the originally realized intention, perhaps better than the author; or to imagine how he would explain it if he belonged to the critic's time and social group. Anti-intentionalists affirm that

> The poem is not a string of knots
> Tied for a meaning of another time
> And country, unreadable, found
> By chance. The poem is not a henge
>
> w.s. graham *Approaches to how they behave*

—though they may find it difficult to deny that how they read is still the poet's business too. 'Freewill of censure' can take some pretty licentious forms.

Variety and extent of intention

So far we have spoken as if intention were a single entity. But in fact the term covers a range of possibilities. It seems easy, after T.M. Gang's efforts, to distinguish everyday or *practical intention* from a specifically *literary intention*. Practical intention is often said to be irrelevant to criticism: 'we should find no trouble in putting to one side the common artistic aim of creating a masterpiece' (Wimsatt). But it is not clear why aspiration to value, perhaps to a certain level of seriousness, is so obviously extraneous. Surely evidence of the level of seriousness has a heuristic application, to say no more? It may at least embolden us in our wilder critical conjectures. If a critic of Conrad ignores the Author's Notes, his own level of seriousness may be thought a bit low. A distinct but overlapping category might be called *generic intention*. This intention, to present a piece of discourse as a work of art, or as a particular kind of work (such as the kind whose artifactual status is deliberately ambiguous), must always have some relevance. To be quite indifferent about it would be like not caring whether Duchamp's urinal was merely a plumber's happy blunder. With some minor experimental genres the sole difference between composed work, *objet trouvé* and natural structure may consist in intention. And it is quite common to find this with individual features. Does this poem happen to use letters only from the top row of the typewriter keyboard quite by chance? Is that other poem limited to the same set of letters out of a minimalist generic intention? We quite properly desire to know. Sufficient evidence to satisfy us may of course reside in the work's ordinary conventional signs. But it may not: it would take an anti-intentionalist quite a while to discover that the lines beginning 'Now I will a rhyme construct/By chosen words the young instruct' are a mnemonic for the value of *pi*. This example is subliterary, but the point it illustrates has a general application. Much of our greatest literature has a considerable element of unobvious generic form.

Most often, critical disputes are about *semantic intentions*, local intentions to mean something by particular words or other constituents. In this context it is customary for everyone except the most scrupulous anti-intentionalists to use *intention* and its variants to distinguish meanings held to be true or valid. The practice seems not without significance for its bearing on authorial privilege. Certainly the usage implies that to say 'the author intends an irony', 'the irony intended here', etc., is different from (and somehow more persuasive than) saying 'I can find an irony here if I use my utmost ingenuity'. However, the custom carries no implication about settling bets by appeal to the author, who may have withdrawn from the work long ago, or forgotten, or never have been conscious of his intention.

The idea of *unconscious intention* seems to some theorists to involve a contradiction. Whether unconscious rationality can exist would be an interesting question. But I do not refer to rational intention. Anyone with even a rudimentary knowledge of psychoanalysis will be familiar with a category of expressions which are highly purposeful, yet nonetheless so far from consciousness as perhaps to be consciously repudiated, once conviction has been brought home. We need not suppose that literary intention is always deeply buried; but it always includes an unconscious or spontaneous component. Every honest writer will confess to effects happier than he meant; no writer knows all of the purpose he reaches out to fulfil. Indeed, he may know almost none of it. That is not important: it is for the author to intend, for the critic to discover and know that intention. The critic may be far better able to rationalize about the work, just as an analyst may be more aware of the motives governing his patient's dream. However, both will at their best avoid overconfidence. Within reason they will listen respectfully to autobiographical disclosures—remembering with a shudder, perhaps, that Eckermann knew better than Goethe whether Goethe loved Lili best. In a thousand unpredictable ways biographical information may have a bearing on unsuspected traits of the work's character.

If intention varies in kind, it also varies in extent: a fact not much discussed. I mean that more or less of a work may be unintended, both consciously and unconsciously. Even pleasing effects, after all, can happen quite accidentally.

He hurried away, while Mary watched him with a doubt of
waking reality, that seemed stronger or weaker as he alternately
entered the shade of the houses, or emerged into the broad
streaks of moonlight.

HAWTHORNE *The Wives of the Dead*

Suppose that a reader is puzzled as to whether the 'doubt' or the
'reality' was stronger in the shade (moonlight can cause uncertainty,
too). He wonders whether this ambiguity is consciously (or unconsciously) intended as a mimetic effect. On the other hand, it
might be adventitious. Such difficulties, which occur very frequently
with stylistic nuances, seem to me quite troublesome. If effects are
adventitious, they form parts of the work only in a very weak sense.
Surely any critic who discussed such accidents would be wasting his
time? Not at all, reply those who see nothing amiss in making random
effects significant. They positively enjoy the disorder of a work's
debatable lands, and welcome the chance to enlarge the realm of
indeterminacy, that is, of dulness. Others take this critique *à outrance*,
arguing that undeniable intentions are no more than effects of
fortuitous causes. These opinions, which militate against the whole
discipline of literary criticism, are scarcely novel. But a new variation
is played by certain structuralists, who hold that the intentional
component of a work is negligible, since significance resides solely
in *langue*. It is the *langue* 'released' by the writer which has meaning
for them, not the work he uses it to make—'What oft was thought',
with a vengeance! When the extent of intentionality is debated, the
issue can usually be resolved into one concerning the critic's freedom.
As we shall see, these disputes are really about the nature of the
reader's contribution.

Diachronic change introduces a farther variable. As the literary
model alters with time, the extent and function in it of the various
intentions also change. For example, the present age has seen many
writers voluntarily submit their art to randomizing mechanisms such
as cutup composition and arbitrary permutation rules. Where
stochastic devices have been set off, or where freedom of vocabulary-
selection, perhaps, has been renounced, intentionality has a somewhat different status. There is no point in treating the intentions of a
William Burroughs just like the intentions of a Milton; and perhaps
Keats's intentions have other limits again. No doubt there is more
continuity than appears between contemporary aleatory effects and
certain schematic forms in the past. But it must be conceded that
intention now claims a different, and sometimes a more restricted,
domain—perhaps just because the domain of consciousness is itself
becoming more extensive. Again, the abandonment of prescriptive

genres (and formal rhetoric generally) has changed intentionality. Genre continues to be functional; but writers are much less likely now to formulate their generic ideas publicly. When they do, their conceptions of genres and subjects and their rank-ordering may be peculiar to this age. What Olson and Creeley have written against subject might be right for some kinds of contemporary poetry. But it hardly applies to Renaissance literature. For example, the over-whelming probability is that Spenser had a definite subject for *Prothalamion*, that he meant to write a fine wedding song for the Earl of Worcester's daughters, and that the intention governed many details of the work that are inexplicable without reference to it. Flexibility will be needed, therefore, in adjusting to historical changes in the mode of intentionality. Features that are consciously formed in one period may in another be left undetermined, without this carrying any implication of special disorder or aleatory intent or even of disregard. In Renaissance poetical manuscripts no conclusion can necessarily be drawn from the absence of punctuation: in the Victorian period the numerological strand of meaning breaks off altogether: and in the modern novel, many seem to think, diction matters so little as to be beneath the intending novelist's notice.

In short, intentionality is not so much a problem as a family of problems. Theorists on both sides have presented general arguments; but as Frank Cioffi has seen there can be no general conclusion, when the issue of intention arises in such a heterogeneity of contexts. However, something might be done to order the different sorts of intention and where possible to establish their relations. In particular the temporal order of the aspects of intention could be explored. Much of the connection between various states of intention will naturally be hidden within the psychological adyta of the writer. But other sequential relations—chronological, logical, linguistic—are not only available, but evident. Indeed, they are so evident as to support the soundness of the intentionalist position. The same idea of composition as a 'collaborative' process that has been used by Morse Peckham and others as an argument against the relevance of intention turns out to be one of the strongest reasons for its relevance.

The sequence of intentions

We may accept (with reservations that need not be entered into now) the idea of composition as an endless process in which editors, compositor and readers all participate creatively, so that continual reactualization or recreation of the work takes place. Let us grant that a compositor participates by deciphering manuscript; that an editor may impose house rules for orthography, and in old works (and some not so old) supply punctuation. Let us farther concede that substantive departures from the text originally intended can very occasionally produce a beauty which the author never thought of, or decided against. Given this situation, what characterizes the good compositor or scribe? In general he is agreed to be one who introduces no new words. Now examine his decision-making as he hesitates between two possible vocabulary-selections. Is not his criterion, rightly, whether the word was intended? There are no two ways about it: at this stage, at least, authorial intention rules. Editorial decisions are normally very little different in this respect. What we ask of an editor is that he transmit the author's vocabulary-selections as faithfully as possible. If he goes wrong and the error makes sense, this is a positive disadvantage. Exceptionally a Maxwell E. Perkins will rearrange or cut his author's text creatively; but then he is either literally a collaborator, or else he meets with approval just because he has rendered his confused author's main intention faithfully. The criterion of competent transmission remains conformity with the writer's vocabulary selections. A few qualifications of this either prove the rule or leave it materially unaltered. For example, oral literature (which has its own somewhat distinct model) may leave performers free to introduce local variations. And in very poorly transcribed texts even of written literature an editor will feel free to select, within limits and brackets, according to his general ideas of the work. Broadly speaking, however, unless one ignores the nature of literary transmission and communication links in general, one must acknowledge the privileged status of the particular set of words intended by the author.

This has never seriously been challenged. In fact, anti-intentionalists have conspicuously avoided the matter of transmission. Perhaps they have half-realized the difficulty of conceding the primacy of intention in this phase while rejecting it in all others. Transmission is indeed the thin end of an irresistible wedge, since vocabulary-choice carries almost every other authorial decision with it.

To see why, we need only think for a moment of the linguistic nature of the work (or, as Peckham prefers, of literary discourse). Choice of words by no means takes place in isolation from other features. It accords with a particular tone, for example; perhaps with a special diction and genre; certainly with many rhetorical structures. The lexical string expresses, in fact, the writer's grammatic and semantic intention; and in turn it binds the recipient to understand one specific communication, in contrast to countless others. There may be ambiguities. But in general the words entail a chain of discourse. If therefore the lexical string enjoys privileged status, so does the work's whole linguistic structure, and ultimately many of its literary features too. Because there is no bulkhead between the linguistic and literary components, there can be none between the privileged arrangement of words and the literary meaning originally implied by that arrangement. Respect for the text of an author seems to constitute *de facto* recognition of the privileged status of his intention.

But it is only the realized intention to which this status is conceded. Why trouble, then, to bring intention in at all? What difference can it make to speak of 'the intended arrangement of words', 'the author's meaning', etc., rather than simply 'the work', 'the meaning'? When the achieved meaning is in doubt, how can it help to invoke a far more shadowy intention? Surely Wimsatt and Beardsley were right to insist that the work's own form is best evidence for its meaning. If the author fulfilled his intention it remains 'in' the work, available as impersonal form. If he did not, his intention is irrelevant. In 'Genesis: A Fallacy Revisited' Wimsatt explains that his argument was never directed against the relevance of such intentions as can be inferred from the work itself. This eirenic clarification appears to satisfy any reasonable apprehension that he might have thrown a baby of value and integral personality out with the slops of wishy-washy biographical speculation. It seems that the anti-intentionalist position freely embraces intention, in the realized form that as we have seen counts for most. Has not Wimsatt conceded quite enough?

If it seems so, that is illusion; for he has really passed over the question of authorial privilege. In this he and Beardsley have unintentionally confused some of their readers. Alan Rodway suggests in *The Truths of Fiction* that most of the intentionalist controversy arises from misapprehension of what Wimsatt and Beardsley originally meant. They 'omitted to use a separate term . . . to distinguish the apparent intention found within the work itself from that imported from outside (by scholarly deduction or the author's own statement). . . . And, of course, only the second sort of intention was declared to be fallacious as a measuring-rod.' Now it is easy to interpret them (as also the Wimsatt *solus* of 'Genesis') in this sense. But on closer consideration they appear never to have conceded that any sort of authorial intention could be acceptable as a *measuring-rod*, that is, a privileged criterion. To permit reference to realized intention is not to assign it any special status among other 'versions' of the work. The authors of *The Verbal Icon* have never recanted the footnote, in which they roundly affirmed that 'the history of words *after* a poem is written may contribute meanings which if relevant to the original pattern should not be ruled out by a scruple about intention.' These are not the words of people who take realized intention as their measuring-rod.

The reason for insisting on intention is that without it the work disappears altogether. Abandon the search for authorial meaning, and there remains no common basis for criticism worth respecting. Intention may be hard, even impossible, to discover; it may have to be inferred and constructed; and it will certainly elude early attempts. But unless our efforts at least aim towards it, we have only Peckham's individualist 'versions' to discuss: a dispersed horde of 'works' competing for attention, each backed by more or less vociferous opinion. That is why it is vital that criticism concern itself with the intended work, and not merely with works.

This is not to say that the critic's sensibility should be repressed; that he should altruistically identify with the author, binding himself to what may after all be no more than a primitive or woolly conception of the work. Conceding authorial privilege means giving the author the first word, not the last. Unfortunately the relation between responsibility to intention and freedom of critical interpretation is obscure, and will perhaps remain so until we have a fuller phenomenology of criticism.

Phenomena of interpretation
The need for a more adequate description of criticism is obvious enough. Above all we need to escape the limiting conception of its role as one of dealing with a given work. The common notion is that criticism starts from a text—'the words on the page'—which it proceeds to interpret and evaluate. But there is no such thing as words on pages, only ink marks. A reader has always to *construct* the words and the work, starting from marks on paper (or sound-waves in air). He does this by interpreting them, according to codes more or less fully shared with their encoder, as indications of the vocabulary choices intended. These choices, in turn, he interprets as signals of intended grammatical (or rhetorical, metrical, numerological, etc.) forms; and so on up the artifactual pyramid. At the top, as it were, above even the intended themes, the work's unity waits to be reconstructed. I have said that the levels are interpreted 'in turn'; but it cannot be overemphasized how complex and organic the process is, whereby a reader's dawning apprehension of a work guides his construction of even its most subordinate elements. Feedback from his general view may fortunately supply the meaning of an unfamiliar usage; unfortunately, he may also misconstrue a con-

stituent because of some ingenious misconception (already at this early stage) of what the work is all about.

We know by hard experience that critics may differ widely about what they have read. Commonly their opinions about the work are said then to differ. But it would often be truer to say that their opinions are about different things: they have constructed works so different, perhaps, that criticism of them must be at loggerheads or cross-purposes. This need not be an impasse. Though one almost hesitates to say it, so unorthodox has the idea become, variation of constructs is due to errors, which can be corrected. Errors in construction really are possible. I refer not to misinterpretation (though that can contribute, as we saw) but to invention of ghost constituents. At any level of the literary communication signals can be wrongly decoded, wrongly identified, or missed altogether. This may soon be obvious, as with the confusion of O.E. thorn and M.E. *p*, or ignorance of an obsolete grammatical rule. But often, as with the stylistic implications of rhetorical indicators, or with obsolete meanings of current words, it is far from clear when construction goes astray. Similarly with contemporary literature: codings may be unfamiliar because they are beyond the reader's emotional, social, or political experience; *avant-garde*; or too conservative to get an alert response. A profound work may be so demanding intellectually that it fails to establish coherent communication. And even with sentiments, though 'a true feeler always brings half the entertainment along with him. . . . 'Tis like reading *himself* and not the *book*', yet there is 'little true feeling in the *herd* of the *world*' (Sterne, Letter to Dr John Eustace, 9 Feb. 1768). In these ways, and many others, literary signals may meet with poor reception; so that the higher-level constituents they are meant to communicate are lost. Of course, the resulting errors are sometimes interesting—even worth consideration in their own right as Pater-like improvisations. But every sensible reader will wish to get the signals right: to put together a construct that is neither random nor idiosyncratic, but that shares with other readers' constructs a common element corresponding to the original work. That original work may not be the whole subject for our different critical views. But it ought to be a component (and I think a main component) of that subject.

How, then, should the work be constructed? This large question has received little attention—not surprisingly, since in the absence of any phenomenology of criticism the constructive phase is confused with the interpretative. One of the few principles advanced to guide construction is Beardsley's 'Principle of Plenitude': namely,

'All the connotations that can be found to fit are to be attributed to the poem: it means all it *can* mean, so to speak' (*Aesthetics* (New York 1958) 144). For Robert Graves, in equally permissive mood, the meaning of a Shakespeare sonnet is the 'one embracing as many meanings as possible, that is, the most difficult meaning'. Indeed, one might call this affluent principle the primary constructive rule in our time. Richness is all.

Yet if it were possible to give general advice, it might well be against the tendency casually embraced by this rule. It is an un-principled principle, which leads in the end to anything meaning anything. If Blake's Satanic mills can be industrial mills (as some have argued in pursuit of plenitude), why should not Spenser's false Una 'framed of liquid air' be chastely cold? Any moderately fanciful reader can easily generate higher-level constituents that satisfy Beardsley's only restraining principle, Congruence. But far more constraints will be needed, to produce a valid construct. It is a common experience to have to change a construct that has proved faulty, yet in which the meanings once *seemed* to fit. And whenever we fault a former construct we acknowledge the artifactual structure to be closed to some congruent realizations. What limits its open-ness? Surely considerations of historical truth, for one thing. The field of criticism has a truth pole as well as an aesthetic interest pole: it matters to us which constitutents are historically 'in' the work. In saying 'the work' I have in effect affirmed that the author's realized intention must exercise a farther constraint. What we try to construct is the original work, in the sense of the intention realized by the author. Scruples about intention will thus rule out many interesting meanings and other constituents. Our criterial questions are Did the author intend this? and, minimally, Can he have meant that? These questions need not constitute appeals to biography. The case of anonymous literature shows that an imagined author can exert con-straint on critical invention. And when we know the authorship it is still the accessible literary *persona* with whom we primarily deal as readers.

Interpretation and evaluation are distinct from construction and logically posterior to it. They are not, however, chronologically sequential phases. There would be far less confusion about in-tentionality if the critic could first construct the author's work and then criticize it. But the matter is less simple. Interpretation, like evaluation, necessarily deals for the most part with what interests the critic or his audience (preferably both). It speaks to their con-dition, even if the work does not. Consequently the focus and power of the reader's attention will vary with time and place in ways that no author can anticipate. Devices, levels of organization, even whole genres, may lose interest or delight (syntactic inversion; strict pentameter prosody; French Biblical epic). And to this Demogorgon of change the critic must, however reluctantly, pay some lip-service. An interpretation faithful to every proportion of the original, but lacking in relevance or interest, would be of very little use. The bearing of this truth on habits of construction is incalculable. How often do we unconsciously meet the choice between falsifying the construct or neglecting the work? It is repugnant to admit that we are temporarily or permanently incapable of receiving anything from what nevertheless was once a great work. But this may often be so. When the literary model alters, the parts of literature for which readers have competence must alter too. Nor are the changes only external or formal. The conception of meaning itself has undergone more than one profound development during the last millenium. In our own age allegoresis, for example, will simply not work as it worked for Dante or even for Shakespeare. And more inwardly still, the critic is exiled from the original work by a feast of knowledge. Inescapable hindsight shuts him out by making him incapable of a simple enough response. How could he ever feel the strangeness of the historically first exploration of an effect familiar to him from its subsequent exploitation and finesse?

The problem is not only a matter of historical stance: criticism's freedom legitimately extends to contemporary works. Living authors are subject to historical contingency too, in the deeper sense of human limitation. Consequently the reader is free to take a broader, deeper, or different view of the work from that of the limited author, if he can. He may well know more, or be more mature emotionally. And he feels perhaps that he can make a valuable contribution of his own in the selective assimilation of the values of the work.

The responsibility of a free critic

This freedom, however, is not so unconditioned as some suppose. Northrop Frye scorns 'the absurd quantum formula of criticism, the assertion that the critic should confine himself to "getting out" of a poem exactly what the poet may vaguely be assumed to have been aware of "putting in" ', that 'it is simply his job to take a poem into which a poet has diligently stuffed a specific number of beauties or effects, and complacently extract them one by one, like his prototype Little Jack Horner' (*Anatomy of Criticism* (Princeton, N.J. 1957) 17–8). But, as we have seen, recognizing the privileged status of intention by no means entails a vague assumption of total consciousness. We are certainly free to talk about features that the author was unaware of, and to talk about any of the work's beauties in terms unavailable to him. In that sense we indeed discourse endlessly of beauties that the author did not 'put in'. But the critic's social contract, it seems to me, is to discuss beauties of existing features, not merely of notional ones. And features do not exist just because we 'invent' or think them. Of course, not all theorists would accept this restriction. That in itself seems significant. Indeed, the intentionalist controversy almost seems as if it may now be starting to resolve itself into a more fundamental questioning of what criticism is about. Does criticism deal with actual literature only, or does it extend also to literature that exists potentially, or speculatively—without, as it were, having previous roots in history?

According to the view set out above, a critic's freedom is conditioned by responsibility to history. This responsibility has several components—not least the duty to avoid being oblivious to his own historical predicament. But from the present point of view the critic's responsibility is to include within his own broader vision the vision of the author. Ideally the original work will be incorporated in his construct, the original values (together perhaps with other critics' evaluations) encapsulated within his values, like the heart and growth rings of a tree. Only then, it seems, can he take his own historical place effectively, so that his interpretation, in turn, contributes to the healthy growth of the work.

This responsibility or 'limitation' (as Frye would call it) is no more confining than thematic relevance to a poet or constancy to a lover. Far from restricting literature as an inexhaustible source of critical discoveries, it directs attention to the headwaters. True, it constrains the critic to distinguish discoveries from inventions. But by doing so, and therefore by obliging the critic to meet the challenges of different minds, it makes for a criticism that is more than just *interesting*.

Not all opponents of intentionalism are formalists or archetypists. Critics devoted mainly to instrumental values tend to dislike a critical exercise that goes farther back than interpretation. They prefer to believe in a work permanently available to the valuer. For them the work has a purely synchronic existence. It is always 'there', in iconic immediacy and isolation, ready for the evaluative act. Even interpretation is a preliminary, to be despatched with a perfunctory word or two. Now, these critics need to be advised that such an attitude, despite its appearance of high seriousness, is really frivolous. The idea that the work continuously exists serves as a comforting defence; for what exists when the valuers come on the scene is a work that they have previously reconstructed themselves or taken over ready-made from other critics. Their wish to 'take it as read' easily covers reluctance to look into the construct's specifications. From time to time an unsound construction collapses spectacularly. Criticism of a *White-Jacket* that contained the phrase 'soiled fish of the sea' lost ground very quickly when the authenticity of the *White-Jacket* retaining Melville's 'coiled fish of the sea' became obvious. But usually bad construction passes unnoticed. It takes a good deal of imagination to realize that not just vocabulary-selection but every component of a construct can be unsound, in ways less obvious but no less disastrous. Yet to a serious critic it makes all the difference whether a statement concerns Melville's work or another one like it.

Are all these counsels of perfection? It must be conceded that we cannot hope to construct an author's work without deficiency or superfluity. Our best attempts are blurred with probabilities and approximations. We cannot even look forward, in the general case, to some distant time when all uncertainties will have been resolved— as one might resolve a particular problem, such as the quality of a rhyme. Criticism's fundamental predicament is that it inescapably concerns itself with an intended work that it must inevitably fail to discover. A similar dilemma may be universally inherent in the nature of meaning. (However precisely a recipient's conception is formulated, it will at best specify a category which the intended meaning belongs to. He can never quite resolve the paradox of simultaneous identity and difference between the author's meaning and what E. D. Hirsch has called the 'intrinsic genre'.) But this dilemma of our contingency should not make us despair or turn to antinomian relativism. There is plenty to be done. Not to know as much as we can about the premises of our interpretations: not to accept every opportunity of learning the codes that form literary communication: not to pursue at least the true Florimel of the work itself: that would be to do less than the reasonable standard of criticism demands. It would be flinching, even, from the difficulties of historical engagement.

Serious critical enquiries are likely to be farthered by habitually orientating thought towards the *locus* of authorial intentions. Eventually, the critic's own unconscious volitions may then be schooled to cooperate in imaginative revivifying of actual literature.

NOTES AND REFERENCES

WIMSATT & BEARDSLEY
The Intentional Fallacy
1. *Dictionary of World Literature*, Joseph T. Shipley, ed. (New York, 1942), 326–29.
2. J. E. Spingarn, 'The New Criticism,' in *Criticism in America* (New York, 1924), 24–25.
3. Ananda K. Coomaraswamy, 'Intention,' in *American Bookman*, I (1944), 41–48.
4. It is true that Croce himself in his *Ariosto, Shakespeare and Corneille* (London, 1920), chap. VII, 'The Practical Personality and the Poetical Personality,' and in his *Defence of Poetry* (Oxford, 1933), 24, and elsewhere, early and late, has delivered telling attacks on emotive geneticism, but the main drive of the *Aesthetic* is surely toward a kind of cognitive intentionalism.
5. See Hughes Mearns, *Creative Youth* (Garden City, 1925), esp. 10, 27–29. The technique of inspiring poems has apparently been outdone more recently by the study of inspiration in successful poets and other artists. See, for instance, Rosamond E. M. Harding, *An Anatomy of Inspiration* (Cambridge, 1940); Julius Portnoy, *A Psychology of Art Creation* (Philadelphia, 1942); Rudolf Arnheim and others, *Poets at Work* (New York, 1947); Phyllis Bartlett, *Poems in Process* (New York, 1951); Brewster Ghiselin (ed.), *The Creative Process: A Symposium* (Berkeley and Los Angeles, 1952).
6. Curt Ducasse, *The Philosophy of Art* (New York, 1929), 116.
7. And the history of words *after* a poem is written may contribute meanings which if relevant to the original pattern should not be ruled out by a scruple about intention.
8. Chaps. VIII, 'The Pattern,' and XVI, 'The Known and Familiar Landscape,' will be found of most help to the student of the poem.
9. Charles M. Coffin, *John Donne and the New Philosophy* (New York, 1927), 97–98.

REDPATH
The Meaning of a Poem
1. A symposium: *British Philosophy in the Mid-Century*.
2. Quoted by Virginia Woolf, *Roger Fry*, Hogarth Press (1940), pp. 240–41.
3. I say 'sometimes', because there are certainly also cases where the poet has new ideas during revision, so that although the old expressions were good enough for the old wine they are not good enough for the new.
4. And even if we take the term 'meaning' more narrowly, the same is true. Even in the narrowest construction of the term 'meaning', as *bare sense*, it is surely unlikely that every poet in writing every poem has realized the full sense of the words he is writing. And we are certainly at liberty to construe 'meaning' more widely than that.
5. John Dewey, *Art as Experience*, New York, 1934, pp. 108–109.

6. 'Honesty' is clearly not enough; but there is no time to take Dewey up on that point.
7. Augustine, *Confessions*, XI, 14.
8. The passage is quoted by Wittgenstein again in his posthumous work, *Philosophical Investigations,* Blackwell, Oxford, 1953, p. 42.
9. For the matter of the relation of the traditional ranges of words to individual uses, see Stern, *Meaning and Change of Meaning,* Göteborg, 1931, especially ch III; Cassirer, *Philosophie der Symbolischen Formen,* Berlin, 1923, I, 22; Ahlmann, 'Das normative Moment im Bedeutungsbegriff', *Ann. Acad. Scient. Fenn.,* Ser. B, Tom. XVIII, Nr. 2, Helsingfors, 1926.
10. Why I say 'a class' is to exclude evaluative experiences *about* the poem, which perhaps the poem *ought* to evoke, but which do not form part of its meaning. Another point about the suggestion which should be emphasized, is that as it stands it is an account of 'the meaning' of the poem in the *fullest sense,* that is, as including the proper effects of phonal, associational, formal, tonal, emotive aspects, and so on, of the poem, as well as the proper effects of the bare sense of the poem, that is, the bare understanding of that bare sense by a reader. One could, however, give a similar account of 'the meaning' of a poem in some more restricted sense, if one wished to. 'The meaning' would then be a sub-class of the whole class mentioned in my suggestion. For instance, 'the meaning' of a poem, if this be construed narrowly as the bare sense of the poem, would be a certain sub-class of similar experiences, which those words in that order *ought* to evoke in a reader familiar with the language (or languages) in which the poem is written.
11. At pp. 226–29.
12. In the Inaugural Lecture called 'Poetry for Poetry's Sake', delivered by him at Oxford on his assumption of the Chair of Poetry (publ. 1901), reprinted in his *Oxford Lectures on Poetry,* 1909 (1923 edition, at p. 4).
13. 'Similar' not, by the way, to any standard experience, but to one another.

HIRSCH
Objective Interpretation

1. *Encyclopädie,* p. 170.
2. Gottlob Frege, 'Über Sinn und Bedeutung,' *Z. für Philosophie und philosophische Kritik, 100* (1892). The article has been translated, and one English version may be found in H. Feigl and W. Sellars, *Readings in Philosophical Analysis* (New York, 1949).
3. Wellek and Warren, *Theory of Literature,* Chap. 12. This chapter is by Wellek.
4. See, for example, ibid., p. 31.
5. Ibid., p. 144.
6. It could also be explained, of course, by saying that certain generations of readers tend to misunderstand certain texts.
7. Wellek and Warren, p. 144. My italics.
8. Ibid., pp. 166–67.
9. Eliot, 'Tradition and the Individual Talent.'
10. Most of my illustrations in this section are visual rather than verbal since the former may be more easily grasped. The example of a box

was suggested to me by Helmut Kuhn, 'The Phenomenological Concept of "Horizon," ' in *Philosophical Essays in Memory of Edmund Husserl*, ed. Marvin Farber (Cambridge, Mass., 1940).

11. See Aaron Gurwitsch, 'On the Intentionality of Consciousness,' in *Philosophical Essays*, ed. Farber.

12. Although Husserl's term is a standard philosophical one for which there is no adequate substitute, students of literature may unwittingly associate it with the intentional fallacy. The two uses of the word are, however, quite distinct. As used by literary critics the term refers to a purpose which may or may not be realized by a writer. As used by Husserl the term refers to a process of consciousness. Thus in the literary usage, which involves problems of rhetoric, it is possible to speak of an unfulfilled intention, while in Husserl's usage such a locution would be meaningless.

13. Edmund Husserl, *Logische Untersuchungen. Zweiter Band. Untersuchungen zur Phänomenologie und Theorie der Erkenntnis. I Teil* (2d ed. Halle, 1913), pp. 96–97.

14. Ibid., p. 91.

15. See Edmund Husserl, *Erfahrung und Urteil*, ed. L. Landgrebe (Hamburg, 1948), pp. 26–36, and Kuhn, 'The Phenomenological Concept of "Horizon." '

16. The phrase, 'piece of language,' comes from the first paragraph of Empson's *Seven Types of Ambiguity*. It is typical of the critical school Empson founded.

17. Vol. 1, *Language*. It is ironic that Cassirer's work should be used to support the notion that a text speaks for itself. The realm of language is autonomous for Cassirer only in the sense that it follows an independent development which is reciprocally determined by objective *and* subjective factors. See pp. 69, 178, 213, 249–50, and passim.

18. Wellek and Warren, *Theory of Literature*, p. 144.

19. Every interpretation is necessarily incomplete in the sense that it fails to explicate all a text's implications. But this kind of incomplete interpretation may still carry an absolutely correct system of emphases and an accurate sense of the whole meaning. This kind of incompleteness is radically different from that postulated by the inclusivists, for whom a sense of the whole means a grasp of the various possible meanings which a text can plausibly represent.

20. Cleanth Brooks, 'Irony as a Principle of Structure,' in *Literary Opinion in America, ed.* M. D. Zabel (2nd ed. New York, 1951), p. 736; F. W. Bateson, *English Poetry: A Critical Introduction* (London, 1950), pp. 33, 80–81.

21. This is the 'synchronic' as opposed to the 'diachronic' sense of the term. See Ferdinand de Saussure, *Cours de linguistique générale* (Paris, 1931). Useful discussions may be found in Stephen Ullman, *The Principles of Semantics* (Glasgow, 1951), and W. v. Wartburg, *Einführung in die Problematik und Methodik der Sprachwissenschaft* (Halle, 1943).

22. See, for example, Cassirer, *Symbolic Forms*, Vol. 1, *Language*, p. 304.

23. T. S. Eliot, 'From Poe to Valéry,' *Hudson Rev. 2* (1949), 232.

24. The word is, in fact, quite effective. It conveys the sense of 'memorable' by the component 'memorial,' and the sense of 'never to be forgotten' by the negative prefix. The difference between this

and jabberwocky words is that it appears to be a standard word occurring in a context of standard words. Perhaps Eliot is right to scold Poe, but he cannot properly insist that the word lacks a determinate verbal meaning.

25. To recall Husserl's point, a particular verbal meaning depends on a particular species of intentional act, not on a single, irreproducible act.

26. This third criterion is, however, highly presumptive, since the interpreter may easily mistake the text's genre.

27. Exceptions to this are the syncategorematic meanings (color and extension, for example) which cohere by necessity regardless of the context.

28. The reader may feel that I have telescoped a number of steps here. The author's verbal meaning or verbal intention is the object of complex intentional acts. To reproduce this meaning it is necessary for the interpreter to engage in intentional acts belonging to the same species as those of the author. (Two different intentional acts belong to the same species when they 'intend' the same intentional object.) That is why the issue of 'stance' arises. The interpreter needs to adopt sympathetically the author's stance (his disposition to engage in particular kinds of intentional acts) so that he can 'intend' with some degree of probability the same intentional objects as the author. This is especially clear in the case of *implicit* verbal meaning, where the interpreter's realization of the author's stance determines the text's horizon.

29. Here I purposefully display my sympathies with Dilthey's concepts, *Sichhineinfühlen* and *Verstehen*. In fact, my whole argument may be regarded as an attempt to ground some of Dilthey's hermeneutic principles in Husserl's epistemology and Saussure's linguistics.

30. Spranger aptly calls this the 'cultural subject.' See Eduard Spranger, 'Zur Theorie des Verstehens und zur geisteswissenschaftlichen Psychologie,' in *Festschrift Johannes Volkelt zum 70. Geburtstag* (Munich, 1918), p. 369. It should be clear that I am here in essential agreement with the American anti-intentionalists (term used in the ordinary sense). I think they are right to exclude private associations from verbal meaning. But it is of some practical consequence to insist that verbal meaning is that aspect of an author's meaning which is interpersonally communic*able*. This implies that his verbal meaning is that which, under linguistic norms, one *can* understand, even if one must sometimes work hard to do so.

31. Bally calls this 'dédoublement de la personnalité.' See his *Linguistique générale et linguistique française*, p. 37.

CIOFFI
Intention and Interpretation in Criticism

1. The allusion here is to the fact that when Shakespeare's *Henry V* is performed in France, Pistol's reference to syphilis as 'malady of France' is sometimes replaced by the expression 'malady of Naples' ('la maladie Napolitaine'). The line of thought is that since our tolerance of such practices does not imply a general indifference to an author's intentions neither need our toleration of anachronistic readings of Blake's *Jerusalem*.

The Scope of the Intentional Fallacy

1. Isabel Hungerland, 'The Concept of Intention in Art Criticism,' *J. Phil.* 52 (1955), 733–42. Miss Hungerland's paper is admittedly exploratory, and is provocative.
2. Leslie A. Fiedler, 'Archetype and Signature: A Study of the Relationship Between Biography and Poetry,' *Sewanee Rev.* 60 (1952), 253–73. Hereafter cited as 'Arche. Sig.'
3. Monroe Beardsley, *Aesthetics: Problems in the Philosophy of Criticism* (New York: Harcourt, Brace and Company, 1958), p. 25. Hereafter cited as A P C.
4. Notice that I do not say 'ought not.' This would raise a question about the *proper* subject matter of criticism which would ultimately force a definition of 'aesthetic'. I do not want to treat this problem here, and so for the sake of the discussion, I accept their notion of the context of criticism as correct. I am really only interested in bringing out the implications involved in their assumption with respect to the intentional fallacy and, more generally, the subject of reasons within literary criticism.
5. 'Arche. Sig.,' pp. 253–273.
6. Ibid., p. 259.
7. Ibid., pp. 259 and 273.
8. W. K. Wimsatt and M. C. Beardsley, 'The Intentional Fallacy,' *Philosophy Looks at the Arts*, ed. J. Margolis (New York: Charles Scribner's Sons, 1962). Hereafter cited as 'Inten. Fall.'
9. 'Arche. Sig.,' p. 256.
10. Ibid., p. 260.
11. A P C, p. 25.
12. 'Arche. Sig.,' p. 259.
13. Charles L. Stevenson discusses these reasons, and others that resemble them, in his paper, 'On the Reasons That Can Be Given for the Interpretation of a Poem,' *Philosophy Looks at the Arts*, ed. Joseph Margolis (New York: Charles Scribner's Sons, 1962), pp. 121–39. I have been heavily influenced by this article, although in the long run my arguments have little in common with Stevenson's. In particular, I disagree with Stevenson when he says, 'My views on this matter are partly borrowed from W. K. Wimsatt and M. C. Beardsley. *But they are concerned largely with the evaluation of poetry, whereas I am transferring their views, with alterations, to the interpretation of poetry* [my italics].' I do not think that Wimsatt and Beardsley are so little concerned with interpretation as Stevenson makes them out to be. In fact, I seriously question whether Stevenson can make his 'transfer' at all. I think that the possibility of a transfer is largely dependent upon what one takes the nature of the intentional fallacy to be. And this is what the present paper is all about. In any case, my debt to Stevenson is certainly a real one.
14. 'Inten. Fall.,' p. 98.
15. Incidentally, this ought to dissuade those who believe that a word gets its meaning by being used in a special way within the context of some poem from pursuing their belief recklessly, but more about this later.
16. 'Inten. Fall.,' p. 97.
17. I do not want this phrase *'conventional* meaning' to commit me to any

given theory of language, but only to the thesis that the words a poet uses (when he uses words and not sounds) have meanings independently of his having used them in his poem. Furthermore, this need not mean that no *poet has ever* or *can ever* create a new word.

18. And this is not to say that a poem is nothing more than words, but only to point out one obvious way in which one can be wrong about a poem.

19. 'Inten. Fall.,' p.98.

HIRSCH
In Defense of the Author

1. The classic statement is in T. S. Eliot, 'Tradition and the Individual Talent,' *Selected Essays* (New York, 1932).

2. See, for example, Martin Heidegger, *Unterwegs zur Sprache* (Pfullingen, 1959).

3. See Ernst Cassirer, *The Philosophy of Symbolic Forms:* Vol. 1, *Language*, trans. R. Manheim (New Haven, 1953), particularly pp. 69, 178, 213, 249–50, and passim.

4. The random example that I use later in the book is the sentence: 'I am going to town today.' Different senses can be lent to the sentence by the simple device of placing a strong emphasis on any of the six different words.

5. The phrase is from T. S. Eliot, *On Poetry and Poets* (New York, 1957), p. 126.

6. It would be invidious to name any individual critic as the begetter of this widespread and imprecise notion. By the 'best' reading, of course, some critics mean the most valid reading, but the idea of bestness is widely used to embrace indiscriminately both the idea of validity and of such aesthetic values as richness, inclusiveness, tension, or complexity—as though validity and aesthetic excellence must somehow be identical.

9. See René Wellek and Austin Warren, *Theory of Literature* (New York, 1948), Chap. 12.

8. For the sake of clarity I should quickly indicate to the reader that verbal meaning can be the same for different interpreters by virtue of the fact that verbal meaning has the character of a type. A type covers a range of actualizations (one example would be a phoneme) and yet in each actualization remains (like a phoneme) the identical type.

9. Plato, *Apology,* 22b–c.

10. Immanuel Kant, *Critique of Pure Reason*, trans. N. K. Smith (London, 1933), A 314, B 370, p. 310: 'I shall not engage here in any literary enquiry into the meaning which this illustrious author attached to the expression. I need only remark that it is by no means unusual, upon comparing the thoughts which an author has expressed in regard to his subject, whether in ordinary conversation or in writing, to find that we understand him better than he has understood himself.'

11. This distinction was not observed in the interesting essay by O. Bollknow, 'Was heisst es einen Verfasser zu verstehen besser als er sich selber verstanden hat?' in *Das Verstehen, Drei Aufsätze zur Theorie des Geisteswissenschaften* (Mainz, 1949).

12. Or at least that of the muse who temporarily possesses him—the muse being, in those unseemly cases, the real author.

WIMSATT
Genesis: A Fallacy Revisited

1. Two friends have specially contributed to this essay—Monroe Beardsley of course, who brought to my attention some of our critics in the journals and who read my early draft, and Donald Hirsch, whose differences from me, whether in conversation or in print, have the unusual character of being always illuminative. His essay of 1960 in *PMLA*, which I cite below and argue with (notes 18, 21, and 53), is one of the best on the subject which I now attempt to reapproach.

2. I leave out his headaches and his gallstones, though there was a time when these too would have been important. For a rich and orderly assortment of artist's drives and motives, conscious and unconscious, during the creative process, see Monroe C. Beardsley, 'On the Creation of Art,' *JAAC, 23* (Spring 1965), 291–304.

3. See below, p. 264 n. 14.

4. See, for instance, Alfred Owen Aldridge, 'Biography in the Interpretation of Poetry,' *College English, 25* (March 1964), 412–20: 'I shall try to indicate a few reasons why biography serves to humanize poetry and therefore to heighten our enjoyment.' 'No purely esthetic criticism has ever stimulated the same public interest,' the same 'extraordinary sensation which has been caused by the recent announcement of A. L. Rowse's biographical study of Shakespeare—with its revelations' (p. 415). Or see John A. Meixner, 'The Uses of Biography in Criticism,' *College English, 27* (November 1966), 108–13; or Carlos Baker, 'Speaking of Books: The Relevance of a Writer's Life,' *New York Times Book Rev.* (August 20, 1967), pp. 2, 31.

5. Leslie A. Fiedler, *No! In Thunder: Essays on Myth and Literature* (Boston, 1960), pp. 312–18.

6. William H. Capitan, 'The Artist's Intention,' *Rev. Int. Phil.*, 68–69 (1964), 331–32. Cf. Joseph Margolis, *The Language of Art & Art Criticism, Analytic Questions in Aesthetics* (Detroit, 1965), p. 99, on stage directions and musical notations. Also see below, p. 212. Margolis is a writer who cheerfully piles up examples that tell in favor of Wimsatt and Beardsley and even quotes passages from them with which he cannot disagree and then with equal cheer somersaults to a guarded conclusion that they 'must be mistaken,' that 'intentional criticism has, to some extent at least, a recognizable and not inappropriate place in the aesthetic examination of art' (p. 103).

7. Capitan, p. 332.

8. Dr F. Cioffi, 'Intention and Interpretation in Criticism' (from *Proc. Arist. Soc.*, 1963–64), in *Collected Papers on Aesthetics*, ed. Cyril Barrett, S. J. (Oxford, 1965), pp. 161–83, esp. 168, 170–71, 172, 174, 175, 179–81. See M. C. Beardsley's review of this volume, with special attention to Cioffi, in *JAAC, 26* (Fall 1967), 144–46.

9. *Massachusetts Rev., 7* (Summer 1966), 584–90.

10. *The Use of Poetry and the Use of Criticism* (London, 1933), p. 140.

11. All the words quoted are from *Tradition and the Individual Talent*.

12. See Richard Ellmann, *The Identity of Yeats* (New York, 1954) and *Yeats: The Man and the Masks* (New York, 1948). The article by A. O. Aldridge cited above confuses the poet's view and the critic's view throughout and refers to much literature which also does. In Slavic countries formalist critics during the 1920s defined a poem as

'a deflection, not a reflection, of experience' (p. 412).

13. 'We ought to impute the thoughts and attitudes of the poem immediately to the dramatic *speaker*, and if to the author at all, only by an act of biographical inference' ('The Intentional Fallacy' [1946], paragraph 7).

14. See Leon Edel, *Literary Biography* (London, 1957); J. Hillis Miller, *The Disappearance of God, Five Nineteenth-Century Writers* (New York, 1965)—De Quincey, Browning, Emily Brontë, Arnold, Hopkins. But for Miller chronology is not important.

15. *Hudson Rev., 12* (Winter 1959–60), 487–507.

16. *Yale Rev., 41* (Autumn 1951), 80–92.

17. *Restoration and Eighteenth-Century Literature, Essays in Honor of Alan Dugald McKillop,* ed. Carroll Camden (Chicago, 1963), pp. 25–37.

18. See this large and interesting work passim, esp. Chap. 8, 'Telling as Showing: Dramatized Narrators, Reliable and Unreliable.' See too Allan Rodway and Brian Lee, 'Coming to Terms,' *Essays in Criticism, 14* (April 1964), 122; and E. D. Hirsch's very subtle and accurate distinction between 'speaking subject' and 'biographical person,' as illustrated in the 'secret awareness' of lying and the 'truth-telling stance' ('Objective Interpretation,' *PMLA, 75* [September 1960], 478–79). See also some good paragraphs on the theme of person and poet in Harry Berger, Jr., 'Cadmus Unchanged,' a review of *Selected Letters of Robert Frost,* in *Yale Rev., 54* (Winter 1965), 277–82. For a range of examples and insights from a different area, see Victor Erlich, 'The Concept of the Poet as a Problem of Poetics,' *Poetics, Poetyka, Poetika* (The Hague, Mouton & Co., 1962), pp. 707–17, and 'Some Uses of Monologue in Prose Fiction: Narrative Manner and World View,' *Stil- und Formprobleme in der Literatur* (Heidelberg, 1959), pp. 371–78.

19. H. W. Garrod, *Poetry and the Criticism of Life* (Cambridge, Mass., 1931), p. 83. Garrod refers to Arnold's 'make-up' of being the greatest English critic.

20. See the excellent article, in effect about anonymous lyric personae, by Arthur K. Moore, 'Lyric Voices and Ethical Proofs,' *JAAC, 23* (Summer 1965), 429–39. 'Lyrics are vouched for simply — . . . through intelligible relationships to activities, conditions, occasions, lives, ideologies, and states of consciousness into which interest enters' (pp. 429–30). See the same author's later 'Lyric Personae and Prying Critics,' *Southern Humanities Rev., 1* (1967), 43–64.

21. *Essays in Criticism, 4* (July 1954), 315, 319. And see below, p. 267, n. 53, *langue* and *parole* as expounded by Hirsch, 'Objective Interpretation,' pp. 473–75.

22. One of the monkeys employed in this experiment once got through the whole poem all right, as far as the last word of the last book, but then he slipped and wrote, instead of 'way.,' 'lxdz.,' and the whole version of course had to be scrapped.

23. 'The Aesthetics of Textual Criticism,' *PMLA, 80* (December 1965), 465–82, esp. 465–68, 475.

24. See Sidney Gendin's sensible short article, 'The Artist's Intentions,' *JAAC, 23* (Winter 1964), 195.

25. Another term which Mr Beardsley (pp. 457, 490–91) puts in this genetic group is 'originality,' which, like 'skill' (see 3c below), is a merit which seems assignable more readily to the author than to his

work. During the neoclassic age, in arguments comparing Homer and Virgil, the latter was sometimes said to have written doubtless the more perfect poem; the former got a good mark for originality. A 1966 Fairlane is a better automobile than a Model-T Ford, but not as original.

26. See Beardsley, *Aesthetics* (1958), p.489. Dr Cioffi (p.164) dismisses this form of the intentionalistic argument with great unconcern. He is no doubt largely unaware of the contexts of literary scholarship and criticism which framed our articles of 1944 and 1946. On 'skill,' cf. Gendin, p.195.

27. See, for instance, John Kemp, 'The Work of Art and the Artist's Intentions,' *Br. J. Aesthetics, 4* (April 1964), 150–51; Capitan, pp.324–26; and Gendin, p.193.

28. Henry David Aiken, 'The Aesthetic Relevance of Artists' Intentions,' *The Journal of Philosophy, 52* (24 November 1955), reprinted in *Problems in Aesthetics,* ed. Morris Weitz (New York, 1959), pp.299–300. Cf. Gendin, p.194.

29. Kemp, p.121, describes this situation very clearly.

30. Capitan, pp.331–32.

31. See his extremely intentionalistic justification of these notes in a lecture on Dante in 1950: 'I gave the references in my notes, in order to make the reader who recognizes the allusion, know that I meant him to recognize it, and know that he would have missed the point if he did not recognize it' (*To Criticize the Critic and Other Writings* [New York, 1965], p.128).

32. The claim for artist's intentions as auxiliaries to works of art will no doubt mean somewhat different things for different kinds and instances of art. See, for instance, Beardsley, pp.20–29; Capitan, pp.327–33; Erwin Panofsky, 'On Intentions,' in *Problems in Aesthetics,* pp.288–95, extracted from Panofsky's 'History of Art as a Humanistic Discipline,' in *The Meaning of the Humanities,* ed. T.M.Greene (Princeton, 1940).

33. See Beardsley, p.20, on painting and sculpture, 'the simplest descriptive level.' Cf. Gendin, p.194.

34. *Preface to Shakespeare* (1765), paragraph 59.

35. Boswell, *Life of Johnson,* 9 April 1778.

36. *Poetical Works of Goldsmith* (Oxford, 1939), p.167.

37. *Goldsmith* (London, 1848), *1*, 369.

38. Beardsley, p.24; Margolis, pp.97,189; David Magarshack, *Chekhov the Dramatist* (New York, Hill and Wang, 1960), pp.188–89, *The Seagull*, p.273, *The Cherry Orchard*. '*The Seagull* is usually interpreted on the stage as a tragedy (a misinterpretation Stanislavsky was the first to impose on the play), and yet Chekhov always referred to it as a comedy' (p.188). 'Practically every producer . . . in spite of Chekhov's unmistakable intentions, regards the play as a tragedy' (p.189). We are here concerned in part with nuances of local meaning, in part also with whole dramatic structure and import. The example of Chekhov might well have been adduced above under 4d. Margolis, p.96, quotes the instance, no doubt unusual in the annals of literature, of Melville's acknowledgment that Hawthorne had revealed to him allegorical meanings in *Moby Dick* which he himself had not specifically 'meant.'

39. Cf. T.S.Eliot, 'What Dante Means to Me' (1950), in *To Criticize the*

Critic, p. 133. The terms are Eliot's. Though he would concede that 'some great English poets . . . were privileged by their genius to abuse the English language,' yet the poets who have best served their language are the greatest, Virgil, Dante, Shakespeare.

40. Number xxxv of the Rossetti manuscript, in Joseph H. Wicksteed, *Blake's Innocence and Experience* (London, 1928), after p. 256, p. 261, and facing p. 285; cf. *Poetry and Prose of William Blake*, ed. Geoffrey Keynes (London, 1932), p. 96.

41. Keynes, p. 75; Wicksteed, after p. 244, and p. 252.

42. E. D. Hirsch, Jr., *Innocence and Experience: An Introduction to Blake* (New Haven, 1964), pp. 263–65.

43. The evidence of the Rossetti manuscript supports the biographical dimension which I introduce for the sake of dialogue with the biographically minded. The distinction between the doctrinaire man and the subtle poem would remain even if the poetic achievement had cost Blake no trouble at all.

44. Wicksteed, p. 190. 'I do not doubt that he continued to accept marriage at its face value even after his mind had learnt to entertain the revolutionary suggestions of the rationalistic and antinomian circles he came to mingle in' (p. 215).

45. *Comparative Literature, 8* (Winter 1956), 28–45, esp. 36–38.

46. Margolis, pp. 103 and 189, citing Isabel Hungerland, 'The Concept of Intention in Art Criticism,' *J. Phil., 52* (24 November 1955), 733–42, and other sources.

47. Dr Cioffi, p. 167.

48. Margolis, p. 103, quoting Beardsley, p. 490.

49. One of our critics, Emilio Roma III, seems to grasp this principle firmly enough and to accept it. ('The Scope of the Intentional Fallacy,' *Monist, 50* [April 1966], 250–65, esp. 250–51, 256, 265). It is perhaps his main reason for recognizing a sort of 'minimal' and 'pitifully easy' meaning in our notion of the 'intentional fallacy.' But he believes that a distinction between what the speaker means and what the 'sentence' means, urged very explicitly by Mr Beardsley in 1958, is not to be found in our essay of 1946. Mr Roma writes with the air (e.g. p. 254) of painfully spelling out what we said. 'Style,' he says, 'is treated [by us] as though it had nothing whatsoever to do with content' (p. 265). To me at least, and I think to Mr Beardsley, this can come only as a matter of surprise. How much of what we have written, in the essay of 1946 and elsewhere, is really understood by Mr Roma?

50. Roma, pp. 251–52, 258, 262; Cioffi, pp. 167, 170 (on excluding 'illicit sources' of interpretation). The word 'motley' in our text just above is from Cioffi, pp. 176, 183, taken by him 'probably' from Wittgenstein.

51. This may involve what Mr E. D. Hirsch calls the 'fallacy of the homogeneous past.' 'The homogeneous critic assumes that everybody in a given cultural milieu shares the same basic attitudes and beliefs. He is content to speak of the Greek Mind, the Medieval Mind, the Victorian Mind' ('Criticism versus Historicism,' mimeograph of a paper read at the meeting of the Modern Language Association, December 1963).

52. Hyatt H. Waggoner, in *What To Say About a Poem, CEA Chapbook*, by W. K. Wimsatt, Jr., and others, ed. Donald A. Sears (College

English Association, 1963), pp. 22, 32.

53. See Mr Hirsch's exposition of Saussure's distinction ('Objective Interpretation,' pp. 473–75), where *langue*, the 'system of linguistic possibilities shared by a speech community,' 'contains words and sentence-forming principles, but it contains no sentences.' A poem or any other verbal text containing sentences cannot then simply 'represent a segment of *langue*' (as modern literary theorists are said to hold) but must be a *parole*, 'a particular, selective actualization from *langue*,' a determinate individual expression. 'Only individuals utter *paroles*,' and '*a parole* of the speech community is non-existent.' 'Meaning requires a meaner.' When we come to the difficulty of the 'bungled text,' the 'freshman essay,' the malapropism (which, let me add, is the basic difficulty of poem and purpose made large and unavoidable), we solve it by saying that the author's text, failing to 'represent the *parole* he desired to convey,' 'represents no *parole* at all.' But such an intuitionist and absolute (or Crocean) conclusion does not sit well in the abstractive and scientific premises (of *langue* and *parole*) with which we have begun. If we are going to have 'words' and 'principles' conceived as prior to *parole*, we must face the possibility of their being badly put together. A 'house' put together of ill-matched cardboard prefabrications would not be no house at all, or nothing, but simply a bad house.

Mr Hirsch's *Validity in Interpretation* (New Haven, Yale University Press, 1967), which urges his views in greater detail and usefully reprints his essay of 1960, appeared only some time after I had completed the present essay. Mr Beardsley, in an essay entitled 'Textual Meaning and Authorial Meaning,' has written what I consider a shrewd critique of the book, scheduled to appear in a symposium in *Genre, 1*, No. 2 (June 1968), a new quarterly issued from the University of Illinois at Chicago Circle.

WATSON
The Literary Past
Select Bibliography: André Morize, *Problems and Methods of Literary History, with Special Reference to Modern French Literature: a Guide for Graduate Students* (Boston, 1922), is a rare example of a methodical account of the procedures of the literary historian, unfortunately outdated in its references. A briefer but more modern version is James Thorpe, *Literary Scholarship: a Handbook for Advanced Students of English and American Literature* (Boston, 1964). For the rise of literary history, see under Chapter 1, above. An article by W. K. Wimsatt and Monroe C. Beardsley, 'The Intentional Fallacy', which first appeared in a periodical in 1946, was revised and collected in Wimsatt, *The Verbal Icon* (Lexington, Kentucky, 1954), and acknowledges a debt to an earlier exchange on a similar theme between C. S. Lewis and E. M. W. Tillyard, *The Personal Heresy* (Oxford, 1939). There could hardly be a single record of the vast expansion of literary history since 1800; but René Wellek, *A History of Modern Criticism 1750–1950* (New Haven, 1955–), is largely concerned with its progress in Europe and North America. On biographical elements, Leon Edel, *Literary Biography* (Toronto, 1957, revised New York, 1959); and for an anthology of the views on biographies themselves, *Biography as an Art*, edited by James L.

Clifford (Oxford, 1962).
1. 'The Lesson of Balzac' (1905), reprinted in *The House of Fiction*, edited by Leon Edel (London, 1957), p.64.
2. Wimsatt and Beardsley, in *Dictionary of World Literature*, edited by Joseph T. Shipley (New York, 1942), p. 327.
3. Lionel Trilling, *Matthew Arnold* (New York, 1939), pp. 134–5.
4. Ferdinand Brunetière, *Manuel de l'histoire de la littérature française* (Paris, 1898), p. iii.

CLOSE
Don Quixote *and the 'Intentional Fallacy'*
1. This article has at various points materially benefited from the perceptive and constructive criticism of Mr Alan Brunton of the Philosophy Department of University College, Cardiff. For his generous help I am extremely grateful.
2. A book entitled *The Romantic Approaches to 'Don Quixote'*, which is about to be submitted for publication.
3. G. E. M. Anscombe, *Intention* (1963 edition)—a work to which this article is basically indebted.
4. W. K. Wimsatt and M. Beardsley, *The Verbal Icon* (University of Kentucky, 1954), and generally the whole first chapter on 'The Intentional Fallacy'.
5. *e.g.* J. Kemp, 'The Work of Art and the Artist's Intentions', *Br. J. Aesthetics*, IV (1964), p. 150.
6. Even Cioffi, in his brilliant attack on the Wimsatt/Beardsley position, uses intention in much the same loose sense as his opponents and, like them, seems to regard intentions as but contingently related to the text. Thus he can talk (pp. 89,90) of author's intentions having varying degrees of relevance to critical interpretation, and of what an author 'meant by a poem' not necessarily being concomitant with 'what makes the best poem of it' (p. 88). While Cioffi is a sophisticated aesthetician, his view of intentions, together with his stress on the importance of a 'biographical' reference in our response to literature, leads him to postulate as examples of acceptable criticism rather dubious cases where 'biographical' criteria supersede the most logically consistent sense of the author's words (see pp. 98, 100). F. Cioffi, 'Intention and Interpretation in Criticism', *Proc. Arist. Soc.* LXIV (1963–4), pp. 85–106.
7. R. Kuhns, 'Criticism and the Problem of Intentions', *Journal of Philosophy*, LVII (1960), p. 14.
8. *The Anatomy of Criticism* (Princeton University Press, 1957) p. 89.
9. Q. Skinner, 'On Performing and Explaining Linguistic Actions', *Phil. Q.*, XXI (1971), p. 15. I am indebted to this article for the suggestion, pursued later, that the identification of intentions in literary criticism can occur via illocutionary redescription.
10. On the admissibility of 'unconscious' intentions see Cioffi, pp. 97–8; also C. Olsen, 'Knowledge of One's Own Intentional Actions', *Phil. Q.*, XIX (1969).
11. Frye, pp. 86,98.
12. Besides citing Frye I have quoted incidentally from L. C. Knights and Paul Valéry. See Knights, 'Idea and Symbol—Some Hints from Coleridge' in *Metaphor and Symbol*, ed. L. C. Knights and Basil Cottle

268

(1960), p. 142; also Valéry, 'Au Sujet du Cimetière Marin' in *Oeuvres* (ed. Pléiade, 1957), I, 1501–7.

13. Anscombe, pp. 80–9.
14. P. F. Strawson, 'Intention and Convention in Speech Acts', *Phil. Rev.*, LXXIII (1964), pp. 439–60.
15. J. L. Austin, *How to Do Things with Words* (1962), Lectures viii and ix.
16. Austin at certain points (*e.g.* p. 104) appears to warn against extending the notion of illocutionary force to literary art when he says that one must distinguish between 'parasitic' uses of language (joking, speaking poetically) and the 'full normal use', between, *e.g.* Walt Whitman's exhortation to the eagle of liberty to soar and a normal order. However, Whitman's 'exhortation' only gets ruled out as an illocution by Austin because it is being contemplated as if it were seeking to perform a function which it would never conventionally be understood as trying to perform. This does not mean that there is not some other illocutionary function which it would normally be regarded as performing, *e.g.* poetically expressing patriotic sentiments. Since Austin offers his doctrine as applicable to all 'serious' and 'normal' uses of language there seems no good reason for not applying it to so serious and normal an area of language as literary art.
17. H. P. Grice, 'Utterer's Meaning and Intentions', *Phil. Rev.*, LXXVIII (1969), pp. 147–77, this being a development of the earlier article 'Meaning', *Phil. Rev.*, LXVI (1957), pp. 377–88.
18. Strawson, *passim*, and Grice, 'Meaning', pp. 386–7.
19. Olsen, pp. 330–1.
20. See note 17.
21. 'Utterer's Meaning and Intentions', p. 151.

HIRSCH
Three Dimensions of Hermeneutics

1. F. D. E. Schleiermacher, *Hermeneutik*, ed. Heinz Kimmerle (Heidelberg, 1959), p. 90. The original reads: 'Alles was noch einer näheren Bestimmung bedarf in einer gegebene Rede, darf nur aus dem dem Verfasser und seinem ursprünglichen Publikum gemeinsamen Sprachgebiet bestimmt werden.'
2. The structure of this distinction I owe to the writings of Husserl and Frege, whose influence I acknowledge in the earlier piece alluded to, 'Objective Interpretation,' *PMLA*, 75 (Sept. 1960).
3. This is a shorthand, not a pejorative term which comprises all non-authorial meaning, whether or not such meaning was possible within 'the linguistic domain common to the author and his original public.' I use the term in preference to 'non-authorial meaning' because the chief disputes have centered, as Schleiermacher's canon suggests, on the question of historicity. Either term would serve.
4. See Ch. Bally, *Linguistique générale et linguistique française*, 2nd. ed. (Bern, 1944), p. 37.
5. Augustus De Morgan, 'On the Structure of the Syllogism and on the Application of the Theory of Probabilities to Questions of Argument and Authority,' *Cambridge Phil. Trans.* (9 Nov. 1846).

SKINNER
Motives, Intentions and the Interpretation of Texts

1. A revised and abbreviated version of an essay which was originally commissioned by *New Literary History* and first appeared as the discussion-article in their issue *On Interpretation* (Vol.3, no.2, 1972). I have been much helped in revising it by the comments I received on the original article from Mr Michael Black. I have since tried to carry my argument a stage further, and apply it to the interpretation of political as well as literary works, in my article 'Some Problems in the Analysis of Political Thought and Action', *Political Theory*, Vol.2, no.3, 1974.

2. H.D.Aiken, 'The Aesthetic Relevance of the Artist's Intentions', *J. Phil.* 52 (1955), p.747.

3. E.D.Hirsch, 'Three Dimensions of Hermeneutics', *New Literary History* 3 (1972), p.246.

4. Morton W.Bloomfield, 'Allegory as Interpretation', *New Literary History* 3 (1972), p.301.

5. The aim announced in Anthony Savile, 'The Place of Intention in the Concept of Art', *Proc. Arist. Soc.* 69 (1968–9) p.101. (Italics added.)

6. See the valuable cautionary remarks in William Righter, 'Myth and Interpretation', *New Literary History* 3 (1972), pp.319–344.

7. Richard Kuhns, 'Criticism and the Problem of Intention', *J. Phil.* 57 (1960), p.7.

8. E.D.Hirsch, loc. cit., p.248.

9. Wolfgang Iser, 'The Reading Process: A Phenomenological Approach', *New Literary History* 3 (1972), p.288.

10. Mario J.Valdés, 'Towards a Structure of Criticism', *New Literary History* 3 (1972), pp.263–5, 272–3.

11. Richard Kuhns, loc. cit., p.7.

12. E.D.Hirsch, loc. cit., p.245.

13. David Lodge, 'The Critical Moment, 1964', *Critical Q.* 6 (1964) p.267.

14. Cleanth Brooks, *The Well Wrought Urn* (London, 1949), Preface.

15. F.R.Leavis, 'The Responsible Critic: or the Functions of Criticism at any Time', *Scrutiny* 19 (1953), p.163. For a contrasting position, however, see Leavis's *Lectures in America* (London, 1969), especially the chapter on Yeats, in which it is conceded that some texts can only be fully understood in relation to the author's life-experiences. See esp. pp.80–81, where literary history is in consequence assigned a role in relation to literary criticism.

16. The discussion has usually focussed on the alleged irrelevance of intentions, but this concept has been standardly used by literary theorists in an extended sense, which in effect covers both motives and intentions. This fact has been pointed out by H.Morris Jones, 'The Relevance of the Artist's Intentions', *Br. J. Aesthetics* 4 (1964), p.143. For some examples, see Kuhns's discussion, which includes such motives as the desire 'to achieve fame' under the heading of intentions (p.6), and John Kemp, 'The Work of Art and the Artist's Intentions', *Br. J. Aesthetics* 4 (1964), pp.147–8 which distinguishes 'immediate intentions' from 'ulterior intentions'. The latter class appears to be identical with the class of motives.

17. W.K.Wimsatt and M.C.Beardsley, 'The Intentional Fallacy,' *Sewanee Rev.* 54 (1946), pp.477–8 and p.484.

18. Wolfgang Iser, loc. cit., p. 279.
19. Wimsatt and Beardsley, loc. cit., p. 483.
20. Morton W. Bloomfield, loc. cit., p. 309. Cf. also p. 301.
21. E. D. Hirsch, loc. cit., p. 249.
22. H. Morris Jones, loc. cit., p. 140. Cf. the comment in A. P. Ushenko, *The Dynamics of Art* (Bloomington, 1953), p. 57 on the work 'speaking for itself'.
23. The connection between this claim and the anti-intentionalist position is noted (but not endorsed) by Aiken, loc. cit., p. 752.
24. Wimsatt and Beardsley, loc. cit., p. 468.
25. R. Jack Smith, 'Intention in an Organic Theory of Poetry', *Sewanee Rev.* 56 (1948), p. 625.
26. T. M. Gang, 'Intention', *Essays in Criticism* 7 (1957), p. 179.
27. Wimsatt and Beardsley, loc. cit., p. 468.
28. T. M. Gang, loc. cit., p. 175. (Italics added.)
29. R. Jack Smith, loc. cit., p. 625.
30. Wimsatt and Beardsley, loc. cit., pp. 470, 477.
31. Ushenko, op. cit., p. 57.
32. Isabel C. Hungerland, 'The Concept of Intention in Art Criticism', *J. Phil.* 52 (1955), p. 733. For an account of the value and limitation of this approach, see Michael Black, 'Reading a Play', *The Human World* 1 (1971), 12–33, esp. the discussion at pp. 13–18.
33. Wimsatt and Beardsley, p. 470.
34. Smith, loc. cit., p. 631. Cf. Black, loc. cit., p. 12 noting the frequent citation of Coleridge's dictum to the effect that a successful work of art contains within itself the reasons why it is so and not otherwise.
35. T. M. Gang, loc. cit., p. 178.
36. Graham Hough, *An Essay on Criticism* (London, 1966), p. 60.
37. This point is well brought out in Frank Cioffi, 'Intention and Interpretation in Criticism', *Proc. Arist. Soc.* 64 (1963–4), esp. pp. 104–6.
38. *Ibid.*, p. 88.
39. For a valuable general analysis of the concept of intention, which distinguishes it from the concept of a motive, see G. E. M. Anscombe, *Intention* (Oxford, 1957) I am much indebted to this account and to Anthony Kenny, *Action, Emotion and Will* (Oxford, 1963), pp. 76–126. My own account of intentions in relation to interpretation has recently been given a partial endorsement (in a discussion which I find generally congenial in its conclusions) by Michael Hancher, 'Three Kinds of Intention', *Mod. Lang. Notes* 87 (1972), pp. 827–851. See esp. pp. 836 n and 842–3 n. It has also been deployed (in what seems to me an interesting practical application) by A. J. Close, 'Don Quixote and the "Intentionalist Fallacy"', *Br. J. Aesthetics* 12 (1972), pp. 19–39. See esp. p. 39.
40. I have tried to give an analysis of the relations between discerning the intention in, and the *point* of, an action, in the second part of my article, 'On Performing and Explaining Linguistic Actions,' *Phil. Q.* 21 (1971), pp. 1–21.
41. See esp. the account posthumously published as *How to Do Things with Words* ed. J. O. Urmson (Oxford, 1962)
42. I have tried to give a fuller account of this point in my article, 'Convention and the Understanding of Speech Acts', *Phil. Q.* 20 (1970), pp. 118–38.

43. For this notion see Austin, op. cit., pp. 101–31. For a deployment of the distinction, relevant to my present argument, see J. O. Urmson, *The Emotive Theory of Ethics* (London, 1968), pp. 27–29.

44. This is the example given in T. M. Gang, loc. cit., p. 177 of 'the intention to produce a certain emotional effect.' One influential source for this way of talking about intentions appears to have been I. A. Richards, *Practical Criticism* (London, 1929), pp. 180–83.

45. For a general account of this issue, see P. F. Strawson, 'Meaning and Truth', *Logico-Linguistic Papers* (London, 1971).

46. Note that the sense of 'meaning' with which I have been concerned is such that my claims apply potentially to other than literary works of art. This point is brought out by Kuhns, loc. cit., p. 7.

47. F. W. Bateson, 'The Function of Criticism at the Present Time', *Essays in Criticism* 3 (1953), p. 16. Hirsch (loc. cit., p. 247) has discussed the traditional claim (the view, for example, of Schleiermacher) that the aim of exegesis must always be to get as close as possible to the 'original meaning'. For recent accounts of the debate between the 'historical' and 'critical' schools, see (for an account inclining to the former side) Lionel Trilling, *The Liberal Imagination* (London, 1951), esp. pp. 185 ff and (for an account inclining to the latter side) Michael Black, loc. cit., esp. pp. 12 ff.

48. Here I retract an overstatement which I made in my essay 'Meaning and Understanding in the History of Ideas', *History and Theory* 8 (1969), pp. 28–30.

49. This point is well brought out both in Cioffi, loc. cit., in discussing Edmund Wilson's interpretation of James's *Turn of the Screw*, and in Morris Jones, loc. cit., p. 141. It seems to me, however, that Morris Jones draws the wrong moral from his story.

50. For a full discussion of this example, see my article in *History and Theory* (cited in fn. 48) at pp. 8–9.

51. C. B. Macpherson, *The Political Theory of Possessive Individualism: Hobbes to Locke* (Oxford, 1962), Ch. v, esp. pp. 206–9.

52. I derive the whole of this example from John Dunn, *The Political Thought of John Locke* (London, 1969), esp. pp. 208–13, 214–20. It is true that Dunn's objections might be partly countered by the suggestion that Locke may have held the belief that his society was likely to become concerned with unlimited capital accumulation, and would thus come to need a justification which he decided immediately to supply. I do not see, however, that this would adequately counter Dunn's third point.

HOUGH
An Eighth Type of Ambiguity

1. Reprinted in W. K. Wimsatt, *The Verbal Icon* (1954).
2. See especially F. Cioffi, 'Intention and Interpretation in Criticism', *Proc. Arist. Soc.*, vol. 64 (1963–4).
3. A. J. Close, 'Don Quixote and the 'Intentionalist Fallacy''', *Br. J. Aesthetics*, vol. 12, no. 2 (1972).
4. Quentin Skinner, 'Motives, Intentions and the Interpretation of Texts', *New Literary History*, vol. 3, no. 2 (1972).
5. Close does indeed mention this in a footnote, but does not make use of it in his argument.
6. F. L. Austin, *How to Do Things with Words* (1962), pp. 9, 22, 92, 104.

7. *Elegies and Songs and Sonnets of John Donne*, ed. Helen Gardner (1965), p. 152.
8. Erwin Panofsky, 'Et in Arcadia Ego: Poussin and the Elegiac Tradition', in *Meaning in the Visual Arts* (1955).
9. *Seven Types*, pp. 22–3.
10. William Empson, *Milton's God* (1961), p. 276.
11. *Paradise Lost*, I, 739–47.
12. Ibid., II, 546–60.

ACKNOWLEDGEMENTS

'The Intentional Fallacy' from W. K. Wimsatt, *The Verbal Icon: Studies in the Meaning of Poetry*, Copyright 1954 by the University of Kentucky Press. Reprinted by permission of the authors and the University of Kentucky Press. First published in *Sewanee Review*, LIV, Summer 1946, 468–88.

'The Meaning of a Poem' from C. A. Mace, editor, *British Philosophy in the Mid-Century: A Cambridge Symposium*, 361–75, Copyright 1957 by George Allen & Unwin Ltd. Reprinted by permission of the author and George Allen & Unwin Ltd.

'Objective Interpretation' from *PMLA*, Vol. LXXV, No. 4, Pt. 1, September 1960, 463–79. Reprinted by permission of the Modern Language Association of America.

'Intention and Interpretation in Criticism' from *Proceedings of the Aristotelian Society*, LXIV (1963–4), 85–106, Copyright 1964 The Aristotelian Society. Reprinted by permission of the author and courtesy of the editor of The Aristotelian Society.

'The Scope of the Intentional Fallacy' from *The Monist*, Vol. 50, No. 2, 1966, 250–66, LaSalle, Illinois, with the permission of the author and publisher.

'In Defense of the Author' from E. D. Hirsch, Jr., *Validity in Interpretation*, 1–23, Copyright 1967 Yale University. Reprinted by permission of the author and Yale University Press.

'Criticism and Performance' from F. E. Sparshott, *The Concept of Criticism*, 162–77, Copyright 1967 by Oxford University Press. Reprinted by permission of the Clarendon Press, Oxford, and the author.

'Genesis: a Fallacy Revisited' from Peter Demetz, Thomas Greene and Lowry Nelson, Jr., editors, *The Disciplines of Criticism: Essays in Literary Theory, Interpretation, and History*, 193–225, Copyright 1968 by Yale University. Reprinted by permission of the author and Yale University Press.

'The Intentional? Fallacy?' from *The New Orleans Review*, Vol. 1, Winter 1969, 116–64, Copyright 1969 by Morse Peckham. Reprinted by permission of the author.

'The Literary Past' from George Watson, *The Study of Literature*, 66–83, Copyright 1969 by George Watson. Reprinted by permission of the author and A. D. Peters and Company for Allen Lane Publishers.

'Don Quixote and the "Intentionalist Fallacy"' from *The British Journal of Aesthetics*, Vol. 12, No. 1, 19–39, Winter 1972, Copyright 1972 by *The British Journal of Aesthetics*. Reprinted by permission of the author and the editor of *The British Journal of Aesthetics*.

'Three Dimensions of Hermeneutics' from *New Literary History*, Vol. III, No. 2, Winter 1972, 245–61, Copyright 1972 by *New Literary History*, the University of Virginia, Charlottesville, Virginia. Reprinted by permission of the author and the editor of *New Literary History*.

'Motives, Intentions and the Interpretation of Texts' from *New Literary History*, Vol. III, No. 2, Winter 1972, 393–408, Copyright 1972 by *New Literary History*, the University of Virginia, Charlottesville, Virginia. Reprinted by permission of the author and the editor of *New Literary History*.

'An Eighth Type of Ambiguity' from Roma Gill, editor, *William Empson: the Man and His Work*, 76–97, Copyright Routledge and Kegal Paul. Reprinted by permission of the author and Routledge and Kegan Paul.